Page 1: Saguaros find company with a carpet of sur blooms. Photo licensed by Shutterstock.com.

Page 2 (top): Phoenix residents know Royal Palms a one of the most luxurious, romantic, and unpretent resorts in the Valley. Photo courtesy of Royal Palms; (bottom): The Valley's Four Seasons Resort is located the scenic foothills of north Scottsdale. Photo court of Four Seasons Resort Scottsdale.

Page 3 (top): Competitive mountain biking is just on of the many outdoor activities available at McDowe Mountain Regional Park. Photo courtesy of Maricop County Parks and Recreation Department; (bottom left): The Desert Botanical Garden at Papago Park is of the most beautiful attractions in Phoenix. Photo t Adam Rodriguez/Desert Botanical Garden; (bottom right, upper): Scottsdale Princess Resort is one of th Valley's most frequented resorts. Photo courtesy of Scottsdale Convention and Visitor's Bureau; (bottom right, lower): Frank Lloyd Wright's Taliesin West in Scottsdale is one of the architect's finest works. Pho by Donna Yeaw/Frank Lloyd Wright Foundation.

Page 4 (top): Tomb of Governor Hunt in Tempe and Phoenix Arizona's Papago Park. Photo licensed by Shutterstock.com; (bottom): The annual Peach Festi at Schnepf Farms in Queen Creek draws thousands visitors. Photo by Michael Ferraresi.

INSIDERS' GUIDE® TO
PHOENIX &
SCOTTSDALE

HELP US KEEP THIS GUIDE UP TO DATE

We would love to hear from you concerning your experiences with this guide and how you feel it could be improved and kept up to date. Please send your comments and suggestions to:

editorial@GlobePequot.com

Thanks for your input, and happy travels!

INSIDERS' GUIDE® TO

PHOENIX & SCOTTSDALE

SEVENTH EDITION

MICHAEL FERRARESI

INSIDERS' GUIDE

GUILFORD, CONNECTICUT
AN IMPRINT OF GLOBE PEQUOT PRESS

All the information in this guidebook is subject to change. We recommend that you call ahead to obtain current information before traveling.

INSIDERS' GUIDE ®

Copyright © 2012 Morris Book Publishing, LLC

Editor: Kevin Sirois
Project Editor: Heather Santiago
Layout: Joanna Beyer
Text Design: Sheryl Kober
Maps by XNR Productions, Inc. © Morris Book Publishing, LLC

ISBN 978-0-7627-7321-3

Printed in the United States of America
10 9 8 7 6 5 4 3 2 1

CONTENTS

Directory of Maps

ABOUT THE AUTHOR

Michael Ferraresi is a Phoenix-based journalist with more than 10 years' experience covering the Valley of the Sun. He worked as a reporter for *The Arizona Republic* and www .azcentral.com, the leading news organization in the state, for several years before leaving in 2011 to join a Scottsdale new media development company. Ferraresi primarily covered law enforcement and municipal government, though he got his start in sports writing. His blogs and online breaking news stories were among the most-read on www.azcentral.com. Ferraresi also taught undergraduate news writing courses at his alma mater, Arizona State University's Walter Cronkite School of Journalism and Mass Communication. He and his wife, Kelly, live in Phoenix and spend their free time hiking and exploring Arizona when they're not freelancing media projects.

ACKNOWLEDGMENTS

I'd like to thank Kate Reynolds and other writers for laying the foundation in previous editions of this Insiders' Guide. Also, thanks to the hardworking public relations team at the Greater Phoenix Convention & Visitors Bureau and their colleagues at neighboring convention and visitor bureaus. Special thanks go to Kelly Carr for her assistance and patience on deadline.

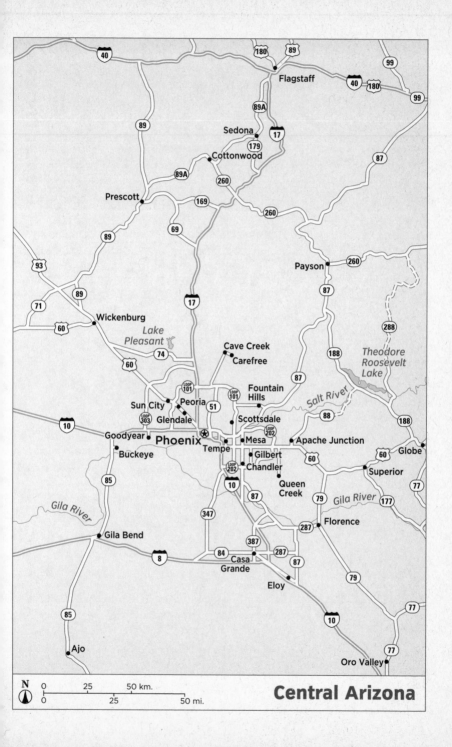

Central Arizona

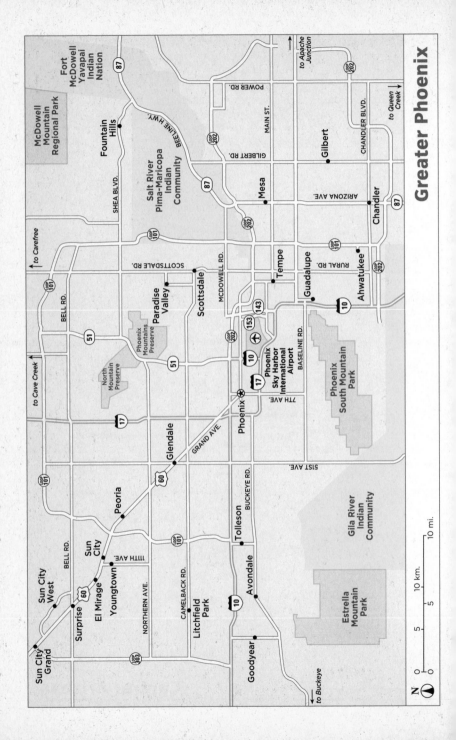

Greater Phoenix

Downtown Phoenix

Chandler

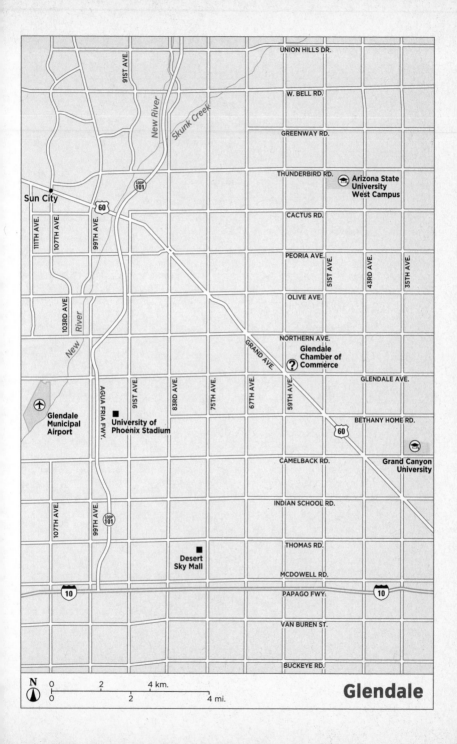

Glendale

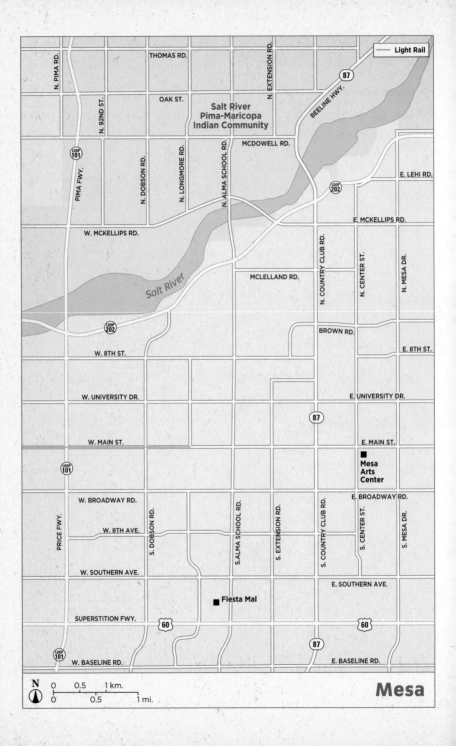

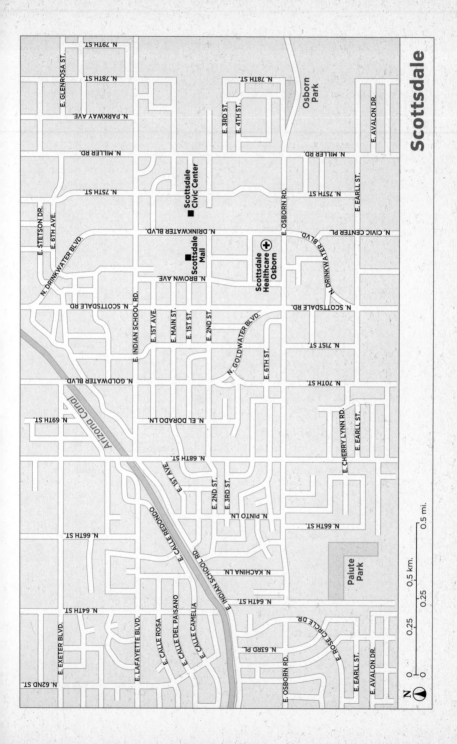

Scottsdale

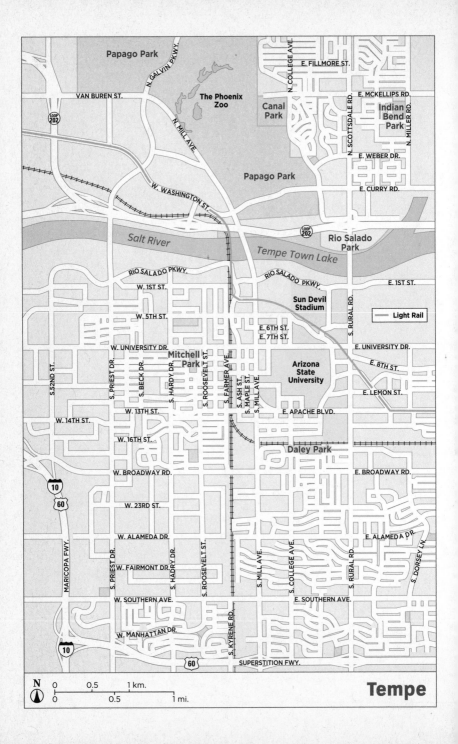

Tempe

HOW TO USE THIS BOOK

This guide consists of data-packed chapters that provide useful information for the weekend visitor and longtime resident alike. You will find a great deal of information in these pages that you will not find in other guidebooks. Not only do we tell you the sights to see, but we fill you in on which neighborhoods are nice places to raise kids and what hospitals have particular facilities. From getting a phone hookup to finding a place to keep the kids (and yourself) entertained, the *Insiders' Guide to Phoenix & Scottsdale* is here to help.

We have arranged the information so that it is easily accessible. If you are flying into Phoenix for the first time, turn to the Getting Here, Getting Around chapter for information on how to navigate the Valley of the Sun once you have landed. Check out the accommodations chapters for choices on lodging (Hotels & Motels, Resorts, and RV Parks & Campgrounds), browse through the Restaurants chapter to locate the best and closest dining options, and flip through the chapters to discover what to see and do while you are here (Nightlife, Shopping, Attractions, Kidstuff, Annual Events, The Arts, Parks & Recreation, Golf, and Spectator Sports). Price codes are supplied in the restaurant and accommodation chapters to further assist you in those selections. The Kidstuff chapter is especially useful for parents looking to give their child a memorable Arizona experience.

You will notice that throughout the guide we refer to five main areas—downtown Phoenix, the Southeast Valley (which includes Chandler, Mesa, and Tempe), the Northeast Valley (which includes Carefree, Cave Creek, and Scottsdale), the Northwest Valley (which includes Glendale, Sun City, and Surprise), and the Southwest Valley (which includes Goodyear). Most chapters are organized by geographical subcategories for your convenience, since the Phoenix metro area is actually several cities. Check out the Area Overview section to find out more.

If you are thinking of moving to this area, you will find the Relocation, Education & Child Care, and Retirement chapters especially helpful. Filled with tips on how to make the transition to life in the Valley as smooth as possible, these chapters tell you how to register your motor vehicle, fill you in on the area school systems, and help you locate the best neighborhood for your needs.

If you are a longtime resident of the Phoenix area, you will find the up-to-date restaurant, nightlife, and annual events listings helpful. Check out the Day Trips chapter for adventures outside the Valley. Whether you are a visitor or a native, don't forget to read the sections on History and Our Natural World. Many city residents aren't fully aware of the rich history and diverse ecozone of the Valley of the Sun.

Generally the title of the chapter will tell you what can be found in it, but some things are a little hard to place. Cafes, for example, are listed in the Nightlife chapter, since they are a popular destination for an after-dinner conversation on our (relatively) cool nights. You will also find some businesses and attractions listed in the Kidstuff and in other chapters. In this case we tailor the information in the Kidstuff section specifically for those taking care of children.

Scattered throughout the various chapters are special Insiders' tips (indicated by an 🄸) for quick insights. The tips are our way of sharing our insider information. You will also find lengthy Close-ups profiling truly unique aspects of the area's lifestyle and culture. Unless otherwise indicated, all listings are in Phoenix proper.

You'll also find listings accompanied by the ✳ symbol—these are our top picks for attractions, restaurants, accommodations, and everything in between that you shouldn't miss while you're in the area. You want the best this region has to offer? Go with our **Insiders' Choice.**

Finally, if you're moving to the Phoenix area or already live here, be sure to check out the blue-tabbed pages at the back of the book. There you will find the **Living Here** appendix that offers sections on Relocation, Education & Child Care, Health Care, and Retirement.

Use this guidebook to get a general idea of the area. Get out and get active; you'll find we have a lot to offer. If you discover something in this book has changed or if you have a recommendation you'd like to share, by all means drop us a line at *Insiders' Guide to Phoenix & Scottsdale*, PO Box 480, Guilford, CT 06437 or you may e-mail us at editorial@GlobePequot.com.

AREA OVERVIEW

Ask around the Valley of the Sun. Most non-native residents remember when they first visited the city named after the mythic creature that rose reborn from the ashes. They will tell you about hummingbirds fluttering around blooming saguaros. They remember the fresh morning sunlight over the patio at brunch at a Scottsdale resort. They'll talk about the refreshing backyard pool in the triple-digit heat or the view of the surrounding purple mountains at sunset.

OVERVIEW

It's difficult to find people who were born and raised in town or who've lived their entire lives in the Phoenix area. For many people, the vast metro Valley is a place to reinvent themselves. They come from Iowa and Massachusetts and Los Angeles for a better lifestyle. Those from the Midwest turn the occasional snowbird vacation into a full-time retirement. New Englanders take jobs in a place where their families won't have to shovel their way to work and school every winter. However, it's not only about the seemingly endless sunshine. City-dwellers from L.A., Chicago, and more-established cities get hooked on the lower cost of living.

The weather can't be beat. In March, you can phone your friends back home and let them know you're sitting poolside in 80 degree sunshine. In fact, the Valley gets sunshine over 85 percent of its daylight hours, according to the National Climatic Data Center. If you've lived here long enough, you'll find yourself shivering or even wearing mittens when the temperatures drop below 50 degrees.

Valley natives have seen Phoenix transition in the last 15 years from a small town to the booming major city it is today. New freeways, housing developments, and commercial centers sprouted up in the 1990s and after the turn of the century before the 2008 economic collapse halted growth. In many ways the Valley exemplified the over-development and over-lending that led up to America's busted housing bubble.

The Valley was also the epicenter for the US immigration debate when Arizona passed a law in 2010 making it a state crime to be in the country illegally. The controversial state bill, known as Senate Bill 1070, fetched international headlines for months. Downtown Phoenix hosted massive protests led by Mexican-American activists and residents concerned for their safety as local police use enhanced authority "when practicable" to detain residents to question them about their immigration status.

Residents were forced to forge their way through the down economy, slumping housing values, and the specter of race-related violence. Now it seems as if Phoenix

Valley Vital Statistics

Arizona governor: Jan Brewer

Phoenix mayor: Phil Gordon (term expires January 2012)

State capital: Phoenix

Other major area cities: Scottsdale, Tempe, Mesa, Gilbert, Chandler, Glendale, Peoria, Surprise, Goodyear, and Avondale

Population: 4.2 million in the greater Phoenix area

Area: 2,000 square miles

Nickname: Valley of the Sun

Average temperatures: January: high 65 degrees F, low 39; July: high 105, low 79.5

Average rainfall: 7.66 inches

Average days of sunshine: 325 days

City founded: October 26, 1870

State founded: Arizona entered the Union on February 14, 1912, as the 48th state. The state flower is the saguaro cactus blossom, the state tree is the palo verde, and the state bird is the cactus wren.

Major universities: Arizona State University, Grand Canyon University, and University of Phoenix

Important dates in history:

  1885—Tempe Normal School founded, establishing the future Arizona State University

  1889—Phoenix named Arizona's capital

  1911—Roosevelt Dam completed, creating a reservoir that helps supply the Valley's water

  1959—Phoenix experiences a boom in new construction and enters a period of steady growth

Time zone: Arizona is on Mountain Standard Time and does not change its clocks for daylight saving time. So Arizona is on Mountain Time half the year and on Pacific Standard Time during daylight saving time.

Major area industries: High-tech manufacturing, tourism, and construction

Sports: Home to 2001 World Series champion Arizona Diamondbacks, and 2007/2009 WNBA champion Phoenix Mercury, in addition to the NBA's Phoenix Suns, NFL's Arizona Cardinals, and NHL's Phoenix Coyotes

Famous sons, daughters & residents:

Frank Luke, WWI ace pilot

Ira Hayes, one of the US Marines who raised the American flag on Iwo Jima

Barry Goldwater, US senator

Frank Lloyd Wright, architect

Steve Allen, entertainer

Marty Robbins, country singer

Paul Harvey, radio personality

Glen Campbell, entertainer

Erma Bombeck, humorist

Bil Keene, cartoonist

Alice Cooper, rock musician

Francine Reed, blues singer

Steven Spielberg, filmmaker

Chamber of commerce:

Greater Phoenix Chamber of Commerce
201 N. Central Ave., 27th Floor
Phoenix, AZ 85004
(602) 495-4195
www.phoenixchamber.com

Major airport: Phoenix Sky Harbor International Airport, served by 17 airlines; www.phxsky harbor.com

Public transportation: Phoenix offers bus service throughout the majority of the metro area. Valley Metro: (602) 253-5000; www.valleymetro.org. A 20-mile stretch of light rail connecting Phoenix with Mesa and Tempe opened in December 2008.

Driving laws: Seat belts must be worn. Children under 5 must be in car seats. High-occupancy lanes are for cars with two or more people or qualified hybrids. Owners of hybrids must first apply to the Arizona Department of Transportation.

Alcohol law: You must be 21 years old to purchase alcoholic beverages. Bars are open until 2 a.m. You can purchase alcohol on Sunday after 10 a.m.

Daily newspapers: *The Arizona Republic* is the state's newspaper of record and the largest daily newspaper in Arizona, with a daily circulation of nearly 499,000. Visit www.azcentral.com for online and mobile editions.

Sales tax: 9.3 percent

Room tax: 13.27 percent in Phoenix, though it varies by community

Visitor center:

Downtown Phoenix
Visitor Information Center
125 N. 2nd St. (across from main entrance of Hyatt)
Phoenix, AZ 85004
(877) CALL-PHX (225-5749)

and its surrounding suburban neighbors are pushing forward into a new era after all the negative national media attention.

The Valley metro area is massive. As it annexed land in past decades, Phoenix's population grew to about 1.4 million by 2010. It totals around 4 million combined with Mesa, Scottsdale, Tempe, Glendale, and other suburbs. While the capital city is Arizona's center of government, industry, and commerce, it's difficult to see where the border lines are drawn. Cities appear to meld into one giant community. Maricopa County has the fourth-highest population of any county in the US.

Obviously, natural resources in a desert are scarce. Valley residents depend on a vast waterworks system that diverts water from the Colorado River 200 miles away. Runoff from varying levels of snowpack in Arizona's northern mountains is stored at Roosevelt Dam northeast of the Valley. Water is a constant source of debate as the Valley's population grows and cities expand to undeveloped outlying areas. Since 2000, the West Valley communities of Buckeye and Surprise have been ranked among the top 5 fastest-growing suburbs in the country.

You'll notice flat, seemingly fertile farmland around the Valley. While the hospitality, tourism, biotech, and manufacturing industries dominate the market, Maricopa County has maintained its tradition as one of the top pima cotton-producing areas in the nation. The Valley's major employers include Arizona State University, which boasts one of the largest overall student populations of any school in the world. Wal-Mart, local governments, the Banner Health hospital system, and the online education giant University of Phoenix are among the others.

By 2008 the median income in Phoenix was $56,555, according to the Greater Phoenix Economic Council. The organization also reported that Phoenix had an 8.5 percent unemployment rate, which had climbed as high as 9.6 percent by 2011. Many of those workers were reeling from layoffs by local construction firms that relied on the real estate boom.

Pro sports are also a major economic force in the Valley. Phoenix hosted Super Bowl XLII at University of Phoenix Stadium in Glendale in 2008, bringing fans of the major-market New England Patriots and New York Giants into town. The 2009 NBA All-Star game was held at the Phoenix Suns' US Airways Center, and the Arizona Diamondbacks hosted the Major League Baseball All-Star game in July 2011. At the college level, the Fiesta Bowl and periodic BCS National Championship are held at the Glendale football stadium, which is home to the NFL's Arizona Cardinals. Each spring baseball fans flock to the Valley to rub shoulders with their favorite ballplayers during the Cactus League spring training season (see Spectator Sports section for more).

The Valley covers about 2,000 square miles. Most of the surrounding suburbs are clearly in the city, but the far-flung communities of Apache Junction (40 miles southeast in neighboring Pinal County) and Buckeye (about an hour's drive west of Phoenix) are considered part of the Valley metro area. The West Valley is crowned by Glendale, though it includes Peoria, Goodyear, the Sun Cities, Surprise, Avondale, Litchfield Park, Tolleson, and El Mirage.

Scottsdale borders Phoenix to the east. The largely affluent community, home to some of the country's top resorts and golf clubs, is neighbored by the cozy towns of

Paradise Valley, Fountain Hills, Cave Creek, and Carefree, in addition to the Salt River Pima-Maricopa and Fort McDowell Indian communities. ASU's hometown of Tempe borders Phoenix to the southeast. The city of Mesa, located about 20 miles east of downtown Phoenix, has the third-largest population in Arizona. Its neighbor, Chandler, has the fourth-largest population. Other Southeast Valley communities include Gilbert and Queen Creek, which is split between Maricopa and Pinal counties. The Gila River Indian Community is the Valley's last stop before you hit Casa Grande on the way to Tucson on I-10.

Sure, there's some regional bias. The East Valley scoffs at the West Valley. People in north Phoenix gossip about the crime in south Phoenix. Kids who grow up in Scottsdale might never spend much time downtown near the capitol. Strip malls in Gilbert look the same as strip malls in Glendale.

Take some time to experience this part of the world and you'll see how shallow those views are. Each community in the Valley has its own character and its top attractions. The calm waters of Tempe Town Lake are so uniquely different than the record-setting vertical stream of water that shoots from Fountain Park in Fountain Hills. The glitzy shopping districts of Scottsdale and the massive suburban malls around Arrowhead Towne Center in Peoria are like night and day. And the Old West history embedded in each of the Valley communities is in striking contrast to the New World mass-developed neighborhoods that have mushroomed from the high Sonoran Desert of the North Valley, down to South Mountain. Remember, it's a dry heat, and you will sweat like you've never sweat before. But it's cooler at night under the desert moon.

The Valley is a place for pioneers and travelers, for vacationers and investors. It's home. It's a getaway. It's a destination. And it's yours to explore.

PHOENIX

In 1985 Phoenix adopted an "urban village plan" as part of the city's general plan. The idea was that the city had nine distinct areas in which city services and business cores were situated or needed to be situated. The city in its annexations had gobbled up many distinctive neighborhoods such as Maryvale, which began as an affordable bedroom community for young married couples and families when it was developed by John F. Long in the late 1950s and early 1960s, and south Phoenix, where the Valley's African-American and Hispanic populations concentrated.

Unlike older and more densely packed metropolitan areas such as New York City, Phoenix swallowed its suburbs and neglected its epicenter. The malls in its far-flung neighborhoods helped keep people from heading downtown to do business. Aside from the office workers who went there, Phoenix's downtown was a ghost town after dark through most of the 1990s. Visitors often wonder about the city's dual skylines. There's one in the downtown area, surrounded by the Hyatt and Sheraton and ballparks. The other is uptown, further north on Central Avenue.

The urban village concept seemed ridiculous to some critics. However, the plan's adoption coincided with major efforts to revitalize downtown, and the project has grown to 15 urban villages. Ever since former Phoenix Suns owner Jerry Colangelo decided to build America West Arena (now

called US Airways Center) in downtown Phoenix, the city center has become more vibrant. Currently referred to as Copper Square, the 90 square blocks from 3rd Avenue to 7th Street, and from Fillmore to south of Jackson, include 95 restaurants and bars, more than 30,000 parking spaces, a free shuttle, and more than 20 arts, cultural, and entertainment venues, including the state-of-the-art Chase Field (home of the Diamondbacks), the newly expanded Phoenix Convention Center, the Herberger Theater Center, the $515-million Arizona Center, the historic Orpheum Theater, and City Hall. With guides on foot or bike 7 days a week and a free shuttle, Copper Square has given people some genuine reasons to head (or stay) there after dark.

Some say Phoenix is rising again. A 31-story Sheraton opened in 2008, followed by other downtown hotels; the $600-million convention center overhaul attracted more major conferences; a 20-mile light rail line gave residents an easier way to commute between Phoenix and the East Valley; the downtown ASU campus is becoming a destination for out-of-state students; and a rising number of young professionals are spending more time at downtown bars than in Scottsdale clubs.

i Grassy green areas are rare in the desert and even scarcer in downtown Phoenix. The city's Civic Space Park on 1st Avenue, which opened in 2009, features solar panels that keep the park lit at night and a rainwater collection system to keep the small lawn healthy.

As a city, though, Phoenix remains a huge suburb with interesting pockets of historic housing in Encanto Village, Arcadia, and the Willo neighborhood. There are some very interesting parks, such as Papago Park, with its oddly shaped red rock buttes, and the mountain preserves of Squaw Peak, North Mountain, and South Mountain. Of course, Camelback Mountain's hiking trails are among the most unique in the city, and the park is right in the heart of the Valley.

i If you are moving to Arizona permanently, you'll want to establish residency. Start by getting an Arizona driver's license. If you have a valid license from another state, you can simply apply and have your picture taken. The written and driving tests are not required. For information about car titles, registration, and personalized license plates, call the motor vehicles division of the Arizona Department of Transportation at (602) 255-0072.

The freeway system has improved mobility around the Valley, but people tend to play and shop close to home, and a number of malls serve that purpose: Desert Sky on the west side; Metrocenter in the north-central section; the Colonnade and Town & Country Shopping Center and the Biltmore Fashion Park, all off Camelback Road and the Arizona 51 freeway; and Paradise Valley Mall in the northeastern section. (We provide an overview of shopping hot spots in the Shopping chapter.)

Phoenix's neighborhoods are built primarily on a grid, and many housing developments are built cookie-cutter style, though the geographic and economic diversity provide character. In the northeastern part of the city, middle-class to upper-middle-class neighborhoods are punctuated by

mountains and foothills, but as you head south toward the Salt River, the increasing tension of crime-ridden neighborhoods can be felt in the flatlands. Nevertheless, along stretches of Baseline Road in south Phoenix, you'll experience an almost pastoral feeling with small remaining farms and orchards. There's a cozy claustrophobia to Phoenix's Paradise Valley neighborhood, different from the upscale town of the same name that sits to the neighborhood's southeast.

Other far-reaching revitalization projects include the Rio Salado Habitat restoration project, a plan to restore the Salt River to its natural state. The area supports native wildlife and plant life and created a revitalized river corridor through central Phoenix. Planners envisioned 10 miles of recreational and interpretive trails; wells and a water delivery system to bring water to the trees and other vegetation; wetlands, canals, ponds and streams; shelter, space, and food for wildlife; and an environmental education center. Gateway, a cyclist and pedestrian plaza on the bank of the Salt River at Central Avenue, features terraced seating, interpretative gardens, and a 40-foot-by-80-foot shade structure. Ongoing construction includes riverbed improvements and the Rio Salado Audubon Center, near the Central Avenue bridge.

One of the six strategic growth areas adopted by the Phoenix City Council is North Black Canyon, located along the I-17 corridor north of Happy Valley Road and Deer Valley Airpark. There are also a variety of short-term and long-term planning and development activities under way to bring housing and retail developments to the area. In other words, this massive city doesn't have a single personality. Each borough is its own unique town within the overall city.

> **i** In November 2005 the 595-acre Rio Salado Habitat restoration project (along 19th Avenue to 16th Street) opened to the public with its 5-mile trail system through the reclaimed riparian area along the Salt River. Information and tour schedules are available at http://riosalado.audubon.org or (602) 468-6470.

SOUTHEAST VALLEY

The Southeast Valley consists of sprawling Mesa, landlocked Tempe, Chandler, Gilbert, and the tiny town of Guadalupe. Some even consider far-flung Apache Junction, a city in Pinal County, to be part of the Valley. The Southeast Valley is one of the key centers of housing growth, with goods and services following new housing. Since so much of this area was agricultural mere decades ago, there are few old commerce centers to serve as anchors. Instead, strip malls sprouted along the major thoroughfares, spaced on a grid of 1-mile squares. Mesa, Tempe, and Chandler all have core downtown areas that are pedestrian-friendly, but in some neighborhoods in the Southeast Valley it's a daunting task to walk almost anywhere, and local mom-and-pop stores or newsstands don't exist.

Mesa

Mesa is the giant of the Southeast Valley and Arizona's third-largest city. Mormons from Utah and Idaho founded the city. They settled on this broad plateau, or mesa, in May 1878 and sought to name the settlement in its honor. However, the post office wouldn't recognize the name "Mesa" because a town named Mesaville existed in Pinal County. The settlers decided to name their community

Hayden, after Charles Trumbull Hayden, who at the time ran a ferryboat across the Salt River. This caused confusion in the mails because of an old post office called Hayden's Ferry, so the settlers renamed their town Zenos, after a prophet in the Book of Mormon, in 1886. When Mesaville went out of existence in 1888, the settlers changed the name of the community back to Mesa.

Mormon culture remains dominant in Mesa, giving it a different ambience from Phoenix and the rest of the Valley. It's not uncommon to see Mormon missionaries, dressed neatly in white shirts and dark ties, riding bicycles and spreading the word. The city also has a large share of snowbirds, young families, and college students who live in less-expensive apartments near the Tempe border.

Given the city's size, the downtown is small and quiet at night. However, the Mesa Arts Center is usually booked with first-class performers. The venue has helped add some flair to the city at night. Mesa is also well known as the offseason home of the Chicago Cubs, whose die-hard fans flood the city and Hohokam Park in March during spring training.

Tempe

Tempe began when Charles Trumbull Hayden built a flourmill and established a ferry service across the Salt River in 1871. A small community soon grew up around the enterprises, and the post office recognized it as Hayden's Ferry and Hayden's Mill. The growing settlement took the name Tempe after the suggestion of "Lord" Darrell Duppa, who had a penchant for Greek names, having named Phoenix. He suggested Hayden's Ferry be renamed Tempe because to him it resembled the Vale of Tempe in Greece.

Hayden became one of the trustees of the Territorial Normal School, which became Tempe's major asset. The Normal School evolved over the next six decades to become Arizona State University (see the Education & Child Care chapter). Today the university is central to Tempe's active downtown scene along Mill Avenue, which has been rebuilt with cafes, restaurants, and stores. The presence of students makes Tempe filled with parties, but also with young thinkers and artists. Tempe was the first major US city to offer border-to-border Wi-Fi to residents and businesses. Like Phoenix and Mesa, it benefited greatly from the construction of the Valley's light rail line, which runs through ASU's campus.

The university's Sun Devil Stadium hosts ASU football and was the site of Super Bowl XXX. The stadium also is one of the few venues to have hosted both a papal mass (Pope John Paul II, 1987) and Rolling Stones concerts. Large concert scenes from Barbra Streisand's *A Star Is Born* were filmed there, as were scenes in U2's *Rattle and Hum*. Other university facilities, such as the Frank Lloyd Wright-designed Gammage Auditorium, also provide easily accessible cultural activities, ranging from touring Broadway plays to classical and pop concerts. The university is also the home of KAET (Channel 8), the Valley's PBS station.

Tempe is unique among the Valley's major cities in that it cannot annex any neighboring land. It is landlocked by Phoenix on the west, Scottsdale on the north, Mesa on the east, and Chandler on the south. However, the city has been making the most of undeveloped land within its limits. The Arizona Mills Mall opened in late 1997 at the junction of the Superstition Freeway (US 60) and I-10. It is one of the largest

malls in Arizona and boasts a range of outlet stores, high-tech play areas, and restaurants, along with an IMAX theater.

The newest Tempe attraction is the Tempe Town Lake, where the once-dry Salt River was dammed to create a 2-mile-long recreation area perfect for biking, jogging, skating, canoeing, sailing, and paddle boating.

Major League Baseball's Anaheim Angels play spring training games at Tempe Diablo Stadium.

Chandler

Chandler is named for Alexander John Chandler, a Canadian who settled in Arizona in 1887. He was the territory's first veterinary surgeon, a post he held until 1892. In the interim he became one of the Valley's largest landholders. His Chandler Ranch covered about 18,000 acres, and in 1911 he sold his land in plots of 10 to 160 acres. The city of Chandler was established a year later. The community retained its agricultural character until about 1980, when a building boom propelled it into its status as one of the fastest-growing communities in the state. Chandler has become home to several high-tech manufacturers, including Intel. The city continues to revitalize its downtown on Arizona Avenue with such projects as the Chandler Center for the Arts, which was completed in 1989, and the 1.3-million-square-foot upscale Chandler Fashion Center, the centerpiece of a 320-acre "urban village." Chandler's population was more than 236,000 in 2010.

Gilbert

Gilbert was established in 1912 on land donated by Robert Gilbert. It was also an agricultural community. In fact, it was known as the Hay Capital of the World until 1920. In 1980, Gilbert had 5,717 residents, which grew to more than 208,000 in 2010. Of course, it suffered some growing pains as one of the fastest-growing communities in the US. The city struggled to build schools and hire teachers as fast as it added families. City leaders have also shifted to attracting high-tech and scientific business to balance residential growth. Banner Gateway Medical Center opened its doors in 2007.

Guadalupe

The tiny landlocked community has one of the smallest populations in the Valley. It boasts one of the more colorful municipal histories. Guadalupe was established by members of the Yaqui tribe who fled Mexico in the late 1800s to escape dictator Porfirio Diaz's attempts to relocate them to the Yucatán, which was far from their ancestral home in northwestern Mexico. The name comes from the Virgin of Guadalupe, the patron saint of Mexico. The town's chief landmarks are the mission-style Our Lady of Guadalupe Church and the Yaqui Temple. Today, Yaqui descendants and Mexican-Americans make up the majority of the town's residents.

Queen Creek

Beyond what is commonly considered the Valley, the farming community of Queen Creek maintains a bucolic lifestyle southeast of Gilbert. The town has received numerous awards for its forward-looking planning strategies, which include the preservation of Queen Creek and Sanokai Washes as public trails and open space. Queen Creek continues to attract newcomers and has grown

from 4,313 residents in 2000 to its current population of 24,000. With Gilbert rapidly growing and Phoenix-Mesa Gateway Airport growing to its north, Queen Creek may soon be enveloped to become part of the Valley's mainstream instead of remaining on the fringe. A new park, library, and equestrian center are among recent improvements.

i For links to websites and information for all Valley cities, go to www.maricopa.gov or call (602) 506-3011 or (800) 540-5570.

Gila River Indian Community

The Gila River Indian Community marks the Valley's southern end. The reservation covers 650 square miles, more than half the size of the Valley, and it houses about 12,000 mostly agrarian residents from the Pima and Maricopa tribes. The reservation is technically outside the Valley, though the northern end houses attractions that draw hundreds of thousands of visitors annually. Firebird International Raceway and a cluster of casinos—including the new Sheraton Wild Horse Pass Resort—have allowed the tribe to improve many community services, such as health care and public safety.

NORTHEAST VALLEY

The Northeast Valley is considered the Valley's most upscale region. It includes large estates in Paradise Valley and newly developed high-end communities located on land recently annexed by Scottsdale. This area is miles from the Salt River bottom. Its foothills become a unique geographic feature as the land slopes gradually upward to the Mogollon Rim.

Scottsdale

Scottsdale is the main Northeast Valley city. On its eastern side, the city mostly borders the Salt River Pima-Maricopa Indian Community, and to the south it is hemmed in by Tempe. Early in its development it squabbled with Phoenix over annexation rights to various tracts on its west side. In the past decade Scottsdale annexed a huge amount of land to the north, which brought communities of ranchers and desert dwellers into its chic fold.

In 1881 Major Winfield Scott homesteaded on the site of the city that would one day carry his name. When Scott retired from the military, he promoted his ranch and the surrounding area as a rest cure and agricultural center. Scottsdale became the official name in 1896, when local settlers sought to establish a school district.

Scottsdale was relatively slow to develop but has boomed in the years since World War II. It was one of the first cities to revitalize its downtown, billing itself as "the West's most Western town." Art galleries abound in downtown Scottsdale, catering to both cowboy-art and modern-art lovers. The downtown is eminently friendly to foot traffic, and Scottsdale Fashion Square and the Borgata of Scottsdale offer upscale shopping not too far from the town center. Aside from the arts, Scottsdale is also known for its nightlife, and the downtown clubs are packed most of the week.

The greenbelt that runs for a dozen miles down the Indian Bend Wash made a virtue out of a flooding problem. Since the wash floods during any significant rain, filling it in for development would have been unwise. Instead, the city devised an alternative plan that turned it into a strip of parkland with jogging and bicycle paths and

🔍 Close-up

Taliesin West: Architect Frank Lloyd Wright's Personal Favorite

Twelve of Frank Lloyd Wright's buildings are listed by *Architectural Record* as among the top 100 in the world, but the architect's personal favorite was his architectural school in Scottsdale—Taliesin West.

From 1927, when he first visited the Phoenix area to consult on the Arizona Biltmore Resort, to his death in 1959 at the age of 91, the charm of the Sonoran Desert lured Wright to Arizona every winter. He built Taliesin West in the late 1930s; during his tenure there he completed one-third of his designs and his controversial style achieved the recognition he had long pursued.

Taliesin West, now a National Historic Landmark, nestles on 600 acres of desert land. A stroll around the grounds, led by informed tour guides—some of them former Wright apprentices—offers insight into Wright's genius. The school trains about 30 students each year. The on-site archives of Wright's drawings and writings draw researchers from around the world. Filmmaker Ken Burns spent 2 years there researching Wright for a PBS documentary that aired in 1999.

The buildings at Taliesin West recline below the mountains, their profile harmonizing with the desert's rocks and plants. Wright's philosophy of organic design found its spiritual home in Arizona, and he believed the cactus epitomized good design. In a 1940 article for *Arizona Highways*, he wrote: "The Arizona desert is no place for the hard box-walls of the houses of the Middle West and East. Here all is sculptured by wind and water, patterned in color and texture."

The desert also supplied building materials. Wright worked side by side with his apprentices in the backbreaking work of gathering rocks and sand to create his unique "desert masonry." Hard, flat-sided rocks found in the area, called Taliesin quartzite, were unsuitable for cutting, but he used them to create a textured surface on the thick, concrete walls throughout the campus.

Hands-on work was an integral part of Wright's education philosophy. Many students continue the tradition of constructing their own desert digs in which they live while studying at the school. One center of social activity was the living room, dubbed "The Garden Room," a 56-foot-long space made even more dramatic by its sloping, translucent roof and spine of windows. Other points of interest on the Taliesin West grounds include the Cabaret Cinema, the Music Pavilion, the Seminar Theater, and Wright's private office. One of Wright's works, the historic Jester House, consists of three large circular rooms framed by glass walls and clustered around a breezeway.

Throughout Taliesin West, redwood timbers crown the buildings and canvas roofs allow sunlight to diffuse through the rooms. The rooms are filled with furniture that Wright designed. The entrances to his buildings are hidden and mysterious; entryways to rooms are low, opening suddenly into spaciousness and light.

Taliesin West was a work in progress while Wright lived, because the master was forever improving on his designs. Today his desert camp provides a glimpse into the creative life of a man whose vision is still ahead of its time.

Taliesin West is located at 1261 Frank Lloyd Wright Blvd. in Scottsdale. Information: (480) 860-2700 or www.franklloydwright.org.

other recreational facilities that would not be unduly affected by the occasional light flood. Waters would irrigate the grass and would be contained by the wide channel.

Central to the city's image as a cultural leader is the Scottsdale Center for the Performing Arts, which features 2 art galleries and an 800-seat auditorium (see the Arts chapter). The arts facility is part of the Scottsdale Civic Center complex, also known as the Scottsdale Mall, which includes City Hall, the Scottsdale Library, and other municipal facilities. It is adjacent to Scottsdale Stadium. The stadium hosts the San Francisco Giants during spring training. Another Scottsdale landmark is Taliesin West, a winter residence built by Frank Lloyd Wright in 1937, making Wright's presence a powerful force in the city's cultural fabric. He's claimed almost as a native son. Scottsdale is also home to the Scottsdale Airpark, a busy industrial park that surrounds Scottsdale Municipal Airport around Frank Lloyd Wright Boulevard.

The neighboring town of Paradise Valley, nestled among the hills between north Phoenix and north Scottsdale, may be the Valley's most exclusive community. Residents can see the back of Camelback Mountain and look up at a formation called the Praying Monk. The large estates of the community, incorporated in 1961, house many of the Valley's celebrities and pro athletes. The town earned some infamy among local drivers when it became the first municipality in the Valley to use photo radar to help its small police force crack down on speeders along Lincoln Boulevard. The mountainside street offers wonderful views of the Valley's lights at night, and it is the main thoroughfare through Paradise Valley from Phoenix to Scottsdale.

i Between 2000 and 2010, Scottsdale added about 14,000 residents. The population spike of more than 7 percent brought the city's total population to more than 217,000. However, other Valley suburbs grew even faster, displacing Scottsdale as one of the top 5 most populated cities in Arizona.

Carefree

As Scottsdale and Phoenix aggressively annex land to the north, the Valley almost includes the foothill towns Carefree and Cave Creek, which are almost always mentioned in the same breath. Gordon Lightfoot's song "Carefree Highway" refers to the highway that connects Carefree to I-17, miles to the west. Carefree, established in 1959, is a planned community of luxury homes that rests in the northwestern shoulder of Scottsdale, just northeast of the very northeastern tip of Phoenix. The home of The Boulders Resort (see the Resorts chapter), the town has huge boulders as topographical features. Carefree's population numbers about 3,300.

Cave Creek

Cave Creek was founded in 1874 when prospectors discovered gold to the northeast. Unlike other communities that became ghost towns after a gold rush, Cave Creek was a good area for ranching. The Cave Creek Wash, which flows year-round, and lush springs nearby helped provide water and grazing areas for cattle. The town, just west of Carefree and north of Phoenix, offers Valley residents a quick, admission-free getaway to the Old West in its Frontier Town, a group of Western-style shops and old-time saloons. Cave Creek's population is around

5,000. The town has a reputation as an artist's colony, but also as a biker haven that housed the Hell's Angels.

Fountain Hills

From northeast Scottsdale, Shea Boulevard travels through a pass in the McDowell Mountains to enter Fountain Hills. The McDowells form a natural boundary between the mountain community and Scottsdale. The bedroom community prides itself on being far from the hubbub and crime of the urban center. When building began in 1970, unincorporated Fountain Hills was seen as being attractive to retirees. The plan called for the then-unincorporated community to expand to 70,000 residents by the time it was built out. Times changed, though, and the market for that type of community evaporated. Now the town, which was incorporated in 1989, offers upscale, low-density neighborhoods. Its population is a mix of retirees, winter visitors, and families, with a population of about 22,500. The town takes its name from its fountain, which can spew a plume of water more than 560 feet into the air. Boosters claim that, when built, it was the world's tallest fountain, rising 10 feet higher than the Washington Monument. It was designed both as a landmark and a means to disperse the town's effluent.

Because of Fountain Hills' growth, the Fort McDowell Indian Community to the northeast of town is slowly being brought into the Valley's sphere. The small community has about 800 registered members. Revenues from tribal enterprises such as the Fort McDowell Resort and Casino, a tribal farm, a gas station on the busy Beeline Highway (AZ 87), Fort McDowell Adventures (a tourist destination that offers horseback riding and other activities in the desert), and Fort McDowell Sand and Gravel have helped the community improve its infrastructure and the income of its members.

Salt River Pima-Maricopa Indian Community

The traditionally agricultural Salt River Pima-Maricopa Indian Community is either at the

very southern part of the Northeast Valley or the very northern part of the Southeast Valley. For the most part, the Salt River marks its southern boundary just north of Mesa and Tempe. The community's chief crops are cotton, melons, potatoes, onions, and carrots. But it is considered the most urbanized of Arizona's reservations. Its Casino Arizona enterprises and the development of Salt River Fields at Talking Stick (spring training home to the Arizona Diamondbacks and Colorado Rockies) have made it more of a destination spot.

Online Info

www.visitphoenix.com
This is a terrific website for visitors and residents alike, developed by the Greater Phoenix Convention and Visitors Bureau. You'll find Phoenix facts, helpful tips, things to do, and useful links to Valley attractions.

www.phoenix.gov
The city's website offers useful information on municipal departments and services. There are also maps, a calendar of events, and pages of local facts. It's a great resource to help navigate the labyrinth of the City of Phoenix.

www.arizonaguide.com
This Arizona Office of Tourism's website will give you tons of information on Phoenix and the rest of Arizona. You can search for information by city, area, or activity. Check out online maps and request free visitor guides.

Along the boundaries with Mesa, Tempe, and Scottsdale, little shops do heavy business selling cigarettes free of state sales tax. The community also benefits from a 140-acre shopping center known as the Pavilions, the largest on Native American land in the nation. The shopping center sits right across from north Scottsdale at Indian Bend and Pima roads.

NORTHWEST VALLEY

The key to the Northwest Valley's development has always been roads. For most of its existence, Grand Avenue—which also doubles as several highways, including US 60—was the main drag that opened commercial development. Acres of industrial buildings line the highway as it progresses northwestward as the only major road in the Valley that proceeds on an angle to the squared-off grid system. Grand Avenue touches on downtown Glendale and downtown Peoria, then offers easy access to Sun City, Sun City West, Surprise, and Youngtown before heading for Wickenburg and Nevada.

The Loop 101 freeway, which begins at Camelback Road and 99th Avenue, heads north to approximately Bell Road and 83rd Avenue before jogging east to connect with I-17. The corridor served by this relatively new freeway has been the center for the Northwest Valley's growth. The Arrowhead Towne Center in Glendale is convenient to residents of Peoria and the Sun Cities and has been the focal point of commercial growth in the area.

Glendale

With a population of more than 226,000, Glendale is the third-largest city in the Valley, the fifth largest in the state, and the major

draw in the Northwest Valley. It was established in 1892 by members of the Church of the Brethren. For the longest time, the city had a reputation as a blue-collar community and the housing was on a par with that offered in Maryvale. The image of downtown was of a railroad crossing tying up traffic at the triple intersection of Grand, Glendale, and 59th Avenues. Glendale's downtown has been revitalized, developing a reputation as a premiere antiquing destination amid the pedestrian-friendly historic area. The city has 2 state-of-the-art sports arenas off the Loop 101 freeway. Jobing.com Arena houses the Phoenix Coyotes, while University of Phoenix Stadium, which hosted the 2008 Super Bowl, serves as home to the Arizona Cardinals. The Westgate City Center added retail and entertainment venues right at the doorstep of both sports complexes.

i Glendale city planners set up a series of 27 bronze plaques around the city to mark historic sites. You can see some of them on foot, and some on part of a driving tour of the city. Information: www.glendaleaz.gov or www.goglendaleaz.com.

To accommodate its rapid growth, Glendale annexed many square miles of unincorporated land to the southwest, including Luke Air Force Base. Unlike Williams Air Force Base (now called Phoenix-Mesa Gateway Airport), which was downsized out of the Southeast Valley due to post-Cold War defense cutbacks, Luke continues to pump money into the economy of the Northwest Valley. However, with Glendale's commercial and residential growth, the base has become a target of noise complaints and safety concerns because of its flight-training missions.

Peoria

Peoria was first settled by Chauncey Clark, who arrived from Peoria, IL, in the late 1800s. A primarily agricultural settlement, the city began to boom in the 1980s, attracting about 400 newcomers a month as housing developments marched over acres previously planted in cotton and other crops. Owing to the city's young-family orientation, the Peoria schools are among the best in the Valley. The city also opened the Peoria Sports Complex, spring-training home to the Seattle Mariners and San Diego Padres, which is just south of Bell Road from Arrowhead Towne Center's many amenities. As Peoria's population grew, Grand Avenue developed as a popular business corridor. The city has reached northward in its growth and swallowed up Lake Pleasant and Lake Pleasant Regional Park, one of the most popular weekend destinations among boating and fishing enthusiasts (see the Parks & Recreation chapter).

Sun City, Sun City West & Sun City Grand

Sun City and Sun City West are unincorporated retirement communities established in the past four decades by builder Del Webb. The primary way to reach these communities is via Bell Road, which runs east to west, connecting Sun City West to north Scottsdale far away to the east. The streets are designed in twisting, sometimes circular mazes that are nearly surrounded by golf courses. The speed limits are low, and golf carts have the right of way. Besides the golf courses, recreation centers form the center of social activity in the Sun Cities, and the communities' recreation boards act as a sort of low-level governmental body

(see the Retirement chapter). Shopping and restaurants are available, but the primary attraction of these retirement communities is the low-key lifestyle, which is augmented by easy access to Phoenix.

El Mirage

El Mirage, on the west bank of the Agua Fria River, was settled by migrant farm workers in the early 1930s. In this working-class community, many residents have roots that reach back to the city's founding. The city grew to 31,700 residents by 2010. Many are Hispanic, and El Mirage retains a proud Mexican-American tradition. Municipal leaders are looking to attract more businesses, particularly distributors and manufacturers. The Santa Fe Railroad and Grand Avenue (US 60) run parallel to each other through the center of El Mirage.

Surprise

Surprise continues to be one of the fastest-growing cities in Maricopa County. In fact, the population, about 96,000 in 2006, nearly tripled between 2000 and 2005. By 2010 it spiked to 117,500. The story goes that one of the city's first settlers back in 1929 said that it would be a surprise if the settlement became a city. Development has been spurred by both family-friendly and retirement communities. However, Sun City Grand, the latest development by Sun City founder Del Webb Corp., could tilt the community's demographic profile toward the older end of the spectrum. The 3,700-acre Sun City Grand sits on a triangle bounded by Bell Road to the south, Grand Avenue to the northeast, and the proposed Estrella Freeway (Loop 303) to the west. Surprise cradles Sun City West to its northeast and touches Sun City

to its east. El Mirage sits to the southeast. Surprise has plenty of room to grow because unincorporated county land stretches from its northwest and southwest boundaries. Picturesque Surprise Stadium is spring training home to the Texas Rangers and Kansas City Royals. A stone's throw away is one of the top municipal aquatic centers in the Valley.

SOUTHWEST VALLEY

Phoenix's headlong growth has pushed its fingers into the Southwest Valley, touching Litchfield Park, Goodyear, Avondale, Tolleson, and Buckeye. The West Valley is perfectly positioned to ride the wave of Arizona's burgeoning population. To central Phoenix residents and those in the East Valley, it might seem like the sticks. But it's cheaper to buy a big house, and you're about an hour closer to Santa Monica or San Diego than your pals in Phoenix or Scottsdale.

> **i** Arizona tourism authorities list scores of statewide events in a single spot. Want the details on Arizona Restaurant Week? Or where to listen to traditional Native American music? Or perhaps the best weekend event for your kids? The answers are found at www.arizonaguide.com/events-calendar.

Litchfield Park

Litchfield Park's main claim to fame is the Goodyear Tire and Rubber Company and its aircraft subsidiary. The company purchased the land that became Litchfield Park and Goodyear during World War I to grow cotton for use in its wartime products. In 1941, as Luke Air Force Base was being established to

the north, the government set up a defense plant run by Goodyear Aircraft Corporation in Litchfield Park. In the late 1960s the city developed a master plan that changed its character from agricultural and defense-oriented to suburban residential. It has since become home to many retired military personnel. The Wigwam Resort is Litchfield Park's major employer and offers a five-star getaway for locals and visitors alike. Life is easygoing out here, even though I-10 puts downtown Phoenix just 25 minutes away. The population is around 5,000.

Goodyear

The completion of I-10 in the early 1990s sparked a building boom in the town of Goodyear. Although the Goodyear company stopped growing cotton here at the end of World War II, the town remains primarily an agricultural community south of Litchfield Park. But that already is rapidly changing. Huge, creatively designed communities like Estrella Mountain Ranch have enhanced the city as destination spot. Years ago, there was nowhere to hang out or spend money. Now the town has the spring training home of Ohio's two big league teams, the Cincinnati Reds and Cleveland Indians. Restaurants and retail sprouted up around the stadium. Family-oriented growth is expected to further deplete the area's expansive farmland, and service industries geared to those residents are already booming. Goodyear's population is more than 65,000 and growing.

Avondale

This is the most heavily populated of the Southwest Valley suburbs, with more than 76,000 residents. Avondale was first settled by an outlaw named Billy Moore back during frontier settlement, but it wasn't incorporated as a city until 1946. It remains mainly an agricultural community, but like Goodyear to its west, it is undergoing a transformation. City planners want light industry and commercial enterprises to balance residential growth. Most agree that Avondale's popularity is owed to the excellent quality of life. Avondale's growth has encompassed Phoenix International Raceway, which used to sit on unincorporated county land. The raceway, a major draw on the NASCAR circuit, generates a good deal of revenue and traffic for all of the Southwest Valley.

Tolleson

At a scant 6 square miles, Tolleson sits just a few miles south and west of Desert Sky Mall in the Maryvale section of Phoenix. It also has a history as a farming community changed by I-10. The majority of Tolleson's largest employers are located within a half mile of the railroad right-of-way in the south half of the city. Tolleson's location makes the city a primary distribution hub.

Buckeye

Once known as the second-fastest-growing suburb in the US, the far-west town has slowed its growth, due to the rising number of foreclosures and postponed commercial development. Buckeye is a giant, 660-square-mile agricultural community with a population of more than 50,800. In 2006 Buckeye broke ground for its first corporate center, with future business development plans high on the priority list.

GETTING HERE, GETTING AROUND

The automobile is still the main method of transportation in the Valley. The freeways are often jammed at rush hours, and a lack of reliable long-distance public transportation between communities forces many motorists to sit in traffic jams every morning and late afternoon. Unlike in some metro areas, there's no commuter rail from the suburbs into the center commercial districts of Phoenix and Scottsdale. Sure, there are public bus routes, but few people with a comfortable car will pass up their own rides to wait in the heat at a bus stop.

High-occupancy vehicle carpool lanes help, and the Arizona Department of Transportation has worked to widen freeways to allow vehicles with two or more people to ease through the gauntlet of brake lights. Highway construction seems to be constant in the Phoenix area. With the expansion of the suburbs, ADOT recently expanded the Loop 202 in the Southeast Valley, linking Mesa with its neighboring suburbs of Gilbert and Chandler. The Loop 303 project in the West Valley has also linked major freeways, and its full expansion is ongoing.

The introduction of the Valley Metro light rail line in 2008 added a whole new dimension to getting around. Suddenly, folks who live in downtown Phoenix, Tempe, and Mesa found it easier to keep their cars parked in the cool of their garages. The first phase of the track, which will expand to other parts of the Valley in the future, runs from neighborhoods north of downtown Phoenix all the way to Main Street in Mesa through Arizona State University.

Critics said light rail was too little too late for a metro area where air pollution is far more serious than in other big cities, but it was a necessary step that has been well received by travelers. A new track will connect light rail to Sky Harbor International Airport, making it even easier to avoid the freeways. But if you don't mind driving, the wide-open space of Valley highways and mountain-bounded state routes also makes for a pleasant trip between destinations.

TRAVELING BY CAR

Interstates & Highways

Driving is nearly unavoidable in the Valley, especially if you're on vacation and looking to explore. Much like Los Angeles, the Phoenix metro area is very spread out and its suburbs are linked to the capital city by several major interstates and highways.

I-10

- **Also called:** Papago Freeway, west of the I-17 interchange in Phoenix; Maricopa Freeway, east of the I-17 interchange.
- **Serves:** The cities of Phoenix, Tempe, and Chandler, in addition to the West Valley communities of Tolleson, Avondale, Litchfield Park, Goodyear, and Buckeye.
- **Connects:** Los Angeles, to the west of Phoenix; Tucson, to the southeast.
- **Orientation:** Mostly east-west, except in Chandler, where it travels north-south before angling southeastward to Tucson. Note that even if you are traveling south for a few miles, the sign still reads EAST.
- **Special notes:** I-10 twice crosses paths with I-17 to form a loop around downtown Phoenix, once at the southern end of I-17 near Phoenix Sky Harbor International Airport and again at a major interchange known as "the stack," about a half mile south of McDowell Road, near 23rd Avenue.

i A gregarious bunch of people known as the Copper Square Ambassadors patrol downtown Phoenix year-round and will answer questions, recommend restaurants, and even escort you to your destination. Look for the people in the orange shirts and khaki pants. Information: (602) 495-1500 or www.downtownphoenix.com/ambassadors.

I-17

- **Also called:** Black Canyon Freeway, north of the junction with I-10; Maricopa Freeway, where it converges with I-10.
- **Serves:** Phoenix, Glendale, Peoria, in addition to the north Valley communities of Anthem and New River.
- **Orientation:** North-south, except where it becomes an east-west corridor through south Phoenix after rounding the Durango Curve, in the vicinity of 23rd Avenue and Durango Street.
- **Special notes:** Provides the most direct route to Sedona, Flagstaff, and other northern points. Inside the Valley it connects central Phoenix to the north Valley to the commercial hubs of Deer Valley Airpark and Metrocenter mall.

US 60

- **Also called:** Superstition Freeway.
- **Serves:** Tempe, Mesa, Gilbert, and Apache Junction, in addition to part of the Northwest Valley.
- **Connects:** The East Valley with Miami, Globe, and Native American communities on the east side of the state. Continues to New Mexico.
- **Orientation:** East-west.
- **Special notes:** Good way to reach Fiesta and Superstition Springs malls, both in Mesa. The western portion of the Superstition converges with Grand Avenue in downtown Phoenix and becomes the Phoenix-Wickenburg Highway. The Grand Avenue stretch of US 60 crawls through Glendale, Peoria, Sun City, and Surprise. This is a primary route to take from the Valley to the freeways that link Arizona to Las Vegas.

AZ 87

- **Also called:** Beeline Highway.
- **Serves:** Chandler, Gilbert, Mesa, and Fountain Hills.
- **Connects:** The East Valley with Payson to the north. Picks up I-10 southeast of the Valley near Picacho.
- **Orientation:** Mostly north-south.

- **Special notes:** This route is a good way to reach Fountain Hills and some of Arizona's cooler northern escapes. North of town, the Beeline Highway becomes a four-lane, sometimes-divided highway, beginning at the intersection of McDowell Road and Country Club on the Salt River Pima-Maricopa Native American Community. In town the Beeline Highway is a regular city street—Country Club in Mesa and Arizona Avenue in Chandler.

AZ 51

- **Also called:** Piestewa or Squaw Peak Freeway.
- **Intersects:** Phoenix and Paradise Valley.
- **Connects:** I-10 and Loop 202 near downtown Phoenix with north Phoenix, in addition to the Loop 101 north of Union Hills Drive.
- **Orientation:** North-south.
- **Special notes:** This scenic three- and four-lane route, with its newly opened HOV lanes, is a good alternative when I-17 is jammed. Previously called Squaw Peak Freeway, elevated portions of this highway offer nice views of the Phoenix skyline and the mountain preserve recreation areas around Squaw Peak. Some of the sidewalls feature public art.

i A popular, enlarged Phoenix map book offers relief for those trying to decipher tiny street names. The map is on a scale 60 percent larger, with easy-to-read sections for densely populated areas. The *Phoenix Metropolitan Street Atlas Professional Edition* is available for $35 from www.maps4u .com or by calling (602) 279-2323. It's also available on Amazon.com.

Loop 202

- **Also called:** Red Mountain Freeway, from Phoenix to Mesa; Santan Freeway from US 60 in Mesa south through Gilbert and Chandler.
- **Intersects:** Phoenix, Tempe, Mesa, Gilbert, and Chandler.
- **Connects:** Downtown Phoenix with Mesa and the Southeast Valley.
- **Orientation:** East-west and north-south.
- **Special notes:** Offers access to Phoenix Sky Harbor International Airport, downtown Tempe, and Arizona State University's main campus. It connects with Loop 101, which in turn links with US 60. Offers a wide view of Tempe Town Lake and ASU's butte-enclosed Sun Devil Stadium.

AZ 143

- **Also called:** Hohokam Expressway.
- **Intersects:** Phoenix and Tempe.
- **Connects:** Loop 202 with I-10.
- **Orientation:** North-south.
- **Special notes:** This short stretch of road offers access to the eastern entrance of the Phoenix Sky Harbor International Airport and parallels AZ 153 for the entire route.

AZ 153

- **Also called:** Sky Harbor Expressway.
- **Intersects:** Phoenix and Tempe.
- **Connects:** Washington and University streets on the east end of the airport.
- **Orientation:** North-south.
- **Special notes:** This short stretch of road offers access to the Phoenix Sky Harbor International Airport and parallels AZ 143 for the entire route.

Loop 101

- **Also called:** Agua Fria Freeway, between I-10 and I-17 on its western end in Glendale; the Pima Freeway, between I-17 and Loop 202 on the northern end in Scottsdale; the Price Freeway, south of Loop 202 on the eastern part of the loop in Mesa.
- **Intersects:** Glendale and Peoria on its western end; Phoenix and Scottsdale on its northern end; Mesa, Tempe, and Chandler on its southeastern end.
- **Connects:** On its western end, I-10 with I-17; on its northern end, I-17 with north Scottsdale; on its eastern end, US 60 in Mesa with downtown Scottsdale and Tempe.
- **Orientation:** North-south and east-west.
- **Special notes:** On the east side, exit the 101 at Indian School Road for direct access to downtown Scottsdale, and at Glendale Avenue in the West Valley to access Westgate City Center.

HOV Lanes

Take note of the lanes marked by diamonds on the interstates, AZ 51, and Loop 202—they function as High Occupancy Vehicle lanes during rush-hour traffic, Mon to Fri, 6 to 9 a.m. and 3 to 7 p.m. Unless you have a passenger, are traveling by motorcycle, or have an automobile that uses alternative fuel, you will pay a fine of nearly $400 for driving in HOV lanes during those specified hours. These lanes are convenient during rush-hour times when commuters slow traffic to a crawl in downtown Phoenix and on freeways leading to the suburbs. One caution: Keep an eye out for cars in the regular lane that are tempted to zip into the HOV lane. If a collision occurs, the difference in the speed of the two vehicles can be deadly.

Driving Tips

Posted limits on freeways vary from 55 to 65 miles per hour within the entire metropolitan area, so watch the signs very carefully. Arizona is a melting pot of people from all over the US, so freeway driving behaviors fluctuate from high-speed Californians to meandering Minnesotans. In addition, the Valley's jam-packed freeways can fluster newcomers, especially since seasoned residents don't yield the right of way as often as they do back East. Passing on the right tends to be a habit for transplants. Be aware of your exits and the possibility that you may have to cut across several lanes of traffic to reach them. Keep an eye out for others who might indulge in high-speed lane changes. Note: You may notice speed-enforcement cameras mounted along some Valley freeways. Don't fret. The technology pioneered on Scottsdale's stretch of the Loop 101 in 2006 expanded to nearly 80 cameras by 2009, only to be shut down by state legislators over concerns about privacy and revenues. Drivers no longer run the risk of being automatically ticketed on freeways, though many Valley cities continue to use fixed- and mobile- photo speed-enforcement cameras in their jurisdictions. Some believe Arizona could reactivate the highway patrol program in the future in a different political climate.

Surface Streets

Most of the Valley is on a grid system, with major thoroughfares marking each square mile. The major exception is Grand Avenue, which is also US 60, linking Phoenix to Wickenburg and points north. Grand Avenue's southern end is at Seventh Avenue and Van Buren Street, and it proceeds at a diagonal northwestwardly across the West

Valley, traveling from downtown Phoenix to downtown Glendale and Peoria and just southwest of the Sun Cities as it heads out of the Valley.

Central Avenue: Although it is not the geographical center of Phoenix, Central Avenue is central to the street-numbering system. The numbered avenues (First Avenue, Second Avenue, etc.) are north-south thoroughfares west of Central. The numbered streets (First Street, Second Street, and so on) are north-south thoroughfares on the east side of Central. Central Avenue is also the major corridor linking downtown Phoenix with uptown Phoenix, two major areas of high-rise business development.

Van Buren Street: An east-west thoroughfare that runs through downtown Phoenix, Van Buren Street is like Central Avenue in that it's the center point for the north-south streets. For example, north of Van Buren, Central Avenue becomes North Central Avenue. South of Van Buren, it becomes South Central Avenue.

PUBLIC TRANSPORTATION

METRO LIGHT RAIL
101 N. 1st Ave., Phoenix
(602) 253-5000
www.valleymetro.org
Phoenix's light rail system debuted in 2008 with a 20-mile starter line that connects Phoenix with Tempe and Mesa. The train runs through the downtown Phoenix entertainment hub and connects multiple Arizona State University campuses. Airport commuters can get dropped off near the airport, but have to catch a shuttle to their terminals. Eventually more of the Valley is likely to be connected, but that could take many years. Trains operate daily, and passengers can

catch one every 10 minutes during peak hours and every 20 minutes off-peak.

The intention is to interconnect the light rail system with the current bus system in such a way that people can get anywhere in the Valley with reasonable ease. It's not as extensive as light rail systems in other US cities, though locals were pleased to have some alternative to driving or waiting for city buses. Still, you must plan on understanding bus schedules if you want to rely exclusively on public transportation to get to most parts of Phoenix. There are 28 light-rail stations on the starter line and 5 transit centers. The transit centers are located at 19th Avenue and Montebello, Central Avenue and Camelback, 44th Street and Washington, Fifth and College, and at Sycamore Center in Mesa. It takes 57 minutes to travel the entire 20-mile route.

There are dozens of bars and restaurants within walking distance of light-rail stops, primarily in downtown Phoenix and along Central Avenue, in addition to those around ASU's main campus in Tempe. The train will also get you within blocks of Sun Devil Stadium in Tempe, in addition to the Suns and Diamondbacks games in downtown Phoenix.

Fares
The average light rail fare is $1.75 per ride. You can also choose from a variety of passes. An all-day pass costs $3.50. You can buy a 3-day pass for $10.50 or a 7-day pass for $17.50. A 31-day pass runs $55. All-day passes expire at 2:30 a.m. the following day. There are no transfers or tokens. Children 5 and younger ride free.

Valley Metro

REGIONAL PUBLIC TRANSPORTATION AUTHORITY

302 N. 1st Ave., Ste. 700, Phoenix
(602) 253-5000
www.valleymetro.org

Valley Metro is the regional identity of the public transit system. This umbrella name was adopted by each city's Regional Public Transportation Authority (RPTA) so that the public could use a seamless, coherent system. Articulated buses (the kind that have two joined sections that flex in the middle) are equipped with bike racks that can hold two or three bikes. Smoking is not allowed. All buses are wheelchair accessible.

Routes

Valley Metro buses link more than a dozen Valley communities with express routes to downtown Phoenix that originate in west Phoenix, Goodyear, Glendale, north Phoenix, Peoria, Scottsdale, Surprise, Ahwatukee, Mesa, Tempe, and Chandler. Bus frequency varies from every 15 minutes to every hour, depending on the route and the time of day. More than 60 local routes run from early morning until early evening. Actual hours of operation differ according to the routes. Connections are usually easy because most routes are generally north-south or east-west and intersect with one another.

Twenty-six express routes connect the aforementioned outlying areas with downtown Phoenix. Designed for business commuters, express buses head inbound to downtown during the morning rush hour and outbound during the afternoon rush. Each bus stops at free park-and-ride lots.

All routes run Monday to Friday, and most local routes run on Saturday. Fewer run on Sunday. Most buses operate on holidays, with the exception of express and RAPID routes, which also don't run on weekends. The *Bus Book*, which contains route and fare information and route maps, can be picked up on any Valley Metro bus, at Central Station at Central Avenue and Van Buren Street in downtown Phoenix, or at the libraries and municipal buildings of the participating cities.

Fares

Fares are $1.75 for a local route and $2.75 for an express route. Bring exact change. All-day passes are around $5 and 3-day passes around $10. Transfers are no longer available, and each ride must be purchased separately. Reduced fares of 85 cents per ride are available for youths 6–18, seniors 65 and older, and persons with disabilities. Children 5 and younger ride free. Other reduced fares are available to ASU students. For information on reduced fares, bus routes, ticket books, and passes, call (602) 253-5000. Buses generally run 6 a.m. to 8 p.m. Sat, 8 a.m. to 5 p.m. Sun and holidays.

i Some riders of RAPID and Express systems can now get help finding a seat. Visit http://phoenix.gov/publictransit/rapid.html to find the average daily passenger counts for each trip. Since buses don't accommodate standing passengers, you can find a less crowded bus and get to work a little earlier or later.

Shuttles

DASH, the Downtown Area Shuttle

This free shuttle service runs every 12 minutes in downtown Phoenix, 6:30 a.m. to 6:30

p.m., and connects the State Capitol with downtown in two separate loops. Call Valley Metro for more information: (602) 253-5000.

FLASH, the Free Local Area Shuttle

FLASH runs through downtown Tempe and around the Arizona State University campus. As the name says, the fare is free. Separate routes run every 10 to 15 minutes and every 30 minutes, generally 7 a.m. to 10 p.m. Service ends earlier Friday to Sunday. FLASH routes running in a clockwise direction are called FLASH Forward, while those running counterclockwise are called FLASH Back. For more information call Valley Metro: (602) 253-5000.

BUS RAPID TRANSIT (RAPID)

RAPID, a Valley Metro park-and-ride bus service, transports commuters to and from downtown Phoenix, traveling downtown in the morning and homeward at night. Four lines operate Monday to Friday. Fees are $2.75 per one-way trip, or $5.50 for an all-day pass purchased in advance. All morning RAPID trips wind up downtown. Routes and schedules are adjusted occasionally by season, primarily in January and July.

RAPID I-10 West operates with 2 morning pickup/afternoon drop-off locations: Desert Sky Mall Transit Center and 79th Avenue/I-10 Park and Ride.

RAPID I-10 East has one morning pickup/afternoon drop-off location: 40th Street and Pecos Road (northwest corner of Pecos Road) Park and Ride.

RAPID I-17 has 3 morning pickups/afternoon locations: Deer Valley Community Center Park and Ride, Happy Valley Park and Ride, and Metrocenter Transit Center.

RAPID SR 51 collects riders in the morning from Paradise Valley Mall and Bell Road at AZ 51 and returns in the early evening.

GUS, the Glendale Urban Shuttle

GUS serves Glendale's central corridor, which includes the bustling Westgate City Center. GUS costs a quarter to ride—10 cents for seniors and ADA passengers 10 a.m. to 2 p.m. GUS 1 operates Mon to Sat 7 a.m. to 6:30 p.m., Sun 8 a.m. to 6 p.m. GUS 2 operates Mon to Fri 9 a.m. to 5:50 p.m. GUS 3 operates Mon to Fri 8 a.m. to 5 p.m. Information: (623) 930-3510; www.glendaleaz.com/transit.

Scottsdale Trolley

The Scottsdale Trolley is a free service that runs every 15 minutes and connects Scottsdale Fashion Square with Loloma Transit Center near Old Town. Its many stops along the way include the Scottsdale Road/Main Street arts district and the Galleria Corporate Center. Ollie the Trolley's new expanded service includes the southern circulator route that collects passengers from several senior centers and drives to Old Town. It operates daily 11 a.m. to 6 p.m. year-round and until 9 p.m. Thurs during Scottsdale ArtWalk. Information: (480) 970-8130; www.scottsdale.gov/trolley.

i Goldwater Bank, located in Scottsdale's Waterfront, caters to the business community and provides in-house concierge service. Yes, someone will make dinner reservations or arrange your shopping. You'll need a minimum balance of $25,000 to keep an account there, but the bank is worth a visit. It's at 7135 E. Camelback Rd. in Scottsdale (480-281-8200).

Rideshare

The Valley Metro Rideshare program was developed to fight vehicle-emitted air pollution, which is infamously familiar to Phoenix residents, who have to live with more bad air days than most Americans. The lingering layer of soot and smog hanging over the city on windless days is known as "The Brown Cloud." The rideshare program can help Valley residents set up carpools, vanpools, telecommuting, and compressed work schedules. For information, sign up at http://sharetheride .valleymetro.org to get matched with ride buddies based on your schedule and needs.

Dial-a-Ride

The dial-a-ride service is available in many communities in the Phoenix metropolitan area. For general information and referrals, call (800) 775-7295. The service is geared to meet the needs of seniors 65 and older and persons with disabilities, though some dial-a-ride systems are available for use by the general public in some communities.

People who have a disability that prevents them from using or accessing the regular bus service may qualify for special service under the Americans with Disabilities Act. They must apply in advance to Valley Metro for certification and must call the respective dial-a-ride at least 1 day in advance to schedule their service. The certification process may take up to 21 days to complete and may require verification of disabilities from a doctor or other medical professional. Others may be required to meet low-income criteria.

East Valley Dial-a-Ride, (480) 633-0101, serves senior citizens and persons with disabilities. Days and hours of operation vary from city to city. Call for details.

El Mirage Dial-a-Ride, (623) 876-4232, serves the general public 8 a.m. to 5 p.m. Mon to Fri with no holiday service.

Glendale Dial-a-Ride, (623) 930-3500, serves the general public 7 a.m. to 6 p.m. Mon to Fri; 7 a.m. to 5 p.m. Sat, Sun, and holidays, which are only available through reservations made by the previous afternoon. Those seeking ADA service should call Glendale Dial-a-Ride at (623) 930-3515.

Mesa Dial-a-Ride service is available only to Mesa residents who are ADA-certified. Call East Valley Dial-a-Ride to reserve. (480) 633-0101.

Paradise Valley ADA Service, handled by Phoenix Dial-a-Ride, (602) 253-4000, serves only persons with disabilities and runs 5 a.m. to 10 p.m. daily.

Peoria Dial-a-Ride, (623) 773-7435, serves the general public 6 a.m. to 6 p.m. Mon to Fri, with no holiday service. Extended ADA service hours are 4:30 a.m. to 9 p.m. Mon to Fri. ADA-eligible trips require as many as 14 days' advance notice to reserve.

Phoenix Dial-a-Ride, (602) 253-4000, serves seniors and persons with disabilities 7 days a week. Weekday service is provided 5 a.m. to 10 p.m. Weekend service is provided from 5 a.m. until 10 p.m. Reservations for ADA service must be made at least 1 day in advance and can be made between 8 a.m. and 9 p.m.

The Sun Cities Area Transit System (SCAT) service, (602) 266-8723, is now operated by Valley Metro in a partnership with Discount Cab. Reservations require 1 day's advance notice and are geared toward residents of the West Valley retirement communities.

Surprise Dial-a-Ride, (623) 222-1622, serves the general public 7 a.m. to 5 p.m. Mon to Fri, with no holiday service.

AIR TRAVEL

PHOENIX SKY HARBOR INTERNATIONAL AIRPORT
3400 Sky Harbor Blvd., Phoenix
(602) 273-3300
www.phxskyharbor.com

Sky Harbor is known as "America's Friendliest Airport" and as one of the top-10 busiest airports in the US. It accommodates 1,500 commercial flights and 100,000 commercial passengers a day for an estimated $90 million daily economic impact. Sky Harbor also serves general aviation, corporate, cargo, and military planes. The airport is seemingly always under construction. A new traffic tower, one of the largest at American airports, began operations in 2007. A state-of-the-art baggage screening system to speed people through security was also added in recent years. Free Wi-Fi service is available near the shops on either side of security checkpoints.

The airport began operating in 1929, and in 1935 the city of Phoenix purchased the airport, which then stood on 300 acres. Terminal 1 opened October 13, 1952, and began Sky Harbor's ascent to its current status. The airport handled 296,066 passengers in the first year Terminal 1 was open. In 1961 it served 920,096 passengers. Terminal 2 was built in 1962 for $2.7 million, just as Sky Harbor broke the 1-million-passenger-per-year mark. The city strove to make the terminal a lovely gateway to Phoenix and commissioned the late Paul Coze to create a three-panel mosaic mural, known as The Phoenix. It still greets passengers in Terminal 2 today. The passenger rate grew to 3 million in 1971, so planning began for the construction of Terminal 3, which opened in 1979. Growth continued, and the Phoenix City Council authorized construction of Terminal 4 in 1986. The $248-million terminal and 4-level parking garage opened in 1990, and Terminal 1 was closed. In 1991 Terminal 4 alone handled 15.4 million passengers, 70 percent of the airport's traffic.

There are more than 120 gates and about 30,000 parking spaces at the airport.

The Valley's 20-mile light rail line (opened in 2008) and the expected 2013 completion of the first phase of a $1.1 billion PHX Sky Train people-mover are expected to make it even easier to navigate the airport, which is generally regarded as one of the most efficient in the country.

> **i** Sky Harbor has a slick paging system, the first of its kind worldwide. Travelers can send and receive messages inside the airport at Paging Assistance Locations (PALs). Names of those being paged are announced and displayed on monitors throughout the airport. Messages may be sent in several ways, including from Braille-enhanced keyboards.

With passenger traffic at about 41 million annually and strict security measures, it's a good idea to arrive at the airport about 2 hours before your flight is scheduled to leave. A free shuttle travels from economy parking to the terminals every 6 minutes.

The airport is about 10 minutes from downtown Phoenix. It's almost centrally located in the Valley and provides easy access to freeways. Keep in mind, however, that the roads around the airport can appear like a labyrinth to visitors. Have your smart phone, guidebook, or other directions ready.

Here are the airlines that serve Phoenix Sky Harbor International Airport and their terminals:

- **Aeromexico**—Terminal 4
- **Air Canada**—Terminal 2
- **AirTran Airways**—Terminal 3
- **Alaska Airlines**—Terminal 2
- **American**—Terminal 3
- **British Airways**—Terminal 4
- **Continental**—Terminal 2
- **Delta**—Terminal 3
- **Frontier**—Terminal 3
- **Great Lakes**—Terminal 2
- **Hawaiian Airlines**—Terminal 3
- **JetBlue Airways**—Terminal 3
- **Southwest**—Terminal 4
- **Sun Country**—Terminal 3
- **United and TED**—Terminal 2
- **US Airways**—Terminal 4
- **WestJet**—Terminal 4

Ground Transportation

All rates listed below are the maximum allowed under contract with Sky Harbor. Passengers are encouraged to negotiate for better rates.

Taxis

AAA/Yellow Cab, Apache Taxi and Mayflower Cab have contracts to provide service to Sky Harbor passengers at the following rates: First mile $5; each additional mile $2; with an airport surcharge of $1. The minimum fare is $15 plus the $1 airport surcharge. There should be no extra charges for more than one passenger in a party or for baggage.

SuperShuttle

SuperShuttle operates 24 hours a day and offers airport-to-door service. Vans depart every 15 minutes to all areas of the Valley 9 a.m. to 9 p.m. and with less frequency 9 p.m. to 9 a.m. Flat rates are charged to each geographical area being served and range from $7 to $35 for a single passenger, with a $7 charge for additional passengers within a group. Call (602) 244-9000 or (800) 258-3826 (outside Arizona) for information or visit www.supershuttle.com. You can make reservations online. To get to the airport via SuperShuttle, call at the same time you make your airline reservations. Reservations from the airport are not required; go to an outer island marked VAN SERVICE.

i Timing is everything at the airport. If you're making a pickup and misjudged the incoming flight time, park at one of Sky Harbor's two cell phone waiting lots. They are open 24 hours a day and provide updated flight information on electronic message boards. There are 90 parking spaces and toilets at each. Rather than circling the airport, flip on the radio, recline your seat, and wait peacefully for the curbside call.

Limousines

All Star Trans, AMP Enterprises, Black Pearl Limo, Mechelle Limousine, Monarch Limousine, and Zion Limousine offer limousine service from Sky Harbor. Their rates are set by zone and range from $35 to $85. These rates include transport of one or two in a party to the same address. Each additional passenger is $10 a head. Feel free to negotiate with the drivers for a lower rate, especially if you wait for other passengers to load and share the fare.

Bus & Light Rail

The light rail drops at 44th and Washington Streets, where a free airport shuttle picks up passengers every 10 minutes. The shuttle stops at each terminal. Valley Metro bus route 13 stops at the airport and provides

connections to the entire Valley. Call (602) 253-5000 for information.

Important Sky Harbor Phone Numbers

Airport Paging
(602) 273-3455
Customs/Immigration
(602) 914-1400
General Information
(602) 273-3300
Ground Transportation
(602) 273-3383
Lost and Found
(602) 273-3307
Parking
(602) 273-4545

Courtesy Rides

Many hotels and resorts provide free pickup and drop-off service for their patrons. To check with your place of accommodation, a courtesy phone center for many hotels and resorts is adjacent to the baggage claim areas in the passenger terminals.

Wheelchair Accessibility

Taxis and limousines will transport passengers using wheelchairs as long as the wheelchairs or other appliances can be folded to fit in the trunk with the luggage. Lift-equipped service for passengers in wheelchairs is available from the SuperShuttle. Passengers should call (602) 244-9000 or, from outside Arizona, (800) 331-3565 for this service. The Valley Metro bus routes that stop at Sky Harbor are also lift-equipped, as are interterminal buses at the airport. Rental cars with hand controls are available from Avis and Hertz. Both need 48 hours' notice. For private

carriers, contact the particular companies to find out their wheelchair accessibility.

Parking

Each terminal has its own parking area, and all are wheelchair accessible.

- **Terminal 2**—The garage sits north of the terminal and features 2,200 spaces. The roof has been converted to 1,100 economy spaces with a daily $11 maximum. Short-term parking on the lower level costs $4 per hour, with a $25 daily maximum. Terminal 2 is the only garage with split-rate parking.
- **Terminal 3**—The garage adjoins the terminal to the east. It features nearly 1,900 spaces and cannot accommodate vehicles taller than 6 feet 8 inches. The rates are $4 per hour, with a $25 daily maximum.
- **Terminal 4**—The garage sits above the terminal and has 6,800 regular spaces on 6 levels. It also features 100 spaces for vehicles over 7 feet tall. Rates are $4 per hour with a $25 daily maximum.

i For a bird's-eye view of the parking picture, go to www.phx skyharbor.com. Look under "Transportation and Parking" to download the Parking Pocket Pal. It's a sanity saver. During busy seasons (January to May and holidays), call the parking hotline, (602) 273-4545, to find parking lots still accepting cars.

In addition, the airport offers 2 long-term economy lots. The lot west of Terminal 2 can accommodate nearly 1,600 vehicles outdoors and accepts vehicles over 7 feet tall. The lot east of Terminal 4 has been expanded to 5,900 spaces in 2 garages

as well as 4,800 surface spaces. Both lots run shuttle service to the terminals. Rates for surface economy lots are $4 per hour, with a daily $9 maximum. Garage economy rates are $4 per hour, with an $11 daily maximum.

The airport offers a 24-hour parking hotline at (602) 273-4545 for information and availability of spots. Hourly parking status is available online at www.phxskyharbor.com.

Rental Cars

As part of Sky Harbor's makeover, a consolidated off-site car rental facility houses all rental agency counters and vehicles in a single location. Located west of the airport, near 16th Street and Buckeye Road, at 1805 E. Sky Harbor Circle South, the rental facility can house up to 5,600 vehicles. A fleet of 62 buses runs to all three terminals about every 5 to 10 minutes. The following companies serve the airport:

- **Advantage**—(800) 777-5500
- **Alamo**—(800) 462-5266
- **Avis**—(800) 331-1212
- **Budget**—(800) 527-7000
- **Dollar**—(800) 800-4000
- **Enterprise**—(800) 736-8222
- **Fox**—(800) 225-4369
- **Hertz**—(800) 654-3131
- **National**—(800) 227-7368
- **Payless**—(800) 729-5377
- **Thrifty**—(800) 847-4389

i Sky Harbor's Rental Car Information Desk, (602) 683-3741, can answer any questions 8:30 a.m. to 5 p.m. Mon to Fri.

Other Valley Airports

In addition to Phoenix Sky Harbor International Airport, numerous smaller airports in the Valley serve general aviation traffic, such as corporate and private planes. These airports, known as "relievers," draw a good measure of the general-aviation traffic that would otherwise be served by Sky Harbor.

CHANDLER MUNICIPAL AIRPORT
2380 S. Stinson Way, Chandler
(480) 782-3540
A general-aviation airport, Chandler handles more than 203,000 operations annually. Its control tower is open 6 a.m. to 9 p.m. There are hangars, shaded tie downs, and open tie downs at the airport, located about 20 miles southeast of Sky Harbor. Airport-based businesses include an avionics shop, full-service fuel pumps, a repair shop, the hangar cafe, and 2 flight schools. Sightseeing tours are available.

GLENDALE MUNICIPAL AIRPORT
6801 N. Glen Harbor Blvd., Glendale
(623) 930-2188
www.glendaleaz.com/airport
The Glendale airport became a hub for the 2008 Super Bowl. It is currently home base for approximately 450 planes, both corporate and private, and handles more than 136,000 airport operations annually. Located about 30 minutes northwest of downtown Phoenix, the airport is home to about 20 businesses, ranging from airplane hangar sales to an aviation insurance adjuster. Airport officials also operate a medical evacuation helicopter, though the airport is primarily for general aviation. A restaurant and a gift shop are on-site. The airport also features a terminal, maintenance services, and rental cars. The control tower operates 6 a.m. to 8:30 p.m. Mon to Fri and 7 a.m. to 7 p.m. Sat and Sun.

MESA FALCON FIELD
4800 E. Falcon Dr., Mesa
(480) 644-2444
www.mesaaz.gov/falcon_field

Falcon Field handles approximately 310,000 general-aviation takeoffs and landings a year. Falcon Field, which opened in 1941, was used originally by the US War Department to train combat pilots for the British Royal Air Force. When World War II ended, the City of Mesa took over the airport. Today nearly 900 planes are based there, along with 30 aviation-related businesses, 50 general commercial enterprises, and 3 restaurants. The control tower operates 6 a.m. to 9 p.m., and the airport features a gift shop, a pilot shop, maintenance, fuel, and rental-car services. It's also home to the Confederate (also called the Commemorative) Air Force Museum. In addition, 4 aerial photography and sightseeing operations run out of Falcon Field.

PHOENIX DEER VALLEY AIRPORT
702 W. Deer Valley Rd., Phoenix
(623) 869-0975
www.deervalleyairport.com

The City of Phoenix Aviation Department, which runs Sky Harbor, has also run this general-aviation airport in the north-central part of the Valley since 1971. Deer Valley, located in north Phoenix about 20 minutes out of downtown, is known as the second-busiest general aviation airport in the US. The control tower operates 6 a.m. to 9 p.m. The airport offers fuel sales, overnight parking, an aircraft maintenance bay, a pilot shop, a restaurant, and a car rental facility.

PHOENIX GOODYEAR AIRPORT
1658 S. Litchfield Rd., Goodyear
(623) 932-1200
www.goodyearairport.com/index.html

The City of Phoenix Aviation Department has managed this airport 24 miles southwest of downtown Phoenix since 1968. The airport was built in 1943 and was originally operated by the US Navy. It served as a support facility for the nearby aircraft division of the Goodyear Tire and Rubber Company. In 1951 the Navy expanded the airport as a base for military aircraft storage, which was its mission until 1965, when the US General Services Administration took over with plans to phase it out. The major tenant is Lufthansa Airlines' Airline Training Center of Arizona. The airport serves the general-aviation needs of western Maricopa County. The control tower operates 6 a.m. to 9 p.m. The airport offers fuel sales, overnight parking, a pilot shop, a flight-planning and lounge area, an aircraft wash rack, and a conference room.

PHOENIX-MESA GATEWAY AIRPORT
5835 S. Sossaman Rd., Mesa
(480) 988-7600
www.phxmesagateway.org

Phoenix-Mesa Gateway Airport (formerly known as Williams Gateway) is a hub for Allegiant Air, which provides affordable flights to western destinations like Missoula, Montana, and Colorado Springs. The airport is on the site of former Williams Air Force Base, which was closed down in post-Cold War Department of Defense budget cuts. It handles approximately 280,000 takeoffs and landings per year—including corporate, cargo, general aviation, and military aircraft. A major economic hub for the area, the airport has about 35 business tenants, including aircraft maintenance, modification, and testing services. It also offers car rental services in the remodeled facility. The control tower operates daily, 6 a.m. to 9 p.m. Facilities include fuel sales, a pilot lounge, VIP lounge, pilot

shop, and an excellent cafe. Arizona State University's east campus is also here.

SCOTTSDALE MUNICIPAL AIRPORT
15000 N. Airport Dr., Scottsdale
(480) 312-2321
www.scottsdaleaz.gov/airport

It's impossible to miss the luxury jets and other small aircraft zooming over the top of your car as you drive along Frank Lloyd Wright Boulevard just north of Scottsdale Municipal Airport. The airport is home base to about 450 planes. It handles approximately 200,000 takeoffs and landings a year surrounded by the Scottsdale Airpark, an industrial park that is home to 30 national/regional corporations and nearly 2,200 small- and medium-size businesses. Commercial charters take off on sightseeing tours from the airport, handling about 10,000 passengers annually. The control tower operates 6 a.m. to 9 p.m. The airport features a large parking lot, an array of specialty shops, a restaurant, maintenance support and repairs, a rental-car company, limousine services, conference rooms, a pilot lounge, and aircraft cleaning and storage. The airport is especially busy in the cooler months during Scottsdale's hectic event season as out-of-town VIPs touch down in their personal planes.

PRIVATE TRANSPORTATION

ARIZONA SHUTTLE SERVICE
5350 E. Speedway Blvd., Tucson
(520) 795-6771, (800) 888-2749
www.arizonashuttle.com

Arizona Shuttle Service runs passenger vans between Phoenix Sky Harbor International Airport and three Tucson locations, in addition to Flagstaff. It has offices in Terminals 2, 3, and 4 at the airport. The company offers 56 trips daily between the three cities and from Sky Harbor 6:15 a.m. to 11:15 p.m. Arizona Shuttle offers a variety of rates, but fares start at $39 one way. Check the website for special fares.

EL PASO-LOS ANGELES LIMOUSINE EXPRESS
1015 N. 7th St., Phoenix •
(602) 254-4101
www.eplalimo.com

El Paso-Los Angeles Limousine Express has 4 buses leaving nightly for El Paso, Los Angeles, and Las Vegas. Tickets for El Paso and Las Vegas are $50 one way and $95 round-trip. Los Angeles fares are $42 and $80. You're advised to purchase tickets in advance, especially for weekend departures, as the buses fill rapidly. Special children's rates are available.

GREYHOUND BUS LINES
2115 E. Buckeye Rd., Phoenix
(602) 389-4200, (800) 231-2222
www.greyhound.com

Greyhound can get you here from anywhere in the US. You'll arrive at its main terminal in Phoenix or around the Valley in Tolleson and Mesa. For information in Spanish, call (800) 531-5332.

SEDONA PHOENIX SHUTTLE
(928) 282-2066, (800) 448-7988
www.sedona-phoenix-shuttle.com

Providing service between Phoenix and the Verde Valley, this company has representatives in the baggage claim area of each terminal in Phoenix Sky Harbor International Airport. It offers nine trips daily from the airport to Sedona, costing $50 one way and $95 round-trip. Children 10 and under

ride free with a paying adult. Fares are $40 one way, $80 round-trip if you only go as far as Camp Verde. The service prefers that you make reservations at least 1 week in advance.

TAXIS & LIMOUSINES

The Phoenix metro area is so spread out, taxis are hardly the most popular option. Nearly everyone drives. Most Valley dwellers use the pay-per-mile taxi as a last resort. Friends will band together to cover the hefty fare in order to avoid driving drunk over 20-mile distances between cities.

Hailing a cab is pretty much a lost art among Valley dwellers. If you want a cab, you'll find them lined up at the airport or in front of your downtown hotel or after last call at the bar. Otherwise you'll have to give the cab company a call. Rates vary from company to company, although fares hover around $2.50 for pickup and $2 for each additional mile.

The following taxi companies serve the entire Valley 24 hours a day:

- **AAA/Yellow Cab**—(602) 252-5252
- **Discount Cab**—(602) 200-2000
- **Paul's Taxi**—(602) 956-8294
- **V.I.P. Taxi**—(602) 300-3000

On the other end of the spectrum, limousines are as popular here as anywhere because they make a nice splurge for a special occasion—at least, for most of us. Limos are generally rented by the hour, with at least a 2-hour minimum rental. Some companies require a higher minimum at busy times, such as weekends and the holiday season. Fares also vary by the type of limo rented. A 10-passenger limo costs more than a 6-passenger limo. You can get a decent town car in Arizona for $75 to $100 an hour, with the 2-hour minimum, not including gratuity and tax. Of course, you can always splurge even more than that—ask for a TV or a bar or food service or all of the above. In addition, most limousine companies also offer van and sedan rentals on similar terms.

Here are some of the limousine companies that serve the Valley:

- **Arizona Limousines**—(602) 267-7097
- **Desert Rose Limousines**—(623) 780-0159
- **The Driver Provider**—(602) 453-0001
- **Sky Mountain Limousines**—(480) 830-3944
- **Valley Limousine**—(602) 254-1955

HISTORY

Since 2008, the Valley and Arizona have earned some unfortunate distinctions. The region has coped with some of the most critical and violent episodes in its recent history, forcing residents to choose sides or hunt for their own facts. Yet in spite of social tensions, Arizonans have fought through the headlines and outside scrutiny to push deeper into a 21st century of tolerance.

Phoenix was dubbed the Kidnapping Capital of America as the city's rising concern over Mexican cartel-related kidnappings and home invasions fetched international media attention. The Valley was ground zero for the national immigration debate, as protestors took to the streets demanding authorities reject state policymakers' controversial Senate Bill 1070, the first of its kind in the US, which makes it a state crime to be in the country illegally. Police and citizens scuffled in Phoenix in a series of incidents, including fatal shootings, which heightened concerns about racial profiling. Then, on a sunny morning in January 2011, US Congresswoman Gabrielle Giffords was shot in the head during an assassination attempt that left six others, including a federal judge, fatally wounded at a Tucson shopping plaza. She narrowly survived, though many early media reports said she was dead, further fueling the confusion and madness of the time.

Outsiders viewed Arizona as the Wild West reborn. Nearly everyone with family and friends in other states found themselves defending their state. Commentators whipped up debates about the economic impact on law enforcement, gun rights, mental illness, and the lack of security around public servants. As the Valley and state's collective consciousness homed in on issues, residents seemed to rally together in understanding. They had no choice but to push forward.

OVERVIEW

Aside from politics and social upheaval, the Valley's runaway growth within the last few decades makes it seem like a young city. Much like with the immigration debate, Phoenix has also been the epicenter for the national housing and mortgage arguments. Rows and rows of incomplete or foreclosed residential properties line streets in the Phoenix suburbs, marking a key element of the national economic crisis.

It's a young city and a changing city, but the Phoenix metro area is heir to a rich and varied cultural history. Very few historical buildings have survived, and strip malls tend to dominate the landscape in a large part of the Valley, but the past is still honored. The desert still preserves the foundations of prehistoric towns and the abandoned mine shafts of prospects gone bust.

Prehistoric Native Americans were the first people attracted to the Salt River Valley. They were hunters and gatherers, living off the land, and their arrowheads can occasionally be found in the more remote areas of the Valley. The first tribes came 20,000 to 40,000 years ago.

i One of the most unique books on Arizona history is *Arizona: A Cavalcade of History* by Marshall Trimble.

The Hohokam (pronounced *hoe-hoe-com*) were the first long-term settlers in the Valley. They farmed the Valley and dug nearly 250 miles of irrigation canals to water their fields. This early engineering feat formed the basis of the modern canal system that helped modern Phoenix rise from the desert. After 1,700 years of tilling the Valley, the Hohokam disappeared less than a century before Columbus sailed to America. Archaeologists cannot agree on why their civilization disappeared, but suggestions include war or economic stresses brought on by bad drought and flooding. Modern Pima in central and southern Arizona trace their ancestry to these ancient peoples. Archaeologists believe that their more decentralized lifestyle proved better suited to the harsh conditions of the desert. After the Hohokam way of life was gone, the Valley remained depopulated. Some ancient hunters camped in the Valley from time to time, but few stayed for long.

New pioneers emerged, further shaping the arid desert landscape into their home.

THE REFOUNDING OF PHOENIX

The Spanish arrived in the area in 1539. They named it Arizona, meaning "arid zone" in Spanish. The Tohono O'odham had a similar, and more optimistic, word for their land—*Ali-Shonak*, or "place of small springs." Conquistadors and Catholic priests explored the area and sent missionaries far to the north into the Hopi and Navajo lands. They claimed the region for Spain, but the Crown's hold on it was tenuous at best. In 1680 Native Americans rose up against the missionaries and soldiers in what is now called the Pueblo Revolt. The Spanish were kicked out for more than 10 years but eventually returned in greater numbers. They founded presidios, or fortified towns, in Tucson and Tubac. Both are still thriving communities. There were several conflicts between the two peoples for the next hundred years, but Spanish influence gradually increased.

Throughout this time the Salt River Valley was virtually ignored. Occasionally Pima and Maricopa Indians would travel from their traditional lands around the Gila River and farm the area, but there was no permanent settlement.

In 1821 Mexico gained independence from Spain. Soon it and the United States clashed as the Americans tried to expand westward. The Americans thought it was their Manifest Destiny to build a country stretching from coast to coast. Anglo settlers in a northeastern Mexican territory instigated and fought a successful rebellion to found the independent Republic of Texas in 1836. It joined the US 9 years later. The US fought Mexico in 1846, and after a short but bloody conflict, the Americans won what is now called New Mexico, California, and Arizona. The Treaty of Guadalupe Hidalgo was signed on February 2, 1848, recognizing the region as American and establishing peace between the two nations. The US government established the New Mexico Territory as an administrative state for the eastern part

of these new lands. In 1854 the US expanded this territory with the Gadsden Purchase, which bought a strip of land that is now southern Arizona and New Mexico.

The territorial capital was at Santa Fe, a long way from Arizona, so there was little official help in times of drought or Apache raids. Locals believed they should become a separate territory so that their concerns could be voiced more directly in Washington. In 1861, while the country was descending into the bloodbath of the Civil War, a group of local boosters gathered in Tucson, then the largest settlement in Arizona, and voted to form a territory in the Confederacy. The government in Richmond agreed and established a garrison in Tucson. In June 1862 a column of federal troops, including famed frontiersman and army scout Kit Carson, marched from California and, after a brief skirmish at Picacho Peak, took the entire territory for the Union. It was the westernmost conflict of the Civil War and led to Arizona becoming its own territory on February 24, 1863.

i Construction teams working on the new Phoenix Convention Center recently discovered the remains of a prehistoric Hohokam village under the old Civic Plaza. Archaeologists were called in, and they discovered pit houses over 3,000 years old. The archaeologists filled about 3,500 sacks with artifacts to be studied later.

In 1865 the US Army established Fort McDowell on the Verde River, 18 miles north of the Salt River, to ward off Apache attacks on the small mining encampments in the area. The supplier for the fort was John Y. T. Smith. He built the first European house in

the Valley and supplied the fort with hay he found growing in the old Hohokam canals. His home, which is gone now, stood near the eastern end of Sky Harbor International Airport.

Although Smith noticed that the damp earth of the old canals was good for growing hay, it took Civil War veteran Jack Swilling to realize their full potential. Swilling was a bit of a shifty character—he fought for both sides in the war and was known for his short temper. Perhaps a life of fighting made Swilling want something more peaceful. He decided to set up a farm in the Valley and, in 1867, started cleaning up the old canals and putting them back into use. He got financial backing from some investors in Wickenburg and established the Swilling Irrigation and Canal Company. Within a year the first European farm in the Valley, owned by Frency Sawyer, began operations. Swilling started a farm as well, first near Tempe and then near Fort McDowell.

After that the town grew quickly. People found that the old canals were so well designed that the Salt River Valley was one of the best agricultural areas in the territory. As more and more people settled there, citizens formed a committee to name their new home. Swilling wanted to name it Stonewall, after Confederate General Stonewall Jackson. Apparently Swilling had fonder memories of fighting for the Confederacy than for the Union. Someone else suggested Salina, in honor of the river that gave the new town life. The name that stuck came from a newcomer named Lord Darrell Duppa, an educated Englishman who passed himself off as nobility to the provincial Americans of the frontier. He said the site should be named Phoenix, after the mythical bird that rises to new life out of its own ashes. It was apt, and

on June 15, 1869, the Phoenix Post Office was established, making the matter final.

Arizona was a true frontier, and Phoenix was still a small and out-of-the-way town. Every necessity or luxury of civilization had to be built, imported, or invented. While this was a major inconvenience for early pioneers, it also provided endless opportunity for the clever and creative. One such person was Samuel Lount. In the days before refrigeration, the only ice available in summer was what had been stored in specially insulated icehouses from the previous winter. When the summer was hot, demand and inadequate insulation meant short supplies. Lount solved the problem in 1851 by inventing a mechanical ice maker. At first it would seem his fortune was made, but there were two drawbacks to the machine: The process was expensive, and Lount lived in Canada, not exactly a place where people would pay top dollar for his product. Realizing the old method of icehouses could still compete over the short summer months in the north, Lount moved his family to Phoenix in the 1870s. It wasn't long before he was one of the richest men in town.

Lount spent his money on real estate in central Phoenix. His business interests expanded, and at his death he was able to leave an immense inheritance to his son and daughter. The daughter, Hattie Mosher, was one of Phoenix's biggest developers and advocates for women's rights. She died in 1945, and there are still a few locals who remember her.

THE YOUNG CITY

Once Swilling, Duppa, and friends got the ball rolling, Phoenix quickly grew in importance. In 1871 it was named the seat of Maricopa County. The city was incorporated in 1878. The canal system continued to be expanded and improved. The Arizona canal, completed by the Arizona Canal Company in 1885, was the largest yet and the first to depart from the old Hohokam routes. New canals fueled new settlements and vice versa. From the 50 or so residents in the Valley when Swilling's company was formed, Phoenix's population climbed into the thousands.

i Arizona State University's Old Main building at the main campus in Tempe marks the site of the first school in Arizona. It was known as Tempe Normal School. Founded in 1885, the school served the earliest settler children of the territory. The building is located at 400 East Tyler Mall at ASU.

Arizona got a regular lifeline to the outside world in the late 1870s when the transcontinental railroad came through the territory. It missed Phoenix, passing through a small depot named Maricopa, 30 miles to the south. City leaders realized what a railroad connection could do for the local economy and built a stagecoach and freight wagon route to the station. By 1886 they needed more than a road and started building a railway track on the route. The Maricopa-Phoenix line saw its first train on July 4, 1887.

After the transcontinental railroad came through Arizona, the region developed at a rapid pace. Established settlements expanded and mining towns popped up like desert wildflowers after a spring rain. Many died just as quickly. But the population was growing and getting richer, which meant more tax revenue and more development.

Tucson fought in the legislature to become the territorial capital, but Prescott was able to keep the title for many years. Instead, Tucson got money for the University of Arizona, which opened in 1891 despite the fact that there were no high schools in the territory. Tempe got a school that eventually would become Arizona State University. The railway link from Phoenix to Maricopa helped the settlements in the Salt River Valley to grow and thrive. Soon it was obvious that the center of power was shifting, and in 1889 Tucson's hopes for the capital were forever dashed when it was moved to its present home in Phoenix.

Soon the Valley was home to offices of the federal, territorial, and county governments, good for business. The jobs they brought and the service industry started a building boom. In the year after Phoenix became the capital, nearly $450,000 was invested in building projects.

There were numerous restrictions on the rights of Native Americans, Mexicans, and immigrants. A city ordinance made it illegal for a Native American to be in town after dark unless he was in the employ of a white resident. In an effort to indoctrinate tribal members, the federal government opened the Phoenix Indian School in 1891. Students were forbidden to speak their native language and required to dress and act "American." Likewise, Hispanics who settled in the city found themselves barred from the Anglo community and power structure, so their lives revolved around their own social and religious institutions. The Chinese, trying to escape prejudice in California, started to move to Phoenix in considerable numbers in the 1880s. While they found a more tolerable atmosphere here, they were still largely relegated to a small Chinatown. Nowadays, Phoenix is home to a wide range of ethnic groups, who celebrate their heritage with special events throughout the year. See the Annual Events chapter for more information.

THE 20TH CENTURY DAWNS

As the new century approached, entrepreneurs opened up railway tracks connecting the capital to various parts of the territory. In 1895 Phoenix became the hub of a line that ran from Ash Fork through Prescott to the Santa Fe transcontinental line.

The new city was doing well, but the harsh conditions of the desert still made life hard for Valley dwellers. The summer heat was almost intolerable. In the 1890s floods raged through the southern half of the city, causing thousands of dollars of damage. In the latter part of the decade, a long drought ruined many farmers.

i Phoenix's first fire department was created in 1886 after a series of bad fires wreaked havoc in the early city. More than 20 men volunteered to help fight fires after a bond was passed to improve the community's water supply.

By the turn of the 20th century, Phoenix had a railroad and many large municipal and private buildings. But the frontier days weren't over. In 1910 two teenage brothers named Oscar and Ernie Woodson, perhaps inspired by reading too many dime novels, decided to make their fortune by robbing a train. There hadn't been a train robbery in the territory for years. The days when a desperado could board a train, blow open the safe, and then disappear into the hinterland with the loot were long past. But the

⊙ Close-up

The Hohokam: The Valley of the Sun's First Settlers

For thousands of years prehistoric peoples had roamed southern Arizona, hunting animals and gathering plants for food. Some experimented with farming, but they never developed elaborate civilizations. That all changed when a people known today as the Hohokam (from a Pima word for "those who came before") arrived in the area a little more than 2,000 years ago and began to build large villages, an extensive irrigation system, and a complex society. Archaeologists divide the Hohokam culture into four distinct phases:

The Pioneer Phase (about 300 BC to AD 550). The origins of the Hohokam are shrouded in mystery. While it is generally thought they arrived in Arizona around 300 BC, many archaeologists argue for a later date. It is also not known where they came from, but most researchers point to Mexico because of the large Mesoamerican influence on their culture. Settling in what is now Phoenix and Tucson, they developed irrigation canals by about AD 300 and lived in small, temporary villages.

The Colonial Phase (AD 550 to 900). During this period the Hohokam spread into central Arizona, eventually stopping on the borders of Anasazi, Sinagua, Salado, and Mogollon cultures. The Hohokam culture area eventually encompassed 45,000 square miles. This was also a time of great artistic flowering, during which the Hohokam developed high-quality pottery with detailed geometric or pictorial designs.

The Sedentary Phase (AD 900 to 1100). Having reached its farthest geographical extent, the Hohokam culture began to develop larger villages and more extensive irrigation canals. They also began to use ball courts inspired by the ritual games in Mexico. Structures, probably for ritual uses but perhaps for houses for the wealthy as well, were built atop mounds of earth. The quality of the pottery decreased at this time, however, because pots were mass produced and the Hohokam's efforts were focused elsewhere. Trade flourished as the Hohokam set up routes across the Southwest and into Mexico.

The Classic Phase (AD 1100 to 1450). Although this period saw the Hohokam at their highest level of population and organization, it was also the period of their decline. Droughts lasting decades hurt the farmers and were followed by floods of the Salt River that destroyed many canals. The towns became impossible to maintain, and the people scattered into bands of hunter-gatherers or small-scale farmers. They eventually developed into the Pima and Tohono O'odham tribes that still live in Arizona today.

VILLAGES & FARMING

The Hohokam built dozens of villages along the Salt River and its tributaries. Archaeologists have traced hundreds of miles of canals, some more than 50 feet wide, irrigating thousands of acres in what was otherwise dry desert.

Their main crops were maize, beans, squash, tobacco, and cotton. They also gathered plants from the surrounding desert, such as saguaro cactus fruit, prickly pear pads, mesquite beans, and agave. Hunters tracked deer and rabbits. The Hohokam were experts at gleaning a life from the desert.

The Hohokam, like many other Southwestern cultures, lived in pit houses. These were usually square or rectangular in shape, arranged in groups around a common

plaza belonging to an extended family. Pit houses get their name from their floors, which were scooped out of the earth. The walls and roof were made of *jacal,* a latticework of branches pasted over with dried mud. This construction technique made the interior cool in summer and warm in winter. It also had the advantage of being quick to make. When the houses became infested with insects or rodents, the Hohokam simply burned them down and rebuilt on the same spot. Archaeologists have found some villages where the houses have successive layers of floors and estimate that the Hohokam burned and rebuilt their houses about once every 25 years.

For an interesting look at a partially reconstructed Hohokam village, check out the Pueblo Grande Museum and Archaeological Park. See the Attractions chapter for more details.

TRADE

The Hohokam had a vast trade network stretching from Utah to Mexico, north to the Great Plains, and west to the Pacific. They made ornaments out of shells from the Pacific coast, which they then exported to other cultures. Other materials not found in southern Arizona, such as turquoise and obsidian, were also highly prized. From Mexico the Hohokam imported tropical birds, obsidian, and copper bells.

RELIGION & RITUAL

Little is known about Hohokam beliefs, but we can tell some things from the ruins they left behind. Many sites include ball courts similar to those found in Central America. Those cultures left written records, and we know that for them the ball games were a religious ritual, where the creation of the world was symbolically replayed, allowing the community to communicate with the hidden world. It is not known, however, if the Hohokam used the ball games for the same purpose.

Large ritual buildings or houses for the elite were built atop platform mounds. It's not certain what went on in these structures, but they are usually found near the start of the larger canals, so they probably had to do with economic or spiritual upkeep.

The Hohokam left a wide variety of petroglyphs (symbols carved onto rocks) that may reflect their religious beliefs. Petroglyphs dot the Arizona landscape and make for fun and interesting trips. The closest site is the Deer Valley Rock Art Center. See the Attractions chapter for more details.

FURTHER READING

The Hohokam: Ancient People of the Desert, edited by David Grant Noble (School of American Research Press, 1999). A short (90-page) introduction to the Hohokam, with chapters written by several experts.

The Archaeology of Ancient Arizona, by Jefferson Reid and Stephanie Whittlesey (University of Arizona Press, 1997). A detailed coverage, more than 300 pages, of the peoples and cultures of the entire state. It includes an extensive discussion of the Hohokam.

Archaeology in the City: A Hohokam Village in Phoenix, Arizona, by David Gregory, Michael Bartlett, and Thomas Kolaz (University of Arizona, 1986). Although it's only 72 pages long, this book provides a good look at the Hohokam of the Salt River Valley.

Woodson boys weren't exactly the sharpest knives in the drawer, and they decided to give it a try. One May evening they boarded the shuttle train running from Phoenix to Maricopa. They had left their getaway horses by the track a few miles out of town. When the train approached the spot, the two desperadoes drew their revolvers and ordered the conductor to stop the train. Then they turned on the passengers and ordered them to empty their pockets. The brothers got a good haul, about $300. Unfortunately, the passengers included many members of the territorial legislature and the sheriff of Gila County. The brothers were now marked men.

The train robbers jumped on their horses and galloped away, heading for the border. It wasn't long before the sheriff of Maricopa County, Carl Hayden, rounded up a posse and set off after them. While his men rode on horseback, Hayden and a friend followed in an automobile. The new invention soon left the rest of the posse in the dust. It wasn't long before they caught up with the Woodsons as they were resting their horses from a hard ride through the May heat. Sheriff Hayden leapt out of the car and whipped out his revolver. The Woodson brothers used their heads for once and surrendered. One of the last train robberies in the history of the West, and the first to be foiled by the use of an automobile, was at an end. The Woodsons did some time and disappeared from history. Hayden eventually became a congressman and then a senator.

FROM TOWN TO CITY

The city's unpredictable supply of water—usually not enough, sometimes too much—led to dam projects sponsored by the federal government. The biggest example near Phoenix is the Roosevelt Dam, about 65 miles northeast of the city at the confluence of the Salt River and Tonto Creek. Construction took 7 years and was completed in 1911. Roosevelt Dam gave the city its first reliable flood-control system, hydroelectric power, and a 16,000-acre reservoir.

Soon Phoenix was wired for electricity, a trolley line served the city's burgeoning population, and by 1910 there were more than 11,000 people living in the Valley. Phoenix was the commercial center for several small but growing towns such as Tempe, Mesa, Scottsdale, Glendale, and Peoria.

Arizona was admitted as the 48th state of the Union on February 14, 1912. By the beginning of the 20th century, Phoenix was developing a reputation as a health resort. Sanitariums offered "rest cures" for those suffering from lung problems, touting the benefits of the Valley's low humidity, mild winter weather, and clean air. While Phoenix was certainly cleaner than the coal-smogged cities of the early modern East, the city now struggles with the "brown cloud" of smog that settles over the area thanks to mass development and over-reliance on freeways increasing pollution, making air quality a persistent issue. The northern-style grass lawns favored by some newcomers add pollen to the air and an extra burden on our precarious water supply.

World War I changed agriculture in the area. The war effort led to a huge demand for cotton, used in everything from uniforms to tires to airplane fabric. Many farms that once grew food crops switched to cotton. It is still an important part of the Arizona economy today. There was also a big demand for rubber, and large rubber factories supplied jobs for hundreds of Phoenix residents. These

two new industries attracted more workers, and by 1920 the city had grown to 29,000 people, the largest in the state.

ℹ️ The Phoenix Street Railway System ran trolleys from 1887 to 1948. In early years horses pulled the cars, but the system was later electrified. Trolleys clanged by every 10 minutes, costing a nickel, but riders and neighbors complained of the hideous noise. The Phoenix Trolley Museum, at 1218 N. Central (across the street from Burton Barr Central Library), is open most of the year. For information call (602) 254-0307.

The influx of people and industry meant that transportation had to be improved. The Southern Pacific Railroad put in a main line to Phoenix in 1926. A year later, commercial airlines took off to Tucson and Los Angeles. Phoenix Sky Harbor Airport opened in 1929. The old dirt roads began to be paved over, and the famous magazine *Arizona Highways* was launched in 1925 to encourage motor tourism.

They weren't the only ones to see Arizona's tourist potential. As early as 1919, the Phoenix-Arizona Club was promoting its city as a tourist destination. "The city where winter never comes" was the club's motto. The San Carlos, the Westward Ho, and—some years later—the Valley Ho of Scottsdale were three of the luxury hotels that drew Hollywood stars to Arizona. The recently refurbished Westward Ho is now a retirement home, but the San Carlos is still in business. The Valley Ho reopened in 2005 with a $70 million renovation, making it equally as chic now as it was in the 1950s and 1960s (see the Hotel chapter).

The Depression didn't hit Phoenix as hard as some other cities, mostly because of Roosevelt's New Deal projects. Large numbers of Arizonans worked on dam projects or on massive archaeological excavations of the surviving Hohokam ruins. The basis of much of what we know about the ancient society comes from this period. One industry that did grow during the Depression was tourism. A local ad agency touted the metro area as the "Valley of the Sun," a far more appealing moniker than the more accurate "Salt River Valley." Another bit of relief came in the early 1930s with the invention of evaporative cooling. This mundane invention rarely makes the history books, though it had a profound effect on life in the desert Southwest. Often called "swamp coolers" by locals, they blow air through moist pads, creating a cool flow of air. Cooler homes and offices make life in the desert more bearable, encouraging people and business to move into the area.

World War II saw GIs training for desert combat to the west of Phoenix and several prisoner-of-war camps throughout the Southwest. Those in Arizona housed German and Italian soldiers. One day, three German POWs from the camp in Papago Park made a break for the border. They had it all planned out. They had managed to steal a map of Arizona and had found that their camp was very close to the Gila River. Tracing its meandering course, they discovered that it met up with the Colorado River, which flowed south into neutral Mexico. They scrounged enough materials to make a raft, and then slipped past their American guards and out into the desert. After evading capture for the first day, they made it to the Gila River—only to find a dry wash. It wasn't long before all three were back in custody.

METROPOLIS IN THE DESERT

The war also attracted defense contractors, a major part of the Valley economy to this day. This trend continued after the war, and by the 1950s Phoenix had a booming economy. Modern air-conditioning was now affordable and provided year-round sanctuary from the heat. New communities sprouted up everywhere, such as Maryvale and Scottsdale for young families and Sun City for retirees. Office buildings and shopping centers vied for space downtown and in the suburbs. It was at this time that Phoenix started its aggressive annexation scheme. By 1960 it had expanded to 187 square miles. Entire sections of town are as large as major cities like Seattle and Atlanta. The city is still growing today, and as you drive in from any direction, you see Phoenix city limits signs long before you see any buildings. Huge sections of undeveloped State Trust land remain ripe for the shovel and bulldozer.

From the 1960s through the 1980s, Valley leaders took the peculiar stance of being pro-growth without developing a mass-transit system or a freeway, and driving became a nightmare. In the 1980s the city government finally decided to build some freeways, including a link to I-10 in 1990.

Like many other modern city centers, downtown Phoenix experienced a decline, with most people preferring the suburbs.

The deterioration seems to have stopped. Shops and bars are now coming back to the area, although parts can still be a bit intimidating after dark. Several big municipal projects such as the Civic Plaza, the US Airways Arena, the Arizona Center, and the Herberger Theater have lured Phoenix residents back downtown.

i Phoenix city officials prepare a palm tree maintenance brochure for residents of the city's central historic districts on how to properly trim the old California and date palms that line many of the traditional brick-home neighborhoods.

Phoenix may be the center of the Valley of the Sun, but its growth fueled the development of other cities—Mesa, Tempe, Scottsdale, Glendale, Peoria, Gilbert, and Chandler. The population of Maricopa County is nearly 3 million. The desert between the towns is rapidly disappearing, and the Valley looks as if it will turn into one big city within a few years. Many locals worry that the water supply won't be enough for so many people, so the population boom may be over soon. This would be good news for Arizonans who know the value of unsullied desert space—and for the few traces of the past that have survived the onset of the 21st century.

HOTELS & MOTELS

There are plenty of options for lodgings in the Phoenix area, so it really depends on what you're into—such as pools, golf, or walking distance to a ballpark. With competition between hotels for your tourism dollars, you almost always have options. Peak months of January to April and October will spike the rates. But you can score some smoking deals outside of those heavier-traveled time periods, and the weather will still be much nicer than back home. One of the biggest decisions you'll have to make is geographic.

This chapter will help you understand the difference between staying in downtown Phoenix, which is much more of a tourist destination now than ever before, and in Scottsdale or other popular suburbs like Tempe and Glendale. For example, you must consider the distances between places. The Valley is very much like Los Angeles: "20 minutes to everywhere." Well, that's only partly true, though you will have to drive most everywhere. Staying in north Scottsdale, for example, puts you more like 45 minutes away from Sky Harbor International Airport and downtown Phoenix.

Keep in mind that Valley hotels are known for their package deals that include golf discounts or spa treatments. Of course, some people might want to stay in a traditional Southwestern-style place, while others prefer a brand-new chic joint with fresh amenities. We have all the options for you to consider before booking your room.

For resorts in the area, see the chapter starting on p. 63.

Price Code

With each location listed in this chapter you will find a pricing guide ranging from one to four dollar signs. The code is based on the price for a 1-night, double-occupancy stay in high season, which is January to April. Rates do not include tax, which is more than 13 percent in Phoenix and varies by city.

$ . . . . Less than $100
$$ . . . . $100 to $150
$$$ . . . . $150 to $250
$$$$ . . . . More than $250

PHOENIX

BEST WESTERN PLUS INNSUITES HOTEL PHOENIX $$–$$$
1615 E. Northern Ave.
(602) 997-6285, (800) 752-2204
www.innsuites.com/phoenix

This location is about 15 minutes away from downtown Phoenix. It's tucked off AZ 51 near Squaw Peak and the scenic north-central city mountain preserves. You're within walking distance to hiking and jogging trails. Amenities at the 104-suite hotel include complimentary breakfast buffet and refreshments, free local paper, free Wi-Fi, a swimming pool, spa, exercise room, and outdoor patio with a basketball court. There's also a complimentary manager's barbecue the first Wednesday every month. There are several types of rooms of various sizes, with options on having a king- or queen-size bed and a sleeper sofa and/or a love seat. The Jacuzzi Suite includes a whirlpool tub. Local calls are free. Pets are allowed.

COURTYARD BY MARRIOTT $$$
2101 E. Camelback Rd.
(602) 955-5200, (800) 321-2211
www.camelbackcourtyard.com

The area near 24th Street and Camelback Road is considered one of the busiest neighborhoods in central Phoenix. Nearby shopping and dining options range from family-oriented to five-star gourmet. Courtyard by Marriott is an economical option in that area and within walking distance of Biltmore Fashion Park and the Esplanade retail/restaurant areas. It adjoins the Town & Country Shopping Center, which includes a locally renowned soul food restaurant and Trader Joe's. The hotel has 143 rooms and 12 suites. Amenities include a swimming pool in the courtyard, a hot tub, an exercise room, free parking, and lots of meeting space. The hotel serves a reasonably priced breakfast buffet.

DOUBLETREE GUEST SUITES $$$
320 N. 44th St.
(602) 225-0500, (800) 222-TREE
www.doubletree.com

Travelers with an early flight will appreciate the close proximity to Phoenix Sky Harbor International Airport. The hotel also is near several office towers known as the Gateway Center, the Pueblo Grande Museum, and the Chinese Cultural Center. It's about 10 minutes to downtown Phoenix, Scottsdale, and Tempe. Plus, 44th Street provides easy access to the freeways and the hotel is only a 1-block walk to the nearest light rail station on Washington Street. The 6-story DoubleTree has 242 two-room suites furnished with microwaves, wet bars, refrigerators, and voice messaging. A complimentary breakfast buffet adds to the amenities, as do the fitness center, the on-site restaurant,

and a large swimming pool surrounded by palm trees.

DRURY INN & SUITES PINNACLE PEAK $$$
2335 W. Pinnacle Peak Rd.
(623) 879-8800, (888) 221-6260
www.druryhotels.com

This 178-room hotel is extraordinarily family-friendly, but also inviting for all ages. The Wet n Wild wave pool is a big hit and draws lots of positive reviews. Guests rave about the complimentary "5:30 Kickback" where the hotel serves a free rotating menu of hot snacks like nachos, baked potatoes, chicken fingers, and mac 'n' cheese. Staying at Drury Inn, located about a half-hour out of downtown Phoenix north of the Loop 101 on I-17, will shave some time off your jaunt to northern Arizona or the Grand Canyon. Rooms include 2-room suites. The hotel offers free Wi-Fi and a free hour of long-distance calls. Hot breakfast, including Belgian waffles and scrambled eggs, is also free.

EMBASSY SUITES PHOENIX-BILTMORE $$$–$$$$
2630 E. Camelback Rd.
(602) 955-3992, (800) EMBASSY
www.embassysuites.com

The pinkish exterior of this hotel draws your attention if you're near the Biltmore Fashion Park shopping center. But you'll be even more dazzled by the interior. A giant atrium called the Sonoran Oasis features waterfalls and 4-story desert-theme murals. Palms and many other trees are in abundance, plus the atrium offers pleasant, brightly colored sitting areas, which make for a pleasant local meeting place. Rooms of this 5-story hotel look out on the atrium, where the hotel's complimentary cooked-to-order breakfasts

are served. The Omaha Steakhouse on the premises is a popular addition to the Biltmore area's dining options. Lodging consists of 232 two-room suites, each outfitted with a wet bar, microwave, refrigerator, well-lit work/dining area, and sleeper sofa. Each room also has 2 telephones with data ports and voice mail, 2 TVs, high-speed Internet, and MP3 connectivity. A fitness room and oversize swimming pool also are at your disposal. Pets are allowed for a fee.

> **i** The Hotel Palomar at the CityScape complex in downtown Phoenix is scheduled to open in 2012 with more than 200 condo-style rooms, making it the eighth four-star Palomar hotel in the US. The luxury boutique lodging at Jefferson and First streets is one of several major downtown hotels, though it's the first built at the CityScape mixed-use development.

HILTON GARDEN INN PHOENIX
AIRPORT NORTH $$–$$$
3838 E. Van Buren St.
(602) 306-2323, (877) 782-9444
www.hiltongardeninn.com

Each of the 192 rooms at the hotel east of downtown Phoenix, just miles from Sky Harbor Airport, includes free Wi-Fi and upgraded amenities. The work areas include large desks and ergonomic chairs, in addition to refrigerators. The entire hotel and common areas have a new feel, since the hotel was built in 2009. The outdoor heated pool and spa, lobby grill, and on-site convenience store are easily accessible. The hotel is located in between downtown Phoenix and Tempe.

HOLIDAY INN HOTEL & SUITES
PHOENIX AIRPORT $$–$$$
3220 S. 48th St.
(480) 543-1700, (877) 859-5095
www.holidayinn.com

This is simply a clean, efficient hotel with outstanding access to some key places. The 114-room hotel, which also includes 24 suites, is within a few miles of Sky Harbor Airport. The light rail station is close to take guests quickly between Tempe and Phoenix. Additionally, the hotel runs a free shuttle to the bars and restaurants on Mill Avenue in Tempe from noon till midnight. Rooms include oversize desks, ergonomically correct chairs, and free Wi-Fi. The Soleil Bistro serves dinner and drinks. An outdoor hotel pool and 24-hour fitness center help you relax and feel at home.

HOMEWOOD SUITES $$$
2001 E. Highland Ave.
(602) 508-0937, (800) 225-5466
www.homewoodsuites.com

This Hilton-operated hotel specializes in extended stays, but you can book a room for just 1 night. Rates decrease for those staying longer than 6 days; there is also a special 30-day rate. All 124 wireless-enabled rooms are suites in this 4-story hotel, which opened in 1997. It's in a prime location near the Biltmore and Camelback Corridor businesses, retail stores, and restaurants. Three shopping malls—Town & Country, Camelback Colonnade, and Biltmore Fashion Park—are within walking distance. It's 8 miles to downtown Phoenix. Regular Homewood suites have 1 king-size or 2 double beds in the bedroom, a fold-out sofa in the living room, plus a well-equipped kitchen and dining area. You can also choose one of the 6 to 8 master suites, each with 2 bedrooms and 2 baths,

a king-size bed, and 2 double beds. The hotel rate includes complimentary breakfast buffet, evening social hour, and use of an exercise room, gas grills in the courtyard by the pool, and a laundry room. A swimming pool, basketball court, and business center with computers are available for guests to use. Another useful feature is the complimentary transportation to anywhere within a 5-mile radius. Pets are allowed for a $100 non-refundable fee.

i Summer is off-season, which means there are serious bargains available June to September. However, rates drop fast as summer approaches. A room you book in January (for July) may be much more expensive than the same room booked in May. Try reserving a no-fee-for-cancellation room in January. As summer arrives, recheck rates. If you can get a better deal, cancel the first reservation.

HOTEL SAN CARLOS $$$
202 N. Central Ave.
(602) 253-4121, (866) 253-4121
www.hotelsancarlos.com

Hollywood "Golden Era" stars Marilyn Monroe, Mae West, Spencer Tracy, and Ingrid Bergman stayed at the hotel when Phoenix was still a charming small city. The San Carlos is full of interesting stories, especially from its heyday in the 1930s and 1940s. It was built in 1928 in an Italian Renaissance Revival design, and it was the city's first high-rise, fully air-conditioned hotel with an elevator. Its commitment to preservation has put the hotel on the registry of Historic Hotels of America. The 1930s-era lobby features dark wood paneling, crystal chandeliers, and old photos of downtown Phoenix. There are 2

restaurants and the supposedly haunted Ghost Lounge, a trendy night spot which offers small bites catered by the hotel's Bistro 202. It also includes a gift shop, a barbershop, and a shoeshine shop on-site. The light rail runs along Central Avenue right outside the hotel, which is a quick walk to just about everywhere downtown. There's also a nice rooftop pool and Dish Network in the rooms. The ground-level coffeehouse is a great spot to have breakfast, and nearby Seamus McCaffrey's is the place to have a pint in the evening. The hotel has 128 cozy rooms and 5 suites, all with complimentary Internet for 30 minutes. An additional $5 gets you unlimited access, including to Wi-Fi in the common areas.

HYATT REGENCY PHOENIX $$$-$$$$
122 N. 2nd St.
(602) 252-1234, (800) 233-1234
www.phoenix.hyatt.com

The Hyatt has been around longer than other high-rise downtown hotels, yet it's still a dominant structure of the skyline—a 24-floor building of dark sandstone and glass. It's topped by a popular rotating restaurant called Compass Arizona Grill and includes a bar, cafe, and Einstein Bros. Bagels. The spacious lobby is a popular place for informal, air-conditioned downtown rendezvous. A recent $15 million transformation updated each of the hotel's 693 rooms, including VIP and business suites, and other amenities. A ride on the glass elevators that slice through the middle of the building affords spectacular views of downtown Phoenix and the Valley beyond. The lobby's huge 7-story atrium is a stunning showcase for hanging abstract sculptures and other artworks. The rooms are tastefully appointed and the meeting rooms are popular for major conventions. You'll also

find an outdoor swimming pool, a whirlpool, exercise rooms, a concierge desk, and a car-rental desk.

RITZ-CARLTON $$$$
2401 E. Camelback Rd,
(602) 468-0700, (800) 241-3333
www.ritzcarlton.com

The 11-story, rose-colored Ritz-Carlton is one of the main buildings to anchor 24th Street and Camelback Road, probably the ritziest intersection in the center city. Hotel brochures point out that a rental car is unnecessary for guests because of all the first-class shopping, entertainment, and dining within walking distance. Guests are within walking distance to Biltmore Fashion Park, the upscale restaurant Christopher's & Crush Lounge, Roy's, and the AMC Esplanade movie theaters, in addition to trendy Stingray Sushi and family options like the Cheesecake Factory. Golf is also quite accessible, as concierges can arrange for tee times at the Biltmore Country Club a few blocks away. The hotel has 281 deluxe guest rooms, including luxurious suites (such as the 1,860-square-foot presidential suite) and a private Club Level with extra services. Dark woods and colors of rose and mauve predominate in the hotel's decor, which is quite ornate, down to the wall moldings, gilded frames on artwork, and the many immense chandeliers. The lobby is a wonderful place for intimate conversations, with the space divided into drawing rooms with overstuffed chairs and museum-quality Old World paintings. Each guest room features a marble bath, a refreshment bar, an in-room safe, plush terry bathrobes, and full maid service twice a day. The hotel has a bistro serving signature martinis on the outdoor patio. The swimming pool area has a summer cafe for alfresco dining, and the Lobby Lounge serves afternoon tea and cocktails.

> **i** Alfred Hitchcock shot parts of his 1960 movie *Psycho* at the Westward Ho when the hotel at 618 N. Central Ave. was considered one of the best places to stay downtown. For the 1998 *Psycho* remake, director Gus Van Sant paid tribute to Hitch by using a helicopter to capture a zooming shot through a window of the Westward Ho. In addition to *Psycho,* Marilyn Monroe's 1956 *Bus Stop* and Paul Newman's 1972 *Pocket Money* were also shot at the Westward Ho.

✳ROYAL PALMS $$$$
5200 E. Camelback Rd.
(602) 840-3610, (800) 672-6011
www.royalpalmshotel.com

Lodging on the lush grounds hidden against the base of the south side of Camelback Mountain consists of 119 guest rooms, casitas, and villas all built around the original 1920s mansion. The hotel's characteristic fountains, gardens, and spacious meeting rooms earned the hotel the reputation as perhaps the best place for a small- to medium-size wedding in the Valley. The deluxe casitas in the West Courtyard are posh, yet unpretentious. They include master bedroom suites, luxurious baths, and patios with fireplaces. Other rooms have custom furnishings, separate living room areas, LCD flat-screen TVs, pillow top mattresses, free daily newspapers, and Wi-Fi. There are also the luxurious Villa and Presidential suites, which are pricey, but worth it if you have the means. Each room at Royal Palms has its own personality, and

the grounds are truly, uniquely Old Phoenix. Located at the hotel is the incredible T. Cook's restaurant, one of the top dining experiences in the Valley. The hotel also boasts a lounge with leather chairs and comfortable sitting rooms, a great place for a half-priced bottle of wine during happy hour in the courtyard, or simply to sip a cocktail or nibble on dessert. (See Close-up in the Resorts chapter, in addition to the Restaurants chapter for more on T. Cook's.)

SHERATON CRESCENT HOTEL $$$–$$$$
2620 W. Dunlap Ave.
(602) 943-8200, (800) 423-4126
www.sheraton.com

The Sheraton Crescent is known for its character and ambiance, a rarity for lodgings along the mostly industrial I-17 corridor in northwest Phoenix. The freeway makes it convenient to central Phoenix attractions (15 to 20 minutes in non-rush hours), and you'll find the large Metrocenter shopping mall just a few blocks from the hotel. The 7-story building sits on 13 nicely landscaped acres, but the interior is downright opulent with its use of marble, stone, glass, and inviting furniture under twinkling chandeliers. There are 342 guest rooms, 12 of which are suites and 2 of which are top-floor penthouse suites. All have been recently renovated. The 2 top floors have controlled elevator access, and guests on those floors have exclusive concierge service, complimentary continental breakfast, and evening cocktails. In the other rooms you'll find high-quality furnishings; a balcony or terrace; a bathroom with Italian marble; 2 telephones with computer-link and voice-mail capability; and a safe. The Indigo Restaurant serves breakfast, lunch, and dinner and specializes in American cuisine. There's also a bar and lounge on the premises. On-site recreation includes 2 lighted tennis courts, sand volleyball, basketball, and racquetball/squash courts, and a health and fitness center with steam rooms and a sauna. Golfers enjoy preferred tee times at nearby courses. At the swimming pool the family will enjoy Monsoon Mountain and its 166-foot waterslide.

✳SHERATON PHOENIX DOWNTOWN $$$–$$$$
340 N. 3rd St.
(602) 262-2500, (800) 325-3535
www.sheratonphoenixdowntown.com

The 1,000-room high-rise on the north end of downtown Phoenix is one of the newest hotels built in the center city. The lobby and common areas are clean, modern, and bright. Rooms include brand-new bathroom amenities, enhanced-comfort beds, and views of your choice of Camelback Mountain, the skyline, or the downtown sports arenas. The hotel boasts 47 suites and 80,000 square feet of meeting space for large groups of business travelers, who take advantage of the short walk to Phoenix Convention Center. Guests tend to gather in the lobby cafe and lounge with complimentary Internet access. The District American Kitchen & Wine Bar, with its generous happy hour, is a popular hangout for downtown businesspeople and young professionals. Microbrews are $3 Mon to Fri 3 to 7 p.m. and 10 p.m. to close, in addition to reduced prices on small plates. The chefs use herbs from their own garden on a 4th-floor patio. The hotel also has a fitness center and a high-rise outdoor lap pool.

WESTIN PHOENIX DOWNTOWN $$$–$$$$

333 N. Central Ave.
(602) 429-3500, (800) 937-8461
www.westin.com/phoenixdowntown

The Westin opened in March 2011 just a couple of blocks from the Sheraton, Hyatt, and Wyndham. Like its competitors, it is located within walking distance to the light rail stations, the Phoenix Convention Center, downtown sports venues, and scores of central places to hang out. Planners designed the 242-room hotel, located in the 26-floor Freeport McMoRan Center, as a sophisticated urban retreat. Each of the guestrooms and the central ballroom features giant windows to maximize views of the surrounding city. The design includes sleek, modern furniture and natural woods in addition to calming neutral colors. Rooms include brand-new bathrooms, innovative Heavenly Beds, and "jack packs" to connect laptops or other personal devices into the 40-inch flat-screen TVs. The Westin also offers a fitness center and a pool with cascading waterfall.

WYNDHAM PHOENIX $$$–$$$$

50 E. Adams St.
(602) 333-0000
www.wyndhamphx.com

Formerly the Crowne Plaza, this 19-story hotel in the heart of downtown was bought and renovated by the Wyndham chain. It underwent a $20 million renovation, further improving the site within walking distance of the Phoenix Convention Center, the Herberger Theater, America West Arena, and shops and restaurants in the Arizona Center. The 520 rooms are spacious and offer the usual amenities. There's more than 60,000 square feet of meeting space for business travelers. The downtown location makes the rooftop terrace and pool all the more enjoyable. All rooms have been upgraded and include free high-speed Internet. The completely redesigned lobby bar, ICON, offers tapas and convenient cocktails to compete with other popular hotel lobby bars within walking distance. Guests can use the fitness center with pool or visit the beauty salon and gift shop. Breakfast is served at Marston's Cafe.

SOUTHEAST VALLEY

ALOFT TEMPE $$$

951 E. Playa Del Norte Dr., Tempe
(480) 621-3300, (877) GO-ALOFT
www.alofthotels.com/tempe

Set at Tempe Town Lake, the fresh, modern hotel blends in with nearby Mill Avenue and the college-town atmosphere. Access to nearby Arizona State University and Sky Harbor Airport is seamless. The hotel's rooms include 9-foot ceilings and extra-large windows for views of Town Lake and nearby buttes at Papago Park. Rooms include walk-in showers, free Wi-Fi with plug-and-play hookups for your tech gadgets, and 42-inch LCD TVs. The big-city urban feel of the hotel also extends to the gym, lounge, snack bar, and outdoor pool. High-tech kiosks allow you to check in and print your airport boarding passes on the go. The hotel is pet-friendly and also offers a day camp for kids under 12.

BEST WESTERN DOBSON RANCH INN $$$

1666 S. Dobson Rd., Mesa
(480) 831-7000, (800) 528-1356
www.dobsonranchinn.com

A pleasant destination in Mesa for about 20 years, the Spanish-style Dobson Ranch

Inn is known for its colorful fountains and flower gardens, in addition to its 10 acres of jogging and walking paths. The recently remodeled inn is convenient to the Superstition Freeway (US 60), which connects Mesa with Tempe and Phoenix. Fiesta Mall is also nearby. Right down the road is the Dobson Ranch Golf Course. The inn has 200 rooms and 13 suites. A standard room offers a sitting area and large dressing area. Executive king rooms include a king-size bed, refrigerator, and coffeemaker. The 2-room suites include a refrigerator, microwave, wet bar, and 2-line phone. The updated hotel has managed to keep its old-Mesa charm while modernizing the rooms and common areas. Other amenities at the inn include a swimming pool, 2 spas, an exercise room, complimentary hot buffet breakfast, complimentary welcome cocktail, free daily newspaper, and free Internet. The hotel restaurant, Cactus Clubhouse, serves barbecue and other Southwestern cuisine. The Dobson Ranch Inn is also the spring training home of the Chicago Cubs, so you very well could be eating breakfast or chilling out poolside next to a pro ballplayer in February and March.

i Arizona does not change its clocks for daylight saving time. So if you are here on the first Sunday in April or the last Sunday in October, national reminders about the time change do not apply to you—at least while you're here.

BEST WESTERN INN OF TEMPE $$
670 N. Scottsdale Rd., Tempe
(480) 784-2233, (800) 528-1234
www.innoftempe.com
Opened in 1997, this 4-floor hotel is popular with business and leisure travelers who want

easy access to the Valley's freeways. It's busy whenever major events at Arizona State University bring people to town, especially since it's only 3 miles to Sky Harbor Airport. The 103 rooms are accessed from interior corridors, and guests have the option of queen- or king-size beds. Wi-Fi and daily newspaper are free. The indoor lap pool has resistance waves for those who like a workout, and the hotel also features an exercise room with 4 spas. A Denny's restaurant shares the property. Small pets are allowed, and there is a free continental breakfast.

BEST WESTERN MEZONA INN $$$
250 W. Main St., Mesa
(480) 834-9233, (800) 528-8299
www.mezonainn.com
Mezona Inn's swimming pool is refreshing and clean, especially for a downtown Mesa pool. Many of the inn's large, refurbished 128 rooms look out on this courtyard. Rooms come with 1 king-size or 2 queen-size beds plus a refrigerator and other typical amenities. Some rooms have irons and ironing boards. The Mezona is in downtown Mesa—easy to reach from the freeway if you are traveling by car. Mesa City Plaza and its surrounding arts center and museums are only a few blocks away. The hotel accepts pets and provides a complimentary hot breakfast and free Wi-Fi.

BEST WESTERN—TEMPE $$
5300 S. Priest Dr., Tempe
(480) 820-7500, (800) 822-4334
www.bestwesterntempe.com
Located in the Guadalupe neighborhood near Arizona Mills shopping center, the 4-story motel has 160 rooms and exceptional access to downtown Tempe and the rest of the Valley. The hotel, which wins awards for its design, offers king- or

queen-size beds. The heated outdoor pool area includes a spa. Another plus is the proximity of Arizona Mills shopping mall. Two rooms are set up for the physically challenged. Pets are allowed, and the hotel provides a dog-walking area. Complimentary breakfast is offered; you're invited to make your own waffles. Wi-Fi is also free.

CLARION INN $$
951 W. Main St., Mesa
(480) 833-1231
www.clarionhotel.com

The cozy, 100-room hotel includes spacious lodgings equipped with free Wi-Fi, flat-screen TVs, microwaves, and fridges. *The Wall Street Journal* is delivered free each weekday. The hotel, located close to the Mesa Arizona Temple and other downtown Mesa points of interest, includes some rooms with balconies. The on-site European Bistro Restaurant and Lounge specializes in German food for lunch and dinner. A pool, hot tub, sauna, and fitness center are also available.

COUNTRY INN & SUITES $$
6650 E. Superstition Springs Blvd., Mesa
(480) 621-8000
www.countryinns.com

Located in East Mesa off US 60 at Power Road, the hotel has great character and feels very homey. It's directly across the freeway from Superstition Springs Center with its shopping, restaurants, and family entertainment. The hotel offers free continental breakfast and Wi-Fi in addition to a free local shuttle.

COUNTRY INN & SUITES $$
808 N. Scottsdale Rd., Tempe
(480) 858-9898, (800) 596-2375
www.countryinns.com

The address is only partly deceiving. Though the hotel is on Scottsdale Road, it's actually in north Tempe. But it's as equally close to downtown Scottsdale as it is to Tempe and Arizona State University. The site features lots of wood in the furniture, stairwells, and bed headboards. Rooms range from standard offerings to extended-stay hospitality suites. Wi-Fi and continental breakfast are free. The heated outdoor pool and fitness center enhance the stay.

DAYS HOTEL MESA COUNTRY CLUB $$
333 W. Juanita Ave., Mesa
(480) 844-8900
www.daysinn.com

Located off US 60 at Country Club Drive in Mesa, this award-winning East Valley hotel is well reviewed by guests. The complimentary hot breakfast, heated pool, Jacuzzi, sauna, and upgraded fitness center enhance any road trip, whether it's for a family vacation or business. The 120 rooms are spacious and linked to free Wi-Fi. Side rooms with patios and family suites are also available.

FIESTA RESORT CONFERENCE CENTER $$$
2100 S. Priest Dr., Tempe
(480) 967-1441
www.fiestainnresort.com

This 12-acre resort-style hotel is close to the freeways and Arizona State University in addition to Sky Harbor Airport. Visiting ASU families can take advantage of the hotel's free local shuttle around the massive campus and surrounding Tempe hotspots. Amenities include a swimming pool and Jacuzzi, an exercise room, and a full-service health club within walking distance of the

hotel. The site's restaurant, Milagro's, serves breakfast, lunch, and dinner. Happy hour in the Kachina Lounge includes complimentary hors d'oeuvres Monday to Friday, one of the fine points the 35-year-old former Fiesta Inn is known for. The 270 refurbished Southwestern-style guest rooms include executive king bedrooms. High-speed Internet and daily newspaper are free.

FOUR POINTS SHERATON $$–$$$
1330 Rural Rd., Tempe
(480) 968-3451, (800) 368-7764
www.fourpointstempe.com
The 187-room hotel is conveniently located in the heart of Arizona State University's campus and within walking distance of restaurants, bars, and shopping. ASU's Karsten Golf Course is also just blocks away. Rooms are consistently clean and inviting. High-speed Internet, bottled water, and daily newspapers are free. The heated, outdoor resort-style pool is a nice addition to a site that's located in the midst of so much youthful activity. A 24-hour business center and gym also enhance the stay.

HOMEWOOD SUITES-CHANDLER
FASHION CENTER $$–$$$
1221 S. Spectrum Blvd., Chandler
(480) 963-5700
www.homewoodsuites.hilton.com
The 133-room hotel offers 1- and 2-bedroom suites complete with fully equipped kitchens with stoves and dishwashers, which makes it great for extended stays. The furniture is modern, sleek, and comfortable. Rooms have 2 TVs, great for preventing family squabbles. High-speed Internet and hot breakfast are free. The hotel pool, basketball court, and fitness center are also excellent vacation amenities. The hotel will rent out

videos for children and audio/video equipment for visiting business guests. Chandler Fashion Center and several major restaurants are nearby.

HYATT PLACE $$–$$$
1422 W. Bass Pro Dr., Mesa
(480) 969-8200
www.phoenixmesa.place.hyatt.com
The 152-room hotel is very new and feels fresh. It's located near the restaurants and cinema at the Mesa Riverview Shopping Center and, in spite of its East Valley address, is only 8 miles to Sky Harbor Airport. Wi-Fi is free throughout the hotel and in the spacious guestrooms, which are loaded with 42-inch flat-screen HD TVs. The rooms include granite counters in the bathrooms and Hyatt "grand beds." The resort-style pool also generates positive feedback from guests.

i To hear about sporting and entertainment events going on while you are here, try calling the Visitor Hotline at (602) 252-5588. The Greater Phoenix Convention & Visitors Bureau updates the message weekly. If you have Internet access during your visit, check out www.showup.com for featured events as well as the latest entertainment information.

HYATT PLACE AIRPORT $$–$$$
1422 W. Rio Salado Pkwy., Tempe
(480) 804-9544
www.phoenixairport.place.hyatt.com
Stylish rooms at the modern facility include sizable work areas, "Hyatt Grand" beds, and oversize sleeper sofas. Wi-Fi is free, and rooms are also equipped with 42-inch HD TVs that provide links to your laptop and other tech devices. Bathrooms have granite

countertops, and the common areas also have that clean, new feel. The hotel will shuttle you for free in a 5-mile radius, which includes Sky Harbor Airport and the many exciting hangout spots around trendy Mill Avenue and near Arizona State University.

i If you're staying in south Scottsdale, aim to be within walking distance of some of the city's key hotspots. Old Town Scottsdale has dozens of restaurants, bars, nightclubs, and other entertainment within a 10-minute walk of the area's hotels. Trolleys, taxis, and pedal-cabs are readily available. Just north of Old Town is Scottsdale Fashion Square, the canal Waterfront development, and other classic Scottsdale hangouts.

☀TEMPE MISSION PALMS $$$–$$$$
60 E. 5th St., Tempe
(480) 894-1400, (800) 547-8705
www.missionpalms.com

The Mission Palms hotel is done in Southwestern mission-style architecture set to the colors of the surrounding Sonoran Desert, yet its rooms and common areas appear quite modern. The photogenic courtyard is marked by dozens of towering palm trees. The 4-story hotel, popular with Arizona State University families and business travelers, has 303 guest rooms recently overhauled as part of an $8 million renovation project that added completely new bathrooms. It's also a sure bet for families on vacation. Several restaurants, coffeehouses, nightclubs, and boutiques are within walking distance of Mill Avenue. Tempe Town Lake, Papago Park, and the Phoenix Zoo are close by. The on-site restaurant, Mission Grille, and Harry's Place cocktail lounge are consistently satisfying.

The hotel offers a bed and breakfast package that includes a king or double room plus breakfast at the Mission Grille. Other amenities include a palm-surrounded rooftop swimming pool and a lighted tennis and basketball court. Tee times and transportation to the nearby ASU Karsten Golf Course can be arranged. Guests also receive complimentary transportation to and from Sky Harbor Airport.

WINDMILL INN OF CHANDLER $$
3535 W. Chandler Blvd., Chandler
(480) 812-9600
www.windmillinns.com/CHANhome.html

The convenience of being so close to the amenities at Chandler Fashion Center is appealing, but the staff and amenities on site also draw rave reviews. The 112-room hotel is known for its affordable value blended with Southwestern resort-style feel. The pool is smaller than you'll find at major hotels, but guests say it does the trick. It offers a library, fitness center, Jacuzzi, and availability for pets upon request. The rooms are double- and king-suites with small microwaves and refrigerators. Wi-Fi and basic breakfast are free.

NORTHEAST VALLEY

BEST WESTERN SUNDIAL $$$
7320 E. Camelback Rd., Scottsdale
(480) 994-4170, (800) 780-7234
www.bestwestern.com

With just 54 well-appointed rooms, the boutique-style hotel provides modern comfort and excellent access to the heart of downtown Scottsdale. Its spacious basic rooms and suites are designed with a contemporary flair. Each is equipped with free Wi-Fi

and high-speed Internet access. The hotel offers an outdoor heated pool, hot tub, business center, and enough parking to set your oversize truck or RV for the weekend. Rooms can be loaded with microwaves or fridges, and some have balconies.

FIRESKY RESORT $$$-$$$$
4925 N. Scottsdale Rd., Scottsdale
(480) 945-7666, (800) 528-7867
www.fireskyresort.com

The FireSky, situated amid palm trees, fountains, and fire pits, is a boutique hotel with 204 large guest rooms and suites, each with private balcony or patio. Enjoy the high-ceilinged lobby and lounge area dominated by a 28-foot fireplace. Rooms include flat-screen TVs, uniquely designed bathrooms, custom bedding, and special bath products. On the grounds you'll find a pool with a sandy beach and a lagoon-style pool. The on-site Jurlique Spa is a destination spot in itself because of the hotel's prime central location. You can dine on an outdoor patio at Taggia, the Italian restaurant on the property. The hotel's 14,000 square feet of meeting space gives large groups room to spread out. The hotel is pet-friendly and provides dog sitters and walkers while you're busy on the town or chilling out by the pool.

GAINEY SUITES HOTEL $$$-$$$$
7300 E. Gainey Suites Dr., Scottsdale
(480) 948-7750, (800) 445-8667
www.gaineysuiteshotel.com

The resort-style hotel is routinely given glowing reviews by guests who love the giant outdoor pool patio and condo-style suites, which include cozy kitchens and spacious living space. In 2008 hotel managers completed a $3.7 million remodel of the 162 rooms, making it even more of a central Scottsdale destination. The bedding and furniture are of the highest quality, including allergen-free covers and elegant marble bathrooms. Rooms include HD TVs and free Wi-Fi, in addition to digital entertainment systems with Nintendo GameCubes for kids who aren't into chilling out by the pool or hitting the nearby spas and shopping centers with mom. The hotel treats guests to complimentary newspapers, breakfast buffet, and evening hors d'oeuvres with beer and wine.

i Downtown Scottsdale is largely for the young and young at heart. Think of the core nightlife area as three parts. There are plenty of bars along Scottsdale Road between Indian School and Camelback roads, but also in Craftsman Court west of Scottsdale Road. To the east of the main thoroughfare, there are plenty of watering holes and clubs on Shoeman Lane, Stetson Drive, and 75th Street. New or renovated bars and clubs pop up constantly, such as the resort-like Spanish Fly Mexican Beach Club. (See the Close-up on Spanish Fly in the Nightlife chapter.)

HOLIDAY INN EXPRESS $$-$$$
3131 N. Scottsdale Rd., Scottsdale
(480) 675-7665, (888) 465-4329
www.hiescottsdalehotel.com

This all-suite, 3-floor hotel has 170 two-room suites where you have your choice of a king-size or 2 queen-size beds. Suites come in several floor plans and include kitchenettes. You can upgrade to a Luxury Business Suite featuring executive desks, well-lit work areas, a Jacuzzi tub, and computer connections. Each suite comes with an iron and ironing board, a microwave, and 2 TVs. The

complimentary breakfast, newspaper. and Internet help you feel at home. For recreation enjoy an exercise room, whirlpool, and an outdoor heated swimming pool. Or you can stroll into Old Town Scottsdale, about a 1-mile walk.

HOTEL THEODORE $$$$
7353 E. Indian School Rd., Scottsdale
(480) 308-1100
www.hoteltheodore.com
You don't get much closer to downtown Scottsdale than the hotel previously known as the Mondrian and James Hotel before that. It has been refurbished by new owners into a tropical paradise with 25-foot bougainvillea "gates" and fountains surrounded by lush landscaping. The 189 chic guestrooms come with Wi-Fi, 42-inch plasma TVs. and a deluxe sound system with iPod connectivity. Suites and apartments are also available, as well as 10,000 square feet of meeting space that's more inviting than the typical chain hotel conference center. Two pools attract different groups; one for sexy pool parties, and the other for serene repose. The Theodore also features a world-class spa and fitness center. The in-house Cielo Italian restaurant serves breakfast and dinner. Teddy's Nightclub and TR's Lounge cater to the techno-dance-party crowd. The names of the hotel and bars pay homage to former US President Teddy Roosevelt.

HOTEL VALLEY HO $$$$
6850 E. Main St., Scottsdale
(480) 248-2000, (866) 882-4484
www.hotelvalleyho.com
The Valley Ho, steeped in Scottsdale history, manages to blend the panache and art of the 1950s with 21st-century state-of-the-art amenities. Today, some guests say the 7-story Valley Ho has more character than some of the more traditional hotels in the Phoenix metro area. The hotel includes a high-tech fitness center, spa facility, and a round courtyard pool. The rooftop terrace, used for wedding receptions and other events, features breathtaking panoramic sunset views. The 194 deluxe rooms and suites offer comfy beds and plush furnishings as well as a small deck for sunbathing and lounging, in addition to 32-inch flat-screen TVs. Plenty of meeting space is available for business guests. Cafe ZuZu offers a casual menu ranging from bacon cheeseburgers to filet mignon and also a happy hour with $5 appetizers like grilled cheese with tomato soup. You can also dine at swanky Trader Vic's, which features upscale Hawaiian/Polynesian cuisine and live local musicians on some nights. The hotel is situated close to Scottsdale galleries, boutiques, restaurants, and nightlife. Kids and pets are welcome. (See the Close-up in this chapter for more on the Valley Ho.)

i The Hotel Valley Ho in Scottsdale prides itself on its environmentally friendly initiatives. Housekeepers use clean, green-certified chemicals, and the spa uses organic, biodegradable products. The hotel claims it saved 20,000 tons of landfill waste by renovating the 1950s-era building rather than tearing it down.

W SCOTTSDALE HOTEL &
RESIDENCES $$$$
7277 E. Camelback Rd., Scottsdale
(480) 970-2100
www.starwoodhotels.com

Just a quick walk from Scottsdale Fashion Square, this stylish and upscale hotel features 224 rooms. Suites are themed, such as the spa suite, WOW suite, and Extreme WOW suite. The "W Residences" within the hotel are like luxury condos. The hotel is especially appealing to those staying in Scottsdale to experience the glamorous nightlife and ritzy lifestyle. W Scottsdale staff provide guests with complimentary chauffer service in an Acura MDX 7 a.m. to 7 p.m. You'll also find 2 multi-level pools, lush landscaping, an elegant spa, and 2 lounges.

i Hotel Valley Ho in Scottsdale, which first opened in 1956, offers 90-minute architectural tours of its buildings and grounds. Tours are given by appointment only and fittingly cost $19.56 per person. Admission includes discounts for hotel services. Call (480) 248-2000 or (866) 882-4484 for reservations.

NORTHWEST VALLEY

BEST WESTERN INN & SUITES OF SUN CITY $$
11201 Grand Ave., Youngtown
(623) 933-8211, (800) 253-2168
www.bestwestern.com

The 96-room, 2-story hotel is consistently clean and recommended by guests who are pleased with the service. For the outlying northwest Valley, it provides a great location. Glendale is about 15 minutes away and downtown Phoenix is about 45 minutes away. Each of the rooms is furnished with either a king-size or 2 double beds in addition to a microwave, refrigerator, and free high-speed Internet. The inn also has mini-suites with 2 queen beds, a sitting area,

and dual vanities. All rooms are eligible for discounted rates for those staying 7 consecutive nights or longer. Guests also enjoy a swimming pool and a complimentary hot breakfast.

HAMPTON INN $$
8408 W. Paradise Ln., Peoria
(623) 486-9918, (800) 426-7866
www.hamptoninn.com

The massive mall of Arrowhead Towne Center is located within walking distance, making the hotel very close to a wide variety of restaurants, bars, shopping, and entertainment. This 5-story Hampton Inn, which opened in early 1998, is considered one of the top lodgings in Peoria. Peoria Sports Complex, site of spring-training baseball games and other events (see the Spectator Sports chapter), is close by. The 112 rooms come with either 2 queen-size or 1 king-size bed. Standard features include microwave and refrigerator. The inn has an outdoor pool, plus a laundry room for guests' use. A hot buffet breakfast is complimentary.

✴RENAISSANCE GLENDALE HOTEL $$$–$$$$
9495 W. Coyotes Blvd., Glendale
(623) 937-3700
www.renaissanceglendale.com

The modern hotel at Westgate City Center appeals to visitors with its bright Southwestern themes and colors, in addition to easy access to Glendale's prime retail/entertainment hub. The 320 guest rooms are known as some of the biggest, newest, and cleanest on the west side of town. They feature down comforters, a 2-line phone, high-speed Internet access, HD TVs, and high-tech connections for your personal electronics. Two on-site restaurants offer American food

Close-up

Hotel Valley Ho: Reviving a Legend

When word of the opening of Hotel Valley Ho reached Hollywood in 1956, celebrities streamed into Scottsdale's hip, luxurious resort. Yet the new hotel also played a surprising role in history. Thanks to the foresight of the original designers, the Valley Ho launched an innovative brand of guest accommodation that helped cement America's post-World War II romance with the automobile. It's a marvelous tale.

"The Valley Ho represented a complete shift in hotel direction," says Joan Fudala, a Scottsdale historian and writer who brings a unique perspective to the hotel. "In previous years wealthy people made a grand entry by train and then stayed for the entire season."

The Hotel Valley Ho had its roots in World War II. Arizona's sunny, dry climate was perfectly suited for flying planes, so in the 1940s training bases sprang up all over the state. Thousands of soldiers were introduced to the area, and sleepy little Scottsdale, then a town of fewer than 1,000 residents, welcomed the airmen. When the war ended and the boys came home, some of them remembered Arizona and returned to raise their families.

About that time Scottsdale began to make a name as an enclave of artistic talent. Painters and sculptors took up residence, and colorful Native American artwork drew big crowds. Shoppers could order jewelry directly from the artist; observe a bracelet, belt, or bolo being fashioned; and then stroll out wearing their art.

Robert and Evelyn Foehl, two hoteliers who took pride in meeting the needs of guests, entered the Scottsdale scene. Robert had trained at the Los Angeles Biltmore, then bought the swanky San Marcos Hotel in Chandler, and later managed the Jokake Inn in Phoenix. Evelyn, one of the few women in the hotel business in those days, had run the Hacienda Del Sol in Tucson. They married and together exemplified gracious Southwestern hospitality; they also knew nearly everybody.

That's when the pieces came together. With the Foehls, Scottsdale had the perfect hoteliers to debut a new resort. Investors hired Edward L. Varney, a student of Frank Lloyd Wright, to design it. He and his associates took inspiration from Wright by creating long horizontal lines and a high-ceilinged lobby that fostered in guests a dramatic, thrilling sense of arrival. They focused the hotel around a central courtyard—a welcoming Southwestern touch—and put in a pool, a lounge, a nightclub, and a restaurant. Oh, and they added something else.

A parking lot.

And so the motor resort came to town, one of the few in the world at the time and the first of its kind in Scottsdale. The notion of car-oriented architecture symbolized mobility and freedom.

Traditionally, says Fudala, guests would spend 80 percent of their time on resort property, with rare excursions. The Valley Ho, with its convenient location, allowed guests to amble into Scottsdale for the evening. Its parking lot added a newer twist—a trip from lobby to lot was easy. Now visitors could drive off to watch a

spring training baseball game, or they could enjoy touring in their own cars at their own pace, without having to wait for public transportation.

Architect critic Alan Hess writes, "Technology had won the war, and it was now erasing seasons, time, and distance."

Motor cars seemed a benevolent technology, one that reflected starry-eyed hope for the future. The hotel was part of the new transportation architecture that facilitated an ever-faster pace. Many people think of the 1950s with mild disdain, as though only hula hoops and baseball cards were created, but what scientists learned in those years redesigned the way Americans lived. No more did there have to be a central downtown area with shops all in one location. Now people could move—fast.

The Valley Ho remained open year-round, the first Scottsdale resort to do so, made possible by the pool and the advent of decent air-conditioning. The Foehls hosted meetings and parties, weddings and proms, and fashion shows on the grounds—hundreds of fashion shows that introduced visitors from around the globe to Arizona culture and style.

The advent of economical cars and improving road networks meant families could travel and vacation together for a week or two. No longer did vacationers spend an entire season camped on a single property.

The Foehls' famous friends found an oasis in Scottsdale, but regular families relaxed there as well. The Foehls welcomed everybody, and everybody came.

The Valley Ho was the place to see and be seen. Accommodations were comfortable, and laid-back Scottsdale residents gave celebrities a chance to be themselves—something not possible in other resort areas.

Bette Davis, Roy Rogers, and Frankie Avalon stayed at the Valley Ho. So did Humphrey Bogart, Betty Grable, Cary Grant, and Tony Curtis. Robert Wagner and Natalie Wood held their private wedding reception on the Valley Ho grounds. When Jimmy Durante couldn't sleep, he'd sometimes slip into the lobby to tickle the ivories—to the delight of other sleepless guests.

The hotel was acquired by Ramada in the early 1970s and remained fashionable for years. But time and neglect took its toll, and the Valley Ho fell into sad disrepair. In 2004 Westroc Hotels and Resorts spent $80 million restoring the landmark property.

The rebuilt hotel maintains much of the 1950s flavor. The soda jerk flips burgers and prepares sodas and banana splits the old-fashioned way, and the Cafe ZuZu serves wonderful '50s-style dishes, such as the blue plate special, chicken and dumplings, and "J's" meatloaf. Dessert? Save room for Mom's apple pie (you'd better, or I'll tell). If you really want a taste of the '50s, order the all-American sampler—a platter that includes a Rice Krispies Treat, a Hostess Cupcake, and . . . well, yes . . . a Twinkie.

The Hotel Valley Ho is located in downtown Scottsdale at 6850 E. Main St.; (480) 248-2000. (See hotel entry for further information.)

and beverages for breakfast, lunch, and dinner. The hotel is a perfect place to stay to be close to games or events at University of Phoenix Stadium and Jobing.com Arena. It also includes a full-service spa.

RESIDENCE INN $$
7350 N. Zanjero Blvd., Glendale
(623) 772-8900

One of Glendale's newest hotels, this one is especially appealing for longer stays. It's close to the excitement of Westgate City Center, yet removed from the main action, which makes it a bit quieter. The 126 rooms are spacious and include wired and wireless Internet access. Kitchen supplies include a conventional oven, a dishwasher, a microwave oven, a refrigerator, pots and pans, and a table and chairs. The granite surfaces are an extra nice touch. Some suites have fireplaces. Rather than eating at one of the many nearby restaurants, you can use the on-site barbecue and picnic area. Pets are allowed. Overall, the hotel is very well rated and is considered a top Marriott property in the Valley.

SPRINGHILL SUITES $$
7810 W. Bell Rd., Glendale
(623) 878-6666

This all-suite hotel located close to Glendale's shopping, dining, and entertainment is very well reviewed by guests. Rooms are quite spacious and include a microwave oven, phone with speaker, and free high-speed Internet access. There are separate areas for eating and sleeping, which is nice for families. You'll find a clean pool area, a gym, a tennis court, and a pool and spa. The breakfast buffet is free.

WINDMILL INN OF SUN CITY WEST $$
12545 W. Bell Rd., Surprise
(623) 583-0133, (800) 547-4747
www.windmillinns.com

The 3-story, all-suite hotel has a few intriguing amenities you don't always find, including the free use of bicycles, free use of a lending library of best-selling books, and free coffee and muffin plus a newspaper delivered to your door every morning. It's perfect for extended West Valley stays. The 127 two-room suites are 500 square feet and come with either a king-size bed or 2 double beds, along with double sinks in the bathroom, a wet bar, a microwave, a refrigerator, 2 TVs, 3 telephones, a desk area, and a sleeper sofa. Guests also have the use of laundry facilities. Adding to the amenities are the swimming pool and whirlpool. Pets are accepted.

RESORTS

There is nothing like the warm, sunny experience of a Valley resort. To people from cold-weather climates, it's paradise. The expansive grounds of the resorts in Phoenix and Scottsdale are especially unique with their mansion-like common areas, condo-like casita rooms, and Sonoran Desert landscapes. Families stay on vacation, honeymooners after their wedding receptions, and business groups as part of annual meetings or ceremonies. But locals also take advantage of the resorts for day trips to the spas, golf courses, bars, restaurants, and other amenities considered among the best in the US.

The Valley's top resorts include the Arizona Biltmore, the Phoenician, the Wigwam, the Boulders, the Four Seasons, and the Scottsdale Fairmont Princess. These are the heavyweights by history, reputation, and consistency. Their world-class offerings are detailed in the following chapter, but other listings outline newer luxury options like the Intercontinental Montelucia in Paradise Valley and reliable family resorts like the Pointe Hilton mountaintop resorts in north Phoenix. While the high-end resorts are worth every penny, and they run their share of tremendous package deals, there's also a lot of value for travelers in some of the lesser-known Valley resorts that are located closer to casinos, ballparks, and downtown nightlife than some of the traditional spots. From golf getaways to wellness-related retreats, there are plenty of seasonal packages to choose from. Bargains between Thanksgiving and New Year's are particularly popular; out of the peak spring and fall travel seasons, the area is still a winter getaway for cold-weather travelers.

State tourism authorities claimed 2009 was one of the worst for Valley resorts as fewer people vacationed or indulged in poolside cocktails and lavish meals in the down economy. Still, more than 35 million people visited Arizona and spent more than $16 billion, state officials said. And that was a down year. By 2011 resort occupancies and average daily room rates were up, according to the Arizona Office of Tourism.

The Valley will always be a national destination, no matter the economic forecast. Arizona is known as being a far better value than California. Its diverse mix of outdoor attractions and major cities sets it apart from other West Coast metro areas. People from Europe, Asia, and South America use Valley resorts as launching points to adventures through the Grand Canyon. But it's the simple details that stand out. The cool of the pool. The green of a desert-framed fairway. The sweetness of that first vacation cocktail. Or the feeling of relaxation from a long-awaited massage. Valley resorts soothe, invigorate, energize, and generate memories with their truly Arizona characteristics.

For hotels and motels in the area, see the chapter starting on p. 45.

RESORTS

Price Code

Resorts were asked for their double-occupancy, daily rates in high season (generally considered January to April, but in some cases including fall months and May). Because resorts tend to offer a variety of accommodations, we have given you dollar codes that represent the range from standard rooms to suites, casitas, and luxury villas. Prices indicated here do not include tax, room service, incidental fees, or fees for golf, spas, and other amenities. Remember that off-season rates can be dramatically lower than what you see here.

$................... $150 to $200
$$ .... $200 to $300
$$$ .... $300 to $500
$$$$ .... More than $500

PHOENIX

ARIZONA BILTMORE $$$–$$$$
2400 E. Missouri Ave.
(602) 955-6600, (800) 950-0086
www.arizonabiltmore.com

The Arizona Biltmore is the stately centerpiece of the ritziest neighborhood in central Phoenix. It's been open since 1929, when it was crowned "The Jewel of the Desert" at its grand-opening gala. Even visitors to town who are not guests of the hotel should see it to understand how it helped lay the foundation for the Valley of the Sun's resort industry and to appreciate it as an architectural gem. Vestiges of Frank Lloyd Wright can be seen all through the interior and exterior since the Biltmore was designed by one of Wright's apprentices, Albert Chase McArthur. (The extent of Wright's own involvement as "consulting architect" is not known, but that just adds to the hotel's mystique.) The

ambience is one of functional elegance. The geometrically stylized image of a palm tree trunk that's sculpted into many of the exterior concrete blocks sets a theme that's used repeatedly in the decor and landscaping. The lobby has remarkable stained-glass windows, balconies, and Wright-inspired furniture and lighting.

Other interesting facts about the Biltmore: Every US president since 1930 has stayed at the Biltmore; chewing-gum magnate William Wrigley and his heirs owned the resort for four decades; and in 1996, the resort completed a 5-year, $50-million renovation and expansion project. The Biltmore continues to be an award-winning resort because its amenities and services keep up with modern times, but face-lifts over the years have not marred its architectural integrity. Additionally, the 24th Street and Missouri Avenue location is part of the uptown/Biltmore area, though it still provides guests with a sense of seclusion from the surrounding urban intensity. It's only 15 minutes by freeway from downtown and is just a skip away from the Camelback Corridor, a prime retail, restaurant, and office district.

The Biltmore's 738 rooms and villas are furnished in a style reminiscent of Wright's. The 1- and 2-bedroom villas have full kitchens, indoor and outdoor dining areas, and fireplaces. The Biltmore's 39 acres make it a relatively compact resort. Still, there's space for the Biltmore Athletic Club, along with 2 championship golf courses at the adjacent Arizona Biltmore Country Club. There's also an 18-hole putting course. The resort's restaurants include Wright's, featuring impeccable New American cuisine, and the new Frank & Albert's, whose chef uses the finest ingredients from specialty farms.

The Biltmore has also been doing high tea for 81 years, a tradition that remains in place from November through May. The resort has 2 bars, 8 pools, 7 tennis courts, and an elegant spa offering therapeutic treatments, fitness equipment, steam rooms, and a full-service beauty salon. The resort has become kid-friendly over the years. The Paradise Pool features a 92-foot waterslide enclosed in twin towers. The Kids Korral offers a range of supervised activities, as well as special programs such as tennis and yoga on weekends. Lawn games include croquet, volleyball, chess, and shuffleboard, and there are pleasant trails for jogging, strolling, and biking. You will also find the poolside private Cabana Club with its swim-up beverage service, salad and sandwich bar, and desserts.

i What is a resort casita? Think of it as a mini-house and a home away from home. Casitas are individual, stand-alone structures or large guest rooms joined in small groupings with other casitas, town house-style, to create a greater sense of privacy. Often they have their own patios, fireplaces, living rooms, and kitchens.

ARIZONA GRAND RESORT $$$
8000 S. Arizona Grand Pkwy.
(602) 438-9000, (866) 267-1321
www.arizonagrandresort.com

The 740-suite hotel near the east side of South Mountain Park is a place for family fun and big business gatherings. The resort includes an 18-hole golf course with permanently preserved mountain views and a water park that's popular with parents. Meeting space is both indoor and outdoor, totaling about 117,000 square feet for groups to

spread out on. The on-site Luxury Spa doubles as a salon for guests. Suites are painted in relaxing desert tones and include bamboo and rattan furniture. Each suite includes a living room with a queen sofa bed in addition to patio or balcony views. The south Phoenix location might seem out of the way, but it's actually closer to Sky Harbor Airport, downtown Phoenix, and Tempe than comparable resorts in the northeast Valley.

THE PHOENICIAN GOLF
RESORT $$$$
6000 E. Camelback Rd.
(480) 941-8200, (800) 888-8234
www.thephoenician.com

No expense was spared in designing and furnishing The Phoenician, the opulent resort located on Camelback Road between Phoenix and Scottsdale. It features a $25 million art collection of paintings, tapestries, antiques, and bronze sculptures, in addition to an oval pool tiled in mother-of-pearl and surrounded by lush landscaping with waterfalls, lagoons, and fountains. Then there are the extra touches such as crystal chandeliers, marble floors and walls, and Italian linens. It's unexpectedly palatial for a metropolitan area with such humble beginnings. Yet guests can easily find serenity and relaxation, along with top-notch services, beautiful nighttime views, great golf, and one of the best restaurants in town—all with Camelback Mountain as backdrop.

The Phoenician is better understood through a quick look at its beginnings. It opened in 1988 as the "house" that Charles Keating built—he envisioned building a resort like no other. But when Keating's savings-and-loan empire crumbled and landed him in federal prison, the resort became the property of the Resolution Trust Corp.

It's owned now by Starwood Hotels and Resorts.

The Phoenician is huge, laid out on 250 acres with 643 rooms, including 119 casitas and more than 50 suites. Most of the accommodations are in the main building, supplemented by more secluded areas with casitas, suites, and villas. Rooms are furnished with expensive rattan furniture, Berber carpets, and oversize bathrooms with Italian marble and oval Roman bathtubs. Rooms are enabled for Wi-Fi and high-speed Internet. The resort boasts 9 pools and a 165-foot water slide.

Guests can stroll through a 2-acre cactus garden. But much of the resort's tropical landscaping actually looks unlike the surrounding Sonoran Desert. Natives of the South Pacific island of Tonga were hired to create the lush greenery. A 27-hole championship golf course, putting green, and clubhouse are also on-site, as is the Tennis Garden with 12 courts, an automated practice court, and a grass court. Staff can arrange for hikes up Camelback Mountain. Croquet, lawn bowling, lawn chess, and billiards provide other amusements. The latest feature is called Canyon Suites, an elegant boutique hotel right on the grounds. Pampered guests are chauffeured in a Mercedes, and a sommelier hosts evening wine tastings.

There are 5 restaurants at the Phoenician, in addition to an ice cream parlor and the relaxing Thirsty Camel Lounge. Many Phoenix residents know about the charming afternoon teas in the Tea Court. The Centre for Well-Being is a large spa, offering over 70 treatments, including massages, scrubs and mud packs, facial care, and exercise equipment. For children ages 5 to 12, the resort runs the Funicians Kids Club, where daily

themes get them swimming, hiking, making crafts, and playing games under staff supervision. You'll also find a beauty salon, a few boutiques, 24-hour room service, concierge service, and airport transportation.

POINTE HILTON SQUAW PEAK RESORT $$–$$$
7677 N. 16th St.
(602) 997-2626, (800) 947-9784
www.squawpeakhilton.com

The resort's proximity to the Phoenix Mountain Preserve and the second-highest point in the city, Squaw Peak, gives a scenic setting to this relatively centralized location. Opened in 1976, it is the older of the two Pointe Hilton resorts in the Valley. Both are about a 15-minute drive to downtown Phoenix and include fantastic views of the city. The Squaw Peak Resort reportedly was the first all-suite resort in the country. Architects gave it a Spanish-Mediterranean look, and the many courtyards and gardens are great for a stroll. The 563 units include mostly 2-room suites and 133 casitas. There are also some boardroom suites, which combine a bedroom with a meeting room for small, executive functions. The resort also includes the Hole-in-the-Wall River Ranch, where families can enjoy tubing amid rocks, fountains, and waterfalls. You'll also find a 130-foot slide and Coyote Camp children's adventure program. Golf is available a few miles away at the Tapatio Cliffs sister Hilton property, and 4 tennis courts are on the premises. The Tocasierra Spa and fitness center are good places to unwind from all the fun. On-site restaurants include the Hole-in-the-Wall, which serves American food in a 1940s ranch house.

POINTE HILTON TAPATIO CLIFFS RESORT $$–$$$
11111 N. 7th St.
(602) 866-7500, (800) 947-9784
www.tapatiocliffshilton.com

Tapatio means "a place of peace and contentment." This resort, with its expanded lobby, is nestled into North Mountain Park, offering tranquil views of mountains, desert flora, and cliffs. The 547 two-room suites of the Spanish-Mediterranean-style resort take advantage of the views. Its best restaurant, Different Pointe of View, allows you to sit at tables in terraced rows, all facing a floor-to-ceiling window for arguably the most gorgeous panorama of the Valley. The restaurant is known for its wine cellar as well as its fine continental food. Three other restaurants serve a variety of fare from steaks to Southwestern. The Falls is a 3-acre water feature of waterfalls, free-form swimming pools, an enclosed water slide, and an open-air restaurant pavilion. The centerpiece is a 40-foot waterfall that cascades into 12 meandering pools, a design inspired by Havasupai Falls in the Grand Canyon. There are 8 recreational pools in all, plus 2 tennis courts, a fitness room, a full-service spa and salon, and the championship 18-hole Lookout Mountain Golf Club course, featuring lush greens amid a desert setting. The on-site Hilton Golf Academy offers intensive instruction and helpful tips to improve your play. Each of the 2-room suites features a private balcony. There are also some boardroom suites, which combine a bedroom with a meeting room for small, executive functions.

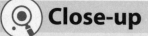

Close-up

Royal Palms

Some Valley resorts feature outstanding golf courses; others, lavish poolside recreation. At Royal Palms Resort and Spa in Phoenix, the amenities are hidden against the south side of Camelback Mountain on meticulously manicured grounds that rival some of the big-name resorts twice its size. There's no golf course on site, and the pools are smaller than at some resorts, but it's one of the most relaxing experiences in town.

Many locals retreat to Royal Palms for dinner or cocktails, knowing the ambiance is so calm and unpretentious. The 119-room resort (also detailed in the Hotels section) is known as the best place in Phoenix for an intimate wedding. Business groups also use it for its meeting areas, which, like its rooms, are set among the on-site citrus groves, water fountains, lawns, and detailed nooks with dozens of romantic hiding places.

Romance is actually the resort's focus. In January 2011 Royal Palms featured its Romantication packages, complete with European-inspired menus at T. Cook's restaurant (see Restaurants for details), lingerie gifts, pampering at Alvadora Spa, and help from the resort's Director of Romance.

Royal Palms dates to 1925, when it was built as the winter retreat for a New York businessman. It's now recognized as a historic site that remains true to its vintage European character. The rooms, common areas, and lounges all carry a European old-world charm that blends with modern Arizona.

The venue is so detail oriented, it is worth checking out, even if only for a cocktail or to stroll the grounds with your lover.

Information: Royal Palms Resort and Spa, 5200 E. Camelback Rd.; (602) 840-3610, www.royalpalmshotel.com.

✳WIGWAM   **$$$–$$$$**
300 Wigwam Blvd., Litchfield Park
(623) 935-3811, (800) 327-0396
www.wigwamresort.com

Some say the Wigwam comes closest to capturing the essence of Arizona and the lure of the West. In recent years the west Phoenix resort's owners have used a $7 million "rejuvenation" redesign to reestablish the Wigwam as a destination over more glamorous spots in Scottsdale and central Phoenix. This once-private club was built in 1918 to lodge visiting executives of the Goodyear Tire and Rubber Co. and was way out in the country back then. By 1929 it opened to the public, with room for 24 guests. The 440-acre west Phoenix resort still carries reminders of a more rugged, cowboy era. Much of the original building from 1918 has been incorporated into the Main Lodge, including a sitting room with a large stone fireplace.

The Wigwam is only 20 minutes from downtown Phoenix. Also distinguishing it from other resorts is the fact that it's the only one in Arizona with three 18-hole golf courses on its property. The Gold and Blue courses were designed by Robert Trent Jones; Arizona's "Red" Lawrence designed the Red course.

Accommodations are arranged in clusters of casitas—331 in all, including 72 suites, decorated with distressed-wood furnishings, stone fireplaces, leather chairs, Mexican ceramic tiles, and Native American-style pottery and baskets. The casitas are Territorial Adobe architecture. They are enabled with Wi-Fi and touch-screens for easy access to the concierge. The Wigwam is home to the elegant Elizabeth Arden Red Door Spa—the first Red Door in the West Valley. The 26,000-square-foot facility boasts 16 treatment rooms, an extensive menu of body treatments, and a complete range of indoor and outdoor programs in plush surroundings. Guests will be pampered in true Red Door fashion.

The new Palm Courtyard outdoor plaza opened in January 2011 to host live entertainment. It is located next to the indoor/outdoor Wigwam Bar, which features classic cocktails and small bites like housemade organic potato chips and buffalo chili. Other recreational amenities include 9 tennis courts and horseback riding. For families on vacation, there's Camp Pow Wow, a supervised recreation program that offers marshmallow roasts and other activities for children ages 5 and older. The resort features a 25-foot tower and waterslide for family fun at its uniquely designed Lodge Pool. The other, the Oasis Pool, is a great place to chill out.

As part of its rejuvenation overhaul, the Wigwam chefs have shifted their focus to fresh and local Arizona ingredients. Innovative chef Chris Bianco, of the internationally renowned Pizzeria Bianco, designed the menu at the resort's new signature restaurant, Litchfield's. It features al fresco dining and a giant exhibition kitchen.

i The Wigwam resort in Litchfield Park west of Phoenix hosts a farmers' market every Sunday for most of the year to showcase the local organic produce, cheese, preserves, and bread used by chefs in the resort's kitchens.

NORTHEAST VALLEY

THE BOULDERS RESORT & GOLDEN DOOR SPA $$$$
34631 N. Tom Darlington Dr., Carefree
(480) 488-9009, (888) 579-2631
www.theboulders.com

The Boulders, set on the edge of Scottsdale in the foothills of the far Northeast Valley, is logistically the best place to get away from it all without leaving civilization. Carefree is a small, laid-back town with beautiful hillside homes about 30 miles north of central Phoenix. The Boulders is on the main route into town and has a 24-hour security gate, separating it from the community of affluent Midwest and East Coast transplants. The resort's name pays tribute to the 12-million-year-old geological curiosity at its center: a 90-foot-high mound of boulders. Other rock outcroppings dot the grounds. The resort was designed and built in the early 1980s with early eco-friendly construction principles in mind. The resort offers on-site geology tours; ask when you reserve. The low-slung adobe-style buildings are painted to closely match the color of the boulders. Almost all the landscaping is indigenous to the area.

A network of trails on resort grounds lets guests enjoy the mountain scenery, including the reported 350 species of birds and other wildlife in the area. The list of amenities is pages long, topped by the Boulders' 2 scenic 18-hole championship golf courses.

In 2010 the resort unveiled its remodeled Bogey's bar at the golf club, setting it apart from other more traditional "19th hole" golf club bars. The Boulders also offers an academy to train with the pros and swing doctors to help you spend less time in the sand on your vacation. Staff members at the Boulders say service is just as important as amenities. With an eye toward anticipating their guests' every need, they keep detailed preference histories—for instance, who likes feather pillows over synthetic.

The 160 guest casitas and more than 60 villas are nestled into the terrain. The most recent interior renovations added warmer colors, regional artwork, Native American artifacts, and vintage-style furniture. Each of the accommodations has a fireplace and private patio or balcony. Families and golf groups can take advantage of the 1-, 2-, or 3-bedroom villas, complete with laundry facilities and kitchens. All units have plugs for personal tech gadgets, wet bars, large dressing areas, upgraded bathrooms, and wood-beam ceilings.

Dining is exceptional, with 6 restaurants to choose from, including the casually elegant Palo Verde and The Latilla, offering a more formal menu and views of a waterfall. There are 8 tennis courts, with tennis pros offering private lessons and weekly clinics. You'll also find 4 swimming pools and rock-climbing sessions that guide you up the boulders formation. The luxurious Golden Door Spa, with its innovative wellness program and state-of-the-art fitness center, features a detox program in addition to yoga and tai chi classes. A "back to the womb" experience and Native American-inspired programs are also offered. It's a short stroll away from the boutiques and galleries of El Pedregal Festival Marketplace or a short drive to the touristy town of Carefree. Complimentary shuttles get you around the 1,300-acre resort. Native American art is showcased in the main lodge and dining areas. Transportation to Sky Harbor and Scottsdale airports is available, or you can fly your private plane right into Carefree Airport.

i Looking for a unique place to stay that's in Scottsdale but not really in Scottsdale? Try the Talking Stick Resort located just over the Scottsdale line east of the Loop 101 freeway. The resort at 9800 E. Indian Bend Rd. includes 497 luxurious modern rooms, 5 lounges, a 15th-floor restaurant with sweeping views, and easy access to Casino Arizona. The Salt River Pima-Maricopa Indian Community operates the resort and casino. Information: www.talkingstickresort.com.

CAREFREE RESORT & CONFERENCE CENTER $$$
37220 N. Mule Trail Rd., Carefree
(480) 488-5300, (800) 637-7200
www.carefree-resort.com

If you like the idea of being close to the mountains, this cozy, hidden-away resort in Carefree is a great choice. You'll enjoy learning the names and whereabouts of such landmarks as Black Mountain, Elephant Butte, and Skull Mesa. The resort's casitas, tennis villas, and restaurants were remodeled and redesigned beginning in 2010. The updated resort has 222 rooms, including standard ones with panoramic views, casitas, and privately owned luxury villas. Several championship golf courses are located close by. The resort offers 2 pools where you can sip the resort's signature

prickly pear margaritas, in addition to 5 tennis courts, an upscale restaurant, a fitness center, and a full-service spa. Through concierge services, you can head out on desert jeep tours, hot-air balloon rides, or horseback riding trips. Other innovative offerings include cowboy-style cooking classes and campfire storytelling. The western-themed Red Horse Saloon was closed and reopened as a meeting facility, further enhancing the venue with 22 meeting rooms. The 11,000-square-foot Opera House is a popular Northeast Valley site for formal programs.

DOUBLETREE PARADISE
VALLEY RESORT $$-$$$
5401 N. Scottsdale Rd., Scottsdale
(480) 947-5400, (800) 222-TREE
www.doubletree1.hilton.com
This is one of the most architecturally attractive resorts on Scottsdale Road. The design incorporates sculpted concrete blocks in a purplish gray for a look that is reminiscent of a Frank Lloyd Wright structure. The central courtyards and pool area of the 22-acre resort are artfully done, with lots of palm trees, fountains, gardens, and waterfalls. The colorful and airy restaurant, enFuego, offers contemporary cuisine with Arizona influences. The more than 300 rooms and suites all have either patios or balconies. Other amenities include a lavish pool, a lounge with live entertainment, a health club, an indoor racquetball court, a putting green, 2 tennis courts, and a gift shop. The city's main mall, Scottsdale Fashion Square, is within walking distance. Golfing at the McCormick Ranch course is a few minutes' drive away.

*FAIRMONT SCOTTSDALE
PRINCESS $$$$
7575 E. Princess Dr., Scottsdale
(480) 585-4848, (866) 540-4495
www.fairmont.com/scottsdale
The Princess was built to resemble a Mexican colonial estate, with lots of arched openings, balconies, railings, and red-tiled roofs. Its terra-cotta color complements the beautiful view of the McDowell Mountains. The Princess is on 450 acres that are now in the heart of north Scottsdale and has about 649 guestrooms, suites, casitas, and villas. Some rooms are like luxury apartments that provide guests with more than 2,000 square feet of space. The resort also has a massive and opulent hotel ballroom, making it a popular place for lavish business conferences. La Hacienda, the resort's much-heralded gourmet Mexican restaurant, and Bourbon Steak, which is led by award-winning chef Michael Mira, are both culinary destinations.

Golf is the big draw here. Guests gravitate to the Princess first for the annual Waste Management Phoenix Open, which is hosted for a week every winter at the nearby Tournament Players Club course. The resort is also equipped to host major pro tennis tournaments on its 7 courts, including a stadium court. Other opportunities for recreation include 5 swimming pools, sand/water volleyball, and a fitness trail. Besides La Hacienda and Bourbon Steak, the resort has The Grill steakhouse, the LV Bistro, and a tapas bar. Shopping is also taken care of, with boutiques carrying sports clothing and other fashions, Southwestern gifts, and Indian jewelry. You can work off calories in the state-of-the-art fitness center, take a dip in the rooftop pool, and then indulge in a massage or a session of aromatherapy. On the grounds of the Princess are several

distinct gardens. Enjoy 2 cactus gardens, a plaza with 300 decorated pots, and a fragrance garden with jasmine, orchid trees, and citrus trees. All rooms have terraces, wet bars, refrigerators, and oversize bathrooms. The 119 casitas are grouped near the tennis courts, while the 72 villas are on the opposite end. Families can take advantage of the Kids Club, which offers supervised activities for kids 5 to 12 daily.

i The affluent north Scottsdale neighborhood of Troon North that houses the Four Seasons Resort is a super-exclusive master-planned community located on a 185-acre mountain preserve dotted with mature saguaro cactus and other native desert plants. The city of Scottsdale plans to complete a 30-acre municipal park in the neighborhood with hiking trails, playgrounds, and basketball courts.

FOUR SEASONS RESORT
SCOTTSDALE $$$$
10600 E. Crescent Moon Dr., Scottsdale
(480) 515-5700
www.fourseasons.com/scottsdale
Despite the fame of the above resorts, the Four Seasons can give any resort in the Valley a run for its money. The location is spectacular—surrounded by acres and acres of pristine desert scenery. With 210 guest rooms, the luxurious accommodations offer views of desert, mountain, and far-off Phoenix. Rooms include 22 suites, mostly 1- and 2-story adobe casitas. A multimillion-dollar casita makeover in 2007 added custom furnishings, MP3 capability, flat-screen TVs, and other amenities. The resort celebrated its 50th anniversary in March 2011. The good news for golf fanatics is that the resort offers

preferred tee times on the 2 renowned golf courses at Troon North, regarded as two of the best in Arizona. The Four Seasons Resort at Troon North made *Condé Nast Traveler*'s prestigious 2008 Gold List. In 2007 the resort picked up the AAA Five-Diamond Award. It boasts 3 restaurants on the premises, including the Talavera, which specializes in seafood and wine. The Onyx Bar and Lounge includes a bar made out of a single, smoothed mesquite tree. A 12,000-square-foot spa and fitness center features 14 treatment rooms, 2 wet rooms, and 2 deluxe spa suites. The resort offers a free Kids for All Seasons program, with daily scheduled events for kids 5 to 12. To top it off, a Kid's Concierge provides personal support and assistance for all youth-related ventures. The pool complex was updated through a recent $1 million overhaul that added entry bridges over natural desert washes and new fences to provide a clearer view of the Valley below the giant patios. Chill out in one of the fully loaded "super cabanas" outfitted with flat-screen TVs and iPod docking stations.

i Mothers and daughters will appreciate the traditionally lavish high tea served in the lobby courts at the Phoenician and Biltmore resorts. But for $35 the Ritz-Carlton in central Phoenix offers custom-blend tea, scones, bite-size desserts, and tea sandwiches that rival the fare served in the better-known resorts. Each of the three high teas is set in stately surroundings and each receives great annual reviews.

✱**HERMOSA INN** $$$–$$$$
5532 N. Palo Cristi Rd., Paradise Valley
(602) 955-8614, (800) 241-1210
www.hermosainn.com

Quietly hidden among the cactus-studded, multimillion-dollar estates of Paradise Valley is the small Hermosa Inn, with 6 lush acres and Lon's, an award-winning restaurant, brimming with hacienda charm (see the Restaurants chapter). The dream project of cowboy artist Lon Megargee, the place was hand-built in the 1930s with adobe bricks, the color of which blends charmingly with the surrounding rock. Megargee turned it into his home, studio, and guest ranch, and called it Casa Hermosa, or handsome house. Megargee's paintings hang throughout the lobby and restaurant. The inn was extensively renovated in the mid-1990s, and today it's popular not only as an inn, but also as the home of Lon's, a secluded restaurant whose chef, Jeremy Pacheco, is known for his innovations with local organic ingredients and traditional European influences. Guests of the inn enjoy a pool, outdoor spas, and tennis. Golf at nearby courses can be arranged. The boutique inn is convenient to both central Phoenix and Scottsdale and affords a lovely view of Camelback Mountain. The 34 hacienda-style guest casitas and rooms underwent a $2 million overhaul to update many of the modern amenities while carefully restoring the Old Arizona details that make the Hermosa such a draw. Casitas come in 3 different types, including 4 Grande Casitas that offer 800 luxurious square feet to call home while in Paradise Valley.

i You don't have to be a guest to enjoy many of the great facilities local resorts offer. Many sell day passes to their spas, golf courses, and fitness centers. Local business executives often rent banquet halls and conference facilities for important functions. Dinner at one of the fine restaurants can make for a romantic evening. Call ahead to see what's available.

HYATT REGENCY SCOTTSDALE RESORT & SPA AT GAINEY RANCH $$$–$$$$
7500 E. Doubletree Ranch Rd., Scottsdale
(480) 444-1234
www.hyattregencyscottsdale.com

This resort, situated well away from busy Scottsdale Road at lushly landscaped Gainey Ranch center, underwent a massive $50 million overhaul that radically changed its character. Key updates were to the lobby, bar, guest suites, casitas, the new Vaquero Ballroom, and Spa Avania. The resort also offers new green initiatives that offer discounts to large groups who follow environmentally sensitive principles. The 27-acre luxury resort offers 493 remodeled guest rooms, including 20 hypoallergenic rooms designed to eliminate nearly all the floating particulates that typically make you wheeze and cough on the road. The Hyatt's collection of art includes Native American works, bronzes, paintings, and other artifacts. Restaurants include the contemporary SWB, a relaxing Southwestern bistro that serves food all day, in addition to a sushi bar with unique sakes and the "alto ristorante e bar" Italian spot. Golf is available at the 3 nine-hole courses of the adjacent Gainey Ranch Golf Club. But guests are likely to get sidetracked by the Hyatt's 2.5-acre water playground with its white-sand beach, 3-story slide that juts out of a clock tower, 10 swimming pools, spa, waterfalls, and other features. The Spa Avania, considered one of the best in Arizona, provides a total immersion treatment experience designed to balance natural biorhythms at specific times of day. Jogging, cycling, and tennis are also encouraged. Deluxe accommodations include private casitas.

i Be sure to consider a visit during shoulder season, which is generally September to December. Temperatures can reach 100 degrees in October, but it's typically beautiful at night and the rates are significantly lower than during high season. The best rates, of course, are in the sizzling months of June to August.

✳INTERCONTINENTAL MONTELUCIA RESORT & SPA $$$$

4949 E. Lincoln Dr., Scottsdale
(480) 627-3200, (888) 627-3010
www.icmontelucia.com

President Barack Obama stayed here in 2009 when he visited the Valley to address the ongoing economic crisis. It marked the first time since Herbert Hoover's administration that a US president stayed anywhere other than the famed Arizona Biltmore Resort & Spa. So you know this place has something uniquely alluring about it. The $325 million project was only a few months old at the time of Obama's visit. Since then it's become more of a household name. Travel+Leisure ranked the resort as the No. 1 hotel in Arizona in 2010. The Montelucia's courtyards, buildings, and corridors evoke memories of Italy or Spain, only set on 34 acres against the gorgeous rock formations of the north side of Camelback Mountain. The resort features 253 guest rooms and 40 suites, some of which are like European villas with private lawns and extensive patios. The complex is more like its own village. Amenities include the 31,000-square-foot Joya Spa, which has to be one of the most relaxing places in the Valley. Men can also experience the tranquil treatments and retire to their luxury man-cave dressing rooms. The golf course, 5 pools, European cafe, and wedding chapel fashioned after a place in Venice also attract guests. Dining includes the award-winning Prado restaurant, which serves contemporary Mediterranean cuisine.

JW MARRIOTT CAMELBACK INN $$$

5402 E. Lincoln Dr., Scottsdale
(480) 948-1700, (800) 242-2635
www.camelbackinn.com

This resort has a lovely, laid-back feel to it, even though it's packed with sophistication and amenities to satisfy all tastes. Guests can relax amid 125 acres in the scenic crook between Camelback Mountain and Mummy Mountain of Paradise Valley. The hacienda-like resort has earned many awards since opening in 1936. Recent renovations have added pueblo-style casitas nestled together to imitate a village, a new lobby bar, and an outdoor courtyard. Casita interiors were redecorated, and a large pool with fun water features was added, among other amenities. The property has 427 adobe-style casitas with private patios or balconies, plus 26 suites. Amenities include 6 tennis courts, a golf pro shop, 36 holes of championship golf, and 5 restaurants, including the BLT Steak restaurant led by chef Laurent Tourondel. The 2 golf courses are a short distance by car. The Spa at Camelback Inn offers 32 treatment rooms and a state-of-the-art fitness center.

SANCTUARY CAMELBACK MOUNTAIN RESORT & SPA $$$$

5700 E. McDonald Dr., Paradise Valley
(480) 948-2100, (800) 245-2051
www.sanctuaryoncamelback.com

Sitting on 53 of the most dramatic acres you'll ever see, right on the slope of Camelback Mountain, this resort has been rated

one of the top resorts in the US since it opened in 2001. The views are considered some of the most spectacular in the Valley. A $3 million renovation in 2010 unveiled a new high-tech kitchen with a raw bar and plancha oven for cooking whole-fish style. Chef Beau MacMillan at the resort's classy Elements restaurant has been featured on the television show *Iron Chef America*. The recent overhaul also included the Praying Monk outdoor year-round dining space, a great spot for panoramic views, and the wine-savvy private dining space of XII, which showcases 800 bottles of outstanding vino. The 98 casitas, with contemporary design, sport such amenities as private balconies, kitchen alcoves, outdoor spas, and even wood-burning fireplaces for a romantic evening. Some casitas have travertine marble showers and oversize tubs, and all offer candlelight turndown service. The resort also offers 7 luxuriously modern private estate homes, each with its own unique character. A state-of-the-art fitness center will help you work off the calories with cardio- and strength-training equipment and a lap pool. The resort also features 5 lighted tennis courts and 4 pools, including 1 infinity pool. You can also take a class in yoga, Pilates, tai chi, or belly dancing. The Asian-inspired spa and meditation garden will de-stress and reinvigorate.

WESTIN KIERLAND RESORT & SPA $$$–$$$$
6902 E. Greenway Pkwy., Scottsdale
(480) 624-1000, (800) 354-5892
www.kierlandresort.com

The 730-acre resort prides itself on its service. But its location is equally excellent. It's located directly across the street from the shopping and dining at Kierland Commons. Other north Scottsdale hotspots are within a few miles. Each of the 732 guestrooms, 55 suites, and 32 casitas comes with Westin's signature "Heavenly Bed" and "Heavenly Bath." Most come with private balcony or terrace and great mountain views. The 27 holes of golf on the Scott Miller-designed courses will help you work up an appetite for a gourmet meal at the on-site Deseo, a Latin-influenced restaurant featuring award-winning chefs. Or, if you prefer, you can choose from one of the other seven restaurants, ranging from casual to upscale. Kids can join the Westin Kid Club for lots of games and activities, slide down the 110-foot waterslide, or meet new friends at Pumpkinville, the fully equipped playground. The resort provides 2 lighted tennis courts and lessons and a 900-foot lazy river for rafting fun. A full-service spa specializes in Native American treatments. A recent property overhaul added 21,000 square feet of additional meeting space, bringing the total square feet of space for big business groups to more than 200,000.

i Kierland Commons, located a quick walk from the Westin Kierland Resort & Spa, offers an upscale Main Street-like dining and shopping experience. It's a great place to pass the time on a warm day in north Scottsdale. Kids can play in the fountains, dad can check out high-end autographed merchandise at Rock Star Gallery, and mom can shop at places like Coach, Talbots, and Brighton Collectibles. Information: www.kierlandcommons.com.

SOUTHEAST VALLEY

THE BUTTES $$$
2000 Westcourt Way, Tempe
(602) 225-9000, (888) 867-7492
www.marriott.com/PHXTM

The Marriott resort, tucked into 25 acres in the curvy red rock buttes in Tempe, is a popular getaway for large business groups. With 345 rooms and 9 suites, there's enough deluxe lodging to host gatherings that fill the site's 40,000 square feet of meeting space. Hillside hot tubs offer sweeping Valley views. The Narande Spa and 5 dining spots are efficient on-site amenities. The resort also offers tennis and volleyball, in addition to easy access to nearby Sky Harbor Airport. The venue routinely hosts local civic gatherings and award ceremonies, including some for nearby Arizona State University. The Top of the Rock restaurant at, well, the top of the buttes, offers a unique panoramic view from its southeast Valley position. New chef Akos Szabo joined in 2011 to rejuvenate the menu.

SHERATON WILD HORSE PASS
RESORT & SPA $$–$$$
5594 W. Wild Horse Pass Blvd., Chandler
(602) 225-0100
www.wildhorsepass.com

With 500 custom-designed rooms inspired by the Gila River Indian Community's heritage, the resort is clearly set apart in character from other top Valley resorts. Its 2 golf courses are managed by some of the most brilliant golf minds in the state, and its Kai restaurant is heralded by some critics as the top fine-dining experience in Arizona (see the Restaurants chapter for more). Wild Horse Pass is located about 15 miles southeast of downtown Phoenix. It features the Aji Spa, with its 17,500 square feet of space and 17 treatment rooms. The Koli Equestrian Center offers riding lessons and horseback adventures through the meandering natural landscape, which is carefully preserved by the Gila River tribe. The resort will accommodate meeting space for groups up to 2,000 people. Between all the amenities and the nearby casino, it's difficult to find time to explore the rest of the Valley. The resort is consistently well reviewed by guests, who are impressed by the clean pool area, impeccable grounds, and comfortable rooms.

RV PARKS & CAMPGROUNDS

For those who like to explore the country from a home on wheels, the Phoenix area provides a great place for a break from the highway, especially during the winter months when the desert sun's power has diminished. Many RV parks nestle in locations with mountain views and come equipped with perks like grocery stores, recreational activities, and spacious shower facilities. Some of the parks are downright luxurious, protected by security gates and enhanced with championship golf courses and resort-like landscaping. The largest of these parks boasts between 1,500 and 2,000 spaces. The range of quality and rates offers something for everyone's taste and pocketbook.

Most of the RV parks are in the outlying communities of the Northwest and Southeast Valley, like east Mesa and the Sun Cities. That's also where most snowbirds, or winter-only residents, like to flock. Apache Junction, a few miles east of Mesa, is composed primarily of retirees who call their RVs and mobile homes home at least part of the year. Consequently, the Valley's RV parks tend to fill with older or retired folks who stay for 2 to 3 months, sometimes longer. They hail from snowy climes such as North Dakota, Minnesota, Iowa, and Canada.

If you're planning to winter in Phoenix at one of these parks, you'll want to make your reservations early—even as much as a year ahead of time. The months of April and October are less crowded than winter. Because space is more available during the hot summer months, you can often find good summer rates if you ask around. If you enjoy your visit to the Valley enough to consider making the transition from resort to RV park, find an RV community you like and reserve a space for the following year.

At the end of this chapter, we list options for those campers who prefer car camping or rough camping.

RV PARKS

Phoenix

NORTH PHOENIX RV PARK
2550 W. Louise Dr.
(623) 581-3969
www.northphoenixcampground.com
The park near I-17 and Deer Valley Road boasts 200 spaces to accommodate RVs. This is an active park, with lots of potlucks and parties and regularly scheduled bingo games. Amenities include showers, 2 laundry rooms, a lounge, a swimming pool, and a store selling propane and other supplies. Pets and children are welcome, and those who desire more seclusion can ask for the no-kids section. Winter rates are $35 daily, $140 weekly, and $325 monthly. Rates are for 2 people; add extra charges for each additional guest, pets, and children.

i On their way in or out of the Valley, RV travelers gravitate to Quartzsite, about 20 miles east of the California state line on I-10. The town hosts a sports/vacation show every January that draws more than 750,000 people, creating seas of RVs. Information: www.quartzsitervshow.com.

Southeast Valley

APACHE PALMS RV PARK
1836 E. Apache Blvd., Tempe
(480) 966-7399
www.apachepalmsrvpark.com
This small, modest park with 80 spaces is modern and friendly and will put you close to the action in downtown Tempe. Amenities include a swimming pool, spa, showers, and a laundry room. Nightly rates are $36 to $40 for 2 people, plus an extra $3 per additional person; $216 to $240 weekly, plus $15 per additional person. Rates go down in the summer. Pets are welcome. Free Wi-Fi and cable TV are available.

GOLD CANYON RV RANCH & GOLF RESORT
7151 E. US 60, Gold Canyon
(480) 982-5800, (877) 465-3226
This RV park features 754 spaces right at the base of the Superstition Mountains. If you like mountain views, this site southeast of Apache Junction might be for you. The 73-acre park is open to people age 55 and older, although most spaces are taken by park models. There's an activity center with swimming and crafts areas, shuffleboard, a 9-hole golf course, pro shop, steam room, sauna, billiard room, card room, and tennis courts. Pets are allowed but limited to one area of the park. Rates are $49 for 1 night,

$250 for a week, $759 for 1 month, and $2,000 for up to 3 months. Free Wi-Fi connection is available in the library.

MESA REGAL RV RESORT
4700 E. Main St., Mesa
(480) 830-2821, (800) 845-4752
A huge, 55-plus RV resort, Mesa Regal offers jewelry-making classes, china painting lessons, and other classes for seniors. There's a beauty salon and barbershop on site. Other perks include 4 swimming pools, a library, a computer room, a restaurant, saunas, and putting and driving ranges. The Mesa Regal usually has room for short-term visitors among its more than 2,000 spaces. Rates are $39 per night, $235 weekly, and $575 monthly. Electricity, cable, and phone are extra. A pet section is available.

i The Arizona Office of Tourism lists RV parks and campgrounds, in addition to other travel resources, on its website at www.arizonaguide.com.

ORANGEWOOD SHADOWS RV RESORT
3165 E. University Dr., Mesa
(480) 832-9080, (800) 826-0909
www.orangewoodshadows.com
This 5-star 55-plus resort prides itself on its recreational amenities and activities for seniors, including group excursions, shuffleboard, 2 pools, hot tub, library, exercise room, and post office. The grounds have a clubhouse, ballroom, and more than 800 orange, lemon, and grapefruit trees that you can pick from (in season, of course). The majority of its residents are winter visitors who return from year to year. Thus, you should call early to reserve one of the 474 spaces. Daily and weekly rates, including electricity, are $40 and $240. The monthly

rate is $525, and the annual rate is $3,780, with electricity extra. No dogs are allowed. Free Wi-Fi is available.

SCHNEPF FARMS RV PARK
24810 S. Rittenhouse Rd., Queen Creek
(480) 987-3100
www.schnepffarms.com
Here's an unusual find off the beaten path: RV spaces set amid a peach orchard. The Schnepf family leases spaces for 25 full RV hookups and a large area for dry camping on their 250-acre farm. Guests can partake of the many attractions that bring out locals and others, including pick-your-own produce, a country store, petting zoo, and picnic area. The farm holds several festivals throughout the year and leases its land for the annual Country Thunder country music extravaganza in April, which means some dates are unavailable for campers. Rates are $35 nightly for a full hookup and $20 nightly for dry camping; $200 per week (for full hookup) and $450 per month. The maximum length of stay, though, is 45 days. Children and pets are welcome. Schnepf Farms is open all year.

i Check your vehicle's tire pressure at least once a month during summer. Tires fail more often than any other equipment, and the Arizona sun is brutal. Each RV needs a different tire pressure because the correct pressure depends on the vehicle's weight.

VIEWPOINT RV & GOLF RESORT
8700 E. University Dr., Mesa
(480) 373-8700, (800) 822-4404
www.viewpointrv.com
This upscale over-55 RV park has dinner theater, live music with national artists, a country store, 2 golf courses, tennis courts, bingo, a computer lab, a softball field, and Wi-Fi Internet access. ViewPoint has been voted the best RV park in the nation several times. The park has around 2,000 spaces, including 453 for RVs and the rest for park models and modulars. Daily rates begin at around $30 in the summer. Weekly rates are $129 to $179. Monthly rates are $450 to $959, depending on the month. You can stay all year for $6,000. Trash, water, and electric are not included.

i ViewPoint RV & Golf Resort in Mesa books the likes of Frankie Avalon, John Davidson, and the Gatlin Brothers. ViewPoint residents get first crack at tickets, but others may attend. Information: (800) 822-4404 or www .viewpointrv.com.

Northeast Valley

WESTWORLD OF SCOTTSDALE
16601 N. Pima Rd., Scottsdale
(480) 312-6802
www.scottsdaleaz.gov/westworld
Horse lovers, take note. This city-owned 160-acre park in north Scottsdale is the site of some of the nation's largest horse shows. About 300 RV sites are open to the public on a space-available basis. If golf is your thing, ask about the 18-hole course at Sanctuary Golf Course (480-502-8200; www.sanctuary golf.com). Pets and children are welcome at WestWorld. Spotless shower facilities are available. Full-hookup nightly rates are $22. There are no weekly or monthly rates since this park is intended for short stays, with a 21-day maximum. Key dates are often blacked out because of the annual shows hosted at WestWorld, such as the Arabian

Horse Show and Barrett-Jackson Collector Car Event.

ℹ️ **For an amazing selection of camping, hunting, and fishing gear, head to Cabela's in Glendale. It's near the University of Phoenix Stadium at Loop 101 and Glendale Avenue. Information: (623) 872-6700 or www.cabelas.com.**

Northwest Valley

PLEASANT HARBOR RV RESORT
8708 W. Harbor Blvd., Peoria
(800) 475-3272, (928) 501-LAKE
www.pleasantharbor.com
This resort is at Lake Pleasant, an intriguing desert setting popular with local boating and fishing enthusiasts. On cool fall and spring weekends, sailors with the Arizona Yacht Club turn out in full regatta, their colorful sails unfurled against a backdrop of the Bradshaw Mountains. The RV park puts you 300 yards from the lake on the east side behind the marina, which is available for those pulling boats. In addition, the 294-space park boasts a clubhouse, an activities slate in high season, pools, spas, an enclosed pet walk, shuffleboard, laundry facilities, a general store, and organized tours. The park is adult oriented, but there are no age restrictions. Many people stay 3 months or longer. All but 40 spaces have full hookups, with rates from $32 nightly, $194 weekly, $560 monthly, $1,546 for 3 months, and $3,993 annually. Discounts are available to those staying longer than 3 months and to people who are members of Good Samaritan Club or Arizona Avenues.

PUEBLO EL MIRAGE RV RESORT
11201 N. El Mirage Rd., El Mirage
(623) 583-0464, (800) 445-4115
www.robertsresorts.com
An 18-hole golf course designed by Fuzzy Zoeller is the centerpiece of this 1,200-space resort, which is geared to winter visitors and year-round residents age 55 and older. In addition to golf, guests can take advantage of the clubhouse, 2 tennis courts, on-site restaurant, Olympic-size pool, hot tub, fitness center, billiards, lawn bowling, arts and crafts, dances, softball field, exercise equipment, and computer club. The park is set on 310 acres located about 20 minutes from Glendale's Westgate shopping and entertainment center. Full-hookup rates are $45 daily and $275 weekly. Monthly rates range from $500 in summer to $800 in peak months. Small pets are allowed.

SUNFLOWER RV RESORT
16501 N. El Mirage Rd., Surprise
(623) 583-0100, (888) 940-8989
This gated resort near the Sun Cities is mostly for 55-plus seniors living in park models, who tend to return every winter. About 250 of the park's 1,203 spaces are available for short-term leases to those seniors with any kind of RV. Amenities are ample: an Olympic-size lap pool, 3 spas, organized activities, shuffleboard, tennis, horseshoes, exercise rooms, a wood shop, a ballroom, a library, and Wi-Fi hotspots at the community center. Pets are welcome. Rates are $49 per day.

ℹ️ **For a list of RV parks that offer free Wi-Fi Internet service, check out www.wififreespot.com/rv.html.**

Southwest Valley

DESTINY PHOENIX RV PARK
416 N. Citrus Rd., Goodyear
(623) 853-0537, (888) 667-2454
www.destinyrv.com

This family park has easy access to I-10, about 5 miles west of Goodyear, and welcomes all ages. Its 282 spaces are open all year, and amenities include a pool and spa, shuffleboard, exercise room, laundry, Internet access, classes, and social get-togethers in high season. The rate for 1 night with a full hookup is $23 to $39, depending on the month. Weekly rates change according to the placement in the park, but range from $138 to $234. Two pets are allowed, but not big dogs. There is a fenced pet walk. Free Internet is available.

> **i** Growing numbers of women are riding the highways in RVs. To learn more, go to www.rvingwomen.org. There is a fee of $45 per year to become a member, but you get a magazine with safety tips and commentary on women's travel issues. The two Arizona chapters have about 2,500 members.

CAMPGROUNDS

The best places for tent camping or rough camping from a truck or RV are in the mountain parks managed by Maricopa County. Not only are they scenic, but they also put you at a distance—though not a great one—from the city's hustle and bustle. The mountains that surround Phoenix aren't terribly tall or verdant with trees, yet they showcase the beautiful Sonoran Desert, with its multitude of cactus species, hardy trees, and wildlife including hawks and coyotes. The parks attract out-of-state visitors and locals for their campsites, hiking trails, horseback riding trails, and picnic sites. All county park campgrounds charge a $6 vehicle entry fee. Usually they ask that RVs be no longer than 35 feet. Note that the heat often forces county campgrounds to close in June, July, and August. Also, Maricopa County does not accept reservations for its campgrounds if you are in a small group or an individual RV. For large groups, reservations are required. Information: (602) 506-2930; www.maricopa.gov/parks.

Southeast Valley

LOST DUTCHMAN STATE PARK
6109 N. Apache Trail, Apache Junction
(480) 982-4485
http://azstateparks.com/Parks/LODU/index.html

You will be in the midst of legends and lore about down-on-their-luck gold miners at this 70-site park for tents and RVs, at the base of the Superstition Mountains, about 5 miles north of Apache Junction. Campers will find shower facilities but no hookups. The cost for sites is $15 to $25, depending on the type.

Northeast Valley

CAVE CREEK REGIONAL PARK
37900 N. Cave Creek Pkwy., Cave Creek
(623) 465-0431
www.maricopa.gov/Parks/cave_creek

The Cave Creek park has picnic areas, a horse staging area, and more than 11 miles of trails within sight of the McDowell and Continental mountains. Several old mine shafts lie within the park, but they are off-limits. The park has 38 camping sites, all with water and

electrical hookups, picnic tables, grills, and fire rings. The comfort stations have showers, and a park host is on the premises. Cost is $25 per night.

MCDOWELL MOUNTAIN REGIONAL PARK
16300 McDowell Mountain Park Dr.
3 miles north of Fountain Hills
(480) 471-0173
www.maricopa.gov/parks/mcdowell
This county park, 15 miles northeast of Scottsdale in the lower Verde Basin, rates as one of the most scenic, with an abundance of mesquite, ironwood, palo verde, and majestic mountain views of Four Peaks. Every now and then, you'll see javelina wallowing in a wash after a rainstorm or hawks dive-bombing their prey in the brush. Elevation within the park ranges from 1,550 to 3,100 feet. Camping areas are divided into 1 general area with 76 spaces and several group campgrounds. This park has 3 competitive mountain biking loops and over 50 miles of multiuse trails. The nightly rate is $25, including water and electricity. Showers are available.

Northwest Valley

LAKE PLEASANT REGIONAL PARK
41835 N. Castle Hot Springs Rd.,
Morristown
(928) 501-1710, (602) 372-7460
www.maricopa.gov/parks/lake_pleasant
A variety of camping options are available in this 23,662-acre park northwest of the Valley. Popular with boaters, this park contains 148 sites for RV and tent camping, some developed and some semi-developed. All sites have covered ramada, picnic table, grill, and fire ring. Developed sites have water

and electricity. Rates are $25 nightly. Some primitive camping sites are available for $10 nightly. There is a group campground, but it requires a commitment of 10 units. Two boat launching ramps with restroom facilities are available.

i Most Arizona fishing is for bass, crappie, catfish, stripers, and bluegills. There's a directory of fishing guides and licensing info at www.azgfd.gov.

WHITE TANK MOUNTAIN REGIONAL PARK
20304 W. White Tank Mountain Rd.,
Waddell
(623) 935-2505
www.maricopa.gov/parks/white_tank
This is the largest park in the Maricopa County park system, comprising more than 29,000 acres of Sonoran Desert mountains. Elevations range from 1,400 feet at the park entrance to 4,000 feet at the highest peak. You'll find plenty of picnic areas, 11 ramadas for use by large groups, a mountain bike trail system, a horse staging area, and 2 wheelchair-accessible trails. The family campground has 40 sites, each with a picnic table and grill. There are no electrical hookups and no dump stations at the park, located about 15 miles west of Peoria. Comfort stations have showers. Cost is $25 nightly for developed sites.

Southwest Valley

ESTRELLA MOUNTAIN REGIONAL PARK
14805 W. Vineyard Ave., Goodyear
(623) 932-3811
www.maricopa.gov/parks/estrella

This was the first park in the Maricopa County regional system. RVers take note—this 19,840-acre area, about 18 miles southwest of Phoenix off I-10, not only offers a few areas for rough camping from a tent but has a campsite with full hookups for 7 RVs. The camp is located near tracks for competitive mountain biking, running, and equestrian use. There is a $6 vehicle entry fee. Amenities in the park include 65 acres of lawns with picnic tables, a golf course, restrooms, 9 ramadas, playground equipment, 2 lighted ball fields, and a rodeo arena. An amphitheater overlooks the picnic area at this park, which is heavily used for group functions. The many trails are for hikers, bicyclists, and horseback riders. The picnic areas, but not the campgrounds, have comfort stations. Full-hookup sites are $20 per night. No reservations taken.

RESTAURANTS

Dining in Phoenix is far different than dining in New York, San Francisco, and other major cities. You will find unmarked gems in the seemingly faceless strip malls built across the Valley rather than in endless lines of great restaurants on city block after city block. You will also have to drive everywhere, between neighboring communities, since walkable shopping districts like Old Town Scottsdale and Mill Avenue in Tempe are rare. Even downtown Phoenix is far more spread out than you might be used to back East or in your hometown big city.

With the wide variety of resorts and posh spots in Scottsdale, the Valley draws its share of top chefs. The area has emerged as a culinary force with artistic, creative restaurateurs expanding sites in the central core of the city. Pizzeria Bianco on the west side of downtown is known as some of the best pizza in the US. The Valley Metro light rail line connects downtown entertainment venues to fascinating restaurants like Hula's Modern Tiki and Fez that are sleek and sophisticated, yet focused on food. More humble downtown hangouts like Matt's Big Breakfast draw hundreds of guests daily, with lines out the door. Places like St. Francis on Camelback Road have reclaimed old Phoenix buildings, using the solid brick as part of the decor that makes them fashionable to everyone from baby-boomer foodies to young people on their first dates.

So many of Phoenix's restaurants are modern, since the city is so new. But it has its share of restaurant history. Los Dos Molinos, arguably the best Mexican food in the Valley, is located in an old mortuary in south Phoenix. T. Cooks at the Royal Palms resort in Phoenix sits on one of the most gorgeous historical sites in the Valley. Other places in Scottsdale are tucked among vestiges of the Valley's Old West roots.

Part of the Valley's allure is its diversity. You'll find Mexican food, but many travelers from Mexico and California claim it's a bit of a melting pot of Mexican cuisine. There's Sonoran flavor, New Mexican, and a blend of cultures in single dishes, like you'll find at the quaint Barrio Cafe in Phoenix. Meanwhile, some of the best home-cooked Mexican food is served at neighborhood ranch markets; the food is unbelievably fresh, yet the markets look oddly mundane from outside (see the Close-up in this chapter for more). Country fare is also huge, with the cowboy culture still prevalent. But Asian noodle houses, sushi, Italian, and other ethnic restaurants are spread throughout the many communities that tie the urban area together.

Price Code

The price code in each restaurant listing gives you a broad idea of the cost of dinner entrees for two, not including beverages, appetizers, desserts, tax, and tip. Obviously,

your bill at a given restaurant may be higher or lower, depending on what you order and on fluctuating prices. These symbols provide a general guide.

$ . . . . **Less than $12**
$$ . . . . **$12 to $25**
$$$ . . . . **$25 to $50**
$$$$ . . . . **More than $50**

RESTAURANTS

Tutti Santi Ristorante Italiano, Phoenix, Italian & Pizza, $$$, 95

Via De Los Santos Mexican Food & Lounge, Phoenix, Mexican, $–$$, 96

Vincent On Camelback, Phoenix, Continental & Fine Dining, $$$$, 93

Vogue Bistro, Surprise, American Fusion, $$–$$$, 111

Wildflower Bread Company, Scottsdale, Sandwich Shops, $, 111

Yasu Sushi Bistro, Phoenix, Sushi, $$–$$$, 100

Yen Sushi & Sake Bar, Glendale, Asian, $$–$$$, 112

Zinc Bistro, Scottsdale, French, $$$$, 109

PHOENIX

American Fusion

✳CHELSEA'S KITCHEN $$$
5040 N. 40th St.
(602) 957-2555
www.chelseaskitchenaz.com

Chelsea's Kitchen offers happy hour drink specials, brunch, and some of the best food in central Phoenix. It's a place locals go, but you'll also find it on hotel concierge recommendation lists. Chelsea's is often crowded, but you can have a drink and a plate of nachos on the patio while you wait for a table. When you get a table, be sure to order the fresh fish or short rib tacos, which are among the best in Phoenix. In general, what you'll find here is a lively atmosphere and a sophisticated twist to familiar foods and signature dishes. You can watch the chefs prepare your meal in the large exhibition kitchen. This is a nice, family-friendly kind of place. Save room for the signature key lime pie and the free chocolate chip cookies as you leave.

COOPER'STOWN $$
101 E. Jackson St.
(602) 253-7337
www.alicecooperstown.com

Alice Cooper, Phoenix's hometown hero of rock 'n' roll fame, opened a casual bar/restaurant near Chase Field and US Airways Center. Billed as "the place where jocks and rock meet," Cooper'stown features not only rock memorabilia, but also sports memorabilia. Fans from Arizona Diamondbacks and Phoenix Suns games tend to wander over before and after games since it's one of only a few decent sports bars within walking distance. Alice offers daily lunch specials, including half-off salads and pasta dishes on some days. He and his partners renovated an old warehouse for this restaurant venture. Joining ribs, chicken, and burgers on the menu are 2-foot-long "Big Unit" hot dogs (former D-Backs pitcher Randy Johnson's namesake), steak, Momma Cooper's Tuna Casserole, and No More Mr. Nice Guy Chipotle Chicken Pasta. You can hear live music here; sometimes famous musicians will sit in with the band. Note that it can be loud. Lunch and dinner are served daily.

CORONADO CAFE $$$
2201 N. 7th St.
(602) 258-5149
www.coronadocafe.com

Nestled in a 1915 bungalow-style house, the Coronado Cafe (really more of a restaurant)

has become justifiably popular as a lunch destination, though its homey warmth is perfect for a romantic dinner. The interior is attractively decorated and there's a delightful atmosphere, but the big attraction here is the food. At first look there's the usual assortment of salads, soups, and sandwiches, but the key is in the preparation. Coronado Cafe uses only high-quality ingredients, making a noticeable difference. For dinner try the ultimate comfort food, the Cafe Meatloaf, or bistro sirloin filet. Coronado is also known for its clean seafood dishes like pan-seared scallops and miso salmon. Wine and beer are available at the cozy spot close to downtown Phoenix.

FEZ $$–$$$
3815 N. Central Ave.
(602) 287-8700
www.fezoncentral.com
Fez is great for drinks and small bites, since it's known as a solid nightlife spot. But the wood-fired Sudanese flatbreads, blue cheese balsamic burgers, and baskets of cinnamon-crusted sweet potato fries are far better than you'll find in most bars. Try the apricot-glazed salmon or lamb kisra. The ultra-sleek, modern dining room makes for a unique dinner experience. The chef's interpretation of American cuisine shows a rustic Mediterranean and Moroccan flair.

MAIZIE'S CAFE & BISTRO $$–$$$
4750 N. Central Ave.
(602) 274-2828
www.maiziescafe.com
The little neighborhood spot off the light rail tracks is known for its refined yet unpretentious bar food. Try the bistro steak salad or blue cheese stuffed burger. The happy hour and brunch specials are popular. The

wine list is also surprisingly excellent. It's a great place to sip a microbrew and munch on fish tacos while watching the traffic from the Central Avenue patio. Maizie's is a prime example of the friendly local restaurants sprouting up through downtown and uptown redevelopment.

PHOENIX CITY GRILLE $$$
5816 N. 16th St.
(602) 266-3001
www.phoenixcitygrille.com
This Phoenix gem is set in an adobe building at Bethany Home Road and 16th Street and is a perfect local neighborhood experience. The food is American with a Southwestern flair. Order one or two small plates, such as the pork carnitas, or skip to full-size entrees, such as the cedar plank salmon with citrus and horseradish or pot roast with caramelized onion bourbon gravy. Some say the salads here are the best in Phoenix. Try to save room for dessert, like the cheesecake or the croissant bread pudding. Parking is limited, so arrive early and plan to have a drink at the bar while you wait.

PITA JUNGLE $$
1001 N. 3rd St.
(602) 258-7482
www.pitajungle.com
The new downtown Phoenix location is one of three in the city and several around the Valley, if that helps explain Pita Jungle's success. But it's hardly a chain restaurant. Each place has its own character. Original local artwork hangs on the walls. and managers change the motif regularly. The Mediterranean dishes like lavosh chicken wraps, falafel, and mahi mahi served with jalapeno hummus are local favorites for lunch and dinner. Aside from the Tempe and other

suburban locations, Pita Jungle is at 4340 E. Indian School Rd. (602-955-7482) and 20910 N. Tatum Blvd. (480-473-2321).

ST. FRANCIS $$–$$$
111 E. Camelback Rd.
(602) 200-8111
www.stfrancisaz.com
Expect to wait for a table, but you won't mind sipping a cocktail at the quaint patio bar facing Camelback Road. The layout of the renovated brick-walled building is impressive. It seems like there are 4 separate dining areas, each with its own character. The food is also worth the wait. St. Francis is known for the chicken it roasts in a special wood-fired brick oven. Other dishes, like the pork chile verde and Moroccan-spiced meatballs, are also cooked in the oven.

Asian

CHERRY BLOSSOM NOODLE CAFE $$
914 E. Camelback Rd.
(602) 248-9090
www.cherryblossom-az.com
This is the place for anything with noodles, including Italian pasta. Cherry Blossom also serves fresh sushi. But it's the ramen, yakisoba, pad Thai, and hot udon soups that make the place so popular. The dining room is very comfortable. If you're visiting Phoenix, it's worth a stop to tell people back home that you ate Italian-Japanese food in Arizona. But in spite of its idiosyncratic menu, the place is legit. It's well reviewed, always fresh, and leaves locals craving more.

CHINA CHILI $$
302 E. Flower St.
(602) 266-4463
www.chinachilirestaurant.com

Light rail construction forced China Chili to a new location that's larger though equally as homey as its original spot on Central Avenue. The food hasn't changed, which is a good thing. Some Valley residents call this their favorite Chinese joint, especially for fire-spicy dishes of Cantonese, Szechuan, and Hong Kong styles. China Chili's top items include the half-sweet, half-spicy Lover's Prawns; the whole striped bass with ginger, scallions and soy sauce; and the Peking duck with pancake wraps. There's a good selection of soups, meat and seafood dishes, and enough vegetarian offerings to keep the nonmeat-eaters happy. No lunch served Sun.

i Chef Johnny Chu of Sens Asian Tapas & Sake Bar is one of the more innovative and approachable chefs in Phoenix. The Hong Kong native, who grew up in Phoenix, opened Sens in 2008 and also runs Tien Wong Hot Pot in Chandler, which features Asian fondue dishes (www.thehotpots.com).

GOURMET HOUSE OF HONG KONG $$
1438 E. McDowell Rd.
(602) 253-4859
www.gourmethouseofhongkong.com
This is the place for authentic Hong Kong and Cantonese dishes. Don't be afraid of the low-income neighborhood or Formica tables and tiled floor. This is a local favorite that's stayed consistently reliable for years. There's no MSG in the food. The lunch "Big Plate" is a bargain, with entree plus egg roll and chicken cream puff for $6. There are lots of noodle dishes for both lunch and dinner. If takeout is your choice, you'll find the service is quite fast. Lunch and dinner are served daily.

PHO THANH $
1702 W. Camelback Rd.
(602) 242-1979

Pho is the specialty here, with chicken, seafood, and beef simmering in arguably the greatest Asian soup broth in the Valley. Also be prepared to sample spring rolls, hearty noodle soups with beef, vermicelli salads, summer rolls, Vietnamese-style grilled shrimp, and other delicacies. The ambience is rather plain, on the order of Formica and vinyl, but tidy enough. Pho Thanh serves lunch and dinner daily. There are dishes under $5, including charbroiled chicken and pork or shrimp banh xeo (savory hot pancakes).

SALA THAI $–$$
10880 N. 32nd St.
(602) 971-1293
www.salathaiaz.com

In spite of its unremarkable location in a north Phoenix strip mall, this is fast becoming the top Thai place in Phoenix. Locals will be disappointed to see this listing, since it's been relatively unknown for years before critics started paying attention recently. Sala serves pad Thai, soups, salads, barbecue, curries, and a homemade nam-sod pork sausage. There's no beer, but the variety of fresh fruit "mocktails" complements many of the dishes.

SENS ASIAN TAPAS & SAKE BAR $$
705 N. 1st St.
(602) 340-9777
www.sensake.com

Chef Johnny Chu, formerly of the restaurant Fate, did a fine job introducing and expanding Sens for downtown Phoenix crowds. You will end up craving Chu's creative twist on traditional dishes, like the spicy wonton with sautéed chicken and pepper jack cheese or warm, comforting soup gyoza. Others include fried quail in Asian spices, bacon lychee yakitori, and edamame in white truffle butter. Sens has a great patio for small bites and cocktails late at night, but the interior dining room is fitting for lunch or an intimate dinner.

Bakeries

AU PETIT FOUR $
2051 E. Camelback Rd.
(602) 852-9668
www.aupetitfour.com

Located right in the heart of the Biltmore area, Au Petit Four does a little bit of everything. It serves salads and panini at lunch, does catering, and offers a wide variety of wines. The $20 dinner special menu on Friday and Saturday provides a starter like mozzarella salad, plus an entree like beef bourguignon, followed by a dessert like chocolate éclair or lemon tart. The tarts, carrot cake, mousse, and other pastries evoke thoughts of neighborhood European bakeries.

BARB'S BAKERY $
2929 N. 24th St.
(602) 957-4422
www.barbsbakery.com

While the trendy coffeehouses with big bakery counters spring up in the suburbs, Barb's Bakery maintains its decades-old tradition near Thomas Road and 24th Street. It has a small sit-down area for coffee and pastries, but mostly this is a take-out place for all kinds of muffins, breads, pies, and sweet rolls. The bakery also does a brisk business in cakes for special occasions. You'll find the sugar cookies and red velvet cupcakes difficult to put down.

TAMMIE COE CAKES $
610 E. Roosevelt St.
(602) 253-0829
www.tammiecoecakes.com

Tammie is a Phoenix institution. Her shops don't have tables, so be prepared to grab and go. You can also order online. The cookies, custom cakes, and cupcakes are some of the best in Arizona. It's a great place to swing by for a snack to go with your Starbucks on a weekend afternoon of bumming around the city. There's a second location at 4410 N. 40th St. (602-840-3644).

i For the absolute latest Valley dining reviews, surf over to www .feastinginphoenix.com for honest, detailed opinions on a variety of eateries. The site is run by Seth Chadwick, a Phoenix native whose foodie review style is like "when Zagat meets Sex and the City."

Barbecue

BOBBY-Q $$–$$$
8501 N. 27th Ave.
(602) 995-5982
www.bobbyq.net

Phoenix isn't known for its barbecue, but Bobby-Q helps locals kill their craving. The north Phoenix restaurant is somewhere between upscale and dive bar casual. The ribs, brisket, steaks, grilled shrimp, and sides are fantastic and worth the trip up I-17. At lunch, there's a $12 sampler with ribs and smoked barbecue pork with a side like mac 'n' cheese. The portions are huge, so it's a great place to go with a group.

Breakfast

THE FARM AT SOUTH MOUNTAIN $$
6106 S. 32nd St.
(602) 276-6360
www.thefarmatsouthmountain.com

Few places are more relaxing for breakfast than The Farm. The restaurant features plenty of outdoor seating near South Mountain Park, so it's a popular brunch stop for locals who finish their early morning hikes. Sit in the fresh, airy, green patio at the Morning Glory Cafe. Breakfast dishes include white truffle scrambled eggs (local eggs, keep in mind), blueberry Belgian waffles, and rustic French toast. The Farm's other restaurants (The Farm Kitchen for lunch and Quiessence Restaurant for dinner) are equally outstanding and worth stopping at, especially if you're on the south side of town.

✳MATT'S BIG BREAKFAST $
801 N. 1st St.
(602) 254-1074
www.mattsbigbreakfast.com

This little restaurant in an old house is all about the details. It serves freshly squeezed orange juice, flavorful bacon and ham, and a light French toast that appears occasionally when chef makes it a "special." Matt's uses only cage-free eggs from humanely raised chickens. Expect to wait up to an hour to sit down. And it's worth it. For a late breakfast, the Chop & Chick (two eggs with a skillet-seared rib chop) will fill you up. The Five Spot is another classic: a rich egg sandwich served on sourdough with thick-cut bacon and a side of hash browns or home fries.

SCRAMBLE $–$$
9832 N. 7th St.
(602) 374-2294
www.azscramble.com

Breakfast and lunch are served daily at this locally owned, reclaimed corner of a Sunnyslope strip mall. The ingredients are as fresh and local as possible, and guests are encouraged not to tip unless they are totally satisfied. Signature dishes include the Brizza, a breakfast pizza with hollandaise, scrambled eggs, cheese, sausage, veggies, and bacon, on hand-tossed dough. Scramble also serves its unique versions of steak and eggs and breakfast burritos. It's unpretentious, innovative, and far enough out of downtown to still be relatively unknown.

Cajun

BABY KAY'S CAJUN KITCHEN $$
2119 E. Camelback Rd.
(602) 955-0011
www.babykayscajunkitchen.com

There are few Cajun dining options in the Valley, so this place does consistent business with its traditional shrimp and crawfish etouffees, hushpuppies, ribs, and crawdaddies. Baby Kay's is easy to find in the Town & Country Shopping Center. Former Phoenix Suns star Charles Barkley used to hang out in the restaurant to satisfy his Southern-born palate. On weekends, just listen for the guitarist playing blues. Outdoor seating on the mall's redbrick plaza is available.

Continental & Fine Dining

CHRISTOPHER'S RESTAURANT &
CRUSH LOUNGE $$$$
2502 E. Camelback Rd.
(602) 522-2344
www.christopheraz.com

The popular restaurant and lounge at Biltmore Fashion Park is led by James Beard Award-winning chef Christopher Gross and sommelier Paola Embry. Seating includes a "kitchen bar," which gives guests the feeling of being at home for a private demonstration. Other dining areas feel like an upscale French bistro. The widely raved-about dishes include salad and pizza prepared with duck confit, smoked truffle-infused filet mignon, lobster pot pie, and scallops prepared differently almost daily.

COMPASS ARIZONA GRILL $$$$
122 N. 2nd St.
(602) 440-3166

This revolving "casual upscale" restaurant atop the 24-story Hyatt Regency in downtown Phoenix is an excellent choice for those wanting to complement a night on the town with a memorable meal. The Herberger and Orpheum theaters and Symphony Hall are within walking distance. The view from the Compass, which makes one clockwise rotation every hour, is an incredible way to see the city. Brass plaques on the windows point out some of the city landmarks. Entrees include veal porterhouse with a spicy salsa and pan-seared snapper with cippolini tomato relish. The Compass is known as a romantic spot with exceptional service.

DIFFERENT POINTE OF VIEW $$$$
11111 N. 7th St.
(602) 866-6350
www.differentpointeofview.com

The hilltop dining room provides far-reaching sunset views. This restaurant at the Pointe Hilton Tapatio Cliffs Resort has a terraced design, allowing every table to experience the panoramic glance at Phoenix below. The chef offers a $19 per-person,

5-course tasting menu. Top entrees include filet mignon with pancetta and sautéed crimini mushrooms and some unique takes on lobster (served with crispy seared herb parmesan risotto torte) and veal (a rosemary port wine braised milk-fed shank served with maple reduction and chervil toasted garlic gremolata). You can sit outside by the fire pit, which is a fantastic spot to enjoy a glass of wine and dessert with a view of the lit-up city.

DURANT'S $$$$
2611 N. Central Ave.
(602) 264-5967
www.durantsaz.com

Durant's is like fine dining in a classic Phoenix supper club, with its sexy dark interior and shiny red leather booths. The food and service are anything but trapped in the 1950s, however. Downtown businessmen still hit Durant's for cocktails and steaks. Young foodies know its reputation and head there for classic dishes like Australian lobster tail, slow-roasted prime rib, and fresh oysters. Durant's serves a consistently solid martini and wines by the glass. It's open for lunch, as well. The Central Avenue location makes it easily accessible on light rail.

✴T. COOK'S $$$$
5200 E. Camelback Rd.
(602) 808-0766
www.royalpalmshotel.com/restaurant

This hotel restaurant is known as one of the best restaurants of any kind in Phoenix. The warm and inviting dining room, complete with hand-painted Italian frescoes, has palm trees shooting out of the floor and through the ceiling. T. Cook's fits the Royal Palms, yet it has its own distinct character. Guests rave about the garlic cream carbonara, paella

with lobster, and pan-roasted sole stuffed with onion marmalade over potato rosti and sautéed artichoke hearts. The restaurant's separate lunch and lounge menus are equally innovative. The lounge menu, for example, serves an outstanding poutine covered in shredded beef short ribs and fried shrimp ravioli with a spicy soy dipping sauce, among other upscale bar food. (See Close-up on Royal Palms in the Resorts chapter.)

ℹ️ If you're itching for a pint of Guinness and a shepherd's pie, belly up to the bar at one of the two McCaffrey's. There's Rosie McCaffrey's, 906 E. Camelback Rd. (602-241-1916 or www.rosiemccaffreys.com) and Seamus McCaffrey's, 18 W. Monroe St. (602-253-6081 or www.seamusmccaffreys.com). The Turf is a newer bar/restaurant, at 705 N. 1st St., run by the same Seamus gang. Information: www.theturfpub.com.

VINCENT ON CAMELBACK $$$$
3930 E. Camelback Rd.
(602) 224-0225
www.vincentoncamelback.com

Chef Vincent Guerithault is so well known and respected that he doesn't have to go to great lengths to promote his namesake restaurant. Vincent has worked in different locations over the years but is now settled into a small, modest-looking restaurant next to a convenience store in east Phoenix. The interior, though, is decorated like a lovely country French cottage. The food is known for Southwestern ingredients prepared in a classic French manner. A basket of warm croissants is served to start. Signature dishes include the duck tamale appetizer and veal sweetbreads with blue cornmeal and red

wine thyme sauce. The menu also features artfully prepared lamb, wild boar, and venison. Don't miss dessert, with wonderful French pastries and a tequila soufflé. Private dining rooms are available. Vincent also runs his Market Bistro at 3930 E. Camelback Rd., which serves breakfast, panini, and a classic French roasted chicken.

Hawaiian

HULA'S MODERN TIKI   **$$–$$$**
4700 N. Central Ave.
(602) 265-8454
Hula's has a great bar, and an awesome happy hour from 3 to 6 p.m. weekdays, but the food is better. Take fish, for example. You can order your choice of ahi, mahi, butterfish, or hapu cooked any one of multiple ways, such as blackened wasabi style with wok-seared shiitake mushrooms. The barbecue pork, black bean burger, and Jamaican jerk chicken are outstanding options. Hula's serves brunch on weekends, and it's also a great lunch stop. It's become a trendy place to hang out for cocktails or a fun meal. Plus, it's just a quick light rail stop away from downtown and some of the best central Phoenix bars.

Italian & Pizza

CIBO   **$$–$$$**
603 N. 5th Ave.
(602) 441-2697
www.cibophoenix.com
Set in a renovated 1913 bungalow, the restaurant is one of the best places in Arizona for an artisan pizza and glass of wine. Some regulars herald the menu as far superior to the more widely recognized Pizzeria Bianco on the other side of downtown Phoenix. Cibo uses only meats and cheeses imported from Italy. The pizza is wood-fired in an oven. The salad and antipasto are served simply with olive oil, salt, pepper, and lemon—nothing too fancy. The ingredients and craftsmanship of the pizza carry themselves. It's worth the wait sitting in the heat on the furniture on the shaded front lawn. If you're going, make sure to save room for the Nutella and mascarpone crepe.

LA GRANDE ORANGE   **$$–$$$**
4410 N. 40th St.
(602) 840-7777
www.lagrandeorangepizzeria.com
Locals recognize La Grande Orange for its upscale neighborhood pizza parlor vibe. The restaurant is next to a gelato spot, wine bar, and cozy grocery/deli. It's a great place to spend a few hours between the different hangouts. But the pizza is the main draw. Specialty pies include those with avocado, goat cheese, and local Schreiner's sausage. Aside from the pizza, there are only a few other menu items, but even those (shrimp ceviche, green chile burger) are fresh and worth ordering in the pizza-centric restaurant. Try The Rocket Man pizza with fresh spicy Fresno chiles, broccolini, roasted peppers, garlic, and oven-dried tomatoes.

THE PARLOR   **$$–$$$**
1916 E. Camelback Rd.
(602) 248-2480
www.theparlor.us
It's not just another fancy pizza joint. The Parlor is set in a comfortably modern dining space, and the patio seating is a great way to enjoy the evening before heading out to a show or drinks. All Parlor pizzas are served with a house blend of cheeses. The signature combos include smoked prosciutto and

olive tapenade, and roasted potato with pancetta, leeks, and Gorgonzola. Pasta, salad, and sandwiches are also on the menu. The Parlor Happy Hour is 3 to 6 p.m. weekdays. Closed Sun.

PIZZA A METRO $$$–$$$$
2336 W. Thomas Rd.
(602) 262-9999
www.pizzaametro.net

If you're from the East Coast, it's hard to find decent pizza that reminds you of back home. The top places are all about hand-crafted and wood-fired. The more casual places and to-go joints can seem like awful imposters. Pizza A Metro is like a back-home neighborhood style that's fast and consistently excellent. The restaurant serves Bolognese meat sauce pizza, meatball pizza, and a full menu with entrees like homemade pasta, salads, and shellfish. The delivery service can get really busy.

PIZZERIA BIANCO $$–$$$
623 E. Adams St.
(602) 258-8300
www.pizzeriabianco.com

The restaurant on the east end of downtown Phoenix is known as one of the best pizza places in the US. Chef and owner Chris Bianco has won much acclaim for his Neapolitan-style pizza made in wood-fired ovens with toppings such as wood-roasted onion and homemade fennel sausage. Individually sized pizzas, inventive salads, and sandwiches make this a great dinner spot, although you'll have to wait in hour-long lines with the Phoenix residents who flock here—but you can always stop at the wine bar next door. The pizzeria is in a historic building that's part of Heritage Square, next to the Arizona Science Center. The farmer's market salad is a nice complement to a Bianco pizza.

TUTTI SANTI RISTORANTE ITALIANO $$$
7575 N. 16th St.
(602) 216-0336
www.tuttisantiristorante.com

Expect a classic Italian meal served with care. The service is typically outstanding, and the dishes are consistently original, yet true to the basics your Nana believed in. The 16th Street location is the original, though Tutti Santi has multiple Valley locations. Seating at the original site is like eating in a big house, and the patio seating is also relaxing. Private dining rooms are available upon request. One of the best dishes is linguine served with clams, mussels, and calamari. A house chicken is served with prosciutto, fontina cheese, and a brandy cream sauce.

Mexican

BARRIO CAFE $$–$$$
2814 N. 16th St.
(602) 636-0240
www.barriocafe.com

Chef Silvana Salcido Esparza's inspiration for Barrio Cafe comes from the culture and traditional ingredients of southern Mexico. The restaurant is comfortable, carved out of a reclaimed central Phoenix building surrounded by modest neighborhoods and humble shops. Don't expect free chips and salsa. But you don't need them. The guacamole with pomegranate is prepared tableside, and it's worth paying for an appetizer. Signature dishes include the *tacos de cochinita pibil*—a Mayan-style slow-roasted pork taco with a Yucatan salsa and a hint of sour orange and queso—and halibut topped with shrimp, lobster, crab, scallops,

and a sauce made with wine, cream, poblano chile peppers, and chorizo. The huevos and machaca rancheros at Sunday brunch are outstanding. Barrio serves lunch and dinner daily except Monday.

CAROLINA'S MEXICAN FOOD $
1202 E. Mohave St.
(602) 252-1503
www.carolinasmex.com
Carolina's is a south-central Phoenix landmark. Carolina Valenzuela's tortillas and tamales are worth a special trip, and many locals refuse to buy either anywhere else. The dining room is more like a cafeteria than a restaurant, so this can be the wrong place for certain occasions. If you want to eat, it's the right place. Carolina is noted for her flour tortillas, delicious in burros or eaten plain. The restaurant also serves classic tacos and enchiladas. You can buy beef chorizo by the pound and tortillas by the dozen. There's a second location at 2126 E. Cactus Rd. (602-275-8231). Both are open for breakfast, lunch, and dinner daily except Sun. For a big, cheap breakfast, grab a breakfast burrito.

i There are lots of great mom-and-pop Mexican joints in the Valley. One example is El Bravo in Sunnyslope, 8338 N. 7th St. (602-943-9753). It's one of those unpretentious dining rooms where you can glance into the kitchen and see the ladies making fresh tortillas and chile sauce.

✳LOS DOS MOLINOS $$
8684 S. Central Ave.
(602) 243-9113
www.losdosmolinosaz.com
The south Phoenix restaurant is known for its New Mexican-style heat. Chilies are in nearly everything, which makes it a favorite for spicy food fans. Los Dos is an interesting place to dine. There's a huge patio to hang out on with a margarita if the wait is long. The restaurant itself is in a renovated mortuary, and the surrounding neighborhood is pretty rundown. Don't let that fool you. This is arguably the best Mexican restaurant in Phoenix. Spicy adovada pork ribs, shrimp Veracruz, and chicken chimichangas are among the excellent dishes. There's a second Phoenix location near Chase Field on Washington Street and another on Alma School Road in Mesa.

THE ORIGINAL GARCIA'S $-$$
2216 N. 35th Ave.
(602) 352-1913
www.garciasmexicanfood.com
Much like Los Dos, The Original Garcia's is tucked away in what many Phoenix residents would consider a low-income neighborhood. Perhaps that's what gives the place such character, and such outstanding food. It's not in a mall or near the latest ritzy retail development. The Las Aviendas (the Avenues) location is in the heart of Maryvale, which is largely Mexican-American. This is the site that spawned the local chain of Garcia's restaurants. It's still family-run, and the recipes are original. Chili con carne, green chile rellenos, and spinach and Sonoran corn enchiladas are some of the specialties. The giant poco pollo lunch special is a favorite. It's like a deep-fried pollo fundito with cheddar and cream cheeses.

VIA DE LOS SANTOS MEXICAN FOOD & LOUNGE $-$$
9120 N. Central Ave.
(602) 997-6239

If you like tequila before or after dinner, this is your place. The Via De Los Santos tequila list is pretty extensive, and the critics love some of the deeper cuts. The cheese crisp appetizer is a great way to start the meal without overloading on chips and salsa (which are also fresh and excellent). The machaca beef is outstanding, as are the green chile corn tamales. The albondigas soup and fajita burrito are delicious and difficult to put down, though the portions are pretty huge. The family-run place is a bit of a dive, and a bit hard to find, which is the way a Sunnyslope restaurant ought to be.

Middle Eastern

EDEN'S GRILL $$–$$$
13843 N. Tatum Blvd.
(602) 996-5149
www.edensgrill.com

You'll find this small family-owned restaurant in a shopping center at the northeast corner of Thunderbird and Tatum. The Mediterranean dishes are authentic and prepared from scratch daily. Among the delicious favorites are hummus, falafel, dolmeh, and a wide selection of chicken and beef kebabs. The lamb is marinated and grilled. The owners pride themselves on good service and a congenial, warm atmosphere that manages to be both casual and elegant. Try to have lunch here; the offerings are similar for lunch and dinner, but the noon prices are cheaper. Dinner is served nightly and lunch Monday to Friday; closed Sunday.

Sandwich Shops

DUCK & DECANTER $$
1651 E. Camelback Rd.
(602) 274-5429
www.duckanddecanter.com

Valley residents call it "the Duck," and it owns a special spot in the hearts of many. It's the kind of relaxed place where you go to sit on the patio with a cool drink and a satisfying sandwich on fresh bread, on slices of everything from rye to cranberry walnut. You can enjoy an espresso or a glass of wine or all sorts of imported delicacies. The restaurant wins awards so often that it's tiresome to list them all. The Camelback location is a bit hard to find because it's tucked away on the southeast side in back of a shopping center. The menu is extensive. It includes a giant list of signature hot and cold deli sandwiches, chili in a bread bowl, plus salads and breakfast sandwiches.

HERO FACTORY $–$$
4233 E. Camelback Rd.
(602) 952-9948
www.azherofactory.com

This New York-style deli is popular with local law enforcement. Expect to see Maricopa County Sheriff Joe Arpaio, US Attorney Dennis Burke, and Phoenix police leaders munching on lunchtime subs. Nicole, the New York native who runs the joint, wears a handgun on her waist as she slices meat and prepares your order fresh. The Italian subs, sausage and peppers, and Cracker Jack (a sandwich with cracked pepper turkey, pepper jack cheese, and Russian dressing) are among the favorites. It's a great place to grab lunch if you're touring downtown Phoenix. Breakfast is also available.

*LOS REYES DE LA TORTA $–$$
9230 N. 7th St.
(602) 870-2967
www.losreyesdelatortaaz.com

Los Reyes serves some outstanding quesadillas, tacos, burritos, and soups. But it's the

traditional Mexican sandwiches that put this place on the national map. This little shop in a Sunnyslope strip mall has been named among the best sandwich shops in the US. It's consistently (amazingly) delicious. The clientele is largely Mexican, and you hear mostly Spanish spoken in the dining room and kitchen. The fresh fruit cocktail drinks are outstanding, especially in summer. The tortas list is about 20 deep. It's hard to pick something that isn't delicious, but the massive Del Rey is worth a shot (with a partner, perhaps, unless you're daring). It includes ham, melted cheese, pork sirloin, breaded beef, sausage, chorizo, and egg.

ROCKET BURGER & SUBS $–$$
12038 N. 35th Ave.
(602) 993-0834
www.rocketburger.com

The Rocket Burger is 3 beef patties on a sub roll with all the fixings and a special rocket-dressing. The greasy-spoon joint is well reviewed locally. The cheesesteaks, cold subs, gyros, and chili dogs bring together a little bit of everyone's hometown. It's some of the best grease in Phoenix. Don't expect anything fancy, and don't expect to leave hungry. Everything is gigantic and reasonably priced. If you have a craving and you're on the west side of town, this is your place.

ROMANELLI'S DELI & BAKERY $–$$
3437 W. Dunlap Ave.
(602) 249-9030
www.romanellisitaliandeli.com

This is a busy, New York-style deli. But it's in Arizona. So the employees smile a little more than they would at your favorite place in the Bronx. The butter cookies and cannoli behind the cases will remind you of home.

This is the place to pick up a pound of thinly sliced Italian mortadella or capicolla. While you're here, grab a few cans of tomatoes to make sauce later in the week. The homemade sausage and peppers and baked ziti are nice changes if you're not into a cold sandwich on fresh bread. Eat at the cafeteria-style seats as you would in Philly, Providence, or any other Little Italy back East.

THAT'S A WRAP $–$$
800 E. Camelback Rd.
(602) 252-5051
www.eatatthewrap.com

OK, so you can't stomach a foot-long salami sub smothered in onions and mustard. No problem. Check out the healthy, unique choices at That's a Wrap. The well-reviewed, vegetarian-friendly sandwich shop is a clean place for a clean lunch. The Buffalo 66 wrap has hot sauce chicken and veggies rolled in an herb tortilla, for example. The salads and side dishes are refreshing and tasty. Closed Sun.

> **i** MacAlpine's Soda Fountain at 2303 N. 7th St. is like having a sundae or milkshake in a time machine. The place serves burgers and homemade seafood chowder, but it's the Egg creams, malts, and other fountain drinks that make it just like your neighborhood 1950s soda jerk. Information: (602) 262-5545 or www.macalpines1928.com.

Soul

LO-LO'S CHICKEN & WAFFLES $–$$
10 W. Yuma St.
(602) 340-1304
www.loloschickenandwaffles.com

It's hard to find a chicken and waffles restaurant in the Southwest. Lo-Lo's serves

all sorts of combinations of this soul food favorite. You can get your chicken Southern style, Southern fried, or smothered in gravy and onions. The chicken and waffles come alone or with grits, eggs, beans over rice, or corn bread. There are also breakfast dishes like chicken omelets and breakfast sandwiches. Breakfast is served all day and night, as is the regular menu. It's a greasyspoon joint with classic chicken, but the salmon croquettes with cheese eggs and "'Hood Classics" like stupid fries (white meat chicken, gravy, onions, and cheese) make it totally unique. This place is a matter of south Phoenix pride, and it's true to its gritty neighborhood roots, but Lo-Lo's also has a Scottsdale location.

MRS. WHITE'S GOLDEN RULE CAFE $$
808 E. Jefferson St.
(602) 262-9256
www.mrswhitesgoldenrulecafe.com
If you like soul food, this is the place. And it's owned by the same family that spawned Lo-Lo's (see above). Since 1964 Mrs. White's has been cooking filling meals of fried chicken, chicken fried steak, pork chops, and fried catfish. Meals come with your choice of sides, such as corn on the cob, mixed greens, and yams. The staff is friendly and welcoming. The walls are autographed by the many NBA players and other athletes who come here for real soul food. The Golden Rule Cafe got its name because patrons get no check at the end of the meal. Instead they are on their honor to tell the cashier what they ate. The building is also a point of Black Phoenix pride. Long a Valley favorite, Mrs. White's is the "best place to eat if you're starting a diet tomorrow," according to the *Phoenix New Times*.

South American

MI COMIDA RESTAURANTE LATINO $
4221 W. Bell Rd.
(602) 548-7900
It's easy to overlook neighborhood restaurants, but this Latin gem is worth a special trip if you are in the northwest corner of town. Rosa and her son Michael run this 6-table restaurant in a small strip mall. The cuisine is primarily Ecuadorian, though other dishes honor Colombia and Peru. They serve banana leaf-wrapped fish for the adventurous, shrimp with plantains in a hearty nut sauce, and a traditional Colombian potato and chicken soup. The Ecuadorian pork tamales are super, and do not miss the coconut flan.

Steakhouse

DONOVAN'S STEAK & CHOP
   HOUSE $$$$
3101 E. Camelback Rd.
(602) 955-3666
www.donovanssteakhouse.com/
phoenix-steakhouse
This fashionable Biltmore restaurant is one of three national locations. The 4 to 8 p.m. Martini Hour is a big draw, as are the steaks. It's a great place for formal parties or for drinks at the wine and martini bar. But the prime filets, New York strips, mixed grill, Cajun rib eye, fish, and chops are all outstanding. It's upscale yet classic, and well-reviewed for some of the best steaks in Phoenix.

THE STOCKYARDS $$$$
5009 W. Washington St.
(602) 273-7378
www.stockyardsteakhouse.com
The Stockyards dates to 1919, when the old cattle feed lot produced the best, freshest

steaks in the young city. It's known as the "original AZ steakhouse," and they're not lying. The prime rib and classic steak cuts are stellar, but the chef also cooks dishes like Sonoran baby back ribs and blue cornmeal-crusted trout.

Sushi

HANA JAPANESE EATERY　　　　**$$–$$$**
5524 N. 7th Ave.
(602) 973-1238
www.hanajapaneseeatery.com
Perhaps the biggest thing here is the service, even more than the ridiculously fresh fish. This is a place where the servers and chefs remember your face. They are genuinely kind and willing to get you whatever you need to make the meal outstanding. The sushi chef will customize meals for diners on some days based on their favorite ingredients. The fish is considered some of the freshest in Arizona. It's hard to believe there's no ocean nearby, because it tastes that fresh. The sashimi melts in your mouth. Tuna, striped bass, halibut, and oysters are equally delicious. Ask for fresh wasabi made from scratch; they'll be happy to give you some. Don't settle for that fake green stuff.

SUSHI EYE　　　　**$$–$$$**
4855 E. Warner Rd.
(480) 820-3376
www.sushieye.com
The Ahwatukee restaurant serves more than 25 colorful, Americanized sushi rolls. The specialties include a spicy chicken roll with baked chicken and spicy sauce, and an ASU roll with spicy tuna topped on rolled shrimp tempura and cucumber with wasabi sauce and jalapeno (perhaps because that's how Sun Devils roll: with as much heat as

possible). Sushi Eye also does deep-fried rolls, traditional maki, and other sushi. A second location is in Chandler.

YASU SUSHI BISTRO　　　　**$$–$$$**
4316 E. Cactus Rd.
(602) 787-9181
Located at Paradise Valley Mall, the unassuming little Japanese joint serves some seriously excellent sushi. But that's actually secondary to the wagyu beef, grilled squid, and other seafood. It has the feel of being upscale without coming across as pretentious, and it's still relatively unknown in an area where sushi is really popular. The tapas-style dishes are a great way to try everything with friends over cocktails. Try the Red Roll of spicy tuna and shrimp tempura.

SOUTHEAST VALLEY

American Fusion

CORK　　　　**$$$–$$$$**
4991 S. Alma School Rd., Chandler
(480) 883-3773
www.corkrestaurant.net
Cork is fast becoming one of the top restaurants in the growing suburb of Chandler. It's modern, chic, and gets quite packed on busy nights. Order a grapefruit basil martini at happy hour. Small bites include wild boar meatloaf and duck fat fries topped with Gruyere. The dinner menu includes a medium-rare elk loin poached in duck fat (clearly, a favorite technique at Cork), plus short rib risotto and an organic lamb T-bone. Cork also offers a chef's tasting menu of 5 courses for $75 per person, which is a great way to experience the menu and get to know the cuisine of one of the more sophisticated restaurants in the Southeast Valley.

✳FOUR PEAKS BREWING CO. $$
1340 E. 8th St., Tempe
(480) 303-9967
www.fourpeaks.com

Four Peaks Brewing Co. is situated in what used to be the Borden's Creamery in Tempe, giving the place a hip, funky industrial warehouse atmosphere. Even the 72-foot-long bar seems lost in all that space. The brewpub caters to college and young urban professional crowds with around 10 different varieties of beer. A favorite is Kiltlifter, a Scottish ale with a rich body, Hefeweizen, and the classic 8th Street Ale. Seasonal beers like the autumnal Pumpkin Porter are incredible. Get a growler bottle for $14 and refill it for $10. It's a brewpub, sure, but the unique menu puts it among the most successful locally owned American restaurants in the Southeast Valley. Locals come here regularly for savory, cheesy chicken beer bread rolls with artichoke hearts, salmon BLTs, pesto veggie pizza, fish and chips, and daily specials like pork adovada with fresh tortillas. A second location on the southeast corner of Frank Lloyd Wright and Hayden in Scottsdale is also open (480-991-1795). Both sites do decent happy hours, and a reverse happy hour 11 p.m. to close.

HOUSE OF TRICKS $$$–$$$$
114 E. 7th St., Tempe
(480) 968-1114
www.houseoftricks.com

The restaurant serves a little bit of everything, from grilled Scottish salmon with unagi glaze to pecan-crusted smoked pork tenderloin. The 2-tiered patio deck with a bar on the top floor and tables at street level offers plenty of seating. If you choose to dine outside, you'll enjoy the shade and the canopy of grape vines, a fountain, and an outdoor fire pit for cool evenings. The renovated old house has lots of character. The restaurant is just off Mill Avenue, so you can eat before heading to the shops or bars. The menu includes quite a few seasonal dishes, giving the chef plenty of room for creativity. Lunch and dinner are served every day but Sun.

✳JOE'S FARM GRILL & LIBERTY MARKET $$
3000 E. Ray Rd. and 230 N. Gilbert Rd., Gilbert
(480) 563-4745, (480) 892-1900
www.joesfarmgrill.com, www.liberty market.com

Joe's Farm Grill and Liberty Market are run by Joe Johnston, one of the most innovative food-minds in the Valley. Everything at the farm restaurant is so fresh because so much is grown at the farm next door. The lettuce for moist hormone-free chicken salads, tomatoes for the locally produced natural hamburgers, hand-breaded onion rings, smoked barbecue sandwiches, and ribs keep guests lined up. Joe's is set amid a citrus grove, with lots of shade and grass, which makes it a destination for anyone who enjoys a relaxing meal. Much like Joe's, the emphasis at Liberty Market in downtown Gilbert is on fresh and local food served with great care. Signature sandwiches like the Arizona Sky (ham, creamy cheese, roasted poblano aioli) and wood-fired pizza like the White Pizza (parmesan cream sauce, smoked mozzarella, grilled chicken, chopped bacon) are worth savoring slowly. Liberty also serves breakfast and dinner, and the bar has a wide variety of excellent beers. Joe's is open daily for omelets, a breakfast burger with a fried egg, waffles, and other outstanding breakfast fare like ham and cheese fritters. Across

the street from Liberty is Joe's Real BBQ for Johnston's sweet, slow-cooked meat over pecan wood. Info: www.joesrealbbq.com.

LANDMARK RESTAURANT $$$
809 W. Main St., Mesa
(480) 962-4652
www.landmarkrestaurant.com

The 1908 Mormon church is now used for weddings, other big events, and a kitchen that serves traditional American fare like meatloaf, salmon, steaks, and sautéed chicken breast with a little Mediterranean flair. The Landmark is great for group dinners. The salad room (it's a full room, not just a bar) offers soups, meatballs, antipasto, and rare items like quail eggs, pickled watermelon, and a huge dessert list that includes spiced apple rings. If you want a bit of Mesa history and a solid family meal, this is the right stop.

Asian

ASIAN CAFE EXPRESS $-$$
1911 W. Main St., Mesa
(480) 668-5910
www.asiancafeexpress.com

This is an authentic Hong Kong-style mom-and-pop hole-in-the-wall joint. It's nothing fancy, but the food is fresh and consistently impressive. The place is growing on Valley foodies, and Mesa residents use it often for carry-out. Fresh salt and pepper Dungeness crab and squid are among the best dishes. Others include noodles with spare ribs in a black bean sauce. The taro coconut tapioca drink is a local favorite. Try the beef with scrambled egg sauce over rice. The owners will prepare your fish or meat for you in their style if you can present a receipt showing it's fresh. For lunch and dinner, the restaurant serves 19 versions of $3.33 special bowls.

i The organic and locally grown hubs of Joe's Farm Grill and Joe's Real BBQ offer free meals to birthday boys and girls. It's a local deal a lot of Valley residents are aware of, because anyone who knows about fresh local food knows that's just about the sweetest deal in town. See above for details on Joe Johnston's joints.

THAI BASIL $$
403 W. University Dr., Tempe
(480) 968-9250
www.thaibasiltempeaz.com

Thai Basil serves consistently tasty noodle and curry dishes, in addition to traditional appetizers like fresh spring rolls and satay chicken with peanut sauce. The sweet heat of the yellow curry is particularly excellent. The pad Thai is mom-and-pop comfort-food-level fare. Arizona State University students and other East Valley residents crave the spicy noodles. The restaurant used to be BYOB. No longer. You'll have to try the delicious Thai iced coffee in the small yet comfortable dining area facing University Drive. It's located just blocks from ASU and the Mill Avenue entertainment district. Thai Basil also does lunch specials and take-out orders.

Breakfast

HARLOW'S CAFE $-$$
1021 W. University Dr., Tempe
(480) 829-9444

When it comes to a filling breakfast, you can't go wrong in a diner built in what appears to be a double-wide trailer. Take a seat surrounded by hungover college students, families with little kids, and workers getting ready for a day in the desert heat.

The family-run cafe is constantly packed. Its omelets, fresh-baked muffins (peach and blueberry are the best), chorizo-packed breakfast burritos, and biscuits and gravy are among the tops in town. The Percy Omelet is a favorite for big appetites. It's like an Italian sausage and peppers dish in an omelet. The Eggs Maximilian is enormous and worth stuffing yourself with; it's eggs, veggies, salsa, potatoes, cheese, and green chilies whipped up on a fresh tortilla. If you're craving a big breakfast in Tempe, don't look any further. Skip Starbucks.

Continental & Fine Dining

✳KAI $$$$
5594 Wild Horse Pass, Chandler
(602) 225-9000
www.wildhorsepassresort.com
Adventurous foodies can expect a daring chef, ingredients not found anywhere else, and a mix of menu and ambiance that has many critics calling this the top fine dining experience in the Phoenix area. Kai features food grown on the Gila River Indian Reservation, the home of the Wild Horse Pass Resort. The menu is a tribute to the native people of the area, with proteins like red deer venison and tribal buffalo featured in entrees. Ingredients like pecans and saguaro blossoms used by chef Michael O'Dowd are grown on the reservation. The menu, beginning with the "birth," or appetizers, plays like a tasteful spiritual journey that ends with "the afterlife"—desserts like an éclair made with mesquite meal choux and lavender custard. Kai is a formal place in very high demand, so be warned when considering reservations.

English

CORNISH PASTY CO. $$
960 W. University Dr., Tempe
(480) 894-6261
www.cornishpastyco.com
It might seem like you're walking into a dark cave in the middle of a strip mall. But that's what a lot of English pubs feel like in the UK, minus the sweltering heat and strip mall next to a convenience store and gas station. Cornish Pasty Co. serves meat pies, but far better than the dry steak and kidney deal you get around London. This place has everything, and there are far too many tasty pasties to list here. The bangers and mash (homemade sausage with sage, red wine gravy, grilled onions, and mashed potatoes served with a side of gravy) and chicken Alfredo (chicken breast, ham, bacon, roasted red potatoes, and creamy Alfredo sauce) are baked with care behind the bar in giant ovens. The crusty, meat-filled pastry pockets date to around 1200, when women cooked them for the poor workers who could afford little else. The Tempe restaurant, which has a sister spot in Mesa, serves a nice variety of imported and local beers. It's easy to find the perfect complement to your hearty pasty dinner.

Ethiopian

BLUE NILE CAFE $$
933 E. University Dr., Tempe
(480) 377-1113
Blue Nile's East African food has been well reviewed for years. The comfortable dining room is something of an Arizona State University hangout, with so many adventurous young foodies in Tempe. It's also a vegan favorite. You don't need utensils here— just some injera, a thin, spongy sourdough

bread, for dipping. The food is spiced, but not overly spicy hot. Blue Nile has some nice combo plates that are perfect on your virgin voyage with Ethiopian food. Vegetables and legumes are common, as are stews, chicken, beef, and lamb. Try the Blue Nile Tebb, a beef dish with onion and green chili, or Tikil Gomen, a savory cabbage and potato dish. Open for lunch and dinner daily.

Mexican

BLUE ADOBE GRILL $$$
144 N. Country Club Dr., Mesa
(480) 962-1000
www.originalblueadobe.com
This New Mexican restaurant in downtown Mesa serves daily blackboard specials for $10. The place is known for its pecan wood-enhanced meats. Christmas style (red and green sauce) stacked enchiladas come with chicken, shredded beef, carne adovada, grilled shrimp, or tenderloin. Another favorite is chorizo-stuffed chicken with chipotle mashed potatoes. The Mesa location is popular, but there's a growing tradition at the Scottsdale location on Frank Lloyd Wright Boulevard.

MUCHO GUSTO $$$
603 W. University Dr., Tempe
(480) 921-1850
www.muchogusto1.com
If you're craving Mexican food, but the average quesadilla-chips-and-salsa joint won't cut it, this is worth a look. Mucho Gusto serves a Twenty Dollar Burrito that's actually $20 and loaded with a 10-ounce gaucho steak, jack cheese, rice, beans, pico de gallo, and guacamole. The Oaxacan tamales (red chile pork or chicken) are steamed in mole sauce. The restaurant also serves classic Mexican fish tacos, Baja chicken, machaca beef,

and frozen margaritas. All the dishes have a unique touch, including the guacamole laced with Grand Marnier. Both the patio and indoor dining room are pleasant.

NORTHEAST VALLEY

American Fusion

BANDERA $$$
3821 N. Scottsdale Rd., Scottsdale
(480) 994-3524
www.hillstone.com
A short menu with some of the best rotisserie chicken in town has made this Old Town restaurant a favorite for years. The lines can be long, especially on Friday or Saturday, but the food is worth it. In addition to its famous chicken, Bandera does ribs, filet mignon, and a Caesar salad with roasted chicken, avocado, almonds, and goat cheese. The Flying Tuna Platter is wholesome tuna on mixed greens with avocado, mango, and miso vinaigrette. The restaurant is open daily for dinner only. If you're in the mood for a take-out dinner, Bandera has a very efficient "flying chicken" drive-through service. Call ahead to order, and they'll have it ready for you when you drive up.

> **i** At Bandera ask for the "cluck and moo" plate. It's not on the menu, but you'll be served some chicken and ribs you'll enjoy.

CAFE MONARCH $$$
6934 E. 1st Ave., Scottsdale
(480) 970-7682
Cafe Monarch seems to get more popular by the day, and it can be difficult to get reservations. It's tucked away in a strip mall near Old Town galleries and shops, so it's not too far off the beaten path. Chef Chris

Van Arsdale serves Asian-inspired dishes like cashew chicken with Japanese black rice, and his entire repertoire has endeared himself to critics and foodies. But keep in mind this is the type of place that's unpretentious and serves almost comfort-like food, in spite of its accolades. Sit on the little patio outside and enjoy a tuna salad plate (with capers, artichoke, and zucchini), a bacon sandwich (with figs, roasted chiles, and green apple), or one of Chef Chris' Smokehouse Sundays barbecue. Chris will also pick a dish for you based on your favorite ingredients, and he often strays from the written menu.

CITIZEN PUBLIC HOUSE $$$
7155 E. 5th Ave., Scottsdale
(480) 398-4208
www.citizenpublichouse.com
The downtown Scottsdale gastropub serves some pretty outstanding bar snacks like Kilt Lifter fondue with the locally brewed dark ale, hunter's sausage, pear, and country bread. Starters include green lip mussel chowder. The entrees are similarly creative and hearty, like coffee-charred short ribs and chicken breast with sweet corn risotto. For dessert you must try the Pig in the Orchard. It's a sweet and creamy bread pudding with Granny Smith apple, applewood smoked bacon, bourbon brown sugar, and cinnamon ice cream. Got room for a drink? Citizen serves lots of artistic signature cocktails. This is a smart menu worth experiencing.

EDDIE'S HOUSE $$$
7042 E. Indian School Rd., Scottsdale
(480) 425-9463
www.eddieshouseaz.com
Chef Eddie Matney is well known around the Valley as co-host of a local TV food show, but also for the dishes at his stylish Old

Town restaurant. His namesake features the popular mo'rocking shrimp appetizer with chili beer dipping sauce with dough balls. Entrees include bacon-infused meatloaf, sesame tuna, and Parmesan halibut. It's open for dinner only. A favorite dessert is chocolate chip tiramisu.

*FNB $$$
7133 E. Stetson Dr., Scottsdale
(480) 425-9463
www.fnbrestaurant.com
Scottsdale is loaded with restaurants of all types, but FnB is one that many critics and locals consider their favorite. Its marketing is also impressive. Check the website for FnB videos with chefs discussing local gastronomic trends and agriculture. The menu is filled with local ingredients. Signature dishes include the braised leek gratin with mozzarella and a fried egg in mustard breadcrumbs. *Food and Wine* called it one of the top dishes of 2010. Like the seasons, the restaurant's ingredients shift. The spring menu has featured items like spaghetti squash, pecorino pasta with local greens, crispy roast jidori (farm fresh) chicken, and lamb tenderloin with a spring ragout. For dessert, try the dulce de leche cake.

ROARING FORK $$$
4800 N. Scottsdale Rd., Scottsdale
(480) 947-0795
www.eddiev.com
Named for a river in Colorado, this restaurant offers rotisserie, wood-fired cooking with a Western flair. Roaring Fork classics include green chili pork stew served with hot buttered tortillas, smoked wood-fired salmon with teriyaki barbecue sauce, braised Dr. Pepper beef short ribs, and the Big Ass Burger with poblano and smoked pepper

Close-up

Phoenix Ranch Markets

The traditional ranch markets of central Phoenix showcase food that rivals some of the top Mexican restaurants in town. This is no-frills Mexican cooking at its finest, whipped up by senoritas with a touch of home-kitchen flair.

That food stand in the back corner of the ranch market with what appears to be a bunch of food that's been sitting under hot lamps overnight? It looks suspect, but those mounds of meat make the best burritos in the neighborhood, with your choice of handmade savory machaca beef, carne adovada pork, and spicy shredded chicken. It's about as far from fast food as it gets. That meat is slow-cooked with care. Locals know their neighborhood ranch markets are the place to go for certain foods based on their specialties. Some are better at short order breakfast burritos than dinner plates, while others are known for their cool fruit cocktail drinks and pastries.

At La Tolteca, a grocery west of 16th Street on Van Buren Street in downtown Phoenix, everything from tacos to tamales is served all day. The place has a bakery, butcher, beer coolers, and a small grocery store with everything from fruit to kitchen cookware. It attracts downtown professionals who know the inexpensive meal is a far better value than an overpriced excuse for a Mexican lunch.

Tolteca is routinely ranked among the best Mexican restaurants in Phoenix, and it's not really a restaurant. You order a plate of seasoned sliced beef with beans and rice (less than $7) or a carnitas torta slathered in fresh guacamole and beans from a lunch counter, then sit in the cafeteria-style dining area after pillaging Tolteca's incredibly fresh salsa bar. The dining area is usually bustling with a mix of young couples, workers, cops, and executives talking over the low hum of Spanish soap operas on the corner TV.

Another example in downtown Phoenix is the Pro's Ranch Market at Roosevelt and 16th streets, just north of Tolteca. It's one of several in Arizona, yet appears absolutely nothing like a chain of Mexican groceries. Locals rave about the individuality of the place and are constantly amazed at the prices. A pound of fresh calamari, perhaps better than what you'd find at big-name supermarkets, goes for less than $2 a pound. An avocado that tastes better than the "organic" items at your neighborhood grocer is 59 cents. The tortillas are made from scratch on-site, the smoky barbacoa beef is addictive, and the roasted chicken tastes better for less money than you'll spend at your typical place.

The Roosevelt Street market is massive. You could spend a whole day wandering through the produce section alone, marveling at the quality of ingredients like jicama and pasilla chiles. The meat counter features tilapia filets, pan dulce sweetbreads, and homemade chorizo.

The neighborhood ranch market is embraced in Phoenix, so if you're visiting or just moving in, get to know the folks at the one closest to home. Aside from gourmet chefs, this is some of the best Mexican cooking in town.

Information: La Tolteca, 1205 E. Van Buren St. (602-253-1511 or www.latoltecamex.com) and Pro's Ranch Market, 1602 E. Roosevelt St. (602-254-6676 or www.prosranch.com).

bacon. The bar here has a strong happy hour following. It serves $3 beers and $5 cocktails and wine 4 to 7 p.m. daily; all night on Sun and Mon. The happy hour includes discounts on Roaring Fork's top dishes like the pork stew and Big Ass Burger. Dinner is served daily.

Asian

MALEE'S THAI BISTRO $$$
7131 E. Main St., Scottsdale
(480) 947-6042
www.maleesthaibistro.com
The restaurant is located in the Scottsdale gallery district, so there's certainly an air of artistic flair to this place. The Thai dishes range from meats in lemongrass and mint to satays to curries. The Drunken Dragon Noodles, the "Thai wife's revenge on drunk husbands," are hotter than usual. Thai iced tea with or without cream makes a most soothing accompaniment if you like your dishes spicy. Other dishes include salads, rice paper rolls, and lettuce wraps with minced pork. Malee's is open daily for lunch and dinner.

TOTTIE'S ASIAN FUSION $$
7901 E. Thomas Rd., Scottsdale
(480) 970-0633
www.tottiesasianfusion.com
Tottie's doesn't look like much, and Scottsdale residents know the space featured struggling restaurants in the past, but this place is comfortable and borderline upscale. Cuisine is inspired by Thai, Vietnamese, Korean, and Chinese food, though Chef Tottie Kaya is from Laos. The green curry, pho, and meaty noodle dishes are raved about. There's a second location at Scottsdale Road and Lincoln Drive. Try the fried plantain and coconut ice cream.

Barbecue

DON & CHARLIE'S $$$–$$$$
7501 E. Camelback Rd., Scottsdale
(480) 990-0900
www.donandcharlies.com
In an area lacking decent barbecue, Don & Charlie's stands out, especially for its ribs. Many locals say this longtime establishment in downtown Scottsdale serves the best-tasting ribs in the Valley. The owner, Don Carson, is originally from Chicago, so he knows something about proper smoke-skills. The prime rib, New York sirloin, and lamb chops are also recommended at the supper club-like restaurant known for its ties to the baseball community. Sports memorabilia is everywhere, so it's also a bit like a museum. It's a great stop for a nice dinner during a Cactus League visit, and you might get a chance to meet Major League Baseball commissioner Bud Selig eating the steak dish named after him. Don & Charlie's is open for dinner only, 7 days a week.

Breakfast

BUTTERFIELD'S PANCAKE HOUSE $$
7388 E. Shea Blvd., Scottsdale
(480) 951-6002
www.butterfieldsrestaurant.com
Scottsdale has its share of solid breakfast places, but Butterfield's is a step above. In summer 2011 the owners planned to open a new breakfast cafe in Scottsdale, but the original restaurant on Shea Boulevard serves breakfast all day and is usually packed. Weekends are especially busy for brunch. The menu from the Illinois-based owners includes Belgian waffles, crepes, omelets, and skillets. Consider it like an upscale, consistently outstanding breakfast chain. The smoothies are a nice addition. Lunch is also served daily.

i Misplaced New Yorkers who need a deli fix can try the Scottsdale Kosher Market at 10211 N. Scottsdale Rd. (480-315-8333). Also try Segal's, located at 4818 N. 7th St. in Phoenix (602-285-1515), or Goldman's Deli at 6929 N. Hayden Rd. in Scottsdale (480-367-9477).

Continental & Fine Dining

BINKLEY'S $$$$
6920 E. Cave Creek Rd., Cave Creek
(480) 437-1072
www.binkleysrestaurant.com

The menu is constantly being changed and modified like any developing work of art. Chef Kevin Binkley's place, located about 45 minutes out of downtown Phoenix, has become a favorite of even the most traditional critics. Binkley is known as a daring, creative, and technically masterful chef, which is interesting because Cave Creek is known more as a chuck wagon Old West town. Try the tasting menu to get a sense of his creations, which include some fantastic takes on rarer proteins like guinea hen, monkfish, venison loin, and filet beef tips. This is the place to dig into cheese and dessert as well. Take your time. There are few better ways to cap an evening in the Northeast Valley than on the cool Binkley patio with a banana bread "puddin'," a signature dessert served with dried cranberries, Brazil nut praline, and dark rum cream.

ELEMENTS $$$$
Sanctuary Camelback Mountain Resort & Spa
5700 E. McDonald Dr., Paradise Valley
(480) 607-2300
www.elementsrestaurant.com

The panoramic views from the restaurant at Sanctuary on the northern slope of Camelback Mountain are memorable, especially combined with the elegant menu. To begin the evening, you'll stroll past the Zen-like fountain at the entrance and step down to the restaurant feeling relaxed already. Try to stop at the Jade Bar before (or even after) dinner to enjoy the amazing desert view. Elements prides itself on preparing sustainable seafood and hormone-free meats. The fare ranges from Asian-inspired sashimi, udon noodles, and miso-glazed salmon to new American dishes and French items. The menu changes monthly. Try to arrange dinnertime so that you can watch the glowing sunset. Patio seating is available. It's one of the most romantic, elegant dining spots in the Valley.

i For a cool break on a hot day, stop by Pop the Soda Shop at 1649 N. 74th St. in Scottsdale (888-305-3877). It carries 1,200 varieties of nonalcoholic beverages, including more than 60 types of rootbeer. Information: www .popsoda.com.

LON'S AT THE HERMOSA $$$$
5532 N. Palo Cristi Rd., Paradise Valley
(602) 955-7878
www.hermosainn.com/lons

You can get away from it all at this intimate Southwestern-style dining room at the Hermosa Inn, which is tucked into a Paradise Valley residential area. The restaurant is named for Lon Megargee, a cowboy artist who developed this property as a hacienda and studio, then turned it into lodging. The artful American cuisine includes grilled beef tenderloin with blue cheese gratin and house-cured bacon, pecan wood-fired

herb-crusted lamb chops, and a Sunday dinner barbecue smoke with delicacies like jidori chicken and "tender belly" porchetta. Lunch and dinner are served Monday to Friday; brunch on Sunday.

French

ZINC BISTRO $$$$
15034 N. Scottsdale Rd., Scottsdale
(480) 603-0922
www.zincbistroaz.com
The name comes from the 25-foot-long zinc bar at the restaurant located right in the heart of Kierland Commons. It's a pleasant place to sit outside, as if Paris were 25 degrees warmer. Daily specials are posted on a blackboard to add to the French bistro atmosphere, and the interior is lined with French books. The chef's onion gratin, a traditional onion soup with bubbling gruyère, is terrific, as is the Zinc Burger, which is served open-faced with bacon and a blue-cheese melt. Scallops with chorizo and crab crepes are unique takes on the recipes. It's also a fine place to enjoy a *fruits de mer* platter. Lunch and dinner are served daily.

Italian & Pizza

PATSY GRIMALDI'S $$
4000 N. Scottsdale Rd., Scottsdale
(480) 994-1100
www.grimaldispizzeria.com/arizona
The first of several Grimaldi's in Arizona, located in the heart of Old Town Scottsdale, serves a fine Caesar salad and fabulous thin-crust pizza. The secret to the success of this pizza lies in the coal brick oven used to bake it. The crust comes out crispy, and garden-fresh ingredients enhance the flavor. Open for lunch and dinner daily, there are three locations in Scottsdale. It's a national chain, but it doesn't taste like it. The downtown Scottsdale location is equally as consistent with its food as those in Peoria, Chandler, and Gilbert.

'POMO PIZZERIA NAPOLETANA $$
6166 N. Scottsdale Rd., Scottsdale
(480) 998-1366
www.pomopizzeria.com
'Pomo serves classic pizza Napoletana, like its Quattro Stagioni. The four-corner pizza gives you a taste of sausage, salami (Italians don't eat pepperoni, you American tourist), mushrooms, and olives. The sweet sauce is pretty outstanding and rivals what's served at the top pizza places in the Valley. But the white pizza is a nice departure from the norm and worth tasting in a more upscale pizza spot. 'Pomo is located at the Borgata shopping center, so there's plenty to do before or after a meal.

Mexican

CARLSBAD TAVERN $$–$$$
3313 N. Hayden Rd., Scottsdale
(480) 970-8164
www.carlsbadtavern.com
Walking into Carlsbad Tavern feels a bit like tripping into the depths of *Fear and Loathing in Las Vegas*. It's bat country. But never mind the spooky motif and "Daily Guano" newsletter, it's quite clean and inviting inside. The New Mexico-style menu also features steak and pasta. The servers are friendly, in a neighborhood tavern kind of way. Top dishes include grilled chicken pasta with andouille sausage and chiles, snapper tacos, and Green Chile Trail plates of items like carne adovada and chile rellenos. The bar serves refreshing margaritas and 35 kinds of tequila. Ask for a patio table. Lunch and dinner are served daily.

RESTAURANTS

i For a quick and tasty lunch worth every penny, head to local chains Paradise Bakery and Wildflower Bread Co. Both sandwich chains are based in Scottsdale. They serve everything from breakfast sandwiches to pastries, soup, salad, and pasta. There are dozens of locations in the Valley. For locations: www.paradisebakery.com or www.wild flowerbread.com.

LOS SOMBREROS $$$
2534 N. Scottsdale Rd., Scottsdale
(480) 994-1799
www.lossombreros.com

There's something for everyone on the menu at Los Sombreros, so this is a nice option for families. Some of the more interesting items include the lamb adobo, a lamb shank with ancho chile sauce, and smoked chicken enchiladas with salsa verde. Los Sombreros is also known for its touches like chipotle cream, Puebla-style mole, and guajillo and pineapple pico. Ask for outdoor seating if it's available.

OLD TOWN TORTILLA FACTORY $$$–$$$$
6910 E. Main St., Scottsdale
(480) 945-4567
www.oldtowntortillafactory.com

In a renovated adobe cottage dating from 1933, Old Town Tortilla Factory offers a pleasant old world atmosphere with a modern twist on Mexican and American fare. With entree items like Shawnee Sea Bass and ancho-raspberry topped red chile pork chops, you can see it's not strictly the cheese crisp-enchilada-taco type of Mexican food. And the Tortilla Factory makes 2 dozen varieties of flour tortillas, using ingredients like sun-dried tomatoes and serrano chiles. The

bar also gets a lot of business, and it's quite popular with tequila aficionados, since the place serves 120 varieties of the Mexican liquor. Some of the high-end tequilas go for $500 a bottle. The restaurant is open for dinner daily. The fountain patio makes for a memorable evening if you're visiting and looking for a great Mexican meal. It's located a quick walk from Hotel Valley Ho and Old Town Scottsdale.

TABERNA MEXICANA $$$–$$$$
7001 N. Scottsdale Rd., Scottsdale
(480) 607-6707
www.tabernamexicana.com

This is upscale Mexican. It's north Scottsdale, so you can expect a little culinary flamboyance. The ceviche and house sangria are not exactly classic South of the Border peasant food. Tacos are filled with filet mignon, scallops, and pork belly. The poblano potatoes make a nice side. Guests rave about the $10 guacamole as well. The recipe includes pumpkin seed and queso anejo. Entrees are equally rich, with innovative twists on chile relleno, cochinita pibil pork stew, and a fajita burger with brisket.

Sandwich Shops

ARCADIA FARMS CAFE $$
7014 E. 1st Ave., Scottsdale
(480) 941-5665
www.arcadiafarmscafe.com

Arcadia Farms occupies two restored homes across the street from each other in downtown Scottsdale and serves American bistro-style dishes. This place has a knack for turning a grilled ham and cheese or albacore tuna into a one-of-a-kind lunch. There is both indoor and outdoor seating, but when the weather is nice it's hard to resist the patio dining amid the lovely trees on the grounds.

The menu ranges from grilled shrimp skewers to seared salmon on French green beans. The homemade breads and desserts are popular. Lunch is served daily.

*DEFALCO'S ITALIAN GROCERY $–$$
2334 N. Scottsdale Rd., Scottsdale
(480) 990-8660
www.defalcosdeli.com

There are few of these original, family-owned Italian delis in the Valley. You have a better shot at finding a mom-and-pop torta shop. So DeFalco's is a treasure. It's located a couple of miles south of downtown Scottsdale, right between Tempe and Scottsdale. The menu is loaded with hot sandwiches and pastas. The store carries take-home dishes, imported Italian canned tomatoes, olive oil, and ravioli. It's also one of the best places in the Valley for imported meats and antipasto. There's a great patio to sit outside with your eggplant parm, salami with vinegar peppers, or chicken cutlet. The family that runs DeFalco's enjoys booming business, so expect a wait. At happy hour imported beers are $3. A personal favorite: "gabbagool" and egg on a toasted Italian roll.

WILDFLOWER BREAD COMPANY $
15640 N. Pima Rd., Scottsdale
(480) 991-5180
www.wildflowerbread.com

Wildflower is a Valley workday favorite for everyone from office executives to moms with young kids. Sandwiches are served on fresh multigrain or ciabatta, focaccia, or wild mushroom. Signature sandwiches include chicken pesto and feta or roast beef and Gorgonzola. Also on the menu are salads—chipotle BBQ, ranch chicken, and almond tuna. Dishes come with a side of orzo pasta salad. There are cookies and biscotti to go

with the good selection of coffees and teas. The Pima Road location southwest of the Loop 101 and Frank Lloyd Wright Boulevard is a popular spot, with so many offices and shops nearby. Check the website for other locations in Scottsdale, Phoenix, Chandler, Gilbert, and Goodyear.

Seafood

MASTRO'S OCEAN CLUB $$$$
15045 N. Kierland Blvd., Scottsdale
(480) 443-8555
www.mastrosrestaurants.com

Located amid the upscale shops of Kierland, the dinner-only seafood restaurant is something of an exclusive spot. It offers private dining, a lounge, and some of the freshest fish in town. You can create your own shellfish tower with oysters, lobster cocktail, and other delicacies. Mastro's also serves steaks and chops. The fish entrees are sophisticated, like Hawaiian big eye tuna, vanilla buttered sole, and Maine lobster.

NORTHWEST VALLEY

American Fusion

VOGUE BISTRO $$–$$$
15411 W. Waddell Rd., Surprise
(623) 544-9109
www.voguebistroonline.com

The quaint French-style bistro in Marley Park Plaza is open for lunch and dinner. The menu is modern and clean, and it has a growing reputation with Northwest Valley folks. The buttery Black Angus steak with brandied peppercorn sauce is a favorite. Other fare ranges from burgers to French rabbit stew with wild mushrooms and other vegetables. It's approachable gourmet done correctly, with its own character.

i Westgate shopping center in Glendale is known for its wide array of eateries that make the average mall food court look like a joke. Successful, little-known national chains include Kabuki Japanese Restaurant, Moe's Southwestern Grill, and Yard House. Information: www.westgatecity center.com.

Asian

SIAM THAI CUISINE $$
5088 W. Northern Ave., Glendale
(623) 931-0658

If you're looking for homemade Asian food in Glendale, this is the place. The Tom Yum Soup with tofu in a fire bowl is a local favorite. The pad Thai, green curry, papaya salad, and other classic Thai dishes are also well reviewed. It's a comfortable mom-and-pop place where you know they'll hustle to maintain their reputation as the top Thai place in town.

YEN SUSHI & SAKE BAR $$-$$$
17037 N. 43rd Ave., Glendale
(602) 978-9022

Solid sushi spots are rare in the meat-and-potatoes Northwest Valley, so you've found a gem here. Yen is known for the casual, fun atmosphere in the lounge-like spot tucked into a Glendale strip mall. The menu provides some unique twists on spicy tuna rolls, Philly rolls, sweet water eel, and other traditional sushi. Oyster shooters and cocktails are also popular. It's a great place to hang out for a large dinner or just for drinks. There are specials after 8 p.m., and happy hour gets crowded.

Breakfast

KISS THE COOK RESTAURANT $
4915 W. Glendale Ave., Glendale
(623) 939-4663
www.kiss-the-cook.com

Just a mile from downtown Glendale's antiques district, Kiss the Cook has been dishing out homemade, country-style breakfast and lunch since 1980. The family-operated restaurant has a cluttered feel, with all the antiques, dolls, birdhouses, and assorted knickknacks on display and for sale. Breakfast includes buttermilk pancakes from an old family recipe and omelets. Also on the table are homemade muffins and apple butter. For lunch the salads are made from scratch. Eggs Benedict and biscuits and gravy are also favorites. The restaurant is open Mon to Sat for breakfast and lunch; breakfast Sun until 1 p.m.

German

✴HAUS MURPHY'S $$-$$$
5739 W. Glendale Ave., Glendale
(623) 939-2480
www.hausmurphys.com

Meat. Potatoes. Heavy beer. How can you go wrong? This restaurant serves schnitzel, sauerbraten, bratwurst, strudel, and other homestyle favorites from Rhineland and Bavaria. Haus Murphy's also hosts live music ranging from traditional Bavarian bands to American rock groups Friday and Saturday nights. The wholesome, home-cooked German food in downtown Glendale has fetched national attention from The Food Network and other media. It's open for lunch and dinner daily. Reservations recommended.

Italian & Pizza

*LA PIAZZA AL FORNO $$
5803 W. Glendale Ave., Glendale
(623) 847-3301
www.lapiazzaalforno.com

This is like the Pizza Bianco of the West Valley. If Haus Murphy's is packed next door, try this place if it's not also wall-to-wall with guests. The excellent addition to historic downtown Glendale features some serious pizza, from classic hand-tossed pizzas with fresh cheese and ingredients to the Italian Stallion with 4 different types of meat and the outstanding Pizza Bianca white pizza. The menu also includes linguine with clam sauce (spicy red or white), lasagna, and Mediterranean ravioli.

SOUTHWEST VALLEY

American Fusion

LITCHFIELD'S $$$-$$$$
300 E. Wigwam Blvd., Litchfield Park
(623) 935-3811
www.wigwamresort.com

The new Wigwam restaurant opened in 2011 as a replacement for Red's Steakhouse. The menu features local ingredients and rivals those of other major Valley resorts. It was established by Chris Bianco, the famed pizza chef of Pizzeria Bianco in Phoenix. Litchfield's uses a wood-grill oven and features dishes that include a beet salad with vegetables from local farms, Arizona trout with pecan sage butter, and grass-fed local beef. The hype around Bianco's new project is part of Wigwam's recent resurgence in the Valley hospitality market, as it adds a modern flair to some of its uniquely Old West features (see Resorts chapter for more). Dinner is served daily.

NIGHTLIFE

The Valley has its share of posh dance clubs in Scottsdale, dive bars in Tempe, and gritty downtown pubs in Phoenix. As in any metro area, there is something for everyone.

Locals tend to switch it up: a wine bar one night, belly up to the neighborhood bar the next. There's enough diversity of late-night hangouts in most communities for even the pickiest drinker. Major entertainment venues are also spread throughout the Valley, so driving to shows never seems to take that long.

Phoenix has been knocked in past years for being soft on live music. Smaller cities like Austin, Nashville, and Cleveland get far more recognition. However, the Valley has its share of concert venues. You can catch national acts at places as small as the hole-in-wall Rhythm Room or as massive as Jobing.com Arena in Glendale. The big acts find their way here, and on any given week you could have your choice of Lady Gaga, the Black Keys, Roger Waters, or Alison Krauss. Major comedy acts are the same way. Huge stars like Jay Mohr, Jimmy Kimmel, David Spade, and Frank Caliendo all have ties to Phoenix.

Some places charge a cover. But so many wouldn't dare. You have options here. It's worth getting away from the major thoroughfares like Scottsdale Road and Mill Avenue once in a while to explore some lesser-known bars. Popular bars and nightclubs are packed for a reason, but going to one doesn't necessarily make for a unique night in Phoenix. If you're single, this is a great area to meet someone on romantic nights out. There are so many young professionals from other parts of the country.

Our recommendations for clubs, bars, live music spots, comedy clubs, breweries, and other hangouts are just a starting point. It's a mix of the trendy and more obscure, from local favorites to places that please Valley rookies. So, cheers. Here's to your night out.

BARS & PUBS

Phoenix

ARMADILLO GRILL
1904 E. Camelback Rd.
(602) 287-0700
www.myarmadillogrill.com
The food is outstanding at this neighborhood bar known for its solid service, great drink specials, and off-track horserace betting windows. "The Dillo" also has 34 TVs, pool tables, and other games to keep you occupied. The cool misters around the patio facing Camelback Road help in the summer if you want to drink outside. Half-price appetizers like calamari, Armadillo Gold chicken

wings, and the bar's excellent Cajun fried pickles are available during happy hour, 4 to 7 p.m. and again 11 p.m. to 12:30 a.m. Each night features different specials, like Mexican Hump Day on Wednesday, with $3 margaritas and $2.50 Mexican beers.

> **i** Not into pub crawls? Coffeehouses are also open late. Check out Copper Star Coffee, 4220 N. 7th Ave. in Phoenix (www.copperstarcoffee.com), a hip renovated space with live music. Lux Coffeebar, 4404 N. Central Ave. in Phoenix (www.luxcoffee.com), is equally artistic and organic-minded about its coffee.

DISTRICT AMERICAN KITCHEN & WINE BAR
Sheraton Phoenix Downtown
320 N. 3rd St.
(602) 817-5400
www.districtrestaurant.com

In most cities, the hotel bar isn't known as the most happening place. The District is different. It's a local hangout, but always filled with visitors from out of town. The drink specials and menu are excellent. You won't spend much money during happy hour, 3 to 7 p.m. and 10 p.m. to close Mon to Sat, when snacks like buffalo sloppy joe sliders and mac-n-cheese with local Schreiner's sausage beer hots are less than $6. There's usually a band or disc jockey playing live in the corner of the modern bar, located right near Arizona Center. Forget the Bud Light when beers like Nimbus oatmeal stout and Oak Creek nut brown ale are $3.

*FILM BAR
815 N. 2nd St.
(602) 595-9187
www.thefilmbarphx.com

This might be the most innovative bar in Phoenix. Film Bar screens independent movies as you sample 30 different craft beers and 15 different wines. Tickets are $7, matinees $5, and $3 Monday. The bar is separate from the soundproof auditorium, which seats 85. The film house opened in February 2011 to wild acclaim in downtown Phoenix, adding to the cultural scene in the walkable urban area near the Roosevelt art galleries. If sitting at the bar and staring at a ballgame bores you, check out this place for art films and cult classics.

Southeast Valley

*CASEY MOORE'S OYSTER HOUSE
850 S. Ash Ave., Tempe
(480) 968-9935
www.caseymoores.com

The name is a bit deceptive, though this popular Arizona State University hangout does serve some decent oysters. Try the baked oysters Rockefeller as an appetizer with a cold beer. Casey's is known for its no-frills atmosphere, huge outdoor patio with tons of dark nooks to hide in, and reputation for being haunted by the spirit of a young woman some believe was killed while the place served as a boarding house after the turn of the 20th century, though stories vary. Dining on the upper floor is worth the trip for the goose bumps. Casey's hosts huge St. Patrick's Day parties, and weekends get busy, but weeknights are very mellow. Beer, cocktails, and bar food are served nightly.

FIBBER MAGEE'S
1989 W. Elliot Rd., Chandler
(480) 722-9434
www.fibbermageespub.com

This classic Irish pub serves Guinness and other traditional European beers, but it's

also known for its live music, poker nights, and other events. Happy hour is 4 to 7 p.m. every day, with half-price appetizers and flatbreads, plus $2 off all beer and wine. Fibber's serves a full menu that includes entrees like an all-day Irish breakfast, seared cod in chorizo broth, and burgers (any of which is $5 Mon).

Northeast Valley

COACH HOUSE
7011 E. Indian School Rd., Scottsdale
(480) 990-3433
www.coachhousescottsdale.com
Coach House is the premier "dive" in Scottsdale, but of course nothing in Scottsdale is truly a dive. It's a far more unassuming bar than the modern, trendy joints around Old Town. It's also popular with everyone from native Scottsdale residents to off-the-plane tourists from nearby resorts. The place dates to 1959 and has retained much of its original character of a tiny wooden house with low ceilings. The big wraparound patio bar is a great place to enjoy a cool desert evening with a cocktail. The bar is also a few blocks from other downtown Scottsdale bars, so it's a perfect addition to a late-night out.

✴OLD TOWN TAVERN
7320 E. Scottsdale Mall, Scottsdale
(480) 945-2882
www.oldtowntavernaz.com
The patio at Old Town Tavern is one of the coolest places to hang out in Scottsdale. The brickwork, outdoor fireplace, and chairs make for an ideal place to sip a cocktail. Live music adds to the warm atmosphere inside and out. It has the feel of an old neighborhood bar with the modern lift of a new Scottsdale hangout. Plus, it's in

walking distance to other Old Town bars, but tucked off the beaten path enough to remain relaxing.

BLUES NIGHTCLUBS

Phoenix

CHAR'S HAS THE BLUES
4631 N. 7th Ave.
(602) 230-0205
www.charshastheblues.com
Char's is a friendly, crowded, smoky nightspot where the blues make you sweat and the brews cool you off. Local journalists have voted it "Best Blues R&B Bar" for years. Arrive early to get a good seat. You're not here to see concerts, but to dance on the postage-stamp-size dance floor when one of the local bands gets really hot. There's live music 7 nights a week. When the bands take a break, the atmosphere is conducive to conversation as in a regular corner bar with a pool table, darts, and TVs.

> **i** Had too much to drink? Call Zingo. They'll pick you up, put their scooter in your car, drive you home, and then take off. It's cheaper than a cab and much smarter than risking a DUI. Call (877) 663-8429 or visit http://zingoaz.com.

RHYTHM ROOM
1019 E. Indian School Rd.
(602) 265-4842
www.rhythmroom.com
As its name suggests, this is the place for rhythm and blues. The dive bar, located in what appears to be an old house/office in a less than desirable neighborhood north of downtown, features national acts and popular local musicians. There's lots of seating

and no fighting for a parking place either. Live music is scheduled almost every night, with shows starting around 8 or 9 p.m. Some shows are free, and those that aren't cost around $10. Drinks are also cheap.

BREWPUBS

Southeast Valley

GORDON BIERSCH BREWERY RESTAURANT
420 S. Mill Ave., Tempe
(480) 736-0033
www.gordonbiersch.com/locations/ tempe-az
The view from the second-floor balcony of this consistently good brewpub chain is part of the draw. You can enjoy a tall glass of a dark microbrew, nibble on some hearty bar food, and survey the crowds on Mill Avenue below. The patio fills up quickly, but the inside rooms have large windows that make for a bright interior during the day. At night it can get packed with college drinkers. There are few things more satisfying than a few rounds of Marzen lager or golden Czech pilsner with a helping of Gordon Biersch's trademark garlic fries. Three other locations are now open. One is in the SanTan Village in Gilbert (480-722-0833). The others are at Westgate Shopping Center at the intersection of Loop 101 and Glendale Avenue (623-877-4300), and in north Phoenix just west of Scottsdale Road at 18545 N. Allied Way (480-342-9860).

SLEEPY DOG SALOON & BREWERY
1920 E. University Dr., Tempe
(480) 967-5476
www.sleepydogbrewing.com
The names of the brews are almost as great as the taste of the brews at Sleepy Dog. The

Dog Pound pale ale, intensely strong St. Bernard barley wine, and Leg Humper hefeweizen are among those that locals love to drink at the brewery or take home. Half-barrel brews and half-barrel kegs are available for purchase of beers like Belgian Agave blonde or chocolate stout. There's enough seating to enjoy a few hand-crafted brews, but the food is limited to appetizers. Sleepy Dog is close enough to other downtown Tempe hangouts that you can spend an hour or two here before heading out to get a bite to eat elsewhere.

> **i** Phoenix is a four-sport town (Diamondbacks, Suns, Cardinals, and Coyotes) and Arizona loyally follows the programs at two major universities (Arizona State and University of Arizona). So there are plenty of places to enjoy an adult beverage and watch the games. Check our Close-up on Valley sports bars in the Spectator Sports chapter for details.

Northeast Valley

✳PAPAGO BREWING
7107 E. McDowell Rd., Scottsdale
(480) 425-7439
www.papagobrewing.com
Papago rotates 30 taps of draught beer daily in its cozy, recently expanded brewpub restaurant. The bar is set next to the big statue of a sleepy, buzzed Trappist monk holding a beer. This place is hidden in the back corner of a strip mall at McDowell and Scottsdale roads, completely unnoticed from the main drag. But it's a local spot with a huge following, both for the beer and the food. Lunch and dinner are served daily, with pizza, burgers, and sandwiches. Papago serves its own beers made by local Sonoran Brewing Co.

The coolers are stocked with dozens of American microbrews and imported bottles. Mix and matching a 6-pack here is cheaper than drinking at most bars, and it gives you the chance to try a lot of unique labels.

COMEDY CLUBS

Southeast Valley

∗TEMPE IMPROV
930 E. University Dr., Tempe
(480) 921-9877
www.tempeimprov.com
Photos of Jerry Seinfeld, Jim Breuer, Dave Chappelle, and other top comedians hang on the walls. Guys with local ties like David Spade and Jay Mohr have performed on the stage. The experience is intimate and engaging in spite of its unassuming presence at the back of a strip mall just blocks from Arizona State University. The Improv, with a capacity of 400, books comedians Thursday to Sunday. Dinner shows are at 8 p.m., and Fri and Sat feature a non-dinner show at 10 p.m. The Improv serves dinner and offers a full bar.

Northeast Valley

THE COMEDY SPOT COMEDY CLUB
7117 E. 3rd Ave., Scottsdale
(480) 945-4422
www.thecomedyspot.net
Located at 3rd Avenue and Scottsdale Road, the Comedy Spot has an unmistakably cozy ambiance. It's a popular Scottsdale date night, and a great place to sink into a chair and laugh with friends. Once a week the venue hosts an open mic night, but you need to sign up months in advance. If you're really hooked, you can sign up for a stand-up comedy class. There's a full bar on site. Shows

are Thursday to Sunday nights. Be sure to check the website for discount coupons. There are also half-price nights for women and students.

JESTER'Z IMPROV COMEDY
7117 E. McDowell Rd., Scottsdale
(480) 423-0120
www.jesterzimprov.com
Jester'z is a family-oriented alternative to other comedy clubs. The shows are free of profanity and vulgarity, which doesn't matter at all. The performers are hilarious enough to get any audience member cackling like a hyena. Like so many great finds in the Valley, the club is tucked away in Papago Plaza at a small, relatively unmarked theater. Jester'z is well reviewed annually as one of the best first-date spots in Phoenix. With friends, it also makes a great night out when combined with dinner and drinks at next-door Papago Brewing (see the Brewpubs section of this chapter for more).

COUNTRY NIGHTCLUBS

Northeast Valley

BUFFALO CHIP SALOON & STEAKHOUSE
6811 E. Cave Creek, Cave Creek
(480) 488-9118
www.buffalochipsaloon.com
This is arguably the top country bar in the Valley. The cowboy boots nailed to the roof are a clue that you're in the right place. Dine on barbecue, dance to live music, and enjoy the country culture of Cave Creek. Buffalo Chip also hosts buffet nights for $10 per giant plate, in addition to other events. There's live bull riding at the rodeo right behind the bar. So be cautious about how many beers or whiskey shots you take

down if you're going here with impulsive friends.

HANDLEBAR-J

7116 Becker Ln., Scottsdale
(480) 948-0110
www.handlebarj.com

The Handlebar-J is another place with a long history. It's been in the Herndon family since 1975. Its hallmark has been the family's music. Ray Herndon, who has played with J. David Sloan, Lyle Lovett, and McBride and the Ride, may be the best known of the Herndon Brothers Band members. Nights are filled with bands, dance lessons, and big parties. The full country menu includes barbecue and steaks. There's a huge patio where you can eat and drink between trips to the dance floor.

DANCE CLUBS

Southeast Valley

BIG BANG

501 S. Mill Ave., Tempe
(480) 557-5595
www.thebigbangbar.com

Live dueling rock 'n' roll pianos get the crowd jumping here. It's cool fun as the pianists play your favorite songs. You'll get music and comedy and dancing all rolled into one. But plan on participating in the mob of party animals in the dark basement bar beneath Mill Avenue. This is the place to go if you don't mind grinding alongside strange singles. The Tempe Big Bang is one of four nationwide, though the Arizona State University hangout might be considered the rowdiest. Events like Trailer Trash Tuesday draw well, and there's an occasional talent show to draw local musicians.

Northeast Valley

AXIS/RADIUS

7340 E. Indian Plaza, Scottsdale
(480) 970-1112
www.axis-radius.com

Bust out your glow sticks for the nightly trance-like techno party at this place, which seems to ooze sex appeal. The 2 clubs, connected by a glass walkway, are longtime favorites for young professionals and college students looking to brush up against each other on the dance floor. Axis is the more laid-back of the two. Decked out with ultramodern furniture, the spacious bars and lounges make a good place to meet with friends over a few drinks and food. Radius is the high-energy dance spot, where the dance floors tend to be crowded on weekends and can get pretty packed on weeknights, too. The clubs offer a VIP lounge with floating bar and a cigar bar as well. Of course, there's a cover every night. No sneakers or logo sports gear allowed.

MYST NIGHT CLUB

7340 E. Shoeman Ln., Scottsdale
(480) 970-5000
www.mystaz.com

If you enjoy big clubs, drop by Myst on the weekends. It's 18,000 square feet, and this place rocks. Myst has a variety of rooms, each with different colors, themes, and music, as well as a kicking dance floor downstairs. The upstairs area has 2 VIP sections, which we've heard are nice, although poor authors like us can't afford the fee. If you do have the money, the Cat Walk VIP Lounge is cool. The crowd tends to be on the young side, as lots of Tempe college students come here on weekends.

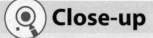

Close-up

Spanish Fly Mexican Beach Club

Many people skip the golf or art galleries and visit Scottsdale for the cool pools. And the sexy nightclubs. Now they have a hangout that combines the two.

The Spanish Fly Mexican Beach Club opened in March 2011 as the only bar in Arizona with a fully functional outdoor swimming pool on its patio, in the middle of the club. Earlier in the day, it's common to see bikini-clad coeds splashing in the pool next to businessmen in dress clothes who've kicked off their loafers to dip their toes in the water. At night, it turns into a poolside dance party with a DJ and multiple bartenders.

Spanish Fly replaced Drift, a popular Scottsdale dive bar, at 4341 N. 75th St. The old Drift parking lot was razed and replaced with the pool patio, which includes a waterfall, palm trees, and a series of comfortable party cabanas with padded seats and flat-screen TVs. You can even order a quarter-barrel keg of beer and sit in the sun all day. They run about $420, so you'll need a crew to pull it off. But it's worth it for special occasions.

Order an ice-cold signature drink like Mamasita, with Parrot Bay coconut and strawberry rum, or a 6-pack bucket of Negro Modelo. Spanish Fly also offers Bikini Drinks, or "low-cal drinks for your hot bod." Punch bowls of mixed drinks are also available.

Unlike many downtown Scottsdale nightclubs, the food is actually very good. You can order until midnight. Order a Mana Roll (mix of ahi tuna and an American alba-core tuna salad) and you know it's going to be fresh. The team that set up Spanish Fly is the same that runs Stingray Sushi across Scottsdale Road in Old Town. Other favorites include carne asada fries, tempura shrimp, healthier wrap sandwiches, and signature Nogi Dogs with chili that are perfect to satisfy the late-night munchies.

If you're looking for a place to party poolside, and the hotel won't let you roll a keg or a bucket of bottles out on the deck, turn to Spanish Fly. It is fast becoming a must-see in Scottsdale.

Information: www.spanishflyscottsdale.com or (480) 949-8454.

THE SHAKER ROOM AT MARTINI RANCH
7295 E. Stetson Dr., Scottsdale
(480) 970-0500
www.martiniranchaz.com

The upstairs Shaker Room features a light show, live music, and plenty of dancing. Sit in romantically dark booths and watch the show floor while sipping a designer martini, or get up and shake your booty on the central dance floor. The venue features local bands some nights, in addition to a DJ spinning rock, hip-hop, and mash-ups. Phoenix tends to be casual, but you'll feel more comfortable here in your very best club attire.

LOUNGES

Phoenix

THE MERC BAR
2525 E. Camelback Rd.
(602) 508-9449
www.mercbar.com

They don't advertise, but look for the Merc at the back of Camelback Esplanade beside Hillstone restaurant. A funky little neon sign with a flashing martini glass lets you know you've arrived. Inside are plush leather sofas and a dark ambience with candlelit tables perfect for intimate conversation. Choose from a long list of specialty martinis. The Merc Bar doesn't exactly have a dress code, but business casual should make you feel at home.

Northeast Valley

*MABEL'S ON MAIN
7018 E. Main St., Scottsdale
(480) 889-5580
www.mabelsonmain.com
This place is a bit like *Mad Men* meets the 21st century. The studded leather chairs, hand-crafted cocktails, and swanky happy hour (5 to 7 p.m. Tues to Sun) enhance a night out in Scottsdale. The lounge is closed Monday. Mabel's is a decent place to enjoy one or two excellent drinks with friends and meet locals, many of whom consider it one of the sexiest lounges in Scottsdale.

Northwest Valley

HELL'S HALF ACRE
Westgate City Center
6751 N. Sunset Blvd., Glendale
(623) 877-8447
Think beer and shots at this joint. It gets crazy at times with wet T-shirt nights and loud local music. Back in the days of the Oklahoma land grab, people lived in tent cities waiting for the great rush to start. One of the most disreputable was named Hell's Half Acre, and it was that concept that inspired this new Glendale nighttime

hangout. The saloon is about 2,500 square feet, and you enter through a custom-made steel fence. Inside, you'll find the bar at the back and a big steel table in the middle of the property. If you sit at the central table, you can strike up a conversation with locals—it's lots of fun. There's live music two or three times per week, and the bar is open daily.

POP CONCERT VENUES

Phoenix

ASHLEY FURNITURE HOMESTORE PAVILION
2121 N. 83rd Ave.
(602) 254-7200
www.livenation.com
And you thought Jobing.com Arena or University of Phoenix Stadium in Glendale were funky names. The former Cricket Wireless Pavilion remains a major draw for national rock acts. When it opened in 1990, this amphitheater (first called Desert Sky Pavilion) was touted as a year-round venue. After all, the Valley's weather would make outdoor wintertime concerts viable. The pavilion holds 22,000 people at capacity. The sound is pretty good, especially at dead center in the covered seats. The Allman Brothers, Red Hot Chili Peppers, Tool, and Kings of Leon have all rocked the crowd here.

i Every April the lawns at Westworld in north Scottsdale are turned into a raging rock 'n' roll party at McDowell Mountain Music Festival. The festival debuted in 2004 with jamband, funk, reggae, and other danceable national acts. Information: www.mmmf.net.

CELEBRITY THEATRE
440 N. 32nd St.
(602) 267-1600
www.celebritytheatre.com

When it opened as the Star Theatre in the 1960s, this venue was the height of chic, a theater-in-the-round setup with a stage that rotates on a turntable (though some acts opt not to have it turn). For many years it was the premier small hall (about 2,500 seats) in Phoenix, especially for acts that could take advantage of its intimacy. The sound system strains when a heavy act plays here, but when the act is more mellow, the effect is absolute magic. Celebrity isn't as well known as other top music venues, but it draws its share of major acts. Catch artists like Lyle Lovett, comedian Mike Epps, or bands like Muse on the cheap.

ORPHEUM THEATER
203 W. Adams St.
(602) 262-7272

The city of Phoenix bought this ancient (in Valley terms) movie theater in 1984 and reopened it in 1997 after $14 million in cleaning and refurbishing. Originally opened in 1929, the theater has furnishings and decor that hark back to the era when movie-going was meant to be an experience. The 1,364-seat theater is now home to a variety of theatrical and dance events and is on the National Register of Historic Places. It even shows the occasional old-time silent film. But the main stage has emerged as an excellent place for low-key national music acts like David Byrne and Monsters of Folk.

US AIRWAYS CENTER
201 E. Jefferson St.
(602) 379-7800
www.usairwayscenter.com

Built as the home of the Phoenix Suns and Mercury basketball teams, the US Airways Center can hold about 19,000 people in the basketball configuration and a few thousand fewer for concerts, depending on the size of the performers' stage. For the best views and sound, you'll want to avoid the floor and the upper bowl. Big shows have included Roger Waters' latest performance of "The Wall," Lady Gaga, and pro wrestling. This is the arena of all arenas in the Valley. There are 3 lounges inside for cocktails.

Southeast Valley

CHANDLER CENTER FOR THE ARTS
250 N. Arizona Ave., Chandler
(480) 782-2680
www.chandlercenter.org

A pleasant community hall of about 1,500 seats, the Chandler Center hosts nostalgic pop events and the occasional contemporary touring act. Two seating sections are on turntables and can be turned around to make the hall smaller and more intimate. Performances include ballet and family-oriented musical gigs. It's operated by the city of Chandler. It was recently reopened after a $6.7 million renovation.

GAMMAGE AUDITORIUM
1200 S. Forest Ave., Tempe
(480) 965-3434
www.asugammage.com

This is the stage at Arizona State University. Frank Lloyd Wright designed this circular building to be built in Iraq, but plans changed, and he ended up unveiling it near Mill Avenue and Apache Boulevard. At roughly 3,000 seats, Gammage Auditorium feels intimate even in the balconies. It's not particularly welcoming to louder acts, but Bruce Springsteen's "acoustic" tour and

Laurie Anderson's controlled technological avant-pop proved that this venue is just as good for live pop music as it is for the arts. You can catch touring theater performances like *Wicked* or *Jersey Boys*, as well as performances by opera divas, classical virtuosos, and pop artists like Beck. Gammage also hosts lectures like the post-9/11 presentation by the late David Halberstam.

✳MARQUEE THEATER
730 N. Mill Ave., Tempe
(480) 829-0707
www.luckymanonline.com

With 1,000 seats, the venue doesn't really have a bad seat in the house (since everyone is standing so close to the stage), and the sound system is among the best in the Valley. If one of your favorite bands is scheduled here, do yourself a favor and buy a ticket immediately. You may never get closer. The theater opened originally for country shows, though it now hosts funk, punk, and other varieties of rock. Marquee is close to Arizona State University and the Mill Avenue nightlife hangouts, so expect a fun crowd.

MESA AMPHITHEATRE
201 N. Center St., Mesa
(480) 644-2178
www.mesaamp.com

There are no seats in this 4,000-capacity amphitheater, just a pleasant grassy slope. So stretch out, watch the stars, and enjoy the music. This is the place to catch acts on their way up and acts on their way down. It's very casual, and people bring blankets. The atmosphere has made it a premier alt-rock venue, drawing major acts like the Black Keys and White Stripes every month.

MESA ARTS CENTER
1 E. Main St., Mesa
(480) 644-6500
www.mesaartscenter.com

As the largest arts venue in Arizona, the Mesa Arts Center is a magnet for top performers. The MAC is known for its acoustics. It's actually four venues within the big venue. Each week marks a unique lineup of music, theater, and other performances. The MAC hosts a mix of classical, folk, rock, country, and bluegrass, among other acts. The overall design, inspired by the Sonoran Desert, features a Shadow Walk with outdoor gardens and an inviting arroyo that flows through the walkway. Located in downtown Mesa, the venue is near plenty of parking and restaurants. The center houses 5 galleries of exhibition space and art studios that offer numerous classes each year in a wide range of crafts. The largest stage is in the 1,600-seat Ikeda Theatre.

Northeast Valley

THE COMPOUND GRILL
7000 E. Mayo Blvd., Phoenix
(480) 585-5483
www.thecompoundgrill.com

Run by the same folks who run McDowell Mountain Music Festival, this north Scottsdale bar hosts some of the most intimate concerts in town. You're able to stand with a pint of beer right in front of the tiny stage, watching top performers up close. After the show performers tend to hang around the bar and mingle with guests. Acts range from Grateful Dead tribute bands to more nationally recognized rock bands. The food and drink selection is also outstanding. The seating and decor are modern, but the place still has a classic bohemian vibe, especially with the acts it books.

SCOTTSDALE CENTER FOR THE PERFORMING ARTS

7380 E. 2nd St., Scottsdale
(480) 994-2787
www.scottsdaleperformingarts.org

At about 800 seats, the Scottsdale Center for the Performing Arts offers an extremely intimate atmosphere for shows by jazz and folk-music performers. A contemporary dance series brings in national companies. Summer brings performances of Native American music and performances for children in the outdoor amphitheater (within walking distance of the Scottsdale municipal complex). The sound in the auditorium is stellar, and all the seats provide excellent views of the stage; the sound in the amphitheater is good. It's also the site for the Scottsdale Arts Festival in March.

Northwest Valley

JOBING.COM ARENA

9400 W. Maryland Ave., Glendale
(623) 772-3200
www.jobingarena.com

The home of NHL's Phoenix Coyotes is similar to US Airways Arena with its major national music acts. From Taylor Swift to Tom Petty, it's the West Valley home of big, spectacular performances. There are 87 luxury suites, plenty of lower bowl seating, and other seats around the edge of the upper deck for great views of the stage. The capacity is about 17,700. The arena opened in 2003, and it's located right at Westgate shopping center for easy access to bars and restaurants before or after the show.

SHOPPING

Parts of the Valley are like Beverly Hills with upscale shopping that draws visitors from around the world. But the Old West vibe of Cave Creek, the sprawling urban malls of Arrowhead Towne Center in Peoria, and the fun assortment of retail at Tempe Marketplace make the Valley a diverse shopping experience.

Scottsdale is probably the best shopping in the Valley, and the best shopping in Phoenix is closer to Scottsdale than anywhere else. Old Town offers dozens of jewelry stores, art galleries, and cool little Old West shops to spend hours in. Just north are Scottsdale Fashion Square and the Camelback Waterfront with some of those Rodeo Drive-type joints we mentioned earlier. North Scottsdale's Kierland Commons area offers everything from Coach to the Apple Store.

Malls are a big part of the Valley's shopping culture. Each community has its own. So if you're staying in Mesa or Glendale, the Fiesta Malls and Westgates of the Valley world should carry what you're looking for, mostly in the comfort of a clean air-conditioned venue. But the Valley also has its share of local shops and unique Arizona gift spots detailed in this chapter.

PHOENIX

Shopping Centers

ARIZONA CENTER
400 E. Van Buren St.
(602) 271-4000
www.arizonacenter.com

The Arizona Center is a 2-story, open-air collection of shops, restaurants, and bars. Incorporated into the design are office towers and numerous gardens, sculptures, and fountains. The main garden in a sunken area near Van Buren Street and 3rd Street offers a shady oasis for lunch breaks and people-watching. The restaurants and bars can get crowded at times, especially with visitors staying at the nearby high-rise hotels, but the more sedate atmosphere in the shops provides a pleasant diversion if you're downtown.

The more than 25 shops include New York & Company, Jayne's Marketplace, and Arizona Beach Company for clothes or gifts. Other specialty shops include Flag World, with an extensive selection of the world's flags; Oak Creek, with Southwestern home accessories; and Sports World, featuring sports apparel.

Many retail carts are scattered about the Arizona Center, selling everything from refrigerator magnets and T-shirts to wind chimes and posters. Restaurants include Sam's Cafe, which has great drink specials and Southwestern favorites, in addition to

a few other choices that are more popular with the downtown lunch crowd. Another attraction is the AMC 24-screen theater, the only movie house in downtown Phoenix. The mall is open daily and provides a Guest Services Center in the food court. Find ample parking in the garage on Fillmore Street, which is open to Arizona Center customers, or try to find a spot along 3rd Street.

BILTMORE FASHION PARK
2502 E. Camelback Rd.
(602) 955-8400, (602) 955-1963
www.shopbiltmore.com

Biltmore Fashion Park's redbrick sidewalks, flower gardens, shaded walkways, fountains, outdoor cafes, and distinctive storefront architecture all exude elegance and Old World charm. It has major national department stores mixed with specialty shops like Ralph Lauren and Apple, but it also offers a pleasant place to hang out with friends.

Macy's and Saks Fifth Avenue are the major department stores, but a big draw for Phoenix residents and international visitors alike is the selection of intimate high-end boutique shops like Chanel, Gucci, Prada, and Fendi. Williams-Sonoma, Pottery Barn, and Urban Living are fun stops for cooking and home-decorating enthusiasts. Lululemon athletica sells high-end yoga gear and other sportswear. Vera Bradley and Calypso St. Barth provide more unique women's apparel.

The Biltmore Fashion Park restaurants are clustered on the east end of the mall. Stores are open daily at the shopping center near Camelback Road and 24th Street. Valet service and free parking, much of it shaded, are available. The Biltmore Fashion Park Concierge Service is open Monday to Saturday near Macy's and the Center Lawn.

i Check out Red Hot Robot at 6042 N. 16th St. You can buy cards, shirts, vinyl toys, an Uglydoll, or a book on graffiti. The store also hosts creative events for children. Information: www .redhotrobot.net or (602) 264-8560.

CAMELBACK COLONNADE
1919 E. Camelback Rd.
(602) 274-7642
www.camelbackcolonnade.com

The Colonnade, one of Phoenix's older shopping centers, has undergone a variety of makeovers through the years to compete with malls in suburban growth areas. It's been transformed into a pleasant, not-too-sprawling mixture of large retail stores in an open-air setting just west of Biltmore Fashion Park. Two of its most unique shops include Last Chance Bargain Shoes & Apparel for smoking deals and Sport Time for sporting goods. You'll also find an Old Navy clothing store; Best Buy appliances, music, and computers; Bed, Bath & Beyond; and Marshall's. If you are hungry, join the locals at the popular Miracle Mile Deli for New York-style bagels and stacked sandwiches. The Colonnade also includes a Phoenix public library branch.

COFCO CHINESE CULTURAL CENTER
668 N. 44th St.
(602) 273-7268
www.phxchinatown.com

This intimate shopping, restaurant, and office complex offers a unique cultural experience where East Asia design meets Western sensibilities. The bold red exterior, green roof tiles, hand-carved pagodas, statues, and an acre of traditional Chinese gardens offer a tranquil refuge. The most interesting store is the Super L Ranch Market, which offers traditional Asian foods and hard-to-find items,

from roast ducks to live clams. Oriental Factory Direct has clothing, books, jade, feng shui products, silk clothes, and other gift items direct from Hong Kong. Some of the shops sell imported herbs and authentic I Ching coins.

i Stinkweed's is the kind of independent music store that is, sadly, disappearing in the US. The shop carries used and new DVDs and CDs. You won't go in without getting trapped listening to rare recordings or chatting about music with interesting strangers. Simply put, it's one of Phoenix's coolest stores. It's at 12 W. Camelback Rd. in Phoenix. Information: www.stinkweeds .com or (602) 248-9461.

DESERT RIDGE MARKETPLACE
21001 N. Tatum Blvd.
(480) 513-7586
www.shopdesertridge.com

Just when you thought there couldn't be any more malls to visit, along comes Desert Ridge, a $170 million, 1.3-million-square-foot "suburban lifestyle entertainment center" featuring several gated communities, commercial businesses, and 5 unique shopping districts with individual shopping themes. Keep in mind, this is northeast Phoenix suburbia, so you'll run through gauntlets of teenagers. As a parent, keep in mind many of the shops are geared toward youths. So the Hollister or American Eagle Outfitters might just keep them occupied for a moment. There are more than 100 stores at Desert Ridge, with books at Barnes & Noble; bikes at Bikes Direct; filling feasts at the Fatburger; headwear at Hat World; shoes at Famous Footwear; and a multiplex theater and eateries, including In-N-Out

Burger, Dave and Buster's, and Yard House. And if that isn't enough retail, the CityNorth development just to the east is also open and growing.

DESERT SKY MALL
7611 E. Thomas Rd.
(623) 849-6661
www.desertskymall.com

In the early 1990s the old Westridge Mall that serves west Phoenix was revamped into fancier digs—including 2 new courts and huge skylights—lending it a clean, airy ambience that fits its mission as a community mall. Nearby is Ashley Furniture HomeStore Pavilion, a popular outdoor concert venue. The mall's department stores include Dillard's, Sears, and Burlington Coat Factory.

i To cater to the largely Hispanic population in west Phoenix, developers added a 77,000-square-foot Mercado with space for more than 200 small-space tenants at Desert Sky Mall. The renovations, which began in 2010, will include Mexican butcher shops, other food vendors, and beauty parlors.

METROCENTER
9617 N. Metro Pkwy. West
(602) 997-8991
www.metrocentermall.com

When it opened in 1973, Metrocenter was not only one of Arizona's first major regional shopping malls but also America's largest shopping mall. It's still no slouch. The 2-level interior has been remodeled with marble inlay floors, palm trees throughout, and 2 dancing waterfalls that often stop shoppers in their tracks.

Among its 200 stores you'll find the major department stores of Macy's, Sears,

and a Dillard's clearance center. Stores include Frederick's of Hollywood, Aeropostale, Sport Chalet, Journeys, and Bath & Body Works. Harkins Theatres, near the food court, offers stadium seating, 12 screens, and the latest stereo sound system. Inquire at the customer service center—on the lower level near Dillard's—for more information about merchants, bus schedules, and stroller rentals. Metro Parkway, which circles Metrocenter, is lined with smaller shopping centers, restaurants, movie theaters, and the popular amusement park Castles 'N Coasters. Among the shops facing Metro Parkway is a large Barnes & Noble bookstore, at 10235 Metro Pkwy. East (602-678-0088).

> **i** The 1950s are back in, so head over to Retro Ranch at 4303 N. 7th Ave. in Phoenix (602-297-1971). You'll find everything from retro furniture to swanky 1950s clothing.

THE SHOPS AT TOWN & COUNTRY
2021 E. Camelback Rd.
(602) 710-2122
www.townandcountryshops.com

The charming blend of red-tiled roofs, courtyards, and fountains makes for a unique shopping experience. About 3 dozen shops, mostly on the small and eclectic side, are connected by walkways lined with red brick. Interesting stops include Chakra 4 Herb & Tea House, which offers a cornucopia of herbs and organic food in its cafe; The Cigar Inn, for cigar and pipe aficionados; and My Sister's Closet, which offers recycled designer apparel. The Trader Joe's in the center is a hub for the area's young professionals and foodie families. You'll find a salad shop, a pita house, and a handful of restaurants on the same corner

of Camelback and 20th Street, including Baby Kay's Cajun Kitchen and Spasso Pizza & Mozzarella Bar.

Outlet Shopping

OUTLETS AT ANTHEM
4250 W. Anthem Way
(623) 465-9500
www.outletsanthem.com

The giant complex of bargain outlet stores is located off I-17 about 45 minutes out of downtown Phoenix in the development of Anthem. The more than 90 stores have a wide enough variety to interest everyone in the family. If you are shopping for kitchen and dining ware, look for Kitchen Collection, Le Creuset, and other stores. Women's apparel includes factory stores for Ann Taylor, Polo Ralph Lauren, and Nautica. For children, stop by the Oshkosh B'Gosh Factory Store or outlets for Gymboree and Carter's. Factory outlets for Banana Republic, Calvin Klein, J.Crew, Columbia Sportswear, Gap, and Nike are particularly popular. Other stores include Sunglass Hut, Bose Factory Store, and Reebok. You also will find a food court and playground. Nearby, the Customer Service Center offers coupon books, stroller rentals, wheelchairs, and tourist information. The shops are open daily and serve as an ideal stopping point between Phoenix and Sedona or Flagstaff.

Antiques Shopping

ANTIQUE GATHERINGS
3601 E. Indian School Rd.
(602) 956-8203
www.antiquegatherings.com

This large store gathers about 50 upscale antiques dealers into one location. Each dealer has a designated space to display

and sells wares. It's impressive how tidy the store is, and it's always an interesting trip to browse even if you have no intention of spending money. You get a quick sampling of the Victorian era, the American West, rural life, and more. Antique Gatherings dealers sell practically everything except the kitchen sink (and maybe that, too), including furniture, house wares, books, dolls, and sports memorabilia. Think everything from fine china to taxidermy.

i For a directory of bookstores in the Phoenix metropolitan area, including stores specializing in used and antiquarian books, check www .matrixbookstore.biz/phoenix_book stores.htm. About 60 stores are listed.

THE BRASS ARMADILLO ANTIQUE MALL
12419 N. 28th Dr.
(602) 942-0030
www.brassarmadillo.com
Here's a fun way to browse for antiques and collectibles in one building. The mall north of Metrocenter off I-17 and Cactus Road showcases items from more than 2,000 dealers over 39,000 square feet of space. Part of a chain of antiques malls headquartered in the Midwest, the Brass Armadillo's easy-to-navigate design includes uncluttered booths and street signs named for states to guide your way. Be prepared to lose track of time among the vast array of furniture, china, toys, glassware, dolls, vintage jewelry, collectible sports cards, and political memorabilia. If you want to learn more about your finds, you can browse the section of reference books on antiques and collectibles. The mall is open daily.

Specialty Stores

BUFFALO EXCHANGE
730 E. Missouri St.
(602) 532-0144
www.buffaloexchange.com
Buffalo Exchange, a national resale clothing store chain, has built a reputation among young adults as the place to find stylish gear on the cheap. Teens love the shoes. But the store has such a good turnover of merchandise and such a wide variety of duds for women and men that we recommend a visit for bargain shoppers of any age. Shopping the Valley locations is an easy way to buy an Arizona memento if you're not into prickly pear lollipops or turquoise jewelry. Buffalo Exchange also pays cash or accepts trades for used clothing in good condition. The store has another location at 227 W. University Dr. in Tempe, near Arizona State University (480-968-2557). The stores are open daily.

COWTOWN BOOTS
2710 W. Thunderbird Rd.
(602) 548-3009
www.cowtownboots.com
After more than 30 years in the business, it's no surprise that almost everything you need to be outfitted in Western style is here at Cowtown, but its specialty is boots. More than 25,000 pairs are on hand at the northwest Phoenix location off I-17, from standard cow leather to more exotic materials like snake, deer, bull, calf, mule, antelope, and ostrich. In addition to the Cowtown label of boots, find popular women's brands like Dan Post and Lucchese. Factory irregulars are usually on sale for a great deal. The store is open daily. Cowtown's other Valley location is at 1001 N. Scottsdale Rd., Tempe (480-968-4748).

SPORTSMAN'S FINE WINES & SPIRITS
3205 E. Camelback Rd.
(602) 955-9463
www.sportsmans4wine.com

This is one of the best liquor stores in the Valley. Not only does Sportsman's offer an impressive range of beer, wine, and spirits, but there's a bar on the premises. Cigars and fine imported cheeses are also for sale. A lot of the products are pricey, but there's also plenty for the slimmer budget. Complimentary wine tastings and classes are hosted regularly. The crowd here is a little more formal than in most places in Phoenix, but no one will turn you out if you dress casually. There's another popular retail shop at 10893 N. Scottsdale Road, Scottsdale (480-922-9463).

TRACKS IN WAX
4741 N. Central Ave.
(602) 274-2660
www.tracksinwax.com

If you're looking for vintage vinyl and you don't want to spend a lot of money, this is the place. Unlike a lot of stores of this kind, Tracks in Wax doesn't cater to the collector so much as the listener. You'll find lots of rare albums here, but the scuffed covers keep them from having inflated collectors' prices. One visit uncovered everything from early Blue Oyster Cult to Pete Seeger playing frontier tunes on the banjo. You'll also find the Pogues, the Byrds, the soundtrack to *Barbarella* (no joke), and even original World War II broadcasts by Tokyo Rose. There are used CDs, too. A second location is at 10410 N. 35th Ave., Phoenix (602-547-0100).

SOUTHEAST VALLEY

Shopping Malls

ARIZONA MILLS
5000 S. Arizona Mills Circle, Tempe
(480) 491-7300
www.arizonamills.com

Arizona Mills opened to much media hoopla in late 1997, partly because it was Arizona's first shopping center from the Mills Corp., the developer of Ontario Mills near Los Angeles and other "Mills" malls. The company brought "shoppertainment" to the Valley of the Sun, mixing outlet stores from dozens of nationally known retailers with a variety of entertainment venues and innovative restaurants. Arizona Mills strives to outshine the ordinary mall by conveying a lively, almost futuristic atmosphere. The walkway through its oval design winds through six theme neighborhoods that evoke an aspect of Arizona, from desert plants to ancient petroglyphs. Arizona artists designed many of the murals, mosaic tiles, metal sculptures, and pottery. Another fixture in the colorful and decor-intense mall is the profusion of video screens overhead, which blare commercials, mall promotions, and music videos. The shopping is fun, but be prepared for sensory overload.

There are more than 180 retailers, restaurants, and entertainment venues at the complex near the junction of I-10 and US 60. Mall anchors include Last Call by Nieman Marcus, Ross Dress For Less, Burlington Coat Factory, JCPenney Outlet Store, Sports Authority, and Saks Fifth Avenue OFF 5th. In women's apparel, other stores include Pacific Sunwear and a Kenneth Cole outlet store. You'll also find factory outlets for Nike, Nine West, Van Heusen, and others. There are a dozen house wares and furniture outlet stores, along with a half dozen cosmetic stores. It may have

more shoe stores than any other venue in the Valley, with options including Skechers, Tilly's, and Journeys, which also has a kids-specific store in the mall.

Other interesting stops include Vitamin World, which offers supplements, packaged foods, and a juice bar. There's a food court with an enormous seating area, plus a 24-screen cinema complex, an IMAX theater, and the popular Gameworks arcade/restaurant. Arizona Mills is open daily.

i One of the largest selections of New Age books and paraphernalia can be found at Vision Quest Metaphysical Bookstore. It's at 2225 N. Scottsdale Rd., Scottsdale (480-949-1888). Avoid calling those pesky late-night infomercial phone numbers and drop in for a tarot reading, Friday night healing session, or to have your aura photographed.

CHANDLER FASHION CENTER
3111 W. Chandler Blvd., Chandler
(480) 812-8488
www.chandlermall.com
Part of a 320-acre urban village, the mall is home to more than 180 shops and restaurants. You'll find anchor stores Nordstrom, Macy's, Dillard's, and Sears, in addition to numerous specialty boutiques. Other shops include the Apple Store, with ongoing demos of the very newest Macs; Disney Store, which opened in 2011; Eddie Bauer; Hollister, with West Coast, surfer-style clothes for teens; Red Rock Trading Post, with Navajo and Hopi crafts; and more. All this, and the mall also has a 20-plex theater and more than 50 eateries and restaurants, including BJ's Restaurant and Brewhouse, Kona Grill, and The Cheesecake Factory.

DANA PARK VILLAGE SQUARE
1758 S. Val Vista Dr., Mesa
(480) 890-0555
www.danapark.com
This brand-new 70-acre property is designed as a high-end village square. The venue at the northwest corner of Val Vista Drive and Baseline Road features wide plazas, promenades, date palm trees, and fountains that remind you of a desert oasis. It's anchored by AJ's Fine Foods, Coldwater Creek, and Barnes & Noble. Restaurants include 8 Oz Burger Bar, Sauce, and Costa Vida Fresh Mexican Grill. Specialty shoppers will find Girly Girlz, a feminine boutique, and Z Gallerie for home accents. Happy hour deals, sales, and special events are listed on the mall's website.

FIESTA MALL
1445 W. Southern Ave., Mesa
(480) 833-4121
www.shopfiesta.com
Fiesta Mall has long provided variety and easy access for Southeast Valley shoppers. In addition to the major department stores of Macy's, Dillard's Clearance Center, Sears, and Best Buy, the mall houses specialty stores such as Express, Champs Sports, GameStop, Forever 21, American Eagle Outfitters, and LensCrafters. There are about 100 stores in all, arranged in a 2-level mall decorated with Southwestern colors. A food court includes In-N-Out Burger and Sep's Mexican Grill. The mall is open daily, and covered parking is available. For moviegoers, 2 cinema complexes are within blocks of the mall.

SANTAN VILLAGE
2218 E. Williams Field Rd., Gilbert
(480) 282-9500
www.shopsantanvillage.com

As the freshest entry to the Phoenix-area shopping center scene, SanTan Village offers about 130 prime retailers to the Southwest Valley. The mall is anchored by Macy's and Dillard's. Best Buy, Barnes & Noble, Coldwater Creek, and Zales are popular stops. But the mall's directory is pretty diverse. It also includes Gordon Biersch Brewery Restaurant, the Apple Store, Old Navy, and Helzberg Diamonds. Solstice Sunglass Boutique lets you choose from nearly 1,000 brands. For children, there's an interactive play area and Build-a-Bear Workshop, where kids can customize their own teddy bears. Some of the latest retailers to the new shopping center include perfume and gelato shops.

SUPERSTITION SPRINGS CENTER
6555 E. Southern Ave., Mesa
(480) 832-0212
www.superstitionsprings.com
The Valley's continued eastward growth ensured the success of this regional mall near Southern Avenue and Power Road, a pleasant destination with about 130 stores. The major department stores are Dillard's, Macy's, Home Sleep Home, JCPenney, and Sears. Several smaller shopping centers sit on the fringes of Superstition Springs Center, making the area a one-stop shopping destination. As for the 2-level mall, its stores include Bath & Body Works, Borders, Fuzziwigs Candy Factory, Gap, and RadioShack. The interior has a contemporary feel, and in good weather it's quite nice to take a breather from shopping by sitting in the outdoor plaza. There's a National Geographic Kids play area. The Picture Show discount movie theater offers shows for $2 all week and $1 Tues. Opened in 2006, the amphitheater offers shows and concerts for the whole family. The customer service venter is on the lower level near the JCPenney entrance, and the stores are open daily.

TEMPE MARKETPLACE
2000 E. Rio Salado Pkwy., Tempe
(480) 966-9338
www.tempemarketplace.com
The marketplace, which opened in 2007, is conveniently located off the Loop 202 east of Rural Road. Critics might say it's a carbon copy of every other shopping mall in the Valley, and superfluous with Arizona Mills located on the south end of Tempe. But it's truly a destination shopping spot. The marketplace sports green laser lights over the parking areas and huge digital billboards. The center is just a mile or two from Arizona State University, so expect to find students eating lunch, enjoying cocktails, and shopping. There's a big focus on entertainment, so be sure to check the website or Twitter feeds (@TMPDistrict) for concerts and event info. Anchored by Sam's Club, Target, and JCPenney, the center contains 120 retailers, including Best Buy, Ross Dress For Less, Barnes & Noble, and Gap. There's a Dave & Buster's, Kabuki Japanese Restaurant, San Felipe's Cantina, and other places to have a cold beer on a hot afternoon. D'Arcy McGee's Irish Pub has developed into a popular late-night hangout with a great bar menu.

Shopping Districts

✴MILL AVENUE
Downtown Tempe
(480) 355-6060
www.millavenue.com
"Mill Ave." as it's known around town features historic buildings, a mixture of shops, restaurants, offices, and a plethora of people-watching opportunities at some of the top Arizona State University hangouts. Several dozen shops line Mill Avenue and the

surrounding side streets, some tucked away in nooks and crannies. The pedestrian-friendly area stretches from University Drive north to Rio Salado Parkway and Tempe Beach Park. Clothing, shoe shops, and other stores that cater to college students abound here. Specialty stores include Urban Outfitters, filled with trendy home accessories, books, gifts, and clothing; Here on the Corner, a clothing and accessories store; Cactus Sports and 2 Campus Corner shops, each great for Sun Devil attire; Lotions and Potions, for healthy body care; and Hippie Gypsy, one of the area head shops that actually sells clothes and gifts that non-stoner students would buy. Bison Witches Bar and Deli, 21 E. 6th St., is an unassuming bar off the beaten path. It's a great place to watch a ballgame with a cheap, cold beer and a stacked sandwich.

Antiques Shopping

ANTIQUE PLAZA
114 W. Main St., Mesa
(480) 833-4844
www.antiqueplazamesa.com
More than 100 dealers are packed into this 2-story antiques mall with 20,000 square feet of exhibit space in downtown Mesa. Find all kinds of furniture from different eras, along with vintage jewelry, table linens, quilts, lamps, Depression glass, trains, toys, and similar small collectibles. Antique Plaza is open daily. There are 8 other antiques shops within walking distance. Free public parking is available, and a number of restaurants are located nearby.

Specialty Stores

BOOKMAN'S
1056 S. Country Club Dr., Mesa
(480) 835-0505
www.bookmans.com

Arizona's largest seller of used books and music has been around for 30 years. Bookman's has stores in Tucson and Flagstaff, but there are only two stores in the Valley. The selection is as complete as any of the book superstore chains—plus it has so many out-of-print titles. There's a section devoted to new books, a large magazine section, and an area for used software. You can preview used CDs at a listening station. A few chairs and couches are available if you become so engrossed in something that you need to sit down. The personnel are willing to patiently sift through books and magazines you bring in for trade. Bookman's awards cash and/or store credit for materials it's willing to take off your hands. The store is open daily. All stores provide free Wi-Fi. A second Bookman's is located at 8034 N. 19th Ave., Phoenix (602-433-0255).

There are few places better than IKEA to shop for furniture for your dorm room or apartment. The store is at 2110 W. Ikea Way in Tempe off I-10 south of Elliot Road. Information: (480) 496-5658.

✳CHANGING HANDS BOOKSTORE
6428 S. McClintock Dr., Tempe
(480) 730-0205
www.changinghands.com
This independent bookstore has a noteworthy selection of new and used books for dedicated readers. The atmosphere here is warm and friendly. Changing Hands offers a number of educational activities for kids and features readings several times a month by local authors. The store hosts book clubs for everyone from science-fiction fans to existentialists. Valley newcomers can keep up to date on activities and new releases

through the store's comprehensive website. The adjacent Wildflower Bread Company makes for a good meeting point for clubs, writing groups, and other literature lovers. Changing Hands is open daily.

COOKIES FROM HOME
1605 W. University Dr., Tempe
(480) 894-1944
www.cookiesfromhome.com

This cookie bakery got its start in 1981 on Mill Avenue in downtown Tempe, then—thanks to a burgeoning mail-order business that has since shifted online—moved to larger quarters in a nearby industrial park. Most agree that these cookies and brownies are as good as homemade. They come in 8 different varieties, and customer favorites include Hunka Chunka, Sugar Momma, and Menage et Trois (white, milk, and dark chocolate chips in a chocolate cookie). The retail store is a great place to buy cookies by the pound or as gift packages, such as the Heartache Repair Kit for your friend who just got dumped. The store is open Monday to Friday.

REI
1405 W. Southern Ave., Tempe
(480) 967-5494
www.rei.com/stores/25

Recreational Equipment Inc. is the top stop for anyone preparing to explore Arizona's outdoors. The store carries equipment and related clothing for camping, cycling, climbing, hiking, and more. Staff members at the Tempe location are particularly helpful about Valley hikes, mountain biking hotspots, or day-drips to more rugged areas an hour or two out of town. If you want to try out a sport, you can rent equipment ranging from climbing shoes to kayaks. If you join the Seattle-based cooperative, you also get

dividends at the end of the year. The store has another location in Paradise Valley, at 12634 N. Paradise Village Pkwy. (602-996-5400). Open daily.

WIDE WORLD OF MAPS
1444 W. Southern Ave., Mesa
(602) 279-2323, (800) 279-2550
www.maps4u.com

This locally grown store carries just about any map your vagabond heart desires and is a vital stop for those who plan on hiking Arizona's rough terrain. If it doesn't carry what you need, Wide World of Maps can map it for you. Its inventory includes travel maps, guidebooks, cookbooks, books on local history, hiking books, topographical maps, atlases, globes, wall maps, CD-ROM maps, and the latest global positioning systems (GPS) and instruction on how to use them. The store also will laminate a map of your choice for maps that will be used a lot. There's another location at 2626 W. Indian School Rd. in Phoenix. The Mesa and Phoenix stores are open Monday to Saturday.

✳ZIA RECORD EXCHANGE
105 W. University Dr., Tempe
(480) 829-1967
www.ziarecords.com

Founded by Phoenix resident Brad Singer in the early 1980s, Zia has grown from a funky little place selling vinyl to a major Southwest music chain. The Tempe location is obviously a hub for Arizona State University students, many of whom are unsatisfied buying big mass-market CDs at nearly $20 a pop. Music lovers appreciate Zia's no-frills approach to providing the widest possible selection of new and used CDs and vintage vinyl. Imports are well represented here, and because the inventory is usually alphabetized without

regard to genre, it's possible to spy a CD by a country singer snuggled next to one by a heavy metal artist. The local music scene mourned Singer's sudden passing in May 1998, but the stores carried on his passion after his untimely death. Find other Zia locations in the Valley at 1940 W. Indian School Rd. in Phoenix (602-241-0313), 2510 W. Thunderbird Rd. in Phoenix (602-866-7867), and 1940 W. Chandler Blvd. in Chandler (480-857-4942). Each of the stores is open all week, mostly until late night.

NORTHEAST VALLEY

Shopping Malls

THE BORGATA
6166 N. Scottsdale Rd., Scottsdale
(602) 953-6538
www.borgata.com
You'll do a double take when you spy this replica of a 14th-century Italian village, complete with brick towers. The Borgata stands out in more than just architecture, though. It guards an elegant array of high-fashion boutiques, jewelry stores, art galleries, and outdoor bistros. The 30 stores include J. Alexander's; Fresh Produce; Femme De Paris; the immensely popular Dolce Salon and Spa; Baudine's for women's shoes and apparel; Saddlebags; Two Plates Full for home decor and gifts; and SLo Foods Organic Cafe. The Borgata's cobblestone courtyard is often transformed into high-end community events. The Christmas season brings an incredible display of twinkling white lights and other holiday decorations. The Borgata is open daily.

EL PEDREGAL AT THE BOULDERS
34505 N. Scottsdale Rd., Scottsdale
(480) 488-1072
www.elpedregal.com

With its Moroccan styling, El Pedregal Festival Marketplace harmonizes with its magnificent desert setting—rock-strewn terrain formed millions of years ago. Located where the new housing developments of north Scottsdale give way to the hills and boulders of Carefree, the shopping development is part of the Boulders resort, a short distance away by foot. More than 30 artisan shops and galleries cluster in this distinctive 2-level building, which overlooks a 1,200-square-foot Courtyard Stage amphitheater for live performances. The more than 125 galleries offer everything from local folk art to African sculpture. Other shops include Stefan Mann and Mila Lingerie Boutique. The Spotted Donkey Cantina serves Southwestern and Mexican specialties.

i When you're in Kierland Commons, don't miss Rock Star Gallery. If you have several thousand dollars, place a bid on an autographed Eric Clapton or Jerry Garcia guitar. If not, drop a bit less on signed photographs or sheet music. The collection is always impressive. The shop is located at 15220 N. Scottsdale Rd., Scottsdale (480-275-4501 or www.rockstargallery.net).

✳KIERLAND COMMONS
15205 N. Kierland Blvd., Scottsdale
(480) 348-1577
www.kierlandcommons.com
The popular shopping center is designed to look like an upscale version of Main Street in a small town, with a spacious plaza, shady trellised arcades, natural stone, and an abundance of flowers and trees. The 450,000-square-foot, mixed-use development is the first "urban village" center to be built in the Phoenix area. It's actually located

in Phoenix, though the location at Greenway Parkway and Scottsdale Road carries a Scottsdale address. Top shops include Restoration Hardware, Anthropologie, Banana Republic, Crate & Barrel, bebe, Bose, Coach, and Sur La Table, along with popular eateries like Zinc Bistro and Mastro's Ocean Club (see Restaurants chapter). Open daily.

✳SCOTTSDALE FASHION SQUARE
7014 E. Camelback Rd., Scottsdale
(480) 941-2140
www.fashionsquare.com
Once a tidy open-air shopping center serving Scottsdale residents, Scottsdale Fashion Square has transformed in the past decade into a nationally renowned ritzy mall that, at 1.8 million square feet, is the largest mall in Arizona. The mall attracts people from all over the Valley, mainly because of its mix of high-powered department stores and classy boutiques.

Scottsdale Fashion Square has Arizona's first Nordstrom and Neiman Marcus. Other anchors include Macy's, Barneys New York, and Dillard's (the largest in the entire national chain). There are 225 stores in all, of which 40 are exclusive stores. In fall 1998 Scottsdale Fashion Square finished construction of an enclosed bridge—filled with 50 stores—that connects Nordstrom on the south side of Camelback Road to the main mall on the north side of Camelback.

The ambience inside the 2-level mall makes for a true Scottsdale shopping experience. It mostly feels upscale, though there's something for everyone's price range. Palm trees tower nearly to the retractable glass ceiling. Fountains throughout the mall make Scottsdale seem more tropical than desert-like, including a 2-story "rain curtain" in the center of the food court, which wraps around an open stairway. The food court is one of the best in the Valley because of its wide selection—from burgers to international fare that includes French, Mexican, Chinese, and Japanese fast food. The numerous sit-down restaurants and cafes in the mall draw evening diners.

Stores include the famous New York jeweler Tiffany & Co., 2 Crate & Barrel sites, Michael Kors, Louis Vuitton, Coach, Guess, Puma, Jimmy Choo, and the Everything But Water swimsuit store.

Also find the Tourneau store that offers 100 brands of watches in thousands of styles, Victoria's Secret or Intimacy for lingerie, Lacoste, Godiva Chocolatier, Sephora, and Pottery Barn Kids. After a hard day of shopping, you can relax at the day spa at Nordstrom or Dillard's or catch a flick at one of the mall's 12 cinemas or a brew at the Yard House. Special services provided by the mall include lockers, stroller rental, valet parking, and a roving concierge. The mall is open daily.

> **i** If you need a little extra heat on your meal, try Southwest Specialty Food Inc., the West Valley-based company behind Whoop Ass hot sauces. The peanuts, popcorn, salsa, and other products sold around the Phoenix area are equally as "kick yo' ass hot" as the habanero pepper sauce. Information: www.asskickin.com.

SHOPS AT GAINEY VILLAGE
8787 N. Scottsdale Rd., Scottsdale
www.theshopsgaineyvillage.com
The Shops at Gainey Village, located on busy Scottsdale Road at Doubletree Ranch Road, are designed as a series of linked outdoor plazas and buildings reflecting an upscale

rustic "village" atmosphere reminiscent of the historic roots of the original Gainey Ranch. The Shops at Gainey Village combine a distinctive blend of upscale stores, boutiques, trendy eateries, and fine-dining establishments. Stores include Oak Creek with Southwestern art and gifts and Rolf's Salon & Spa. Hungry? The Village Tavern offers American fusion cuisine and popular cocktail deals. The bar is a major draw for local professionals who know it as the "Best Happy Hour in Town."

Shopping Districts

5TH AVENUE
Downtown Scottsdale
www.scottsdale5thave.org
A number of shopping districts thrive in downtown Scottsdale, each with its own special personality and charm. The merchants of 5th Avenue cater to tourists and locals alike with a plethora of boutiques and art galleries, many with merchandise unique to the Southwest. The 5th Avenue shops run along 3 blocks of mostly shaded walkways; the fountain with 4 horses near the center of activity makes a prominent landmark. Shops line both sides of the street, and it's worthwhile to explore the establishments on 3rd Avenue, Stetson Drive, Marshall Way, Craftsman Court, and Main Street. The shops are interspersed with many top-notch art galleries for which Scottsdale is famous. (See The Arts chapter for more information.)

Here are a few stops along the way to keep in mind as you browse. Kactus Jock, at 7121 E. 5th Ave., features sportswear made from natural fiber. Southwestern gifts can be found at Fifth Avenue Trading Post, 7090 E. 5th Ave. Angel Wings & Other Things is an angel-themed gift shop at 7121 E. 5th Ave.

i 5th Avenue merchants host a Thieves Market twice a year to sell end-of-the-season items for up to 70 percent off. There's no sale like it. This is Scottsdale, people. Don't expect too much of a reduced rate. Information: www.scottsdale5thave.org.

MAIN STREET
West Main Street, downtown Scottsdale
www.downtownscottsdale.com
The art gallery strip along West Main Street in Scottsdale boasts outstanding collections of *objets d'art* and antiques. We'll explore the area's reputation more thoroughly in the chapter on The Arts, but note that masterpieces by many of the Old Western masters are represented here, as well as works by folk artists, Native American artists, and contemporary artists. Guidon Books, now located at 7109 E. 2nd St. 2 blocks off Main Street, features a serious collection of antique Western and Civil War books as well as collectible posters and maps. Turkey Mountain Traders, at 7008 E. Main St., specializes in antique Native American artwork. Arizona West Galleries, at 7149 E. Main St., offers an amazing collection of Western antiques and cowboy collectibles.

MARSHALL WAY ARTS DISTRICT
Downtown Scottsdale
www.downtownscottsdale.com
The Marshall Way Arts District—between Craftsman Court and 3rd Avenue west of Scottsdale Road and north of Indian School Road—is an art lover's heaven. The galleries feature a diversity of media, from limited-edition prints to art you can wear, all in a tree-shaded, upscale setting. Many internationally recognized artists have displayed their work here. If you are looking for distinctive jewelry, you might want to check out

SHOPPING

Jewelry by Gauthier, at 4211 N. Marshall Way, and Art One Gallery, at 4120 N. Marshall Way, which represents artwork from students at Arizona colleges and universities. If you get an urge to be creative yourself—or want to pen a perfectly elegant description of your travels to someone you left behind—stop by the Paper Place for fine stationary and writing instruments at 4130 N. Marshall Way.

OLD TOWN
Downtown Scottsdale
www.downtownscottsdale.com
Old Town Scottsdale encompasses many of the city's oldest buildings in about 4 blocks around Main Street and Brown Avenue. The historic shopping district, with more than 150 stores, begins at the corner of Scottsdale Road and Main Street and fans out a couple of blocks to the east and north. Across Scottsdale Road to the west are the 5th Avenue shops, another fun shopping district mentioned earlier. Between the two, you are sure to find the perfect memento of your trip to this area or the perfect gift for a friend or relative.

A few Old Town Scottsdale shops to explore include Saba's Western Store, at 3965 N. Brown Ave., which has been outfitting cowboys and cowgirls since 1927, and Bischoff's Shades of the West, 7247 E. Main St., for everything from local hot sauce to Southwestern decorations. The classic Rusty Spur Saloon, 7245 E. Main St., makes for the perfect pit stop to suck down a cold beer and enjoy some live guitar music out of the sun.

SCOTTSDALE PAVILIONS
9175 E. Indian Bend Rd., Scottsdale
(480) 834-8500
www.thepavilionsattalkingstick.com
The Pavilions, run by the neighboring Salt River Pima-Maricopa Indian Community, has

such a good selection of stores that it has stayed a popular destination since it opened more than a decade ago. In the past few years, the upgrades have included revamped restaurants, shops, and hangouts around Salt River Fields, the new Cactus League complex of the Arizona Diamondbacks and Colorado Rockies. The field opened in 2011 to sellout crowds that will surely continue each March as more baseball fans make the Pavilions a destination point. The open-air mall combines large, freestanding stores flanked by smaller stores, all on both sides of Indian Bend Road. Best Buy, Target, and Home Depot are some of the bigger retailers. New or updated places within walking distance to the ballpark include YC's Mongolian BBQ and Ultra-Star Cinema. Most of the stores and entertainment venues are open daily.

SCOTTSDALE SEVILLE
7001 N. Scottsdale Rd., Scottsdale
(480) 998-4774
www.scottsdaleseville.com
This pastel-colored, Southwestern-style shopping center has several high-end boutiques, including Draper's and Damon's and the Leopard Spot. Home decor shops include Azadi for fine rugs and Distinctive Interiors & Design. Here you'll also find a selection of good restaurants, including Ruth's Chris Steak House. Enjoy the day and a cocktail or coffee at any of the several other eateries. Most stores are open daily at the center near Indian Bend Road.

Specialty Stores

CHIEF DODGE INDIAN JEWELRY & FINE ARTS
1332 N. Scottsdale Rd., Scottsdale
(480) 970-1133, (800) 553-5604
www.chiefdodge.com

For more than 30 years, the family-run establishment at Papago Plaza in south Scottsdale has offered a wide selection of Native American arts and crafts, allowing customers to buy directly from the artisans for a significant savings. Turquoise jewelry is abundant here, as are crafts such as Navajo kachina dolls, sand paintings, pottery, and baskets.

JACADI-PARIS
15024 N. Scottsdale Rd., Scottsdale
(480) 443-3921
www.jacadi.us
Jacadi-Paris, located in Kierland Commons, is an upscale children's boutique where shoppers can find clothing, shoes, and nursery items. As the name implies, the store has roots in Paris, and styles have a European flair. The core belief is that introducing a child to fashion is a way of teaching good taste, so attention to detail is paramount here. Don't even think about wash-and-wear.

POISONED PEN BOOKSTORE
4014 N. Goldwater Blvd., Scottsdale
(480) 947-2974
www.poisonedpen.com
It's no mystery where book lovers go to buy their favorite whodunits. The Poisoned Pen is one of the largest mystery bookstores in the country. In business for more than a decade, the store not only tallies more than 12,000 titles, but it brings in top-rated mystery writers for book signings, hosts book clubs, and even runs its own Poisoned Fiction Review blog.

i After all that shopping, you'll need to cool off. Head over to the Sugar Bowl ice cream parlor at 4005 N. Scottsdale Rd. (480-946-0051). Order a chocolate milkshake or a hot fudge sundae at the classic soda-jerk style counter 7 days a week.

SMOCA STORE
Scottsdale Museum of Contemporary Art
7374 E. 2nd St., Scottsdale
(480) 874-4666
www.smoca.org
Art books, gifts, and other items purchased from the SMoCA store in the heart of Scottsdale's arts center, near the city's Civic Center, help fund the museum's programs. Voted "Best Museum Shop" by Valley publications, its eclectic assortment of eye-popping home accessories, jewelry, art, T-shirts, and educational (but fun) toys should please just about anybody on your shopping list. Many of the works are handmade by local artists.

SPHINX RANCH GOURMET MARKET
3039 N. Scottsdale Rd., Scottsdale
(800) 482-3283
www.sphinxdateranch.com
Date farming is quite successful in Arizona, and Sphinx Ranch has one of the best reputations in the state. Personnel offer samples of several plump date varieties to help you make your choice. Other products, such as cactus jellies and locally made candies, are also available. But the date milkshakes are a flavorful way to cool down in the summer. The store occupies the original home on the date ranch, though the dates come from local farms.

NORTHWEST VALLEY

Shopping Malls

ARROWHEAD TOWNE CENTER
7700 W. Arrowhead Towne Center, Glendale
(623) 979-8928
www.arrowheadtownecenter.com
Arrowhead Towne Center serves Glendale, Peoria, the Sun Cities, and other parts of

northwest Phoenix. Dillard's, Macy's, Sears, and JCPenney anchor the mall, a high-tech-looking, steel interior featuring a profusion of plants, skylights, and benches. Stores include Dick's Sporting Goods, Forever 21, Coldwater Creek, Lane Bryant, Victoria's Secret, the Children's Place, Disney Store, GNC, Gymboree, and Kitchen Gourmet. In addition to the 170 stores, shoppers can enjoy an outdoor amphitheater, multiple restaurants in the food court, and a movie theater. Nearby are the 4,500-acre master-planned community of Arrowhead Ranch and the Peoria Sports Complex, spring training headquarters for the Seattle Mariners and the San Diego Padres. There are plenty of bars and restaurants in the plazas around 75th Avenue and Bell Road near the mall.

✳WESTGATE CITY CENTER
6770 N. Sunrise Blvd., Glendale
(623) 772-4000
www.westgateaz.com

It's hard to imagine Westgate City Center used to be miles of flat farmland. Now it's a shopping center, a dining spot, and a place to visit before or after a sporting event. Westgate is home to the Phoenix Coyotes at Jobing.com Arena, site of some of the Valley's biggest concerts, and the Arizona Cardinals at University of Phoenix Stadium. The sports venues are a quick walk to restaurants, theaters, and lots of shopping right off the Loop 101. Here you'll find the Body Shop, Quiksilver, Fossil, and Ridemakerz custom toy cars. Diners can lift a cocktail glass at Margaritaville, cool down at Ocean Blue Frozen Yogurt, or grab lunch at Moe's Southwest Grill or

Shane's Rib Shack. Westgate also hosts a Saturday farmers' market October to May.

Antiques Shopping

HISTORIC DOWNTOWN GLENDALE
Vicinity of 59th and Glendale Avenues, Glendale
www.historic-glendale.net

The historic core of the Northwest Valley was named by *USA Today* as one of the top antiques destinations in the country. With its restored bungalows and white picket fences, Glendale's pedestrian-friendly downtown appears to have sprung from a Norman Rockwell painting. You can find dozens of antiques stores in the 16-square-block area. Shops that feature antiques, crafts, tearooms, and even a candy factory are often housed in carefully restored buildings from the early part of the last century. You'll see streets lined with old-fashioned storefronts, streetlights, and park benches in Old Towne and the Historic Catlin Court shopping districts. Old Towne surrounds historic Murphy Park.

Many of the stores are open 7 days a week, but it's best to call ahead if you're interested in a particular store. Though the stores are too numerous to name, a few of the approximately 100 antiques and specialty shops include The Apple Tree, 5811 W. Glendale Ave. (623-435-8486), with one of the larger selections of antiques and collectibles; A Mad Hatter's Antiques, 5734 W. Glendale Ave. (623-931-1991), with vintage toys, dolls, coins, advertising art, and folk art; and Coury House Shoppes, 5802 W. Palmaire Ave. (623-435-1522), with fine used and out-of-print books.

ATTRACTIONS

A rizona is a place where the ancient world meets the modern. Classic museums like the Heard Museum in downtown Phoenix and Deer Valley Rock Art Center provide a look at the culture and sacred art of the Valley's first settlers. Ruins on the outskirts of town at Casa Grande and Montezuma's Castle give you a glimpse of life before American settlers arrived from the East. The Valley also has its share of modern art and science museums—enough, if fact, that you can easily fill a week's stay. Unique spots like the Desert Botanical Garden at Papago Park, the hiking trails in the mountain preserve areas around the city, and the family-oriented Old West features at Rawhide draw as many locals as they do tourists.

Museums range from the Arizona Science Center to the Phoenix Art Museum. Districts like Old Town Scottsdale and Papago Park provide enough destination spots in themselves to take up entire days. Keep in mind that most of the year the weather is so gorgeous that walking around outdoors is a primary draw when you're not sitting by the pool.

Think about maximizing your time here by seeing multiple attractions in a day. For example, a hike in the Superstition Mountains in the Southeast Valley is easily followed by a stop at nearby Goldfield Ghost Town. A hike through the red rock buttes of Papago Park is paired nicely with a stop at Phoenix Zoo. Stop at the Pioneer Living History Museum in north Phoenix on the way to or from Out of Africa wildlife park in Camp Verde.

See the Parks & Recreation chapter for more ideas on how to enjoy the Arizona outdoors. The Kidstuff chapter will give you a child's-eye view of our best museums and other attractions. Browse The Arts chapter if you'd like to take in some additional culture while you're here. The Day Trips chapter also offers more ideas if you want to shoot up to the high country or down to the Old Pueblo of Tucson.

Price Code

With each attraction listed in this chapter you will find a pricing guide ranging from one to four dollar signs. The code is based on a single adult admission. Some admissions vary; for example, if there are a basic admission and a deluxe admission, there may be a range of price codes. If there is no dollar sign, the attraction has no entry fee.

$	Less than $5
$$	$5 to $10
$$$	$10 to $15
$$$$	More than $15

PHOENIX

✳ARIZONA SCIENCE CENTER $$$
600 E. Washington St.
(602) 716-2000
www.azscience.org

With about 300 interactive exhibits to explore, plus a giant-screen theater and planetarium, you could spend an entire day at the Arizona Science Center. It has exceeded attendance expectations since opening in 1997 and continues to draw children and adults alike. Phoenix leaders rightfully consider the futuristic 4-story structure a major factor in the resurgence of downtown. Rising into the sky is a 9-story triangular peak, also called a fin, covered with aluminum.

The planetarium at the Science Center has undergone major renovations and has a new "seamless" dome—the first in the world. The Irene P. Flinn Theater has a 3D-capable IMAX theater.

The exhibits are cleverly organized into galleries that explore human physiology, physical forces, transportation, geology, technology, and applied sciences. Almost all the exhibits are hands-on, which is what makes the center so absorbing. You can slide through a human being's innards in the All About Me gallery, learning about the body's many unseen functions, or better understand the benefits of green energy in the APS Solar Gallery.

Make time to check out the nifty games, puzzles, posters, books, and other gifts in Awesome Atoms. The cafes of Heritage Square are just next door, and others on the west side of downtown are blocks away.

Admission is $12 for adults and $10 for seniors and children 3 to 17. Tickets combining the exhibits and admission to the IMAX theater and/or planetarium are more expensive.

ARIZONA STATE CAPITOL MUSEUM & WESLEY BOLIN MEMORIAL PLAZA
1700 W. Washington St.
(602) 926-3620
www.lib.az.us/museum

As capitols go, Arizona's is a fairly modest granite building with a striking copper dome. The white winged figure atop the dome is called Victory Lady. The Capitol Museum is made up of all 4 floors of the original capitol building, which dates from 1900. In fact, it was built 12 years before Arizona became a state. The Arizona Legislature, having outgrown the building in 1960, meets in newer quarters behind the capitol. Stroll through the capitol to see various murals executed over the decades to depict Arizona's history and scenery and its progress as a state. Also view the old House chambers, historical photos, and a statue of the state's first governor, George W. P. Hunt. More sights can be found on the capitol grounds and the adjoining Wesley Bolin Plaza, a grassy, 2-block area of sculptures and monuments. It is named after a former Arizona governor. On the eastern end of the plaza rests an anchor from the USS *Arizona*, sunk during the Japanese raid on Pearl Harbor in 1941. The anchor serves as a memorial to those who died aboard the battleship. You'll also find memorials to veterans of just about every recent war, including the Korean and Vietnam Wars as well as Desert Storm. The plaza is accessible during daytime hours. Admission is free. Call to inquire about guided tours, which are given twice daily, usually at 10 a.m. and 2 p.m.

BURTON BARR CENTRAL LIBRARY
1221 N. Central Ave.
(602) 262-4636
www.phoenixpubliclibrary.org

Several major metropolitan libraries with architectural significance have been built since 1990, and Phoenix's central library is one of them. Opened in 1995, the 5-story, multimillion-dollar structure was paid for through a city bond election for arts and cultural improvements. Residents looked at its simple exterior of corrugated copper and gray concrete and either loved it or hated it. Then, slowly but surely, the public trickled in, and by viewing it more closely, they began to understand the concept behind local architect Will Bruder's organic design. It is a design inspired by the majesty of Arizona's many copper-colored mesas and rugged gray canyons, and it skillfully uses natural light in opposition to the notion that public libraries have to be dark and stuffy. The north side of the building has computer-controlled shades, or "sails," outside the windows that rotate and adjust to let in the right amount of light according to the time of day. This makes it one of the most energy-efficient buildings in a state where wasteful construction methods are still the norm. Another remarkable feature is the main entry, where a glass elevator swooshes up and down the 5 floors while reflecting colored lights into the pool below it. The Great Reading Room on the top floor is considered the largest such room in North America.

The Phoenix library system celebrated its 100th anniversary in 1998 and has grown to 15 branches in addition to the new Burton Barr library, named for a longtime Arizona legislator. It replaces the old central library at McDowell Road and Central Avenue. The new library includes a good children's area, the Rare Book Room, and the Arizona Room, with resources on the history of the Southwest. This library offers free Wi-Fi.

CITYSCAPE
1 E. Washington St.
www.cityscapephoenix.com

As downtown Phoenix evolves, CityScape will be a destination point and revenue-generating tool for the city. The $900 million, modern mixed-use complex at Washington Street and Central Avenue opened in 2010. Since then, more downtown residents and tourists have found their way to the Lucky Strike Lanes bowling alley, to Stand Up Live comedy club, to lunch spots like Five Guys Burgers and Fries, and restaurants like The Arrogant Butcher. By 2011 planners hoped to lock down even more eateries. Downtown residents and students who live at Arizona State University's downtown dorms were thrilled at the opening of the CVS drug store. The upscale Oakville Grocery also gives downtown folks another option than Circle K or the big supermarkets miles away. CityScape is a comfortable place to sip a coffee and chill out in the urban wilderness. But it's also a place envisioned for big events. The opening weekend in 2010 featured free block-party concerts by Macy Gray and Third Eye Blind.

DEER VALLEY ROCK ART CENTER $$
3711 W. Deer Valley Rd.
(623) 582-8007
http://dvrac.asu.edu

The Deer Valley Rock Art Center serves as a sanctuary for the 1,500 ancient petroglyphs to be found on this 47-acre desert preserve. Operated by the Arizona State University School of Human Evolution and Social Change, it provides public access to the Hedgpeth Hills petroglyph site via a quarter-mile nature trail. Signs along the way help interpret what you're seeing. You'll come away with a better understanding of

the cultures that made the rock art—the Hohokam and Patayan who inhabited the area from A.D. 300 to 1450. Morning viewing is recommended. The visitor center has various exhibits, a video room, and a gift shop. Admission is $7 adults, $4 students and seniors, $3 for ages 6 to 12, and free for children younger than 6.

*DESERT BOTANICAL GARDEN $$$
Papago Park
1201 N. Galvin Pkwy.
(480) 941-1225
www.dbg.org

There's no better place to see the Sonoran Desert in full, colorful bloom than the Desert Botanical Garden. It is one of the nation's few public gardens dedicated to desert plants. Its winding trails pleasantly take you through veritable forests and introduce you to 4,000 species of cacti, succulents, trees, and flowers. In spring, native wildflowers are also in bloom.

The garden opened in 1939 as both a showcase and conservation headquarters. Today its collection includes several rare, threatened, and endangered Southwestern species in addition to common plants. After a leisurely morning or afternoon in the garden, you will be able to recognize and reel off names of flora such as the ocotillo, the jumping cholla, desert marigolds, the creosote bush, the palo verde tree, the yucca plant, and more. Each trail has signage not only bearing the names but also explaining the plants' hardiness and desert life in general. Often you will find garden volunteers at information stations displaying specimens you can touch.

The garden is organized around multiple trails. They explain how desert plants are used for food, fibers, and construction. The Sonoran Desert Nature Loop Trail is a quarter-mile hillside trail focusing on the interactions among plants, birds, reptiles, insects, and mammals sharing the desert. The Desert Discovery Loop Trail features thousands of desert plants from around the world. On the trail are the Cactus and Succulent galleries, which showcase plants inside greenhouses. At the garden you'll find a visitor center, a gift shop, a cafe, and a plant shop, which has a wonderful selection of plants to buy—instructions included. Also on the grounds is Webster Auditorium, one of the few remaining authentic examples of Pueblo Revival architecture in central Arizona.

Online admission is $15 for adults, $13.50 for seniors, $7.50 for students, $5 for children ages 3 to 12, and free for those younger than 3. The garden frequently offers guided tours, schedules outdoor concerts, and hosts other nature events or art exhibitions; more information is available on the garden hotline, (480) 941-1217.

HALL OF FLAME MUSEUM OF
FIREFIGHTING $$
6101 E. Van Buren St.
(602) 275-3473
www.hallofflame.org

The Hall of Flame houses almost 100 restored pieces of hand-to-hand, horse-drawn, and mechanized firefighting equipment dating from 1725 to 1961. The collection includes several well-preserved fire engines, including a fire truck that is safe for children to climb into and pretend to drive. Wannabe firefighters can dress up in coats, helmets, and other gear, or simply browse the galleries to learn more about the lifesaving profession. There's a gallery devoted to helmets, an area showing more than 2,000 fire department badges, fire safety exhibits, a

game area, and an art gallery of firefighting-related scenes. Admission is $6 for adults, $5 for seniors, $4 for children 6 to 17, $1.50 for children 3 to 5, and free for children younger than 3. There's plenty of free parking.

HEARD MUSEUM $$$
2301 N. Central Ave.
(602) 252-8848
www.heard.org

The popular cultural center has an internationally renowned collection of Native American fine arts and crafts with an emphasis on the indigenous peoples of the Southwest. It was one of the first true cultural attractions in Phoenix. The more than 32,000 works of art and ethnographic objects span several centuries and are handsomely and informatively displayed. All exhibits are presented with a quiet reverence for Native American ways of life.

The Heard Museum was founded in 1929 by Dwight B. and Maie Bartlett Heard, a prominent Phoenix couple who moved to the Valley from Chicago in the mid-1880s. The Heards were avid collectors of Native American artifacts and art, especially those of Southwestern cultures. Their decision to build a museum to share their exemplary collection was visionary. Today the Heard Museum annually attracts 250,000 visitors from all over the world. It has outgrown its original building—of charming Spanish colonial-style design—and has completed a multimillion-dollar expansion, adding 3 new galleries, a new auditorium for performances of Native American dance and music, and an Education Pavilion, among other things.

Visitors should spend time at Native People in the Southwest, the Heard's permanent exhibit chronicling the cultures of a number of tribes through art, artifacts, maps,

information boards, and videos. Also see the Barry Goldwater collection of 437 historic Hopi kachina dolls. Other galleries concentrate on jewelry, contemporary paintings, prints, and sculptures by Native Americans.

The Heard Museum shops showcase Native American jewelry, textiles, pottery, and kachina dolls for sale. If you are a serious collector of Native American art, this is your place. The staff is knowledgeable about the things they sell and can often point you to the finer pieces.

See the Annual Events chapter for special events at the Heard, such as the World Championship Hoop Dance Contest, the Guild Indian Fair & Market, demonstrations of traditional Navajo weaving, and other events.

The Heard is located a half-mile north of Phoenix Art Museum, 4 blocks north of McDowell Road, right on the light rail line. Admission is $15 for adults, $13.50 for seniors, $7.50 for students and children 6 to 12, and free for children younger than 6. For questions, call the recorded information line at (602) 252-8848.

HERITAGE SQUARE $–$$
115 N. 6th St.
(602) 262-5071
www.phoenix.gov/PARKS/heritage.html

Heritage Square is a cherished city block that contains the only remaining residential structures from the original town site of Phoenix. Listed on the National Register of Historic Places, it's a grouping of eight restored Victorian houses in a pedestrian-only enclave. You can find it in the shadow of the Arizona Science Center and Chase Field.

The most eye-catching is the Rosson House, built in 1895, with its expansive

veranda and an octagonal gray turret topped by an elaborate finial. The Rosson House's 10 rooms feature pressed-tin ceilings and parquet floors. Tucked next to it is the Forest's Carriage House, which serves as the ticket office and gift shop. The charge for guided tours is $7.50 for adults, $6 for seniors and students, $4 for children 6 to 12, and free for children younger than 6.

The Arizona Doll & Toy Museum is inside the Stevens House. It showcases antique and modern dolls, dollhouses, and toys. An authentic-looking 1912 schoolroom features antique dolls propped in desks like students. Admission is only a few dollars.

Heritage Square also features the Teeter House, now home to the Nobuo Asian-style teahouse; the Silva House, now home to the Rose and Crown English pub; the Lath House Pavilion, erected in 1980 to facilitate the many outdoor festivals and markets held at Heritage Square; the Duplex, a small house that serves as city offices; and the Baird Machine Shop, dating from 1929 and now home of Pizzeria Bianco (see the Restaurants chapter for details on what many consider the best pizza joint in the US).

i The Tovrea Castle, built more than 80 years ago, was originally intended to be a European-style grand hotel. The city of Phoenix recently restored the little chateau, noticeable from the Loop 202 freeway. It's impossible to miss the castle that resembles a 3-tiered wedding cake sitting in the middle of the cactus grove.

MUSICAL INSTRUMENT MUSEUM $$
4725 E. Mayo Blvd.
(480) 478-6000
www.themim.org

The latest addition to the Valley's museum scene is located just west of Scottsdale Road in north Phoenix. With a collection of 12,000 musical instruments and other items from around the world, there is plenty to gawk at, including Eric Clapton's guitar and the Steinway piano that helped John Lennon create "Imagine."

The MIM is set in a gorgeous, modern 192,000-square-foot facility built through a $250 million project. The galleries are filled with natural light, almost urging you to pick up an instrument and begin writing a song. The museum is a hub of world music education and hosts performances in its theater. Performers during the inaugural 2010 season came from Sierra Leone, China, Israel, and other countries. The MIM's spacious design by award-winning architects features 2 floors of galleries, a recording studio, a classroom for demonstrations, a cafe, and a coffee shop.

The 450-foot river-like corridor called El Rio connects the various exhibits, which range from mechanical music of the early 20th century to the hands-on Experience Gallery where guests can pluck and strum versions of the instruments displayed in the galleries.

MYSTERY CASTLE $
800 E. Mineral Rd.
(602) 268-1581

Built in 1930 in the foothills of South Mountain Park, Mystery Castle has been open for public tours ever since a 1948 *Life* magazine article put it on the map. The 8,000-square-foot castle, made from recycled bottles, old bricks, and other random materials, was built by an eccentric father as an act of love for his young daughter. It has 18 rooms and 13 fireplaces. The daughter, Mary Lou Gulley, still

lives there and conducts tours from 11 a.m. to 4 p.m. Thurs to Sun. The admission gate closes at 3 p.m. sharp. The castle is closed from July to September. Admission is $5 for adults, $3 for children ages 6 to 15, and free for children younger than 6.

PHOENIX ART MUSEUM $$
1625 N. Central Ave.
(602) 257-1222
www.phxart.org

The central Phoenix museum has generated more buzz in recent years with its permanent collection of 17,000 works, which span several centuries and represent many artistic styles and media. Curators have also secured traveling exhibits of works by world-renowned artists like photographer Ansel Adams and impressionist Claude Monet. The museum officially opened in 1959, although it had thrived as a small community arts center for two decades before that. By the 1980s the museum began to outgrow its space, but in 2006 a $50 million expansion helped quite a bit. The museum features 11 collections, including Western American Galleries (which features works by Georgia O'Keeffe), a fashion design collection, contemporary art, classic European works, and Latin American artists.

Admission is $10 for adults, $8 for seniors and students, $4 for children ages 6 to 17, and free for children younger than 6. Admission is free 3 to 9 p.m. Wed.

PHOENIX ZOO $$$$
Papago Park
455 N. Galvin Pkwy.
(602) 273-1341
www.phoenixzoo.org

A little-known fact about the Phoenix Zoo: At 125 acres and 1,300 animals, it is the largest privately owned nonprofit zoo in the nation. Open since 1962, it is also internationally known for its efforts on behalf of saving endangered species. For instance, a zoo breeding and redistribution project begun in 1963 has increased the number of the Arabian oryx—a type of antelope—from 9 to its present world population of about 1,100.

Set among the rolling hills, cactus, and red rocks of Papago Park, the Phoenix Zoo draws about 1.5 million visitors a year. Some Valley families visit the zoo several times a year. Exhibits and events are continually being updated. They include recent showcases on Komodo dragons and koalas, and the "Rock the Zoo" 80s-themed musical tour. The zoo specializes in animals that enjoy warm climates. Exhibit spaces closely resemble the animals' natural habitats. You can see how the spaces change as you move along the zoo's 4 distinct trails: the Tropics Trail, which is great for bird-watching; the Africa Trail, with lions, tigers, and elephants; the Children's Trail and Harmony Farm, featuring the Wallaby Walkabout, farm animals and farm equipment, a small butterfly garden, and playground; and the Arizona Trail, a must-see for out-of-state visitors. Here you can view Mexican wolves, coyotes, desert birds, bats, and a spine-tingling array of snakes, scorpions, and other small creatures.

The Safari Train is a popular way to tour the zoo. It offers a 25-minute narrated tour by open-air bus. The zoo hosts special shows, guided walks, and classes year-round. Ask about the day's events at the gate. If you're visiting in the summer, it's best to arrive early in the morning before the animals take an afternoon siesta.

Admission is $18 for adults, $9 for children 3 to 12, and free for those 2 and younger. The Safari Train costs extra. Check

our Annual Events chapter for details on ZooLights at holiday time.

PIONEER LIVING HISTORY MUSEUM $$
3901 W. Pioneer Rd.
(623) 465-1052
www.pioneeraz.org

A mix of authentic buildings and historically accurate reproductions, Pioneer Arizona immerses you in life in the territory at the turn of the 20th century. Its 90 acres feature an 1880s schoolhouse, an 1890s exhibition hall and dress shop, and an 1870s opera house. A stroll down the dusty streets will also lead you to a blacksmith shop, sheriff's office and jail, church, ranch complex, and other buildings. Be sure to sling open the swinging doors of the Whiskey Road to Ruin Saloon, dating from the mid-1800s. Some of the buildings were moved to the museum from other parts of Arizona, and some were constructed using building plans of the time. Adding to your visit will be the many costumed interpreters, including cowboys, lawmen, and Victorian ladies. The actors demonstrate crafts and stage melodramas. Pioneer Arizona is said to be the largest living-history museum west of the Rockies. It is about 30 minutes north of central Phoenix, just off I-17 at the Pioneer Road exit. Admission is $7 for adults, $6 for seniors, $5 for students and children, and free for those younger than 5.

PUEBLO GRANDE MUSEUM
  ARCHAEOLOGICAL PARK   **$$**
4619 E. Washington St.
(602) 495-0901
www.pueblogrande.com

Whenever we modern-day residents need a reminder that we were not the first to civilize this desert valley, we head over to Pueblo Grande. There we can learn to understand and appreciate the world of the Hohokam Indians, who flourished in this area for several centuries before mysteriously disappearing in the mid-15th century. Visitors learn about the Hohokam's many crops, their extensive canal system for irrigation, their use of adobe construction, and their arts and crafts. Most important, once you've seen the indoor exhibits, you'll follow trails around the actual ruins of a Hohokam village unearthed by archaeologists. The Pueblo Grande also has an excellent gift shop with Native American arts and crafts. Admission is $6 for adults, $5 for seniors, $3 for children, and free for kids younger than 6.

i Stay in the NOW on your smart phone with the Greater Phoenix Convention & Visitors Bureau's blog, The Hot Sheet. It breaks down new restaurants, upcoming events, shopping deals, and more info from travelers. Go to www.thehotsheetblog.com.

SOUTHEAST VALLEY

DOWNTOWN TEMPE
Tempe Convention & Visitors Bureau
51 W. 3rd St., Tempe
(480) 894-8158, (800) 283-6734

The downtown area near Arizona State University blends coffeehouses, nightclubs, trendy restaurants, boutiques, bookstores, offbeat little stores, and office towers, primarily concentrated on Mill Avenue. All this activity makes for a thriving community of students, workers, and tourists who take to the streets all day and into the evening. In fact, downtown Tempe is bustling with nightlife, especially on weekends. But there's also a historic side to Tempe. Several

brick buildings built in Victorian or Spanish colonial revival styles have been preserved, and new construction does a good job of harmonizing with them. A walking tour should include stops at the Hayden Flour Mill, recognizable by its 4 silos; Monti's La Casa Vieja Steakhouse, the former home of Charles Hayden, founder of Tempe; Tempe City Hall, a modern, upside-down pyramid of glass and steel; the Andre Building, one of the city's best examples of preservation; and the Laird and Dines Building, a Tempe landmark that now incorporates restaurants, shops, and bars. On the way in or out of town, notice the Old Mill Avenue Bridge, dating from the 1930s.

GOLDFIELD GHOST TOWN
4650 N. Mammoth Mine Rd., Apache Junction
(480) 983-0333 •
www.goldfieldghosttown.com
Goldfield was a booming town back in the 1890s, thanks to a gold strike at the base of the Superstition Mountains. For 5 years, millions of dollars worth of high-grade ore was excavated by eager miners who dreamed of striking it rich. In Goldfield's heyday it boasted a hotel, boardinghouse, and 3 saloons. The boom went bust, of course. Now, as a tourist attraction, Goldfield offers mine tours, gold panning, a nature trail, and exhibits of antique mining equipment. It is also the site of Arizona's only operating narrow-gauge railroad, which takes you on a short scenic tour of the town. The town's Main Street has a steakhouse/saloon, an ice cream parlor, and several shops to find an Arizona memento. If you're there on a weekend, you might catch a gunfight (staged, of course). From Apache Junction in the far East Valley, Goldfield can be reached by driving

north on Apache Trail (AZ 88). Admission is free, with mine tours and other attractions priced individually.

THE MUSEUM AT PAPAGO PARK $
1300 N. College Ave., Tempe
(480) 929-9499
www.arizonahistoricalsociety.org/ museums/tempe.asp
The Arizona Historical Society's museum on the Tempe side of Papago Park opened in 1996. Exhibits include multimedia maps, historic photographs, and a few hands-on exhibits looking at the agriculture, mining, and urban development of central Arizona in the 19th and 20th centuries. One gallery focuses on World War II and its impact on the Valley, including personal letters and photographs from participants in the war effort. A new exhibit through March 2013 provides a history of Cactus League baseball. Admission is $5 for adults, $4 for seniors and students; children under 12 are free. There's free admission the first Saturday each month.

NORTHEAST VALLEY

CAREFREE/CAVE CREEK
Carefree/Cave Creek Chamber of Commerce
748 Easy St., Carefree
(480) 488-3381
www.carefree-cavecreek.com
These two neighboring communities south of Tonto National Forest make for fun excursions because of their scenic surroundings, boutiques, Western shops, and easygoing ambience. The half-hour drive from Scottsdale is pleasant in itself. Head north on Scottsdale Road, and you'll see how acres of new development are interspersed with stretches of unspoiled desert. The McDowell

Mountains draw your eye to the east, and the northern view spotlights the hills of the national forest. Several miles of Scottsdale Road north of Scottsdale have been designated the Desert Foothills Scenic Drive, and small signs tell you the names of the various desert plants that flourish in the area.

Using this route you'll reach Carefree first. The planned community was founded in 1956, and today it's dotted with expensive hillside homes. The world-class Boulders Resort is in Carefree, as is the upscale boutique/art gallery enclave called El Pedregal Marketplace. Several boutiques and galleries are in the town center, along with the K.T. Palmer Sundial, one of the largest sundials in the world. In tune with the town name, Carefree has fun with street names. Walk along Ho and Hum roads, for instance, or Easy Street.

Find neighboring Cave Creek by following the signs that point west to Cave Creek Road. You'll know you're there when you start to see storefronts and restaurants that hark back to the Old West, motorcycle enthusiasts, and bohemian artists. Modern residential development is springing up all around Cave Creek, though town center is able to retain its traditional character. Like Carefree, it's a fun place for souvenir shopping and antiques hunting. Take a break at one of the saloons on Cave Creek Road before heading back to the metropolis.

COSANTI
**6433 E. Doubletree Ranch Rd.,
Paradise Valley
(480) 948-6145
www.arcosanti.org/expCosanti**

Paolo Soleri's Cosanti foundry in Paradise Valley allows visitors a chance to see Soleri's trademark ceramic and bronze wind bells

made on site, cast from the elements and forged in fire. Soleri, a Frank Lloyd Wright apprentice who built the Arcosanti colony in northern Arizona (detailed in the Day Trips chapter), established the foundry in 1956. It looks the same way it did decades ago, a place that seems both futuristic and historically familiar. It has a very organic vibe. Soleri designed the domed apses, which the artisans sit beneath in the shade to shape and cast the bells.

Cosanti bells make ideal gifts. If cowboys, Indians, salsa, or scorpion-embedded paperweights won't cut it, this is definitely worth a stop. Each bell is a colorful piece of original Arizona artwork, beautifully wrapped and boxed for a gift. Cosanti bells range from $30 to $850; proceeds help to complete Arcosanti. There are no set tours at Cosanti, but you have the chance to walk the grounds and see the bells being cast. Apprentices working on site are happy to explain Soleri's history, his place in Arizona, and his philosophies on art and sustainable living.

i The Scottsdale Convention & Visitors Bureau website has a live chat feature, so you can ask questions before you visit. Go to www.scottsdale cvb.com. Click on "Contact."

✳**DOWNTOWN SCOTTSDALE**
**Scottsdale Convention & Visitors Bureau
4343 N. Scottsdale Rd., Scottsdale
(480) 421-1004, (800) 782-1117
www.scottsdalecvb.com**

Downtown Scottsdale is better seen by foot than by car. Scottsdale Road and the east-west roads that cross it are jam-packed with stores, restaurants, and galleries. Besides, traffic on Scottsdale Road slows to a crawl in high tourist season, so you might as well

leave the car in one of the many public parking lots. Look at the lampposts and elsewhere, and you'll see signage that designates the different areas of downtown, including Old Town Scottsdale, West Main, Marshall Way, and 5th Avenue. The latter three areas are the domain of shoppers and art connoisseurs and are well worth your time if you are interested in souvenir hunting or in browsing the galleries. See the Shopping and The Arts chapters for more information.

You get a sense of the city's Old West heritage on a walking tour suggested by the Scottsdale Historical Society that includes these sites: the intersection of Brown Avenue and Main Street, site of the first general store and post office; the Little Red Schoolhouse on the Civic Center Mall, preserved from 1909 and home of the Historical Society; Cavalliere's Blacksmith Shop at 3805 N. Brown Ave.; and the building at 3933 N. Brown Ave., built in 1923 as a pool hall.

Be sure to walk around the Civic Center Mall, a modern complex of government buildings, a public library, a performing arts center enlivened with gardens, fountains, and sculptures, and the Scottsdale Museum of Contemporary Art. It is a comfortable place to walk, or to sit and relax at an outdoor festival or concerts.

i College football fans should check out the Ziegler Fiesta Bowl Museum at the Scottsdale Waterfront. The museum celebrates the game's history, as well as the Xs and Os of past bowls and the local celebrations surrounding the event.

OUT OF AFRICA WILDLIFE PARK $$$$
4010 N. Cherry Rd., Camp Verde
(928) 567-2840
www.outofafricapark.com
Think of Out of Africa not as a zoo but as a small version of Sea World that substitutes exotic tigers for killer whales. The big cats can be seen in natural habitats developed for them at the park. Yes, they romp in the water with staff members and perform various tricks. Species include white tigers and Bengals. There are 9 animal shows in all, which give the park a chance to show off its other inhabitants, including lions, foxes, bears, cougars, wolves, pythons, and exotic birds. Watch caretakers toss 800 pounds of meat to eager carnivores. Ride a safari Jeep among the giraffes and zebras. The park is about 90 minutes north of central Phoenix on I-17. Admission, which includes the shows, is $36 for adults, $34 for seniors, and $20 for children ages 3 to 12. Children under 3 are free.

TALIESIN WEST $$$–$$$$
12621 N. Frank Lloyd Wright Blvd.,
Scottsdale
(480) 860-2700
www.franklloydwright.org
Frank Lloyd Wright's brilliance in creating organic architecture that harmonizes with its surroundings is perfectly exemplified at Taliesin West, which served as Wright's winter home, studio, and architectural campus from 1937 until his death in 1959. The 600-acre site is nestled amid cactus and scrub, with wide-ranging views of Phoenix to the south and mountains to the east.

At first glance, you may think Taliesin West looks strange. But the eccentricities of its design quickly grow on you as you learn how Wright and his apprentices gathered

rocks from the desert floor and sand from the washes to use as building materials. You also will come to appreciate Wright's attention to detail and how he used light and space. Taliesin West offers multiple guided tours 9 a.m. to 4 p.m. daily. They range from 1 to 3 hours and from $18 to $60. Times and rates vary by season and day of the week, so check the Wright Foundation's website for specifics. The 1-hour Panorama Tour takes visitors around the campus, through the Cabaret Theater and Music Pavilion, and includes a peak at Wright's office. The 3-hour Behind the Scenes Tour takes a much more intimate look at the grounds, and you're treated to tea in the Dining Room.

i City slickers who want to experience life on the range are in luck. The Arizona Cowboy College in Scottsdale offers classes, usually during the spring and fall. Keep in mind, this is a camp where you will work and sleep under the stars. Information: (480) 471-3151 or www.cowboycollege.com.

NORTHWEST VALLEY

DOWNTOWN GLENDALE

Glendale Chamber of Commerce
7105 N. 59th Ave., Glendale
(623) 937-4754
www.glendaleazchamber.org
The awnings, the shade of many trees, the brick sidewalks, and the well-preserved buildings all lend a pleasant ambience to downtown Glendale near 59th and Glendale Avenues. It is an antiques hunter's paradise, with about 4 dozen antiques shops within a few blocks of each other. It is said to be the largest concentration of antiques dealers in Arizona. The shops sell everything from

Victorian-era furniture to automobile memorabilia to vintage telephones to elegant collectible figurines (see Shopping chapter for more). Storefronts bear the names Arsenic & Old Lace, Strunk's Hollow, and Grandma's House. Also scattered throughout downtown are plenty of specialty shops selling everything from angel figurines to hand-blown glass. Visitors gravitate toward the 4-block area known as Catlin Court, where century-old bungalows have been preserved and turned into shops and restaurants. Look for trolley stops if you would like a mobile tour of downtown the old-fashioned way. Glendale stages a farmers' market and crafts fair in Murphy Park, Saturday only, November to May.

For refreshments, your options include ice-cream parlors, tearooms, and family-style restaurants. Or you could skip such formalities entirely and head straight to Cerreta Candy Company, 5345 W. Glendale Ave. (623-930-1000), where you can watch chocolates and other candies being made in this small, family-owned factory.

i If you haven't been to the Desert Botanical Garden recently, drop by to see the cactus and succulent house. The new space is eco-supportive and designed to showcase the large variety of plants, as well as to facilitate thousands of visitors each year. It's at 1201 N. Galvin Pkwy. in Phoenix (480-941-1225).

SAHUARO RANCH PARK

9802 N. 59th Ave., Glendale
(623) 930-4200
www.glendaleaz.com/parksand
recreation/sahuaroranchpark.cfm

Listed on the National Register of Historic Places, the 17-acre park is designed to preserve one of the Valley's oldest and finest homesteads. The land was once part of a 640-acre fruit farm developed by a family from Illinois in the late 1800s. In the 1970s the city of Glendale saved several acres from development and turned Sahuaro Ranch into a tourist attraction. You can explore 13 original buildings and a lavish rose garden. More than 100 peacocks roam the grounds. Also on display is a small re-creation of the original fruit orchard, as well as a miniature cotton gin, a restored vineyard, artifacts in the Main House Museum, blacksmithing tools, and various artworks. The park itself is accessible from 6 a.m. to sunset every day, but free guided tours of the 1895 main house are given by volunteers and are limited to Wed to Sat 10 a.m. to 2 p.m. and Sun 10 a.m. to 4 p.m.

SOUTHWEST VALLEY

RAWHIDE
5700 W. North Loop Rd., Chandler
(480) 502-5600
www.rawhide.com
The 1880s-style Western town keeps Arizona traditions alive with shows by costumed characters and authentic-looking storefronts on Main Street. Rawhide is one of the Valley's most popular attractions, annually drawing thousands of foreign tourists. Featured are stagecoach, train, and burro rides; gold panning; a shooting gallery; several shops selling Old West gear; plus hourly stunt shows complete with explosions, fistfights, gunfights, and falls from buildings. Admission is free, though various activities cost extra.

i The white mansion on the hill near 24th Street and Lincoln Drive in Phoenix's ritzy Biltmore Estates neighborhood belonged to chewing gum magnate William Wrigley Jr. He built the mansion in 1931 as a 50th anniversary present for his wife. Information on tours and events: www.wrigleymansionclub.com.

WILDLIFE WORLD ZOO & AQUARIUM $$$$
16501 W. Northern Ave., Litchfield Park
(623) 935-9453
www.wildlifeworld.com
Billed as the place to see exotic animals, Wildlife World Zoo is worth visiting if you like an informal zoo that lets you encounter animals up close. The collection, about 350 species total, includes everything from giraffes and rhinos to penguins and an albino alligator. Many visitors come to see the impressive array of birds, such as toucans, macaws, cockatoos, and ostriches. Most of the birds are in a large, walk-in aviary. At the giraffe feeding station, kids can mount a platform that puts them at eye-level with the giraffes. They can also feed the lories (small parrots) with apple wedges. Admission prices are $27.50 for adults and $14.25 for children ages 3 to 12. It's free for children younger than 3.

KIDSTUFF

Phoenix is very much a young city, and that's reflected in the youth of so many of its residents. Young families with little kids have their share of favorite activities, along with young professionals and snowbirds.

Based on the weather, you have air-conditioned or outdoor options. Either is sure to expand your child's mind. With so many natural wonders around the city, there's plenty to explore in wildlife, landscape, and ancient Native American art. While your pals back East or in the Midwest are waiting for the thaw, you and your son will be able to toss the ball around in one of the dozens of city parks that stretch across the Valley.

The museums and entertainment choices slanted toward kids are also outstanding in Phoenix. The Arizona Science Center, Challenger Space Center, and Museum of Natural History will keep young people occupied for hours. With so many family-oriented shopping areas, there's plenty of laser tag, arcades, and children's theater. Plus, the water parks of Big Surf and Golfland make exciting full-day outings for the family.

For more ideas see the Spectator Sports chapter for places to watch professional sports year-round. See the Parks & Recreation chapter to scope out ideal sites for desert hikes or for whiling away an afternoon. Keep in mind that other kid-friendly attractions like Goldfield Ghost Town, the Maricopa County regional parks, and other sites for all ages are detailed in other chapters.

Price Code

With each attraction listed in this chapter you will find a pricing guide ranging from one to four dollar signs. The code is based on admission for an adult and one child. Please note that small children often get in cheaper or for free. Some admissions vary; for example, if there are a basic admission and a deluxe admission, there may be a range of price codes. If there is no dollar sign, the attraction has no entry fee. For restaurants the price is for a meal for two, not including drinks and dessert.

$	Less than $5
$$	$5 to $10
$$$	$10 to $20
$$$$	More than $20

INDOOR PURSUITS

Museums

ARIZONA MUSEUM OF NATURAL HISTORY $$$
53 N. Macdonald St., Mesa
(480) 644-2230
www.azmnh.org

At the Mesa Southwest Museum, visitors can explore Arizona without ever leaving town. It features a 200-million-year-old *Camarasaurus*, in addition to other giant prehistoric fossils. A 3-story mountain presents a life-size peek at the Mesozoic era—just watch out for the animated dinosaurs and the flash floods. Kids can hunt for their own dinosaur bones in the Paleo Dig Pit. Admission is $10 for adults, $9 for seniors, $8 for students with ID, $6 for children 3 to 12, and free for children younger than 3.

ARIZONA MUSEUM FOR YOUTH   **$$**
35 N. Robson St., Mesa
(480) 644-2467
www.arizonamuseumforyouth.com
You can really kid around in this downtown Mesa museum, where youth enjoy an introduction to fine arts. Visitors can experiment with hands-on activities that stimulate creativity and artistic savvy. Kids under 5 will especially enjoy Artville, a tiny town designed to teach awareness of colors, shapes, and textures. Admission is $7 for everyone over 1.

i Each year Phoenix hosts the Itty Bitty Open, a free golf tournament for kids ages 3 to 5. The tots get instruction and a free set of plastic clubs and other gear. Mom and Dad get bragging rights. The event is usually held in January, a couple of weeks before the Waste Management Phoenix Open pro tournament. Information: (602) 944-6168 or www.jgaa.org.

ARIZONA SCIENCE CENTER   **$$**
600 E. Washington St., Phoenix
(602) 716-2000
www.azscience.org

The folks at the Arizona Science Center have childlike fun down to a science. The multimillion-dollar structure houses 4 floors worth of hands-on, engaging exhibits that make learning seem like second nature. Look for a planetarium with one of the largest domes in the West; a theater with a 5-story screen using IMAX technology; and 350 exhibits cleverly organized into galleries that explore human physiology, physical forces, transportation, geology, and technology. Exhibits change frequently, so families can stop by more than once. Experiments allow your budding Einsteins to get their first introduction to bioscience. Admission is $12 for adults and $10 for seniors and children 3 to 17. Tickets combining the exhibits and admission to the IMAX theater and/or planetarium are more expensive. The center also runs special workshops for children 6 and up. (More information is available in the Attractions chapter.)

CHALLENGER SPACE CENTER   **$$**
21170 N. 83rd Ave., Peoria
(623) 322-2001
www.azchallenger.org
Part of a network of 100 centers worldwide, this location is run in association with the Smithsonian Institution. Kids of all ages will love the planetarium, but the most intriguing thing here is the Technology Flight Deck, which is designed like Johnson Space Center. Wannabe astronauts can participate in 2-hour simulated space missions Sat 10:30 a.m. to 10 p.m. The missions include a trip to Mars and a "rendezvous with a comet." Reservations are required, so call in advance; tickets cost $22.50 for adults and $19.50 for students and seniors. Admission is $8 for adults, $5 for children, $7 for seniors. Kids under 4 are free.

CHILDREN'S MUSEUM OF PHOENIX $$$
215 N. 7th St., Phoenix
(602) 253-0501
www.childrensmuseumofphoenix.org
The goal of the new Children's Museum, located in the historic Monroe School, is to engage the minds, muscles, and imaginations of children. Interactive exhibits designed for kids 10 and under include an art studio to encourage creative expression, the Desert Den to introduce kids to native Arizona plants, and one of the most extensive jungle-gyms parents have ever seen. The museum has received multiple local awards since 2008 and is considered one of the most thrilling, engaging educational experiences for kids in the Valley. Admission is $11 for everyone except seniors ($10) and children under 1 (free).

Theater for Young Audiences

CHILDSPLAY $$$–$$$$
Tempe Center for the Arts
700 W. Rio Salado Pkwy., Tempe
(480) 350-2822
www.childsplayaz.org
Childsplay has been entertaining the young and young-at-heart since 1977 with theatrical performances of classic children's stories like Charlotte's Web and Dr. Seuss tales. Other kid-friendly plays, like A Year With Frog and Toad, are spirited and engaging for kindergarteners. The theater also hosts classes for children. Ticket prices are $19 to $26 depending on the show time ($19 to $21 for kids).

COOKIE COMPANY $$$
Greasepaint Theatre
7020 E. 2nd St., Scottsdale
(602) 254-2151
www.phoenixtheatre.net
An affiliate of Phoenix Theatre, the Cookie Company built a stellar reputation for taking old stage favorites and putting a modern spin on them. The theater, made up primarily of adult actors, enjoyed its 30th season in 2011. Performances of If You Give a Mouse a Cookie and Unstoppable Me! included free activities for the kids an hour prior to curtain. The theater is aptly named—audiences chomp on cookies and milk after each performance during a meet-the-actors reception. Admission is around $15. Call the box office for updated prices.

GREAT ARIZONA PUPPET THEATER $$
302 W. Latham St., Phoenix
(602) 262-2050
www.azpuppets.org
These puppeteers have been delighting audiences since 1983. They use a variety of characters, including rod puppets, hand puppets, and marionettes. The shows often celebrate Arizona culture. Productions have included Cinderella and The Three Billy Goats Gruff. The theater also occasionally hosts guest puppeteers from around the country, such as the Magical Moonshine Theater, and Chinese puppet master Yang Hui. Performances vary with the season and show, so call ahead. Tickets cost $6 per child, $8 per adult.

*JESTER'Z IMPROV COMEDY $$$$
Theater 168
7117 E. McDowell Rd., Scottsdale
(480) 423-0120
www.jesterzimprov.com
Jester'z improvisational theater is funny enough for adults but clean enough for kids. Its shows steer clear of raw language and crude situations. Alcohol and smoking are prohibited on the premises. Performances are

fast paced and interactive, and members of the audience yell out suggestions for scenes, games, and exercises. The 90-minute shows are scheduled every Fri and Sat at 8 and 10 p.m. All tickets cost $12 except the 6 p.m. Sat show ($10). Reservations required. If your kids get an itch for show business after the show, sign them up for classes and workshops.

Shopping

ARIZONA MILLS
5000 S. Arizona Mills Circle, Tempe
(480) 491-7300
www.arizonamills.com
This mall is full of manufacturers' outlets that appeal to adult shoppers, but it also has a kid-friendly side, notably because it contains Gameworks arcade restaurant, an IMAX theater, and a 24-screen movie theater. The Rainforest Cafe delights with the sights and sounds of a simulated Amazon rain forest. The mall has several toy and game stores, including Toy Mart and Game Daze. Your kids will also enjoy browsing The Disney Store Outlet. Arizona Mills can be reached from I-10 near the junction with US 60.

i The Valley has a rich youth baseball tradition, so there are plenty of air-conditioned indoor facilities to send your kids for extra practice. One state-of-the-art center is The Cages at 2511 E. Bell Rd. in Phoenix. It features several cages, pitching alleys, and space for instructional clinics with former pros. Information: www.thecagesfacility.com or (602) 923-0607.

ATOMIC COMICS
1120 S. Country Club Dr., Mesa
(480) 649-0807
www.atomiccomics.com
This is the Valley's original comic book store. Its customers range from kids to childlike adults. Aside from traditional comics, Atomic also features comic-related video games, collectible cards, and action figures. Atomic Comics has three other Valley locations: 2815 W. Peoria Ave., Phoenix (602-395-1066); 12621 N. Tatum Blvd., Phoenix (602-923-0733); and 3155 W. Chandler Blvd., Chandler (480-940-6061).

SUPERSTITION SPRINGS CENTER
6555 E. Southern Ave., Mesa
(480) 832-0212
www.superstitionsprings.com
This mall makes a nice destination for a family outing, not only because it houses several major department stores and dozens of specialty stores, but also because it has a couple of nice features for those moments when you're shopped out and need a respite. Children can take a break by riding the carousel near the food court or by exploring the indoor toddler play area near the Sears lower level. Westcor runs a Kid's Club every Thurs at 10 a.m., usually with singing and dancing shows.

Kid-Friendly Restaurants

AMAZING JAKE'S PIZZA FACTORY
1830 E. Baseline Rd., Mesa
(480) 926-7499
www.amazingjakes.com
This facility is an indoor adventure with all sorts of entertainment and fun to go along with an all-you-can-eat buffet. Activities include go-karts, laser tag, mini golf, and video games. There are gentler rides for the little ones, but the kids need to be at least 4 years old. All rides cost extra.

MIMI'S CAFE
Desert Ridge Marketplace
21001 N. Tatum Blvd., Phoenix
(480) 419-5006
www.mimiscafe.com

This restaurant chain is rich in New Orleans French Quarter ambience. It's a charming change of pace among the eateries at Desert Ridge. Mimi's brunch is a favorite of all ages, but it's also a consistently good chain for lunch and dinner. The dozen or so kids' menu options include spaghetti Alfredo and a kiddie turkey dinner. Other Valley locations are at 2800 W. Chandler Blvd., Chandler (480-899-5612); 4901 E. Ray Rd., Phoenix (480-705-4811); 7450 W. Bell Rd., Glendale (623-979-4500); 10214 N. Metro Pkwy. West, Phoenix (602-997-1299); 1250 S. Alma School Rd., Mesa (480- 833-4646); 8980 E. Shea Blvd., Scottsdale (480-451-6763); and 1220 N. Dysart Rd., Goodyear (623-935-9760).

ORGAN STOP PIZZA
1149 E. Southern Ave., Mesa
(480) 813-5700
www.organstoppizza.com

The original Organ Stop Pizza opened in Phoenix in 1972, featuring a huge Wurlitzer pipe organ rescued from oblivion. The larger structure in Mesa was built to accommodate the crowds and the largest Wurlitzer theater organ in the world (more than 5,000 pipes). Kids love dancing to the live organ music and all the special kaleidoscope lighting effects.

Other Indoor Retreats

✳ALLTEL ICE DEN   **$$**
9375 E. Bell Rd., Scottsdale
(480) 585-7465
www.coyotesice.com

In addition to offering public skating, this facility sponsors figure skating and hockey classes for kids and adults, and has a pro shop, a concession area, and a cafe. Usually there are DJ light shows Friday and Saturday nights; Friday is Teen Night, and Saturday is Family Fun Night. Public sessions vary by the season but usually last 2 hours every weekday. Admission is $5 to $8 depending on your age; rentals cost a bit extra.

CERRETA CANDY COMPANY   **$$**
5345 W. Glendale Ave., Glendale
(623) 930-1000
www.cerreta.com

This redbrick building is a landmark in downtown Glendale known for its handmade chocolates and candies. Tours are available Monday to Friday; Cerreta also hosts a Chocolate Pizza Tour where kids can make their own creations for $10. Boxed candies and chocolates by the pound are available for purchase.

DAVE & BUSTER'S   **$$$**
2000 E. Rio Salado Pkwy., Tempe
(480) 281-8456
www.daveandbusters.com

Recess is calling! That's the slogan at Dave & Buster's, and if you haven't taken the kids there yet, it's time. There are approximately a zillion games, all cool, and both kids and adults love this place. You can buy a package deal, where you get dinner and a card good for 10 games. The kids can play while you relax in the restaurant or bar area. There's a second Valley location at 21001 N. Tatum Blvd., Scottsdale (480-538-8956).

JAMBO! PARK $$$
2726 S. Alma School Rd., Mesa
(480) 820-8300
www.jambopark.com
Jambo! Park has the feel of a mini state fair with amusement park rides, video games, mini golf, mini bowling, and colored lights. Fortunately, for families looking for something to do on a hot day in the Valley, they're all indoors. The play lands are geared to children 12 and younger, offering small but fast roller coasters, carousels, and other kiddie rides. Preschoolers like the 3-level soft playground with tunnels, chutes, and ladders. A $10.99 Jambo! Passport gets you some unlimited rides and other perks. There's another location at 15230 N. 32nd St., Phoenix (602-274-4653).

KIWANIS PARK WAVE POOL $$
6111 S. All-America Way, Tempe
(480) 350-5201
www.tempe.gov/pools/kiwaniswavepool
This indoor pool at Kiwanis Community Park is not a full-fledged water park, but it has continuous waves and a giant waterslide. It's popular when it's too hot to be outside, yet you can take away a bit of the chill from swimming with a few moments of sunning on the pool's outdoor deck. Admission is $6 for anyone 12 and up and $3 for children 2 to 11. The pool is not recommended for toddlers. Tube rentals, snacks, and beverages are available.

LASER QUEST $$–$$$
3335 W. Peoria Ave., Phoenix
(602) 548-0005
www.laserquest.com
Kids can chase each other around an 8,000-square-foot maze, tagging one another with laser beams. The mazes include multiple levels, making for great games of Manhunt. General admission is $8, though groups vary by package. Another location is at 2035 S. Alma School Rd. in Mesa (480-752-0005).

OCEANSIDE ICE ARENA $$
1520 N. McClintock Dr., Tempe
(480) 941-0944
www.oceansideicearena.net
At a cool 50 degrees Fahrenheit, Oceanside provides a nice escape for East Valley residents. Public skating sessions vary week to week, though, and sometimes there is no public skating at all, so call ahead for hours. Admission is $7 for adults and $5 for children 3 to 17. Figure skate rentals are $3. Hockey skate rentals are the same. Inquire about lessons for beginning skaters or children's hockey.

SCOTTSDALE CIVIC CENTER LIBRARY
3839 N. Drinkwater Blvd., Scottsdale
(480) 312-2474
http://library.scottsdaleaz.gov/kids
This large library is a focal point of Scottsdale's Civic Center Mall, and its colorful children's area is one of the best in the Valley. Programs include family story time, kids' reading practice sessions with the dogs from Tail Waggin' Tutors, and specific sessions for toddlers.

FUN IN THE SUN

Amusement Parks

CASTLES 'N COASTERS $$$$
9445 Metro Pkwy. East, Metrocenter, Phoenix
(602) 997-7575
www.castlesncoasters.com

This amusement park catches your eye from I-17 in north Phoenix. The best way to get there is to take the Dunlap Avenue exit. The park's name comes from its castle replica, which anchors the center of the amusement park, and the 2 roller coasters, including one of Arizona's largest, Desert Storm. The park also runs log rides, bumper boats, go-karts, a smaller coaster and carousel, along with 4 miniature-golf courses. Inside the castle are video games and snack areas. An unlimited ride day pass is $20.35.

CRACKERJAX $$$$
16001 N. Scottsdale Rd., Scottsdale
(480) 998-2800
www.crackerjax.com

Miniature-golf aficionados like this place for its 2 courses with different degrees of difficulty. You can also try your hand at real golf on the 2-level driving range. The park keeps kids happy with bumper boats, go-karts, sand volleyball, batting cages, and an arcade. The park has extended hours Fri and Sat. An unlimited ride pass goes for $20 to $25 depending on the day. The Bungy Dome, with its bouncy 30-foot drops, costs $10.

ENCHANTED ISLAND AMUSEMENT
PARK $$$
Encanto Park
1202 W. Encanto Blvd., Phoenix
(602) 254-1200
www.enchantedisland.com

Encanto Park stretches for several blocks between Thomas Road and Encanto Boulevard. The amusement park within the 222-acre city park continues to be a favorite gathering place for families, especially those in central Phoenix. Enchanted Island's most nostalgic attraction is a carousel that has graced the park since 1948. Another longtime favorite is the C.P. Huntington train that winds around the park. For more amusement, there's a parachute tower, bumper boats, and more. There are also plenty of picnic areas adjacent to Enchanted Island. At Encanto's lake try a little paddle boating, canoeing, or fishing. You can rent boats by calling (602) 254-1520. An unlimited ride pass costs $13.65 for guests less than 54 inches tall and $8.10 for those above. Individual tickets cost $1.10.

FIDDLESTICKS FAMILY FUN PARK $$$$
1155 W. Elliot Rd., Tempe
(480) 961-0800
www.fiddlesticksaz.com

Fiddlesticks offers miniature golf, bumper boats, go-karts, batting cages, and video games. The Tempe location has a lighted driving range popular with golfers of all ages. Unlimited ride wristbands cost $17.49 each, though the park runs discounts.

Water Parks

BIG SURF WATERPARK $$$$
1500 N. McClintock Dr., Tempe
(480) 994-2247
www.bigsurffun.com

The massive pool, as big as 4 football fields, lets you ride the waves every 90 seconds. Its surrounding landscaping and decor lend the park a Polynesian theme. Big Surf has 8 giant slides and assorted other slides. Little ones will enjoy a wading pool with sprinklers and easy slides. General admission is $26; $15 from 3 to 6 p.m.

GOLFLAND/SUNSPLASH $$$$
155 W. Hampton Ave., Mesa
(480) 834-8319
www.golfland.com/mesa

The gigantic wave pool includes a "river" that you can lazily float on in an inner tube. The kiddie area is quite big, with easy concrete slides, a waterfall, sprinklers, and hoses for lots of safe water play. Admission to the water park and other features varies. The best value is $36 for an unlimited pass to the water park, mini golf, laser tag, and other features.

WET 'N' WILD PHOENIX $$$$
4243 W. Pinnacle Peak Rd., Glendale
(623) 201-2000
www.wetnwildphoenix.com

The water park and wave pool are popular with folks in the West Valley. The newest attraction is the Constrictor, an enclosed flume slide that shoots you through corkscrew turns and spirals. Little ones have a great time on the easy slides and in the play pool. For adventurous older kids and adults, there are several larger slides of the super-speedy, scream-eliciting variety. General admission is $35; $20 for admission after 5 p.m. There are discounts for some children and seniors.

i Looking for an evening out with the family? Check out the Movies in the Park series at Kiwanis Park, Mill Avenue and All-America Way in Tempe. The kid-friendly movies (think *Toy Story 3* and *Despicable Me*) are free on Friday evenings in the cooler spring months. Take a picnic and a few chairs and enjoy the evening out on the lawn. Call (480) 350-5200 for a schedule.

Other Parks

DESERT BREEZE RAILROAD $
Desert Breeze Park
660 N. Desert Breeze Blvd. East, Chandler
(480) 893-6652
www.desertbreezerr.com

Ride on a reproduction of an 1880s train in this small but pleasant park in a suburban neighborhood. There's also plenty of playground equipment in the park and a carousel. The train primarily runs 10 a.m. to 7 p.m., though some hours vary. A train ride costs $6; the park runs holiday specials.

i The Arizona State University Center for Meteorite Studies is home to the largest university-based meteorite collection in the world. To see the collection, visit the Bateman Physical Sciences Building—C-wing, room 139, on the Tempe campus (480-965-6511).

INDIAN BEND WASH BIKE PATH
Hayden Road, Scottsdale
(480) 312-7275

This is an easy, meandering bike path along a greenbelt, but the route stretches for 11 miles. So decide beforehand how much of it you want to tackle. There are several good starting points, such as north of downtown Scottsdale at Chaparral Park at Hayden and Jackrabbit Roads, or the Bike Stop Rest Area on Thomas Road between Miller and Hayden Roads. You can head north toward Shea Boulevard or south toward McKellips Road in Tempe. The greenbelt and its small lakes and golf courses make pleasant surroundings. In-line skaters, strollers, joggers, and dog walkers share the route. The greenbelt is slightly below street level because it's the place that catches the flow of rainwater after big storms and thus prevents flooding of nearby homes.

MACDONALD'S RANCH $$$$
26540 N. Scottsdale Rd., Scottsdale
(480) 585-0239
www.macdonaldsranch.com

Take a horseback ride among desert scrub and saguaros with the McDowell Mountains as your backdrop. For decades MacDonald's Ranch has been teaching people about horses through lessons and day rides. The ranch also specializes in stagecoach rides, cowboy cookouts, and hayrides. Reservations are required, and the ranch suggests these activities for children ages 7 and older. There are free pony rides at the ranch for those younger than 7. A 1-hour guided trail ride is $40 to $45 per person.

*MCCORMICK-STILLMAN RAILROAD PARK $

7301 E. Indian Bend Rd., Scottsdale
(480) 312-2312
www.therailroadpark.com

Valley families with little kids know and love the park's main train, a model of the Rio Grande Western Railway. It chugs a little over a mile through 30 acres of parkland. You board at Stillman Station, a replica of a historic Arizona train depot. Railroad buffs should head to the corner of the park housing displays of railroad memorabilia. There you'll find a Pullman car that was used by several US presidents, a 1906 Baldwin locomotive, a 1914 Santa Fe baggage car, and a machine shop dating from 1903. There's also a 10,000 square-foot Model Railroad Building. For most of the year, rides on the train and carousel are offered daily, starting at 10 a.m. and running until dark. A ride costs $2; children younger than 3 ride free. A Southern Pacific caboose houses a snack bar. The park hosts free concerts and other events in the cooler months.

SUPERSTITION FARM $$

3440 S. Hawes Rd., Mesa
(602) 432-6865
www.superstitionfarmtours.com

Casey and Alison Stechnij, a brother-and-sister team, grew up on a farm in East Mesa. After years spent following other pursuits, they joined forces and decided to show kids what farm life really means. This working 28-acre dairy ranch offers tours Sat 10 a.m. to 4 p.m. The petting zoo is open most of the week. You'll ride a hay wagon as you learn all about life on the farm. There's a milk bar with 12 flavors. Groups are welcome if you call ahead. Tours cost $7.50 and $5.50 for kids under 13.

ANNUAL EVENTS

The constant sunshine makes recurring festivals, sporting events, and other outdoor gatherings pretty easy to plan in Phoenix. Even holiday events like ZooLights at the Phoenix Zoo and Glendale Glitters go off without a touch of rain or snow. With thousands of annual events, you'll find plenty of options, especially during the high tourist seasons in the cooler months. From cultural events like Cinco de Mayo to art walks and other art events like Phoenix Film Festival, something pops up in the local listings nearly every weekend.

These are great opportunities to combine entertainment and shopping, or music and art, or other blends of your favorite things, in one event. Our listings are universal for all age groups, because young children, teens, seniors, and everyone else should be able to find something engaging at the Barrett-Jackson car show or the Peach Festival in Queen Creek. So figure out when you'll be here and carve out a full day to enjoy some of the Valley's top annual attractions.

JANUARY

BARRETT-JACKSON COLLECTOR CAR EVENT
WestWorld, 16601 N. Pima Rd.,
Scottsdale
(480) 663-6255
www.barrett-jackson.com/events/
scottsdale

Rightly dubbed "the Oscars of the collector-car world," this is an auction and show of hundreds of classic cars, almost all in excellent original or restored condition. Along with the Waste Management Phoenix Open and the Arabian Horse Show, the Barrett-Jackson Classic is one of Scottsdale's top 3 events, attracting high-rolling auto enthusiasts from around the world. The 2011 event marked Barrett-Jackson's 40th anniversary with a classic car road-rally through Scottsdale. Past events featured a 2009 Chevrolet Corvette ZR1, 1965 Shelby Cobra 4000 Roadster, and 1964 Dodge Hemi Charger Concept Car valued at $750,000, among many others. The event runs for a week in mid-January, with daily general admission tickets ranging from $25 to $55 per day or $160 for the week.

CELEBRATION OF FINE ART
Loop 101 and N. Scottsdale Road,
Scottsdale
(480) 443-7695
www.celebrateart.com

This open-air exhibition and festival hoists its big white tents every year for about 11 weeks, starting in January. It provides a chance to see the on-site studios of more than 100 artists, including painters, jewelers, photographers, weavers, ceramists, and

a sculpture garden. One of the attractions at the event is the chance to see artists in action. It is no wonder that *Art & Antiques* magazine called this "one of the West's premier art events." It is usually open during daytime hours, and admission is $8 for adults, $7 for seniors and military; children under age 12 are free.

i For a larger overview of annual events in the Valley, visit www .phoenix.eventguide.com.

P.F. CHANG'S ROCK 'N' ROLL ARIZONA MARATHON AND HALF MARATHON
Wesley Bolin Memorial Plaza, Phoenix
(800) 311-1255
www.rnraz.com
Thousands of racers, walkers, and supporters line the Valley streets for this charitable event, which has raised more than $28 million for the Leukemia and Lymphoma Society and other charities over the years. The course (26.2 miles for the marathon and 13.1 miles for the half) winds through Phoenix, Scottsdale, and Tempe. Numerous bands and cheering squads lift spirits along the way. Spectators and racers join the fun by wearing colorful costumes, so take your camera. Racers finish near Arizona State University, where a free post-race party at Tempe Beach Park draws top-name performers. The event is usually held the second weekend in January.

✳WASTE MANAGEMENT PHOENIX OPEN
Tournament Players Club of Scottsdale
17020 N. Hayden Rd., Scottsdale
(602) 870-0163
www.wastemanagementphoenixopen .com

The Phoenix Open is considered the world's most-attended golf tournament, though many spectators go for the food, cocktails, and people-watching more than the actual tournament. It's unlike any other golf experience with the rowdy crowds on the stadium-like par-3 16th hole and late-night Bird's Nest party tent. The tournament course is one of the most picturesque in the West. On a sunny day it's relaxing to sit on the lawn and watch some of the top golfers in the world. Tickets at the gate cost $25 per person; children 17 and younger are admitted free when accompanied by an adult. The TPC course is adjacent to the Scottsdale Princess Resort (see the Resorts chapter).

FEBRUARY

FOUNTAIN HILLS GREAT FAIR
Avenue of the Fountains, Fountain Hills
(480) 837-1654
www.fountainhillschamber.com
The town of Fountain Hills looks forward each February to welcoming thousands to this 3-day outdoor fair featuring the creations of 480 professional artists and craftspeople. Also on the bill are food courts, live entertainment, carnival rides, games, and an early-morning hot-air balloon race—all taking place on the expansive park in the center of Fountain Hills. You can't miss it—this is where you'll see one of the tallest fountains in the world, shooting 500 feet into the air at set intervals. From the intersection of Scottsdale Road and Shea Boulevard in north Scottsdale, head 12 miles east to Fountain Hills. Admission is free.

i Glendale's Chocolate Affaire, held each February, is like Graceland to chocoholics. For more information, call the city of Glendale at (623) 930-2299.

LOST DUTCHMAN DAYS
1590 E. Lost Dutchman Blvd., Apache Junction
(602) 540-6524
www.lostdutchmandays.org
The legend of Jacob Waltz—the Lost Dutchman—and his futile quest for gold in the Superstition Mountains has been celebrated since 1964 in Apache Junction. Lost Dutchman Days features a parade, a senior pro rodeo, various vendors, a carnival, gold panning, and food booths. The series of events are held around the end of February. Ticket prices vary based on the events.

i Old Town Scottsdale hosts a 2-day Feng Shui Festival each March and October. Admission and classes are free. Information: www.fengshuiaz.com or (480) 854-6961.

MATSURI: A FESTIVAL OF JAPAN
Heritage and Science Park
115 N. 6th St., Phoenix
(602) 262-5029
www.azmatsuri.org
You will have many ethnic and cultural festivals to choose from during a Phoenix winter, but this is perhaps the best. Since 1984 Matsuri organizers have brought together the sights and sounds of Japanese classical dancing, taiko drummers, natives dressed in beautiful kimonos, and artists displaying unusual crafts. Martial arts play a big part in the festival, too, with demonstrations in judo, Shotokan karate, swordsmanship, and tae kwon do. Exhibits include bonsai demonstrations, origami folding, kite construction, fabric art, and cooking demonstrations. You can also participate in a traditional tea ceremony. Booths serving Japanese food are in abundance. Matsuri usually takes place the last weekend in February. Admission is free.

PARADA DEL SOL
WestWorld
16601 N. Pima Rd., Scottsdale
(480) 990-3179
www.paradadelsol.us
This Scottsdale tradition salutes the city's Old West heritage. During Parada del Sol Week, cowboys, pioneer women, and mountain men reclaim their place in local history. Events include the Hashknife Pony Express, in which riders deliver mail via horseback on a 225-mile ride from Holbrook to Scottsdale; the Parada del Sol Parade through downtown Scottsdale, a Saturday morning spectacular that's believed to be the world's largest and longest horse-drawn parade; the Parada del Sol Rodeo, 3 days of bronco riding, steer roping, rodeo clowns, and more, sanctioned by the Professional Rodeo Cowboys Association; a Rodeo Dance; and a Trail's End Celebration, featuring food, drinks, kids' activities, and gunfight performances. Parada del Sol events usually take place in February, though the rodeo events happen in early March. The parade is free.

SCOTTSDALE ARABIAN HORSE SHOW
WestWorld
16601 N. Pima Rd., Scottsdale
(480) 515-1500
www.scottsdaleshow.com
Founded in 1955, the Scottsdale Arabian Horse Show attracts more than 200,000 spectators. It's one of the world's largest Arabian horse shows, with 2,400 of the world's finest steeds competing for more than $1 million in prize and scholarship money. A main arena and 2 secondary

arenas run simultaneously classes in halter, English pleasure, trail horse, hunter, jumper, dressage, Western pleasure, and other categories. Two huge tents become display space for more than 250 exhibitors from around the world selling clothing, jewelry, fine art, food, and horse accessories. Daily admission to the 10-day extravaganza is $10 per day. Seniors pay $7; children under 13 are admitted free.

WORLD CHAMPIONSHIP HOOP DANCE CONTEST
Heard Museum
2301 N. Central Ave., Phoenix
(602) 252-8848
www.heard.org
The popular early-February event draws more than 40 Native American hoop dancers from the US and Canada. The hoop dance was part of a healing ceremony meant to restore balance and harmony. In Native American tradition the hoop symbolizes the cycles of life. You'll see members of various tribes in their colorful buckskin costumes. Dancers use as many as 50 hoops to form shapes and suggest images while showing off their fluid grace and precision. Admission is $12 for adults, $7 for kids 4 to 12, and free for children 3 and under. Tickets include admission to the museum.

i Each February, Hellzapoppin' Senior Rodeo features senior bronco busters and cattle ropers in the Buckeye rodeo. For tickets call (623) 386-2727 or visit www.buckeyevalley chamber.org.

MARCH

CHANDLER OSTRICH FESTIVAL
Tumbleweed Park
2250 S. McQueen Rd., Chandler
(480) 963-4571
www.ostrichfestival.com
This 3-day family festival recalls the days of ostrich farms in the Valley. Ostrich-themed events include jockeys riding ostriches as if they were thoroughbreds. Numerous food booths give you a chance to sample ostrich burgers. The event features live family-oriented musical performances, pig races, a dog show, and a parade. The Ostrich Festival usually takes place the second weekend in March. General admission is $10, with discounts for seniors and kids. A variety of passes are available.

THE NATIONAL FESTIVAL OF THE WEST
WestWorld
16601 N. Pima Rd., Scottsdale
(602) 996-4387
www.festivalofthewest.com
From old-time fur traders to modern-day ranching, this festival commemorates the romance, lore, and legend of the American cowboy and the settling of the American West. Over 4 days in mid-March, the festival presents Western music and movies, cowboy poetry, and costume contests. Western heroes and peddlers dressed in period costumes stroll the festival grounds. One of the highlights of the show is the Chuck Wagon Cook Off, in which chuck wagons from across the country come to compete for prizes. Visitors can sample their old-fashioned cooking. Each year the festival honors individuals who have helped preserve the Western lifestyle. Past honorees have included Gene Autry, Ben Johnson,

and Denver Pyle. Admission is $14 for adults with discounts for children, students, and seniors. A 4-day pass costs $45.

SCOTTSDALE ARTS FESTIVAL
Civic Center Mall
7380 E. 2nd St., Scottsdale
(480) 994-ARTS
www.scottsdaleartsfestival.org
The work of more than 185 artists and artisans is featured in this juried outdoor show that is ranked among the top art festivals in the country. Adding to the ambience are musical performances on 2 stages, food and beverage booths, and an area for children. The event takes place on a Friday, Saturday, and Sunday in mid-March. General admission is $7.

THE TEMPE BEER FESTIVAL
Tempe Beach Park
54 W. Rio Salado, Tempe
www.azbeer.com
This fun 2-day festival introduces you to hundreds of Western microbeers and tasty dishes prepared by some of the area's slickest restaurants. Sip Moose Drool Brown Ale, or quaff a Scape Goat Pale Ale or Pete's Wicked Ale. Designated drivers can choose from a variety of sodas. General admission is $40. General admission includes 24 tickets that can be exchanged for samples. VIP admission, which includes professionally catered nibbles, private restrooms, and private shade seating, is $80 per person. Every penny supports the Sun Sounds Foundation, a charitable group that helps the blind and nearly blind. The festival is often held in mid-March.

TEMPE FESTIVAL OF THE ARTS
Downtown Tempe
(480) 921-2300
www.tempefestivalofthearts.com
The 3-day outdoor festival of juried works on the last weekend of March shows everything from jewelry and pottery to photography and blown glass. The streets of downtown Tempe, including several blocks of Mill Avenue, are blocked off to traffic for pedestrians. Adding to the festive atmosphere are street musicians and performers, booths offering a wide range of food, and activities for kids. Admission is free.

APRIL

COUNTRY THUNDER WEST
20585 E. Price Rd., Florence
(866) 802-6418
www.countrythunder.com
As many as 30,000 country music fans show up each day of the 4-day festival. Country Thunder takes place in mid-April at a large campground site, enabling those traveling in RVs to stay close to the festivities. There are activities for kids, shows of glowing hot-air balloons, and food booths to go along with the concerts. Ticket prices vary based on the package, and tickets bought at the gate cost a lot more, so plan ahead.

MY NANA'S BEST TASTING SALSA CHALLENGE
Tempe Beach Park
80 W. Rio Salado Pkwy., Tempe
(602) 955-3947
www.salsachallenge.com
Visitors go through nearly 3,000 pounds of tortilla chips each year in the spicy foodie event, which raises money for the Arizona Hemophilia Association. The flavors span the

salsa spectrum from sweet and fruit-flavored to 4-alarm-fire varieties. The early-April event also includes live music and activities for kids. Admission is $8.

PHOENIX FILM FESTIVAL
Cine Capri
7000 E. Mayo Blvd., Scottsdale
(602) 955-6444
www.phoenixfilmfestival.org
The Phoenix Film Festival is held every spring and brings together independent and experimental filmmakers from the local area and around the world. It runs for a week and showcases some art films with bigger budgets, though the emphasis is on the more cutting-edge, marginalized filmmakers. Visitors have a chance to mingle with the directors, actors, and writers and share ideas on their favorite medium. Individual screenings are as low as $10, but a festival pass is a better value. Passes run from $30 for 1 day to $150 for the whole festival.

PHOENIX IMPROV FESTIVAL
Herberger Theater Center
222 E. Monroe St., Phoenix
(480) 389-4852
www.phoeniximprovfestival.com
The festival attracts national talent and local troupes. The festival showcases theatrical improv as well as comedy, so you'll see a wide range of forms, with each performance created on the spur of the moment. In true improv fashion, actors in the 3-day festival create entire scenes based on random suggestions by the audience. There are also workshops for the public. Tickets cost $10 to $15.

✳SCOTTSDALE CULINARY FESTIVAL
Scottsdale Civic Center Mall
7380 E. 2nd St., Scottsdale
(480) 945-7193
www.scottsdaleculinaryfestival.org
This long-running annual event is a week-long salute to the culinary arts, featuring some of Arizona's top chefs. Events include special dinners for close to $200, including some with wine pairings. The annual Great Arizona Picnic offers food from dozens of Valley restaurateurs. Admission to the picnic costs $10. Live music adds to the festivities, and there's usually a beer garden in one corner of the mall.

i Each year Schnepf Farms sponsors Dinner Down the Orchard in their peach orchard, with feasts featuring celebrity Valley chefs. Information: (480) 987-3100 or www.schnepf farms.com.

MAY

CINCO DE MAYO FESTIVAL
Downtown Phoenix
101 1st Ave.
(602) 279-4669
The weekend near the 5th of May brings a huge Mexican-theme street celebration to downtown Phoenix. The live entertainment includes mariachi bands, folklorico dancers, and headliner acts from the US and Mexico. Performers have included Laura Flores, Los Lobos, and Freddy Fender. The celebration, which includes numerous food booths, children's activities, local bands, and various contests, usually begins about noon each day and continues into the late evening. Admission is $5 for adults; free for children 12 and younger.

QUEEN CREEK PEACH FESTIVAL
24810 S. Rittenhouse Rd., Queen Creek
(480) 987-3100
www.schnepffarms.com

The second and third weekends of May mark taking the kids out to pick their own fresh peaches, snacking on a brunch of homemade peach pancakes, and grabbing handfuls of organic produce from the Schnepf Farms gardens. The country store is stocked with fresh fruit preserves, stuffed olives, homemade granola, and other locally produced food. A slice of peach pie or peach ice cream is the ultimate way to end a jaunt to the farm, which celebrated its 70th year in 2011. Organizers usually schedule celebrity chef demonstrations and have a sampling pavilion, in addition to crafts vendors. You can save a few bucks by picking your own peaches or select peaches from the bushels near the checkout line. Admission is free. Hay rides, train rides, and food are extra.

JULY

FABULOUS PHOENIX FOURTH
Steele Indian School Park
300 E. Indian School Rd., Phoenix
(602) 534-FEST

Many Valley residents celebrate the Fourth by watching fireworks above Arizona's Capitol building with a 25-minute fireworks show and numerous events scattered in the park. Nearly 250,000 people have turned out for past events in spite of the heat. The event features various stages of entertainment, food vendors, and crafts displays. In the past few years, Fabulous Phoenix Fourth has managed to book top-name country entertainment, including The Dixie Chicks, Alabama, Toby Keith, and The Mavericks. Fireworks start at 9:30 p.m. Admission is free.

SUMMER SPECTACULAR ARTWALK
Arts district of downtown Scottsdale
www.scottsdalegalleries.com

For more than 10 years, shortly following the Fourth of July, the dozens of galleries of downtown Scottsdale collaborate on a Thursday evening ArtWalk filled with artists' receptions, refreshments, musical entertainment, and other special events. An after-dark stroll through the galleries of Marshall Way, Main Street, and other avenues offers a good way to beat the heat, especially because the galleries roll out the red carpet by presenting works from nationally known artists. The ArtWalk is free.

WINTER IN JULY
Phoenix Zoo
455 N. Galvin Pkwy., Phoenix
(602) 273-1341
www.phoenixzoo.org

Each year the zoo trucks in tons and tons of snow to help cool off Valley residents who suffer through triple-digit temps for most of the summer. Animals (where appropriate) get fresh snow in their cages, and some taste "bloodsicles." It's all part of a program to enrich the lives of captive animals by encouraging natural behavior and stimulating their native intelligence. Activities are free with regular zoo admission.

OCTOBER

ARIZONA STATE FAIR
State Fairgrounds
1826 W. McDowell Rd., Phoenix
(602) 252-6771
www.azstatefair.com

The Arizona State Fair runs for about 3 weeks; giving attention to the hundreds of agricultural, livestock, fine arts, crafts, and

collectibles displays can take a day. But if you want just a daylong outing, make sure you leave time for enjoying the midway rides and games. You also want time to indulge in barbecue, meat on a stick, Navajo fry bread, and a variety of bizarre deep-fried foods that include Twinkies and scorpions. The music lineup has included Lynyrd Skynyrd, Snoop Dogg, and Trace Adkins. Expect to pay around $12 for adults, $6 for seniors and kids ages 5 to 13; kids younger than 5 are free. Ride tickets and games cost extra. The concerts are free with admission; reserved seats for the concerts are available for an extra fee and can be purchased in advance. Discounts are available online.

NOVEMBER

GLENDALE GLITTERS
Downtown Glendale
(623) 930-2299
www.glendaleaz.com/events
All the buildings in a 10-block area are decked out in more than 1 million lights, extending into Murphy Park. In Catlin Court, an antiques shopping district, the buildings sparkle with icicle lights. On Friday and Saturday evenings, the antiques shops and restaurants stay open late. There's also music, arts and crafts, and carriage and trolley rides. On other nights you can stroll and enjoy the quiet beauty of one of the Valley's nicest neighborhoods. The lights are switched on with much fanfare and fireworks on the night following Thanksgiving and stay on until mid-January. The event is capped off in style with Glendale Glitter and Glow, another nighttime street festival. Bands and street performers gather for a giant block party during which dozens of hot-air balloons light up the night. All events are free.

DECEMBER

APS FIESTA OF LIGHT ELECTRIC PARADE
Begins at North Phoenix Baptist Church
5757 N. Central Ave., Phoenix
(602) 262-6862
Phoenix has dozens of holiday events put on by both public and private sponsors. This is the biggest. Up to 300,000 people crowd 3 miles of sidewalk along Central Avenue on the first Saturday of December to watch more than 100 brightly lit floats. This has been going on since 1987, and it just seems to keep getting bigger. Admission is free.

INSIGHT FIESTA BOWL BLOCK PARTY
Downtown Tempe
(480) 350-0900
www.fiestabowl.org
This is no neighborhood block party. Named one of the top 8 places to spend New Year's Eve by *USA Today*, more than 150,000 people ring in the New Year in the Southwest's version of Times Square. The event has entertainment for the whole family, including interactive games and magic shows for the kids and 10 performing stages with live music for adults, as well as large dancing areas and several beer gardens. Food and beverage booths line both sides of the street. The city blocks off downtown streets and clears the way for live entertainment from nationally known performers like REO Speedwagon and Jimmy Eat World. Food and beverage booths, kiddie rides, and fireworks displays round out the event, as well as a pep rally with each visiting team's marching band and drill squad. The action begins about 4 p.m., with the pep rallies starting after dark. Two rounds of firework displays top the event, at 9 p.m. and again at midnight. Admission is $20.

LAS NOCHES DE LAS LUMINARIAS
Desert Botanical Garden
1201 N. Galvin Pkwy., Phoenix
(480) 941-1225
www.dbg.org

For more than 30 years, volunteers at the stunning Desert Botanical Garden have marked the holiday season with Las Noches de las Luminarias. Southwestern-style luminarias are paper bags weighted down with sand, with each bag containing a lighted candle. It's a holiday tradition to place luminarias along a path to brighten the way in the dark nights of winter. During this 17-night event, usually held after Thanksgiving and on weekends in early December, the garden paths glow with 7,000 luminarias, making for quite a sight. Musical entertainment adds to the scene. This is a popular event, so buy tickets as soon as possible.

ZOOLIGHTS
Phoenix Zoo
455 N. Galvin Pkwy., Phoenix
(602) 273-1341
www.phoenixzoo.org

The Phoenix Zoo strings more than 600,000 lights along the pathways and up in the trees. Look carefully and you'll see light displays of butterflies, birds, spiders, snakes, and larger creatures. Some displays are "animated," such as frogs that jump across a lake, and some displays move in time to holiday music. It's a great family outing and a fantastic way to see the zoo. Admission is $10 at the gate; discounts are available online. Children ages 2 and under are free.

THE ARTS

Phoenix, Scottsdale, and Tempe have deep artistic traditions. Phoenix, for example, began building a foundation for arts and culture early in the 20th century. The Heard Museum opened in 1929 as perhaps the premier exhibition of Native American art, and the Phoenix Art Museum traces its beginnings to the 1930s. Frank Lloyd Wright and other creative thinkers have left their imprint in Scottsdale, while Arizona State University students have forged their own modern path at studios in Tempe and along the gritty art walks in revitalized neighborhoods in central Phoenix.

In this chapter we give an introduction to the arts—though a comprehensive listing would be longer than this book. There are also additional details on art museums, venues, and theater for kids in the Attractions and Kidstuff chapters.

OVERVIEW

Cowboy art is an important tradition in the Valley. The Cowboy Artists of America was founded in 1965 in Sedona, and its annual auction is a premier Valley art event. Modern art has found a haven here as well, but perhaps the best combination of the two styles is the work of Ed Mell. This Arizona native draws on Western themes for his cubist renditions in oil and bronze.

Another form of art that has allowed people around the world to enjoy Arizona's natural wonders is photography. The photographers of the magazine *Arizona Highways*—in print for more than 85 years—have established the benchmark for this type of landscape work. Its first color cover featured a photograph taken by one of Arizona's famous politicians, Barry Goldwater, who documented Native American life.

Theater is also huge in Phoenix, and the wide variety of venues provides national acts with plenty of options. Film, too, is a burgeoning medium in Phoenix as more filmmakers take advantage of better tax incentives than they have in California. Musicians and actors from the East and West coasts have made the area home, and the Valley scene has blossomed to include an estimated 60 professional and community theater companies, ranging from the mainstream to experimental. There are also active theater departments on the main and west campuses of Arizona State University. The film program at tiny Scottsdale Community College is regarded as one of the top film programs in the state, and Scottsdale also hosts the Phoenix Film Festival each year.

After many rough years, the Phoenix Symphony is in a period of relative financial stability that continues to draw residents regularly to the downtown Herberger Theater Center. Arizona Opera has gone beyond traditional performances to attract a new generation of fans. For those who

like rock, pop, alternative, and New Age music, Phoenix has packed in more national acts than it has in years. It attracts most of the major tours, from the Rolling Stones to Kenny Chesney. The jazz scene also sizzles, thanks to local music promoters who bring in regional and national artists known for classic jazz, easy-listening jazz, Dixieland, and other styles. (See the Nightlife chapter for jazz and pop music venues.)

Outside the Valley, art also flourishes. To the north, Sedona is home to approximately 200 working artists, many of whom have fled urban areas to draw inspiration from the town's red-rock vistas. Jerome, near Sedona, and Bisbee to the south are both former mining towns that have also retooled themselves as art communities. Tourists find plenty to see and do in these areas, as the chapter on Day Trips illustrates in more detail.

THEATER

ACTORS THEATRE OF PHOENIX
Herberger Theater Center
222 E. Monroe St., Phoenix
(602) 253-6701
(602) 252-8497 (box office)
www.actorstheatrephx.org

Formed in 1984, this professional theater aims for five productions per season. Past hits included a "slightly off-center" version of *A Christmas Carol* and *The Lieutenant of Inishmore*. Ticket prices range from $31 to $47.

ARIZONA THEATRE COMPANY
Herberger Theater Center
222 E. Monroe St., Phoenix
(602) 253-6701
(602) 252-8497 (box office)
www.arizonatheatre.org

Arizona Theatre Company, the state's nonprofit resident theater, puts on 6 mainstage productions in Phoenix and Tucson. In choosing plays, ATC says its mission is to offer a broad range of theatrical styles, confront a spectrum of issues, and deepen ATC's commitment to cultural diversity. Past productions included *The Pajama Game* and *To Kill a Mockingbird*. Expect first-class costumes, lighting, and sound and stage design from ATC. Single-ticket prices range between $31 and $59.

PHOENIX THEATRE
100 E. McDowell Rd., Phoenix
(602) 258-1974
(602) 254-2151 (box office)
www.phoenixtheatre.net

Phoenix Theatre claims to be the state's oldest theater company. Its season runs September through May, and it presents productions that exhibit a commitment to little-known gems along with big-name works. Past productions included *Crazy for You* and *Altar Boyz*. A popular sidelight is the Cookie Company, a troupe that performs theater for children—and serves cookies too. (See the Kidstuff chapter for more.) Call for ticket prices.

SOUTHWEST SHAKESPEARE COMPANY
Mesa Arts Center
55 E. Main St., Mesa
(480) 962-1299
www.swshakespeare.org

The goal of this company is to create a modern-day "people's theatre," whereby audience members take an active role. Past productions have included *Macbeth*, *A Shakespeare Christmas,* and *The Merry Wives of Windsor.* Each production usually runs two weekends in a row. Season tickets cost around

$135; adult and senior single-ticket prices are around $30. Group discounts are available.

ℹ️ **Arizona Theater Company gives teens a chance to be theater critics. The Teen Critic Program teaches students to appreciate theater and also how to construct professional theater reviews. Participating students receive preferred press seating and attend opening night events. Information: (602) 256-6899.**

MUSIC

ARIZONA OPERA
Phoenix Symphony Hall
75 N. 2nd St., Phoenix
(602) 266-7464
www.azopera.com
Arizona Opera's innovative productions include theatrical and technical advances, such as supertitles (for those who need to brush up on Italian) and rear projectors. Past productions have included *The Magic Flute* and *Gems*. The opera season is October through April. Season tickets are available, and individual tickets range from $25 to $119.

THE PHOENIX SYMPHONY
Phoenix Symphony Hall
75 N. 2nd St., Phoenix
(602) 495-1117 (office)
(800) 776-9080 (box office)
www.phoenixsymphony.org
Founded in 1947, the symphony has won recording awards from the American music industry, plus continental Europe's equivalent of the Grammy. Its musicians play classics, chamber, and family concerts. They also provide music for Ballet Arizona, the

Arizona State University Choral Union, and the Phoenix Boys Choir, along with other performance groups. The Phoenix Symphony's season runs September through May. Tickets range in price from $19 to $80. The symphony is generous with its time and gives occasional free concerts in the park. Some concerts are preceded by lectures discussing the music to be performed.

DANCE

BALLET ARIZONA
3645 E. Indian School Rd., Phoenix
(602) 381-0184
(602) 381-1096 (box office)
www.balletaz.org
Ballet Arizona is one of Arizona's largest performing-arts companies. Its repertoire has included demanding classical ballet works, major 20th-century works, world premieres of new works, and cutting-edge choreography. Its annual performance of *The Nutcracker*—performed at Symphony Hall, 75 N. 2nd St., Phoenix—draws thousands of families who might otherwise not be interested in ballet. The company's major performance venues include the Orpheum Theatre, 203 W. Adams St., Phoenix; and Symphony Hall at 75 N. 2nd St., Phoenix. Single tickets range from $17 to $121, with discounts for seniors and students.

ℹ️ **The Scottsdale Artists' School offers an ongoing series of fascinating art lectures that are open to the public and often free. Talks are given in various venues. Information: www.scottsdaleartschool.org or (480) 990-1422.**

CENTER DANCE ENSEMBLE
(602) 997-9027
(602) 252-8497 (box office)
www.centerdance.com

The Herberger Theater Center created the Center Dance Ensemble as its resident modern dance company. The small company has become highly respected through emotional performances of works like *Snow Queen*, based on a Hans Christian Andersen fairy tale. The ensemble performs four times a year at the Herberger, 222 E. Monroe St. in Phoenix. Admission is generally $21 for adults, $17 for seniors, and $9 for students.

VENUES

CHANDLER CENTER FOR THE ARTS
250 N. Arizona Ave., Chandler
(480) 782-2680
www.chandlercenter.org

The high-tech Center for the Arts has contributed to the coming of age of downtown Chandler. Its concerts, road shows, and theatrical productions draw people into what not too long ago was a sleepy city center. Past performers included Bill Cosby, John Tesh, Mickey Rooney, and Burt Bacharach. More than 24 regional arts organizations regularly use the center. In addition to the more than 1,000 activities held each year in its 3 state-of-the-art theaters, the center continuously runs visual arts exhibitions and educational programs.

GAMMAGE AUDITORIUM
Arizona State University
1200 S. Forest Ave., Tempe
(480) 965-3434
www.asugammage.com

One of the Valley's architectural jewels, Gammage was designed by Frank Lloyd Wright and completed in 1964. A redesigned adaptation of Wright's never-built Baghdad Opera House, the auditorium has 50 concrete columns supporting the round roof, which has a pattern of interlocking circles. The 3,000-seat auditorium had an extensive renovation and continues to be known for its acoustic excellence as well as its beauty. This is the place to see touring Broadway shows; Gammage has hosted *Wicked*, *The Color Purple*, and *Sweeney Todd*. It also books smaller theatrical performances and pop and classical music concerts. The stage accommodates a full symphony orchestra and a massive pipe organ.

✳HERBERGER THEATER CENTER
222 E. Monroe St., Phoenix
(602) 254-7399
(602) 252-8497 (box office)
www.herbergertheater.org

A block north of Phoenix Symphony Hall, the Herberger has 2 stages designed to provide an intimate theater experience. The popular venue underwent major renovations in 2010, adding new lighting to the lobby and a chandelier-like lighting feature in the center of rotunda. A new patio with outdoor seating, second-floor Gallery Lounge, and other updates to common areas were established through a 2006 voter-approved bond. The Center Stage seats 802 on 2 levels, and Stage West seats 320 in a proscenium, or horseshoe, configuration on 3 levels. When the orchestra pit is not being used, it can be raised or lowered to accommodate set designs. Acoustics are designed to facilitate the spoken word, making the Herberger a popular venue for theater. With four resident companies and several rentals to community groups, the Herberger bursts with about 600 performances a year.

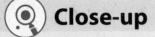 # Close-up

First Fridays

Don't expect polished turquoise jewelry or oil paintings of statuesque cowboys and Indians.

Pounding the pavement along Artlink's First Friday gallery tour in downtown Phoenix is a departure from the tourist hubs of Old Town Scottsdale. The monthly phenomenon is a gritty, organic, heartfelt introduction to urban central Phoenix.

Artlink is a free, self-guided exploration of the revitalized neighborhoods and warehouses around Roosevelt Street and Grand Avenue just north of downtown. Many have been turned into cool little galleries. For years, the local artists who reclaimed the old buildings have built reputations for consistently thoughtful shows hosted from 6 to 10 p.m. the first Friday of each month.

Visitors tread over barren dirt lots, around busted chain link fences, and into houses, some of which look at first glance like dingy frat houses or like something out of *Hoarders*. They are anything but. The folks who have renovated dozens of broken-down properties used for the urban art walk are some of the smartest artists in Arizona. What began with about 10 spaces in 1998 has exploded into more than 100 spaces between established galleries, street fair-style vendors, and other spots. They've reclaimed sections of the city and filled the wasted space with sculpture galleries, spaces for live music, and artsy shops where local thinkers talk about the state of the city.

There's usually a heavy social commentary that ebbs and flows through many of the stops along the Artlink path, with many artists expressing their feelings on immigration enforcement, sex, violence, urban decay, and the ongoing rebirth of downtown.

While many of the galleries feature everything from urban contemporary to avant-garde found art, others feature fine art that comes with Scottsdale-like price tags. Free shuttles pick up and drop off at Phoenix Art Museum. Also, you're never too far from some of the top restaurants and bars in the center city, like Pizzeria Bianco, Sens Asian Tapas & Sake Bar, and FilmBar. (See the Phoenix sections of the Restaurants and Nightlife chapters for more.)

First Friday galleries do an exceptional job of creatively filling their space. The Roosevelt Row sites are particularly popular these days, including Modified Arts, 407 E. Roosevelt St., with its exposed brick backdrop and live performances; Eye Lounge, 419 E. Roosevelt St., which is known for its edgier contemporary exhibits; and MonOrchid Gallery, 214 E. Roosevelt St., one of the largest First Friday sites, which showcases both local and national artists.

Maps are available at galleries and at the nonprofit Artlink office at the Carriage House at Heritage Square, 115 N. 6th St. (602-256-7539).

KERR CULTURAL CENTER
6110 N. Scottsdale Rd., Scottsdale
(480) 596-2660
www.asukerr.com

Tucked in amid the glitzy resorts and shopping centers of Scottsdale Road, Kerr Cultural Center is a 300-seat adobe studio designed for chamber music. Today Kerr's

programming includes jazz, folk, world music, theater, lectures, cameo theatrical events, and family concerts. It is run by Arizona State University. The entrance to Kerr is a little tricky. Follow the signs at the stoplight at Rose Lane near the Borgata Shopping Village.

i The Mesa Arts Center invites art and music lovers to its free concert series, often held Thursday at noon in the outdoor Shadow Walk Plaza. "Out to Lunch" offers a wide range of musical talent. The center is located at 1 E. Main St. in downtown Mesa. For a current schedule visit www.mesaartscenter .com.

✳**MESA ARTS CENTER**
1 E. Main St., Mesa
(480) 644-6500
www.mesaartscenter.com
Billed as the most comprehensive arts center in Arizona, the Mesa Arts Center (MAC) lives up to its promise by sponsoring just about every sort of program imaginable in the world of arts. The campus sits on 7 acres in downtown Mesa. Inside are 4 theaters, from small, intimate studios to the grand and 1,600-seat Ikeda Theater. In the center's art studios and classrooms, students learn everything from ceramics and printmaking to photography and acting. The center also sports 5,500 square feet of exhibition space, including several galleries. It books around 600 to 800 performances annually, including Broadway musicals, rock concerts, and major theatrical performances.

ORPHEUM THEATER
203 W. Adams St., Phoenix
(602) 262-6225
(602) 262-7272 (box office)
The Orpheum was built in 1929 as an ornate Art Deco theater to showcase vaudeville acts and movies. Later it attracted Broadway shows and all kinds of stars. Now it's a hotspot for the fine arts, intimate rock concerts, international ballet, and regional theatrical productions. The Orpheum's history, renovations, and events have been key in the revitalization of downtown Phoenix.

PEORIA CENTER FOR THE
** PERFORMING ARTS**
8355 W. Peoria Ave., Peoria
(623) 815-7930
www.theaterworks.org
The city built the $13 million arts center in 2007 as a major step in revitalizing the downtown area. It features a 250-seat main stage auditorium—an intimate setting to enjoy community theater and other performing arts. The auditorium consists of a proscenium theater with an orchestra pit for live music. In addition to theatrical productions, the resident company, Theater Works, holds a variety of workshops at the center for adults and children.

i On most Thursdays and Saturdays from January through April, the Scottsdale Convention & Visitors Bureau sponsors a free lunchtime Native Trails festival at the amphitheater adjacent to the Scottsdale Center for the Performing Arts. Programs feature an introductory talk by a representative of the Fort McDowell Yavapai Nation, followed by traditional music or dance. Information: (480) 421-1004.

SCOTTSDALE CENTER FOR THE PERFORMING ARTS
7380 E. 2nd St., Scottsdale
(480) 994-2787
www.scottsdaleperformingarts.org
The Scottsdale Center for the Performing Arts and Scottsdale Museum of Contemporary Art (SMoCA) contribute to the city's reputation as a fine-arts destination. The performing arts center hosts more than 60 music, dance, and theater performances, as well as several screenings of independent films throughout the season. Performances by the Phoenix Chamber Music Society, the Phoenix Symphony Chamber Orchestra, and the Scottsdale Symphony Orchestra take place on a regular basis. Some concerts are held under the stars in the center's outdoor amphitheater. Ticket prices vary based on the type of performance.

i Kerr Cultural Center sponsors a free series of lectures and performances called Coffee at Kerr. They are usually held on various weekdays at 9:30 a.m. For details and schedules, call (480) 596-2660. Space is limited, so be sure to RSVP if you plan to attend.

SYMPHONY HALL
75 N. 2nd St., Phoenix
(602) 495-1117 (office)
(800) 776-9080 (box office)
www.phoenixsymphony.org
The home of the Phoenix Symphony Orchestra and the Arizona Opera also hosts touring performers and Broadway shows. The hall, which has the largest proscenium stage downtown, is known for its good acoustics, plush interior, and stunning chandeliers. It seats 2,600 on the main floor and in the balcony.

TEMPE CENTER FOR THE ARTS
700 W. Rio Salado Pkwy., Tempe
(480) 350-5287
(480) 350-2822 (box office)
www.tempe.gov/tca
The $63 million performing arts center is located on Tempe Town Lake, just blocks from Mill Avenue and the city's core. Its 88,000 square feet feature a 600-seat 4-tiered theater that accommodates dance and drama. A more intimate studio seats 200. The center also houses a gallery and meeting rooms. The center is home to the Actors' Renaissance Theater, the Arizona Academy of the Performing Arts, Childsplay, the Desert Dance Theater, and the Tempe Little Theater, among others.

VISUAL ARTS

Art Museums

ARIZONA STATE UNIVERSITY ART MUSEUM
51 E. 10th St., Tempe
(480) 965-2787
http://asuartmuseum.asu.edu
The campus art museum is linked with the Herberger Institute for Design and the Arts at the Nelson Fine Arts Center. The light rail connection to Tempe and ASU provides easy access to the museum's contemporary art exhibitions, which include touring national works. Programs encourage free expression of social issues through a variety of media, including new media. Free admission.

HEARD MUSEUM NORTH
32633 N. Scottsdale Rd., Scottsdale
(480) 488-9817
www.heard.org/north
The northern branch of the famed Heard Museum (detailed in Attractions chapter)

includes 2 exhibition galleries that feature changing exhibitions of Native American art. It also hosts guest artists and special events. The museum shop offers the highest-quality arts and crafts by Native American artists. Admission is $5 for adults, with discounts for seniors, students, and kids.

SHEMER ART CENTER & MUSEUM
5005 E. Camelback Rd., Phoenix
(602) 262-4727
www.shemerartcenterandmuseum.org
The small museum makes its home in the first house built in Arcadia, a stately neighborhood at the base of Camelback Mountain. It has been expanded and renovated over the years but maintains an "old Phoenix" character. Inside you'll find contemporary works by local artists. Bold steel sculptures and a citrus orchard enliven the center's grounds. In addition to a variety of art classes for all ages, the museum sponsors an Artists' Cafe series where local artists can keep abreast of trends and issues. Admission is free for most shows.

WEST VALLEY ART MUSEUM
17420 N. Avenue of the Arts, Surprise
(623) 972-0635
www.wvam.org
The Surprise museum's collection of ethnic costumes from more than 75 countries, acquired from all over the world, is worth seeing, as is the sculpture garden. It has an extensive permanent collection featuring more than 50 Japanese woodcuts and more than 300 prints by Andy Warhol and other American artists. The museum offers art classes, a concert series, and other events.

Galleries

BENTLEY GALLERY
4161 N. Marshall Way, Scottsdale
(480) 946-6060
www.bentleygallery.com
The Bentley specializes in abstract and minimalistic contemporary painting and sculpture. This is where interior designers find marvelous steel sculptures.

CERVINI HAAS GALLERY
7007 E. 5th Ave., Scottsdale
(480) 429-6116
www.cervinihaas.com
A gallery like this helps you appreciate the artistry and variety in the realm of crafts. You'll find high-quality contemporary crafts in wood, ceramics, basketry, and glass, plus jewelry and clothing. The gallery runs a blog that takes viewers behind the scenes with featured artists.

GEBERT CONTEMPORARY ART GALLERY
7160 E. Main St., Scottsdale
(480) 429-0711
www.chiaroscuroaz.com
This gallery displays work from a variety of contemporary artists and is viewed by locals in the art scene as one of the best contemporary galleries. The focus here is on sculpture of various materials, but there is also an interesting array of paintings and photography. Work includes evocative stoneware and elaborate floral paintings.

GILBERT ORTEGA MUSEUM GALLERY
3925 N. Scottsdale Rd., Scottsdale
(480) 990-1808
Ortega, a 4th-generation trader in Native American arts and crafts, boasts a dozen locations around the Valley. If you're in the

market for authentic Native American jewelry, baskets, rugs, and pottery, it's a good idea to get a sense of the variety by stopping in at one of these stores. The museum gallery is the biggest and best location, combining a retail store and display area for several museum-quality pieces from Ortega's private collection.

JOAN CAWLEY GALLERY
7135 E. Main St., Scottsdale
(480) 947-3548
www.jcgltd.com
Another veteran of the Scottsdale gallery scene, Joan Cawley showcases American contemporary and Southwestern art. Claiming "we know West," the gallery boasts landscape, wildlife, abstract, Native American, and Latin art, among other forms. The Scottsdale gallery features around 50 artists and rotates its presentation monthly.

> **i** The Dancin' Dads, a group of men with daughters taking classes at Marilyn's Academy of Dance in Peoria, perform during Phoenix Suns games, Christmas pageants, and a host of other events. It's hilarious to some, artful to others. And you can hire them to bust a move at your own party. Information: www.dancindads.com or (623) 412-8883.

LISA SETTE GALLERY
4142 N. Marshall Way, Scottsdale
(480) 990-7342
www.lisasettegallery.com
This gallery, loved by serious contemporary collectors, represents national and even international artists. Even those who don't know much about art will appreciate works

such as those by William Wegman, whose clever dog photos have picked up commercial appeal.

OVERLAND GALLERY OF FINE ART
7155 E. Main St., Scottsdale
(480) 947-1934
www.overlandgallery.com
Overland is known for its collection of early-20th-century Russian impressionism. This is the place to pick up Western and American representational art for your home's formal living spaces. Merchandise includes hand-painted original stone lithographs.

RIMA FINE ART
7130 E. Main St., Scottsdale
(480) 994-8899
www.rimafineart.com
This gallery features contemporary Russian painters but also has a nice collection of French impressionists, plus 20th-century masters of the Southwest. Among the more interesting pieces are rare sculptures by Auguste Rodin. Rima is routinely reviewed as one of the best galleries in Scottsdale.

RIVA YARES GALLERY
3625 N. Bishop Ln., Scottsdale
(480) 947-3251
www.rivayaresgallery.com
The Yares Gallery is set a bit apart from the crowd, both geographically and philosophically. Two blocks south of most of the galleries, its high-tech exterior looks freshly transplanted from New York City. That metropolitan attitude carries over to the gallery's collection, which emphasizes abstract and contemporary art.

Art Walks & Festivals

✳HIDDEN IN THE HILLS STUDIO TOUR
Cave Creek
(480) 575-6624
www.sonoranartsleague.org/hidden.php

Once a year over two weekends in November, the artists who live and work in the hills around Cave Creek open their studios for a public tour. The tour is presented by the Sonoran Arts League and represents more than 100 artists. The event offers a chance to see sculptures, paintings, glasswork, and pottery, some by nationally known artists. It's also an ideal way to see the artists at work in their personal workshops. Maps to the studios are available from area retailers or the Cave Creek Chamber of Commerce by calling the number listed. Also, a downloadable map is available on the website.

MAGIC BIRD ARTS & CRAFTS
FESTIVALS
Locations vary
(480) 488-2014
www.magicbirdfestivals.com

The festivals hosted in the Valley's cooler months usually feature dozens of booths, imported wares, food, music, and family entertainment. Locations include major parks and spring training baseball complexes, such as Salt River Fields and Surprise Stadium. Admission and parking are free.

i For a map of a self-guided tour to Scottsdale's public art sites, contact the Scottsdale Cultural Council at (480) 994-ARTS or download a map at www.scottsdalepublicart.org/maps.php.

SCOTTSDALE ARTWALK
Downtown Scottsdale
www.scottsdalegalleries.com

On Thursday evening several streets in downtown Scottsdale are typically loaded with pedestrians hopping from gallery to gallery. Head for Marshall Way, 5th Avenue, 1st Avenue, Main Street, and Craftsman Court for a free art-gazing experience. The ArtWalk is presented by the Scottsdale Gallery Association. The 75-plus members open their doors year-round for free entertainment, refreshments, and artist demonstrations.

i The city of Phoenix built a large panel to preserve more than 160 petroglyphs at 19th Avenue and Greenway Road. In Tempe find petroglyphs along the hike up "A" Mountain near Arizona State University. The Petroglyph Trail in the Superstition Mountains in the Southeast Valley is one of the best hikes in the Mesa area. For more information on petroglyphs, visit the Deer Valley Rock Art Center or call (623) 582-8007.

THUNDERBIRD ARTISTS FINE ART &
WINE FESTIVALS
Various locations
(480) 837-5637
www.thunderbirdartists.com

Those interested in buying paintings or sculptures, especially in the Southwestern genre, should check out the juried fine art and fine crafts festivals organized by Thunderbird Artists. The group, which represents about 150 US artists, often exhibits work in conjunction with various festivals according to theme. The Carefree Fine Art & Wine Festival, held on various weekends from November to March, turns the streets

of Carefree into one big art gallery. Other festivals are held in Scottsdale and Fountain Hills. The free shows usually run during the day on weekends in the cooler months.

ARTS ORGANIZATIONS

ARIZONA ARTISTS GUILD
18411 N. 7th Ave., Phoenix
(602) 944-9713
www.arizonaartistsguild.net
The nonprofit Arizona Artists Guild provides a nurturing environment for artists. It meets the third Tues of each month, Sept to Apr, at 7 p.m. Meetings include talks and demonstrations by nationally known artists, which non-members can attend. Members with an interest in a specific medium, such as sculpting, get together regularly. Other activities include juried exhibitions, critique groups, and a fund-raiser.

ARIZONA COMMISSION ON THE ARTS
417 W. Roosevelt St., Phoenix
(602) 771-6501
www.azarts.gov
The Arizona Commission on the Arts is a state-funded agency. It has sponsored such projects as "Voices: Community Stories Past and Present," which strives to collect and preserve oral history and also various performing arts exchanges. The commission also runs the creative azarts417 blog on its website, which gives viewers news and insight into the Valley arts scene.

PHOENIX OFFICE OF ARTS & CULTURE
City Hall
200 W. Washington St., 10th Floor,
Phoenix
(602) 262-4637
www.phoenix.gov/arts

The city arts commission's mandate has been to enhance the arts in Phoenix and raise the public's awareness and involvement in preserving, expanding, and enjoying the arts. The commission also directs a public art program—outdoor sculptures, murals, and other works—and fosters arts education in the schools. Many of the city's cultural activities are funded by matching grants from the commission. Its website is a helpful resource for city events.

SCOTTSDALE ARTISTS' SCHOOL
3720 N. Marshall Way, Scottsdale
(480) 990-1422, (800) 333-5707
www.scottsdaleartschool.org
Since 1983 the nonprofit Scottsdale Artists' School has been a small oasis of art instruction, attracting adults of all skill levels from all over the country and abroad. One reason the school is so popular is its roster of working artists who serve on the faculty. Students have a chance to learn portraiture, still-life painting, figure sculpture, and dozens of other techniques. Annual enrollment is about 3,000, and early registration is recommended.

SCOTTSDALE CULTURAL COUNCIL
7380 E. 2nd St., Scottsdale
(480) 874-4610
www.sccarts.org
The Scottsdale Cultural Council is a nonprofit arts management organization contracted by the City of Scottsdale to oversee its cultural affairs, including management of the Scottsdale Center for the Performing Arts, SMoCA (Scottsdale Museum of Contemporary Art), the Scottsdale Public Art program, and the Scottsdale Arts Festival. The council has been recognized with accolades and awards for its contributions

to the community, including an Arizona Humanities Council Distinguished Organization Award.

WEST VALLEY ARTS COUNCIL
13423 W. Founders Park Blvd., Surprise
(623) 935-6384
www.westvalleyarts.org
The arts scene in the West Valley is small but poised to grow as new residents pour in. Keeping on top of the situation is the West Valley Fine Arts Council, which receives funding from the Arizona Commission on the Arts and elsewhere. It is entrusted with developing, enhancing, and promoting quality arts and arts education in the entire West Valley, a region that encompasses everything west of I-17. The council's annual Native American Festival is a showcase of authentic crafts, music, and hands-on activities for families. The council also organizes regular concerts ranging from classical to pop music.

OUR NATURAL WORLD

Visitors tend to the think of the desert as a harsh, unforgiving place. Others simply come to Phoenix for the golf and resort swimming pools. But none of that accurately depicts the Sonoran Desert's place in America.

The sun is shining nearly every day, and the temperatures most certainly shoot into triple digits several months of the year. But the feel of a nature walk in the foothills in March or October, or a day or two after a monsoon rain, gives you a much better sense of the landscape. One glimpse at a hillside of blooming saguaro cacti and it seems like a different planet, far removed from the faceless commercial developments and cookie cutter homes that clutter so much of the New West.

Hiking in Arizona is unlike hiking anywhere else in the world. This is the Grand Canyon State. And while that massive chasm in northern Arizona is the greatest outdoor experience in the state, the Valley is scattered with parks and preserves that will help you refocus your own personal energy in a natural setting just miles from the city. You won't have to go far to reconnect with nature. Tarantulas, coyotes, mountain lions, bobcat, rattlesnakes, and Gila monsters are among the creatures that call these parks home.

The city has plenty to offer, but so does the desert. Keep in mind that the patch of sand outside your hotel doesn't count. In any direction, about 20 or 30 minutes out of downtown Phoenix or Scottsdale, you will find your path and agree there's something soothing about this arid climate.

A ROCKY DESERT

Phoenix and the Valley of the Sun sit at the northern extreme of the Sonoran Desert, an ancient seabed that's now almost devoid of moisture. Mentioning a desert may call to mind movie panoramas of windblown sand dunes, but that's the wrong picture. Before humanity's intrusion, the Sonoran Desert was an endless tract of eroded, brown mountains punctuated by valleys of patchy desert grass, palo verde trees, saguaro cactus, and creosote bushes. The sand is brown, reddish-brown, or a gravelly gray. It doesn't accumulate in dunes or even seem like sand really, but rather a surface grit.

At a distance the desert's precipitous mountains look like piles of precariously balanced rocks ready to come tumbling down if a crucial stone is pulled out. This is an illusion created by erosion. The topsoil has been stripped away by the eons, and today we view the bedrock, the skeleton of these mountains. The smoothness of their surfaces recalls their origins at the bottom of an ancient sea.

Other mountains, still brown, slope more gently toward the sky. More hospitable than the rock-faced giants, these mountains' sides are dotted with cacti, and the surfaces seem coarse and pebbly. Some of the mountains are relics of ancient volcanic activity, but today those forces of nature sleep soundly. Although Arizona is the next-door neighbor of seismically active California, it's relatively inactive as far as earthquakes are concerned.

THE LAY OF THE LAND

Essentially, the Valley of the Sun is the Salt River Valley. The metropolitan area is bisected and bounded by rivers about 1,000 feet above sea level. The Salt River, or Rio Salado, cuts across the Valley, and its ready supply of water was Phoenix's initial reason for being. To the east of the Valley, the Salt meets the Verde River as both wend their way down from mountain ranges. To the west the Salt flows into the Gila River, which continues westward to the Colorado River on Arizona's border with California. Like a western boundary line for the Valley of the Sun, the Agua Fria River flows from the north into the Gila. The nearly imperceptible slope of the Salt River Valley gives the Phoenix metro area the appearance of a plain ringed by gigantic, jagged teeth.

Phoenix looks northwest to the Bradshaw Mountains; its topography to the north and east gradually rises to the steep ascent known as the Mogollon Rim (pronounced *muggy-OWN*). To the south, South Mountain creates a wall within the city only recently girdled by new housing developments spreading southward. The Estrella and White Tank mountains rise to the southwest and west. The majestic Superstitions dominate the southeast, while the Northeast Valley's McDowell Mountains separate the luxury neighborhoods of north Scottsdale from others in Fountain Hills.

Humanity has made South Mountain, which sits south of the Salt River, among the Valley's most identifiable summits. Broadcast towers blinking their red warnings to aircraft are clustered atop the mountain. On a clear night they can be seen from the ground more than 50 miles away, like a homing beacon for returning travelers.

Other easily identified rock giants include Camelback Mountain and Squaw Peak. As its name implies, Camelback huddles like a sleeping camel in the middle of the city, surrounded by mansions and resorts. To the west Squaw Peak provides a vexing sensitivity problem. In 2003 Arizona Governor Janet Napolitano and the Arizona Board on Geographic and Historic Names instigated a name change from Squaw Peak to Piestewa Peak in honor of Lori Piestewa, the first Native American woman to die in combat. The heated debate over the seemingly politically correct reaction to complaints from activists distracted the Valley briefly from the scenic hiking and biking trails the park is known for.

i The Sonoran landscape is dotted with old abandoned mine shafts, especially in the mountains outside Phoenix. Authorities warn that it's dangerous to explore the old holes in the ground, many of which were dug by inexperienced Easterners who had more ambition than technical skill. A hundred years later they are prone to cave-ins.

From a distance the Papago Park buttes, which today overlook the Phoenix Zoo

and the Desert Botanical Garden, look like smooth bumps separating Phoenix from Scottsdale and Tempe. Their reddish-brown surfaces make them look like close cousins to Camelback well to the north. You can climb through the red rock formations and peer out of the Window Rock at sunset.

WEATHER & CLIMATE

Many people complain that it's hotter than hell in Phoenix in the summer. Without knowing the forecast in hell, we admit the air temperature can feel pretty similar. Climbing into a black car with no tint on the windows is a terribly painful experience. People are also fond of saying, "It's a dry heat," though you'll find you sweat nearly as much in the Valley as you would in lower temperatures in more humid climates.

The hottest days peak at more than 120 degrees Fahrenheit. Summer ignores the calendar here, with 100-degree days sometimes stretching from May to October. On the upside, the lack of humidity means the shade of a leafy tree offers considerable relief. Swimmers emerging from a pool on a hot summer day may suddenly feel chilled because the water evaporates so quickly off their skin. As long as the air is dry, many say that 105 degrees in Phoenix is more comfortable than 95 degrees in a humid climate.

A desert undergoes vast temperature fluctuations each day. The scorching midday heat gives way to a chill in the dead of night. The desert doesn't have an insulating coat of humid air (dry heat makes way for dry cold) or a thick blanket of vegetation to hold the day's heat close during the night.

Such is not the case for the Valley of the Sun, except on its very fringes. A "heat sink" effect is a direct result of the Valley's

staggering growth. In 1940 Phoenix was a cow town of 65,000 and Scottsdale was a hamlet of 1,000. Now, the sun beats down on the city pavement, sidewalks, and buildings all day. These structures store the heat, and at night they radiate it back into the air. Average summer low temperatures have been climbing for decades, and it is not unusual to experience 100-degree temperatures well after dark. This is a major change from the days when agriculture was the dominant industry.

Believe it or not, with irrigation provided by the federal Salt River Project, certain crops grow extremely well in this climate. Desert soil that had never seen the plow proved rich in nutrients. In 1915, soon after the completion of Roosevelt Dam, creating Phoenix's primary water source of Roosevelt Lake, there were 250,000 acres of alfalfa, cotton, citrus, grain, and other crops under cultivation. The large number of irrigated fields provided significant cooling at night.

During the winter, temperatures creep down to below freezing in the Valley's colder locations, and people have to protect frost-sensitive citrus and other plants and flowers. These low temperatures usually occur only in the dead of night, and any accumulated frost or ice melts away by midmorning. On rare occasions some snow may dust the outlying mountaintops of Four Peaks, the Superstitions, or the Bradshaws. You can smell the snow in the air, feel a little chill, and still work or play outside in shirtsleeves. Winter is also the most likely time to see fog in Phoenix, as cool air close to the ground holds the winter moisture.

During the winter a warm air mass traps the cold air close to the surface like an invisible bowl held over the Valley, creating what TV weather forecasters call an "inversion

layer." The surface air stagnates, and pollutants accumulate to unhealthy levels, waiting for a weather front to push them out. In an effort to fight this situation, Maricopa County declares no-burn days when wood-burning stoves and fireplaces, long popular accoutrements for Valley homes, may not be used. Also, the use of oxygenated fuels is mandated for Valley vehicles in the winter months. Ordinances banning the installation of wood-burning fireplaces in new construction have also been passed by Valley municipalities.

THE MONSOON

In early- to mid-summer humidity builds up into a rainy season known locally as "the monsoon." The presence of the monsoon is not determined by the presence of storms but by the measure of moisture. When the average dew point hits 55 degrees for 3 days in a row, the monsoon season is considered to be up and running.

Like its namesake in southern Asia, the Arizona monsoon depends on a shift in the prevailing winds. During the rest of the year, these winds come from the east, but as the monsoon builds, sometime in late June or early July, the prevailing winds begin to come out of the west. Moisture flows up through Mexico from the Pacific Ocean and the Gulf of California, stirring up torrential rains, impenetrable dust, and purple streaks of lightning.

The surrounding mountains and the Valley's superhot air seem to form a barrier that has to be hammered away by the increasing strength of the monsoon system. Each day the thunderheads creep closer but then dissipate in rain over the mountains. The Valley almost resists the incursion of these summer storms, even as Valley dwellers wish the tease would end and the rains begin. After all, the humidity is building, and desert living is at its most uncomfortable. Everyone anticipates the welcome release of the rain, knowing it will refresh the landscape and wash away the city dust and soot.

i One good way to avoid becoming lost on a desert hike is to choose an arroyo (dry riverbed) to follow. You can hike along the riverbed, enjoy a picnic lunch, and turn around when you are tired. Be careful to avoid walking along an arroyo during rainy season, though, as the riverbeds are prone to flash floods.

These storms cause flash flooding through the normally dry channels of washes and arroyos. In a matter of minutes, gentle trickles become full torrents. This is the natural course of storms in the desert, where the vegetation is sparse and the rock-hard surface resists rapid percolation of the water. The ground refuses to absorb the water, so it runs off, accumulating in the washes. The gathered waters flow rapidly to a low point—in this case the Salt River. The Valley's building boom aggravated those natural tendencies, and new developments are required to have flood-retention basins to prevent flash flooding in neighborhoods.

The monsoon storms generally occur in the late afternoons and early evenings, after the atmosphere has had the whole day to saturate itself with moisture. The National Weather Service's storm warnings usually expire no later than midnight. In the early morning, the cycle begins again as the moisture deposited earlier starts to evaporate and form clouds.

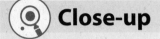

Close-up

Saving Our Wildlife

Kachina the coyote was taken in by a human family as a cub because she was small and adorable. The family tried to raise her, but as she grew she tore the house apart. The family decided Kachina couldn't stay and called the Southwest Wildlife Rehabilitation & Education Foundation in Scottsdale.

Linda Searles, executive director of the facility, often sees this happen. She and 75 dedicated volunteers care for wounded or orphaned birds, coyotes, javelinas, bears, wolves, mountain lions, bobcats—almost every sort of creature in the Sonoran Desert.

The center is open for wildlife emergencies 24/7, and its mission is to save the desert one life at a time. The center rescues, rehabilitates, and then releases native creatures whenever possible. In most cases the center is an animal's last chance for life.

"Feeding a coyote by hand is a death sentence for the coyote," says Lynne Locascio, a foundation volunteer. "It'll approach the wrong person and be shot." Kachina the coyote must live her life at the center because she is caught between two worlds—both wild and tame.

Usually the center succeeds in returning an animal to the wild. The facility owns a fully equipped operating room and a small pharmacy and has passionate people willing to track wounded animals, dart them with a sedative when necessary, and get medical care. They've saved thousands of birds and animals. The community helps, too. Boy Scout troops build cages on the 10-acre lot.

The center's second mission is education. Tours are available by appointment. To arrange a tour or to report an injured animal, call (480) 471-3621.

The nonprofit Southwest Wildlife Rehabilitation & Education Foundation can be contacted at PMB #115, 8711 E. Pinnacle Peak Rd., Scottsdale 85255, or www.south westwildlife.org.

Often the thunderstorms are preceded by pillars of blowing dust whipped up from the desert surface to thousands of feet in the air. An approaching dust storm looks like an ominous thick wall of airborne dirt that blocks the sun. In the worst case, visibility goes down to zero, making it extremely dangerous to drive. In some rare instances, the dirt stays in the air even after the rain hits, and the water showers everything with tiny blobs of mud.

There's no official measure of when the monsoon ends. The humidity suddenly stops anywhere from late August to mid-September. Compared with the monsoon storms, most other rains in the Valley are gentle. In some years the monsoon season is much drier than in other years. Even less dependable is the winter rainy season, which can fluctuate wildly in intensity. Generally, the winter rains are soft. Yet the worst flooding in the 1990s and early 2000s resulted from winter storms fanned by the Pacific Ocean weather condition known as El Niño. Despite all the stormy weather, the average annual rainfall is listed as a mere 7.66 inches.

THE DESERT AS GARDEN

Visitors are often stunned at the bright springtime colors of the desert in bloom. The palo verde tree's bright green bark and leafless, bony branches explode into bright yellow blooms. As the ironwood tree blossoms purple, the yucca wears white, the ocotillo sports red, and the saguaro crowns itself with waxy white flowers high above the desert floor.

Varieties of cacti abound precisely because they are so adapted to the undependable rainfall of the desert. Cacti fall under the classification "succulents" because they store water in preparation for bone-dry years. The saguaro is among the largest of cacti, and mature plants can grow to be 50 feet tall and weigh up to 20 tons—98 percent of which is water. Its white bloom is Arizona's state flower; the majestic plants, which run wild through the foothills of the Sonoran Desert, are as significant an Arizona symbol as the Grand Canyon. Sixty miles north of Phoenix, the saguaro disappear as the ground level rises.

Another familiar sight is the barrel cactus, particularly since it's quite popular as a landscaping plant. The barrel cactus grows to about 5 feet tall. Its spines are not thin and fine like hair, yet they resemble hair in the way they cover the barrel's stubby body. This is the cactus a lost desert traveler could dig into for water.

Most people already know the prickly pear cactus, which comes in 300 varieties that have been cultivated around the world. Unlike most cacti, it is not tubular. Its flat pads look like thorny, oval-shaped oven mitts. Fruit and flowers bud atop the edges of the pads.

The cholla (CHOY-uh), especially the breed known as the teddy-bear cholla (or jumping cactus), has numerous barbed spines, which make the plant look like an unkempt, hairy hermit. The spines dig into flesh and, because of their barbs, are hard to get out. The jumping cactus likes to trick the unsuspecting: People tend to misjudge the spines, walk too close, and brush against them. The teddy-bear joints detach easily upon contact. First-timers will say the cactus jumped out to get them, hence the name.

Another desert plant that's popular in landscaping is the ocotillo (oh-ca-TEA-oh), which is not a succulent. Its strategy of defense against long dry periods is to remain dormant most of the time, its thorny arms like octopus tendrils praying for water. After a rain its brown arms sprout thousands of tiny green leaves and then shed them to prevent water loss by transpiration.

The agave (ah-GAH-vay), or century plant, lives up to 75 years to bloom just once. At the end of its life, the agave sends up a stalk that might grow to be 30 feet high. The stalk holds the precious blooms, and once that work is done, the agave dies. Yuccas, which bear a close resemblance, also show up in desert landscaping.

Arizona's state tree, the palo verde, generally grows in desert washes. It bears leaves for a short time but sheds them, as the ocotillo does, to conserve water. Photosynthesis continues, though. The tree's bark is green because of the presence of chlorophyll, the catalyst of photosynthesis, and the surfaces of the branches sustain the tree the way leaves do on other trees.

Mesquite (mess-KEET) trees are not native to the Sonoran Desert. They were imported from Texas. They can grow up to 30 feet tall, though most in Arizona are smaller. Their root systems will spread out as much as twice that distance to trap as much water as

Desert Safety Tips

Many Arizonans are avid fans of one or more outdoor sports such as hiking, rock climbing, and mountain biking. But it is important to remember that the desert is also a harsh and unforgiving place. Every year people are injured or even killed because they ignore basic safety tips:

- **Bring plenty of water.** A liter per person for every 2 hours is recommended. Freeze water bottles overnight or load them with ice to make the water more refreshing on hot days. Drink frequently, not just when you get thirsty. If you are thirsty, you are already a bit dehydrated. It's also a good idea to hydrate before you set out.

- **Bring a pair of tweezers.** Many desert plants have thorns, so look, but don't touch. If you get stuck by one, don't try to pull out the thorns with your fingers. Working without tweezers may just transfer the thorns to your fingers and hurt a lot more.

- **Dress appropriately.** Loose-fitting, cool clothing that covers most of your skin and a broad-brimmed hat are best. Sturdy shoes or hiking boots are important, and long pants will help protect you from thorns.

- **Use an effective sunscreen.** Arizonans have a very high rate of skin cancer. The desert is not a place to work on your tan. Sunburn can happen before you know it and can lead to dehydration or heat-related illness.

- **Never hike alone.** See the film *127 Hours* for a startling reminder.

- **Never touch or handle wildlife.** Many will bite or sting if threatened, and some are poisonous.

- **Never stick your fingers or toes anywhere you haven't looked in first.** Snakes and scorpions often hide in dark nooks and crevices.

- **If you are bitten, remain calm.** Even rattlesnakes and scorpions are rarely fatal. Have your fellow hikers drive you immediately to the nearest ranger station or hospital. While snakebite kits may provide some help, they are no substitute for proper medical attention.

- **Tell someone where you are going and when you expect to be back.** Find out about your hike first. Outdoor shops and national parks can provide maps and information for a wide variety of hikes.

- **Stay on the trail.** This will reduce your chances of getting hurt or lost. It will also help preserve the desert's fragile ecosystem.

possible during a rain. Grazing cattle, eating the tree's beans and depositing them elsewhere in their droppings, helped the trees multiply rapidly in Arizona's rangeland.

The creosote bush dominates the Sonoran Desert. Its survival strategy seems to be birth control. The plants are widely spaced so that they don't vie with one

another for water. Scientists believe this happens partly because the mature plants produce substances that inhibit seedlings.

CRITTERS GREAT & SMALL

Without air-conditioning and irrigation, only hardy creatures can survive the Sonoran Desert's extremes of climate. Before humanity got here, inhabitants developed their own means to cope with the desert's undependable rainfall and extreme heat. In a land where food is scarce for all creatures, they developed vicious defenses against becoming food themselves, whether the spiny barbs of the jumping cactus or the poisonous sting of the scorpion. The desert includes 16 species of rattlesnake and more than 20 species of scorpion, not to mention 4 species of skunk and the Gila monster, the only species of poisonous lizard in the US. Two poisonous spiders—the Arizona brown spider (cousin to the brown recluse) and the black widow—also make their home in the desert's dark spots, where flies serve as plentiful food.

i Gilbert's 110-acre Riparian Preserve at Water Ranch is considered one of the best bird watching spots in a state noted for extraordinary birding. The preserve is on Guadalupe Road, east of Greenfield Road, next to Southeast Regional Library in Gilbert. Information: (480) 503-6744 or www .riparianinstitute.com.

Spend some time with interpretive park rangers or other wildlife experts and you'll learn to appreciate the beauty of these creepy crawlers. The black shell of the black widow is almost luminescent. The skin of the Gila monster looks like an exquisitely beaded belt. The scorpion's claws and venomous stinger make it appear like the gladiator of desert arachnids.

i For answers to all your questions about desert plant care, call the Desert Botanical Gardens hotline at (480) 481-8120. Experts are available weekdays 9 a.m. to 4 p.m.

The relentless sun can heat the desert floor to 150 degrees Fahrenheit; so many desert creatures are nocturnal. Foremost among these is the coyote, the wily trickster from Native American lore. Perhaps the notion of being a trickster comes from the coyote's speed, which can fool those unfamiliar with it. Another factor in the coyote's trickster image is that coyotes hunt in packs in clever fashion. One will chase the prey while others rest, and then one of the rested will take up the pursuit if necessary. The prey never gets to rest, of course, and eventually tires. Coyotes also are opportunistic, so they don't often work hard to find food. They eat carrion, diseased animals, and even plants. Coyotes are generally gray and weigh in at between 15 and 45 pounds. The Valley's relentless growth has driven back the coyote to the fringes, but outlying homeowners and campers know not to let domestic cats or small dogs out where they will become easy prey. Most people who've lived here have heard the unmistakable howls of a coyote in the distance.

Roadrunners are rarely seen in the Valley since they've mostly been driven out by settlement, but every now and then you'll spot one dashing across a road in an outlying area. They're noticeable with their Mohawk-like headdress and long legs.

Like the coyote, predators such as the mountain lion, the bobcat, and the badger don't hang around the Valley much, though those animals and others, like bear or deer, will find their way into urban areas every so often. Most of the remaining wildlife in the Valley is pretty good at hiding itself. Fleet-footed jackrabbits and cottontails tend to jump out of the brush, even in the city. People don't see owls much, but they're up there, waiting to come out at night to catch rodents. Any number of small lizards dwell in your backyard, and toads occasionally show up.

The Valley's diversity of birds is great, but you're most likely to see pigeons, sparrows, finches, woodpeckers, doves, ducks, and geese. Every yard seems to have a mockingbird. Set out a hummingbird feeder, and the spoon-size birds will show up hungry. It takes a lot of fuel to power those rapid-fire wings. The state bird is the cactus wren. It is the largest North American wren, but it prefers the open desert to the confines of civilization. The wren loves to nest in cholla, where its home is protected from predators by the cholla's spines. The Gila woodpecker and the gilded flicker, on the other hand, cut holes into a saguaro cactus and nest inside. Some hawks make their nests in the crook of the saguaro's arm, although they're not likely to do it in your backyard. Bats also lurk here. They're prized by some for their ability to keep the insect population down.

Poisonous snakes such as the Western diamondback rattlesnake, which can grow to more than 6 feet long, prefer to stay away from humanity. However, Valley residents have occasionally found rattlesnakes on their doorsteps or in their garages in the spring. Usually, such snakes are halfway dazed as they come out of hibernation and have wandered someplace they don't really want to be in search of a place to sun themselves. If you see one, don't assume it will give you a warning before it strikes. They are very quick and don't necessarily rattle their tails before striking. Call an animal-control officer first, rather than the fire department. However, both are prepared to handle snakes.

The Valley harbors the poisonous black widow and Arizona brown spiders. The black widow female is usually about a half-inch long, a glossy black with a red hourglass on her underside. The male is seldom seen and carries red marks along the sides of its abdomen. (Maybe he's seldom seen because the female has a habit of eating him after mating.) Widows will eat other spiders along with other insects. They are easily provoked when guarding an egg sac but otherwise calm. The spider is found in the warm regions of all 48 contiguous states. The spider's venom causes muscle spasms and on rare occasions can be fatal, mostly in children, seniors, or others with weaker immune systems.

The Arizona brown spider is about $2/5$ of an inch long, with a yellow-orange hue and a violin shape on its back. Like a true desert dweller, it is nocturnal, and it paralyzes small insects with its poison to trap them before feeding. Its bite is rarely fatal, but this is a creature you don't want in your house. They have been known to bite sleepers, leaving ugly round scars where the venom kills the skin.

If you want to get a human Valley dweller upset, talk about a scorpion bite. Scorpions don't bite. They sting. They have pincers that make them look something like tiny lobsters, but the sting is in the tail. Scorpions are found under rocks in the desert, so be careful if you're turning over a stone. Generally, the smaller the scorpion, the more

dangerous its sting. *Centruroides sculpturatus* is the deadliest in Arizona and can kill humans, although this rarely happens anymore. This tiny scorpion is distinguished by a thin tail and straw-colored body about 2 inches long.

> **i** Don't panic at the bite of a venomous bug or snake. Stay calm and call the Banner Good Samaritan Poison and Drug Information Center hotline: (602) 253-3334 or (800) 222-1222.

Relative newcomers to the pantheon of Valley pests are the Africanized honeybees, commonly known as "killer bees." These bees arrived in Arizona from Mexico in the late 1980s and by the early 1990s had extended their range to include the Valley. They are uncommonly aggressive in defense of their hives and will swarm over a perceived intruder and sting relentlessly. Depending on the susceptibility of the victim, even the gentler European honeybee can kill, so the killer bees' threat is greatly exaggerated. Still, caution is advised. The basic preventive measure is to watch for bee activity and call a beekeeper if a hive is forming on some part of your property.

PARKS & RECREATION

The Valley's continuously warm climate makes for an idyllic setting most of the year. Few places in the US provide more opportunity for golf, baseball, hiking, mountain biking, or just about anything else you do outdoors. Winter sports are the exception. But believe it or not, it snows in the high country, and you're able to snowboard or ski up there, too.

Everyone knows there's plenty of mountain hiking, rock climbing, and other hillside recreation available here. But the Valley is also known for its lakes, which are loaded with fish and perfect for water sports. Horseback riding is also a major draw in the Valley, and the thriving equestrian culture enables visitors to see the desert from the saddled back of a four-legged guide. Municipal parks and aquatic centers provide more options for everything from softball and tennis to wave pools.

To give you an overview of the Valley's outdoor hotspots, we've divided this chapter into two sections. The first is Parks, in which we list the major parks in and around the Valley of the Sun and the variety of recreational offerings each one affords. The second section is Recreation, which focuses on specific recreational activities, like horseback riding and soaring. For information on camping in the Valley, see the RV Parks & Campgrounds chapter. Some sites, like Papago Park (Phoenix Zoo, Desert Botanical Garden), McCormick-Stillman Railroad Park for families with young children, and Sahuaro Ranch in Glendale Park are detailed in the Attractions and Kidstuff chapters.

PARKS

National Forest

TONTO NATIONAL FOREST
www.fs.fed.us/r3/tonto

Tonto National Forest is adjacent to the Valley, bordering north Scottsdale and Mesa and Valley points in between. The forest covers nearly 3 million acres of wilderness, and the Forest Service says it is one of the most heavily visited national forests. You might wonder what makes it a forest since there are so few tall trees, but there are actually some pine-covered areas further into the wilderness and lower desert trees closer to civilization. Elevations range from 1,300 to almost 8,000 feet. There is a $6 day-use fee plus $4 per watercraft, plus charges for camping and other activities.

Many Valley dwellers are attracted to the water-based activities in the forest on the Verde and Salt rivers and reservoirs like Saguaro Lake. They are also fond of the cool climate of Payson in summer. (See blurbs on Saguaro Lake and Payson in the Day Trips

chapter and under the Boating, Fishing, and Tubing headings in this chapter.)

Tonto National Forest offers 900 miles of hiking and equestrian trails. Those closer to the Valley are better suited to novices. Other trails are deep in remote areas and will challenge the most experienced hiker and rider.

It's always a good idea to check on conditions and fire restrictions out in the wild before starting on a backcountry trip. The Mesa District Ranger Station, 5140 E. Ingram St., Mesa (480-610-3333), offers a convenient place to pick up trail maps and other forest recreational information. The Cave Creek Ranger Station, 40202 N. Cave Creek Rd., Cave Creek (480-595-3300), is the ideal place to visit before taking day trips into the expanse of the Tonto beyond Scottsdale and the Northeast Valley.

State Park

LOST DUTCHMAN STATE PARK
6109 N. Apache Trail, Apache Junction
(480) 982-4485
www.azparks.gov/PARKS/LODU

Jacob Waltz, known as the "Dutchman," traveled through the Superstition Mountains east of the Valley in the 1880s, searching for gold. The name of the park is a bit of a misnomer because it makes it sound as though the Dutchman was lost. Waltz claimed he found gold in the Superstitions, and as proof he used gold to buy supplies when he returned to civilization. Waltz always eluded anyone's attempts to follow him to the mine, and when he died, the location of the mine was "lost"—if it wasn't a figment of Waltz's imagination, which seems most likely. Ever since, people have searched for the "Lost Dutchman Mine." Some people have died trying, and local media often do stories on rescues of stranded hikers in the nearby Superstition Wilderness of Tonto National Forest. For the record, Waltz was German, not Dutch.

The park was established in 1977 after the US Bureau of Land Management sold the Lost Dutchman Recreation Site to the state. The 320-acre park's facilities include a visitor center, picnic areas with tables and grills, a campground with 35 units, a dump station, trails, restrooms, showers, and group-use areas. Saguaros are everywhere in this desert park. At night the lights of the Valley are visible. A hiking and equestrian trail leads into the rugged Superstition Wilderness. Park rangers advise that the grade of the trail makes it tough on horses and recommend the park's lower-level trails, on which hiking, mountain biking, and horseback riding are all permitted. One of the most accessible hikes is a pretty tough 4.5-mile round-trip route that gives stunning views of Weaver's Needle, an imposing outcrop of volcanic rock. The entrance fee is $7 per vehicle with up to 4 adults. To get to the park, take the Superstition Freeway (US 60) east to the Idaho Street (AZ 88) exit. When AZ 88 becomes the Apache Trail, follow it about 5 miles northeast to the park entrance.

Maricopa County Parks

The Maricopa County Parks regional network of recreation areas is described as the largest county parks system in the country. It offers access to hiking, camping, swimming, and many other activities. Daily hours of operation vary, so call the county for information at (602) 506-2930 or go to www.maricopa.gov/parks. The daily fee is $6 per vehicle. Fees for watercraft, archery, campsites, and other amenities are detailed on the website.

CAVE CREEK REGIONAL PARK

37900 N. Cave Creek Pkwy., Cave Creek

(623) 465-0431

www.maricopa.gov/parks/cave_creek

This 2,922-acre county park is within the town of Cave Creek. Its entrance is on 32nd Street, 1.5 miles north of Carefree Highway (AZ 74). Interesting rock formations and scenic views are the park's hallmarks. There are a number of old mine shafts in the park, and visitors are advised not to enter them because they are hazardous. The park includes 51 individual picnic sites available on a first-come, first-served basis. Four large ramadas for group picnics can be reserved for a fee. There are 38 individual campsites plus a group campground that is available by reservation only. A horse-staging area and trail rides can be booked in the cooler months. The park has 6 well-maintained trails, totaling 11 miles. The trails close at sunset. All are multiuse, unless otherwise marked. To get to the park from downtown Phoenix, take I-17 north to the Carefree Highway exit and head east to 32nd Street. You can also reach the park from north Phoenix by taking Cave Creek Road, or from Scottsdale by taking Scottsdale Road. When you reach the Carefree Highway from either road, proceed west to 32nd Street.

ESTRELLA MOUNTAIN REGIONAL PARK

14805 W. Vineyard Ave., Goodyear

(623) 932-3811

www.maricopa.gov/parks/estrella

The 19,840-acre Estrella Park features 65 acres of turfed area with picnic tables, grills, restrooms, playground equipment, 2 lighted ball fields, a rodeo arena, and the only grass picnic area in the Maricopa County parks system. An amphitheater nestles against a hill overlooking the picnic area. Eight ramadas with electricity can be reserved. Group camping is available with reservations. Water is available in picnic areas. The park has 33 miles of trails for hiking, horseback riding, and biking. A competitive track with 2 loops that total 13 miles is intended for high-speed training for mountain bikers, equestrians, and runners. To get to the park, take the Estrella Parkway exit south from I-10. About 5 miles south of I-10, head east on Vineyard Avenue. The park entrance is on your right.

LAKE PLEASANT REGIONAL PARK

41835 N. Castle Hot Springs Rd., Morristown

(928) 501-1710

www.maricopa.gov/parks/lake_pleasant

This 22,662-acre park surrounds Lake Pleasant, which was formed when the New Waddell Dam was built to store water brought into Maricopa County by the Central Arizona Project canal. The lake is nearly 10,000 acres and is 225 feet at its deepest point. The park has 2 boat ramps—a 10-lane one at the south end of the lake and a 4-lane boat ramp accessible through the north entrance. Two campgrounds are open for tent or RV camping. Reservations are not accepted for the 148 sites, many of which have electrical and water hookups. Nearby restrooms have showers, and all sites have picnic tables, ramadas, and firepits. Shoreline camping is allowed in the summer and fall months. A Desert Outdoor Center is available for rent. Lake Pleasant is located 20 miles northwest of Phoenix in Peoria. From central Phoenix, take I-17 north to Carefree Highway (AZ 74). Exit Carefree Highway and travel west 15 miles to Castle Hot Spring Road. Head north to the park entrance.

✳MCDOWELL MOUNTAIN REGIONAL PARK

16300 McDowell Mountain Park Dr., Fountain Hills
(480) 471-0173
www.maricopa.gov/parks/mcdowell

This 21,099-acre park in the McDowell Mountains features 88 picnic tables, comfort stations, a youth-group camp area, and family and group campgrounds. The campgrounds offer 76 sites with a dump station, water, electricity, and shower facilities. Water is available in the picnic areas. Advance registrations are required for the group and youth-group camp areas. The park features hiking, mountain-biking, and horseback-riding trails. A competitive track offers 3 loops of varying difficulty for competitive training away from recreational users. Mountain bikers, equestrians, and runners are invited to use this track. From central Phoenix, take Loop 202 east to the Beeline Highway (AZ 87). Continue northeast on AZ 87 to Shea Boulevard. Travel west on Shea Boulevard to Saguaro Boulevard and turn north. Continue through the town of Fountain Hills to Fountain Hills Boulevard; turn right and travel 4 miles to the park entrance.

✳SPUR CROSS RANCH RECREATION AREA

44000 N. Spur Cross Ranch Rd., Cave Creek
(480) 488-6601
www.maricopa.gov/parks/spur_cross

Cave Creek Regional Park gets a lot of attention because of its size and amenities, but Spur Cross is far more picturesque. The 2,100-acre conservation area is ideal for hiking over the big rocks of the riparian zone that lines Cave Creek, which flows pretty freely, especially after heavy rains. It's also an ideal place to see the rugged high-Sonoran Desert terrain by horseback. Local groups organize riding trips in the spring along the creek. Hikers are treated to foothills covered in wildflowers and saguaro cactus. There are about 7 miles of trails to explore. The Elephant Mountain Trail leads visitors into the neighboring Tonto National Forest. Spur Cross is one of the more lush and green parks in the Phoenix area. Park rangers organize hikes that are listed on the park's website. Driving north from Scottsdale, take Cave Creek Road through the town of Cave Creek to North Spur Cross Ranch Road. The entrance to the park is about 30 miles from central Scottsdale.

WHITE TANK MOUNTAIN REGIONAL PARK

20304 W. White Tank Mountain Rd., Waddell
(623) 935-2505
www.maricopa.gov/parks/white_tank

This park, among the White Tank Mountains just to the west of the Valley, seems almost a secret to Valley dwellers. It's rarely crowded and makes for an ideal place to explore the desert. The 30,000-acre park includes 240 picnic sites with grills, tables (a few have small covers), and restrooms; a 40-site campground; and a group campground that requires reservations. There are 11 group picnic areas available. The park also has a horse-staging area, a 10-mile competitive mountain-biking course, and 25 miles of shared-use trails plus 2.5 miles of pedestrian-only trails. The park has 2 barrier-free trails, which lead to ancient Native American petroglyphs. Numerous sites dot the park, and educators can provide information on guided hikes. To get there from downtown Phoenix, take I-10 west 18 miles to AZ 303.

Proceed north on AZ 303 to Olive Avenue. Travel west 4 miles on Olive to the park entrance.

Municipal Parks

In a place with more than 300 days of constant sunshine, parks are an important part of life. The Phoenix Parks and Recreation Department, (602) 262-6861, administers almost 26,000 acres of desert and mountain parkland within Phoenix city limits. Suburban cities like Tempe, Scottsdale, and Glendale take equal pride in their local green spots. Some parks preserve the natural desert and offer incredible hiking.

i The Phoenix Parks and Recreation Department allows residents to view its class schedule and register online. First visit www.phoenix .gov/parks. To sign up for a class or event, click on "Classes and Programs" on the menu.

ECHO CANYON RECREATION AREA
East McDonald Drive at Tatum Boulevard, Phoenix
(602) 261-8318
When Phoenix was small, Camelback Mountain's south side was its familiar face and the north side was as mysterious as the dark side of the moon. The north side is where the Echo Canyon Recreation Area sits. The rock here, which rises some 200 feet in places, is redder than in most Phoenix mountain parks, except for Papago Park. This area doesn't have the usual park amenities—the only water available is a water fountain at the trailhead—just hiking trails and the opportunity to go rock climbing. The views of the city are truly incredible, especially a day or two after a heavy rain clears the lingering smog.

Experienced rock climbers and hikers enjoy the exercise. Be warned: It's a tough vertical ascent on Cholla Trail in places, and you will get winded if you're not in the best shape. But it's a great park to push yourself into better shape. Some Valley residents run the trail daily, every morning.

ENCANTO PARK
2605 N. 15th Ave., Phoenix
(602) 261-8991
www.phoenix.gov/PARKS/encanto.html
A lush, grassy enclave in the heart of Phoenix, Encanto Park is the easiest way for people caught up in the swirl of urban life to take a breather. It's also a spot for family picnics and recreation. There are boating and fishing on the small lake, a children's amusement park at Enchanted Island (see the Kidstuff chapter), a lighted basketball area, tennis courts, a nature trail, golf, a playground, and softball fields.

FOUNTAIN PARK
12925 N. Saguaro Blvd., Fountain Hills
www.fh.az.gov/fountain-park.aspx
A 64-acre park surrounds Fountain Lake, where Fountain Hills' namesake fountain can shoot water up to 560 feet into the air. Normally, the fountain's plume, created by two 600-horsepower turbine pumps, is 330 feet. (A third pump is kept idle as a backup, and it's only on the rare occasion when the third pump is turned on that the 560-foot stream is possible.) The fountain has a utilitarian purpose: to help evaporate effluent (treated wastewater). Through most of the year it operates for 15 minutes at the top of the hour 9 a.m. to 9 p.m. The schedule can increase during winter when there's more effluent to evaporate. The fountain's plume can be seen from the Beeline Highway

shooting up over mountaintops. The park is a perfect place for picnicking on the grass, jogging, and playing on playground equipment. It's home to an 18-hole championship disc golf course, restrooms, and a chilled drinking fountain. Families with small children find it to be one of the more relaxing parks in the Northeast Valley.

INDIAN BEND WASH
Along Hayden Road, Scottsdale

The greenbelt that is Indian Bend Wash can be looked at as one huge park, although it's not. An 11-mile path used by bicyclists, joggers, walkers, and skaters connects a series of golf courses and city parks in one vast stretch of green, roughly through the center of Scottsdale. Four city parks sit among the golf courses: Chaparral Park, at 5401 N. Hayden Rd.; Indian School Park, at 4289 N. Hayden Rd.; Eldorado Park, at 2311 N. Miller Rd.; and Vista Del Camino Park, at 7700 E. Roosevelt Rd. The facilities include softball fields, tennis courts, basketball courts, volleyball courts, playgrounds, and picnic areas. For more information on facilities, call the number above. Both Chaparral and Eldorado Parks have municipal pools; see our Aquatics section for more details. Fishing is permitted at Chaparral and Eldorado Parks; see the Fishing section. The Indian Bend greenbelt is an ideal place for flat, relaxing cycling (see Kidstuff chapter for more).

i The Phoenix area is home to some fantastic fishing at lakes Pleasant, Saguaro, Roosevelt, and Bartlett. The state game and fish department keeps an up-to-the-minute Arizona fishing report at www.azgfd.net/fish.

KIWANIS COMMUNITY PARK
6111 S. All America Way, Tempe
(480) 350-5200
www.tempe.gov/kiwanis

The facilities at green Kiwanis Park are extensive, including lighted softball/baseball fields, batting cages, lighted sand volleyball courts, a lighted basketball court, picnic tables, playground equipment, a lake, a wave pool, horseshoe courts, soccer fields, and a recreation center that includes 15 lighted tennis courts. For information on recreation center activities, call (480) 350-5201. Boat rentals are available for Kiwanis Lake. Tempe residents may reserve picnic ramadas, ball fields and volleyball courts up to 11 months in advance. Fishing is also permitted.

i Zenergy Yoga, 8241 E. Evans Rd., Scottsdale, specializes in yoga for the whole family and offers several options for kids and teens ages 3 to 18. The classes, designed to be fun and playful, teach kids to incorporate yoga into everyday life. Information: (480) 905-8801 or www.zenergyyoga.net.

NORTH MOUNTAIN RECREATION AREA
10600 N. 7th St., Phoenix
(602) 495-5540
www.phoenix.gov/PARKS/northmtn.html

The hiking and mountain biking hotspot is situated on and around North Mountain and covers a small section of the North Mountain Preserve. From the higher points on North Mountain, you can look down over Sunnyslope and see downtown Phoenix to the south. The rec area also offers basketball and volleyball courts, a playground, a ramada and picnic area, and restrooms. The North Mountain Visitor Center (www.northmountainvisitorcenter .org) is a must if you're in the area. Preserve

Bark Parks—Where Your Pooch Can Run Wild

Chaparral Park
5401 N. Hayden Rd., Scottsdale
(480) 312-2353
www.scottsdaleaz.gov/Parks/OffLeashAreas
This park features 3 grassy runs. The runs are rotated so that two are always open, while the third is closed to give the grass a break. There's an area for passive pooches and another for the aggressive types. Each run has over an acre. Owners relax on benches under the trees.

Cosmo Dog Park
2502 E. Ray Rd., Gilbert
(480) 503-6200
www.gilbertaz.gov/parks/popups/cosmo-park.cfm
Dog Fancy magazine has ranked Cosmo Dog Park as "best dog park in the country." It boasts 4 fenced acres, separate areas for active and timid dogs, pet drinking fountains, a swimming area, a doggie beach, an obstacle course, area lighting, and mutt-mitt waste disposal stations.

PetSmart Dog Park at Washington Park
21st Avenue, north of Maryland, Phoenix
(602) 262-6971
www.phoenix.gov/PARKS/dogparks.html
A 6-foot-high perimeter fence guards the mutts in this 2.65-acre grass-surface park. The park has a water fountain and 2 doggie watering stations, mutt-mitt dispensers, garbage cans for waste material, and separate gates for large and small dogs.

Rose Mofford Sports Complex Dog Park
9833 N. 25th Ave., Phoenix
(602) 261-8011
www.phoenix.gov/PARKS/dogparks.html
Rose Mofford Park has lots of trees for shade to cool our four-legged friends as they sniff and smooch their new buddies. The dog area is 2.5 acres of grass.

experts offer information on the history and landscape of the area. There's a huge exhibit hall, and nature programs are hosted regularly.

PHOENIX MOUNTAINS PARK & RECREATION AREA
2701 E. Squaw Peak Dr., Phoenix
(602) 262-7901
**www.phoenix.gov/recreation/rec/parks/
preserves/locations**

Like Camelback, North, and South mountains, the rugged landscape around Squaw Peak (Piestewa Peak) at the south end of Phoenix Mountains Preserve makes for outstanding urban trail outings. It's almost like being outside the city. The Summit Trail and other trails attract hundreds of people daily. You'll see athletic types running up trails that you find difficult to walk, so there's something for everyone. The

cul-de-sac trailhead area includes picnic ramadas.

RED MOUNTAIN PARK
7745 E. Brown Rd., Mesa
(480) 644-2351
www.mesa.gov/parksrec

At Red Mountain Park you get away into a marshland against the backdrop of the Superstition Mountains. At the center of the park's artificial lake is a marsh environment where ducks and other birds hide out when they're not out on the water. The park offers picnic ramadas that can be reserved, playground equipment, a cement volleyball court, soccer fields, and basketball courts—all lighted. Reservations are required. Across Brown Road and to the east of the main developed portion of the park is the park's lighted softball complex. Fishing is also permitted.

SOUTH MOUNTAIN PARK
10919 S. Central Ave., Phoenix
(602) 534-6324
www.phoenix.gov/recreation/rec/parks/
preserves/locations

At 16,000 acres, South Mountain Park is billed as the largest municipal park in the country. More important than that to Valley dwellers and visitors, it offers an easy way to get an overview of the Valley. You can see virtually everywhere in the Valley from Dobbins Lookout, and a "compass" points you in the direction of such landmarks as Four Peaks, a mountaintop in Tonto National Forest to the northeast, and the Estrellas to the southwest. A park road hairpins up and down the mountain to serve vehicles and daredevil bicyclists. In addition, the park offers an interpretive center to learn about all the desert flora and fauna, an activity complex, ramadas

and picnic areas, restrooms, and a network of hiking and riding trails. See the Horseback Riding and the Hiking and Biking sections in this chapter.

ℹ️ DreamCatcher Park was designed as a safe haven for families with special needs children. The softball diamond has a urethane-coated base, allowing for easy wheelchair access. To learn more about the adaptive recreation programs at the Surprise facility, call (623) 220-2000.

THUNDERBIRD CONSERVATION PARK
59th Avenue and Pinnacle Peak Road,
Glendale
(623) 930-2820
www.glendaleaz.com/Parksand
Recreation/ThunderbirdPark.cfm

Thunderbird Park boasts 1,185 acres that offer great views of the Northwest Valley. The natural desert foothills area includes nearly 15 miles of hiking, biking, and equestrian paths; 15 covered picnic areas with grills; and wildlife-viewing blinds. There are 50 different bird species viewable from the park.

RECREATION

Ballooning

ADVENTURES OUT WEST
5002 E. Sweetwater Ave., Scottsdale
(480) 991-3666
www.adventuresoutwest.com/arizona

Adventures Out West has been flying people over the desert in hot air balloons since 1973. The company offers a balloon and Jeep safari package that's about 4 hours total. Flights cost around $175 per person. Group rates are also available. Flights take off from the Northeast Valley over State Trust

lands every morning at sunrise and in the late afternoons from November through March. Reservations are required.

HOT AIR EXPEDITIONS
(480) 502-6999, (800) 831-7610
www.hotairexpeditions.com

Groups meet daily in the cooler months at Deer Valley Airport in Phoenix to drive out to a North Valley launch site to climb aboard hot air balloons. After dawn you'll be floating anywhere from treetop level to 1,000 feet high over 200 miles of open desert. You'll touch down 45 to 90 minutes later and enjoy a champagne brunch in the desert as you and other passengers reflect on the flight. Then the company drives you back to your car. Rates are $133 to $183 per person. Gift certificates and group rates are available. Food includes quiche, pain au chocolate, fresh fruit, and other food prepared by Vincent on Camelback (see the Fine Dining section of the Restaurants chapter).

Boating

Arizona is among the top states in per-capita boat ownership, and water sports are as immensely popular in the Valley as they are in California or the Midwest. In Arizona all aquatic vehicles—from sailboards to Jet Skis to large boats—must be registered with the Arizona Game and Fish Department. The only vehicles exempted are nonmotorized inflatable boats that are less than 12 feet in length. Registration for residents costs $20 for a craft up to 12 feet. Longer boats have a sliding fee that goes up to $66 for boats longer than 64 feet. Nonresident fees begin at $100 for boats 12 feet or shorter and get as high as $495 for boats over 64 feet. For more information on fees, safety, fishing hotspots, and more, go to www.azgfd.gov.

✳BARTLETT LAKE
Bartlett Lake Marina
20808 E. Bartlett Dam Rd., Scottsdale
(602) 316-3378
www.bartlettlake.com

As the closest lake to Scottsdale, Bartlett Lake steals boaters and wakeboard fans from some of the more crowded Valley water sport hubs. The boatable surface is less than 2,900 acres, which is still more than Saguaro and Canyon lakes combined. Parts of Bartlett Lake appear to be surrounded by high cliffs, almost like boating through a saguaro-studded canyon. It's a gorgeous spot to relax in a boat while fishing or sipping a cocktail. However, it is a major draw for young people who like to go fast and flip tricks on the open water. The marina is located about 50 miles from downtown Phoenix. There are camping and fishing as well.

i It's not for the faint of heart, but if you're looking for a thrilling family adventure that involves great views of the Valley seen for a few minutes while plummeting to earth, check out Skydive Arizona. The company runs short, guided sky dive flights out of Eloy southeast of the Valley. Pay a bit extra to have a videographer capture your adrenaline-filled free fall. Information: www.skydiveaz.com or (877) 313-JUMP.

LAKE PLEASANT
AZ 74, Peoria
(928) 501-1710
www.maricopa.gov/parks/lake_pleasant

At 10,000 surface acres, Lake Pleasant tends to be crowded with boats and Jet Skis on weekends. But it's also home to the Arizona Yacht Club, whose members use the lake for their weekend regattas. The lake, formed

by the Waddell Dam, offers gorgeous views of the surrounding mountains. The massive regional park around the lake crawls with wildlife, including coyotes, burros, and nesting bald eagles. The lake permits parasailing as well as boating. You pay $6 per motor vehicle to get into the park, plus $4 for vehicles pulling motorized watercraft. The park's main entrance (the first as you come up from the Valley) gives access to a 10-lane boat ramp, which is adjacent to parking for 355 vehicles with boat trailers. The second (north) entrance is 3 miles past the first and gives access to a four-lane ramp at Scorpion Bay, which has space for 112 vehicles with boat trailers. Information: www.pleasantharbor.com or www.scorpionbaymarina.com.

SAGUARO LAKE RECREATIONAL AREA
Off Bush Highway, in Tonto National Forest about 10 miles northeast of Mesa
(480) 986-5546
www.saguarolakemarina.com
Saguaro Lake reservoir gets crowded on summer weekends, and it remains one of the most popular water sport draws in the Valley, especially with families in the Southeast Valley. There are two Forest Service boat-launch ramps on the north end of Saguaro Lake. You can come straight up and launch, park your land vehicle nearby, and take the boat on out. When coming from Mesa, the launch ramps can be reached by taking the turn off Bush Highway for the Sheriff's Aid Station and the Saguaro Lake Marina. The lake is closed to parasailing (it's just as well, since the surrounding mountains close off the lake from prevailing winds). Those with boats and personal watercraft should be considerate of water-skiers and kayakers. Boating maps are available at the Mesa District Ranger Station, 5140 E. Ingram St., Mesa (480-610-3300), and

at the Tonto National Forest Office, 2324 E. McDowell Rd., Phoenix (602-225-5295). The entry fee is $6 per day, per vehicle, with $4 extra charged for watercraft.

i Arizona is a top destination for rock climbing, attracting international climbers. For information on climbing in the Valley, check out *Rock Climbing Arizona* by Stewart M. Green. If you want to get some practice in a good indoor gym, try the Phoenix Rock Gym at 1353 E. University Dr. Information: www.phoenixrockgym.com or (480) 921-8322.

Climbing

CAMELBACK MOUNTAIN
Echo Canyon Recreation Area
East McDonald Drive at Tatum Boulevard, Phoenix
(602) 261-8318
Camelback Mountain offers quick access to great climbs in the Valley, but the crumbly sandstone walls make the situation a bit dicey. The 80-foot tower called the Praying Monk, one of the most popular climbs, offers a sheer angle, a great view of the Valley, and permanent—though aging—bolts fixed along the route. The east face is rated at 5.4; the southeast corner at 5.6. Hikers beware—do not climb these rocks without the proper gear, protection, and instruction.

Extreme Sports

BOB BONDURANT SCHOOL OF HIGH PERFORMANCE DRIVING
Firebird International Raceway
20000 S. Maricopa Rd., Chandler
(800) 842-RACE
www.bondurant.com

Racing on the Loop 101 will get you arrested. Here, it's encouraged. In fact, instructors teach you how to do it safely and effectively. The Bob Bondurant School is committed to professional driving instruction. The facility has access to 4 racetracks and features a 15-turn, 1.6-mile track on the school grounds. An 8-acre course is used for advanced skills. The school has more than 200 race-prepared cars, and the classes range in length from 1 to 4 days. Courses are offered year-round, 5 days a week.

DCB EXTREME ADVENTURES
2487 S. Gilbert Rd., Gilbert
(480) 460-5052
www.dcbadventures.com
Are you looking to train for a triathlon event? Extreme Adventure features numerous training events throughout the year, beginning with a 2.4-mile swim in Tempe Town Lake, a primer for an Ironman event. The company offers mountain bike races, swimming, and running. Costs vary, depending on the event, so call or check the website.

EXTREME ARIZONA
6061 E. Cave Creek Rd., Cave Creek
(480) 488-8529
www.extremearizona.com
This shop rents all sorts of extreme adventure vehicles, including dirt bikes, Jeeps, ATVs, Tomcars, and a variety of watercraft. The store will deliver the watercraft to Bartlett Lake and Lake Pleasant for a fee. The security deposits are steep, but this is your chance to enjoy the Sonoran Desert on its hundreds of miles of trails. Maps and other help are provided. Please remember to respect the land.

WESTWORLD PAINTBALL ADVENTURES
4240 W. Camelback Rd., Phoenix
(602) 447-8200
www.westworldpaintball.com
At 30,000 square feet, Westworld Paintball Adventures has the largest indoor facility in the Southwest. Courses include dirt, bunkers, and sniper towers, as well as a regulation airball field. An on-site pro shop sells paintball supplies and features a friendly, helpful staff. You don't need a reservation to join in the open play. Reservations are $30 and include the equipment rental and 100 rounds of ammo. The company also runs the outdoor Splatter Paint Ranch on the southwest corner of Jomax and Scottsdale roads.

Fishing

If you're 14 or older and plan to fish in Arizona, you need to be licensed by the state Game and Fish Department. Some local jurisdictions require a separate special permit, so it's good to check on local regulations before you decide to test a new fishing spot.

Licenses are issued annually to residents for $18.50 to $54 depending on the type, but several license options are available for nonresidents. A tourist can pick up a 1-day license for $17.25, a 5-day license for $32, and a 4-month license for $39.75. These licenses entitle you to catch warm-water fish in any body of water in the state, including the Valley's canals. Trout privileges are considered separate, though they are built into some of the fees. The exception to this rule is the Urban Fishing program, which costs $16 annually for residents and visitors alike. An Urban Fishing License entitles you to fish only at certain park lakes in the Phoenix and Tucson areas. To fish anywhere else in the Valley or the state, you need the general

license. The advantage of the Urban Fishing program is that the license fees pay for the stocking of these specific lakes with catfish in summer and trout in winter. Licenses are available online at www.azgfd.gov and at many sporting goods stores. The game and fish department can also be reached at (602) 942-3000.

LAKE PLEASANT
2 miles north of AZ 74, Peoria
Lake Pleasant presents the angler with bass, catfish, and crappie. Because the lake is so popular, the serious but bleary-eyed angler is going to be out in the water well before dawn.

ROOSEVELT LAKE
Off the Apache Trail, AZ 88, about 30 miles northeast of Apache Junction in Tonto National Forest
Serious anglers recommend Roosevelt Lake. From central Phoenix, Roosevelt Lake is the farthest of the lakes formed by dams along the Salt River. Despite being the highest of the lakes, it's fairly warm because it's shallow, and the fish grow well. Spring is the best time to catch bass; crappies are abundant, too. Catfish are best caught in spring and summer. You can fish the lake year-round, though, and still turn up some good catches.

SAGUARO LAKE
Off Bush Highway, about 10 miles northeast of Mesa in Tonto National Forest
Saguaro Lake is a challenging place for anglers because the lake is so popular. It's tough to make a good catch here. The best time to fish Saguaro Lake is in winter, when most of the boating traffic dies down. Anglers who can't wait for winter will get up

well before dawn or stay up into the wee hours to partake of Saguaro Lake's bounty of bass and catfish in some secluded cove.

Bicycle Rental & Repair

Sure, everyone drives in the Valley, but a bike is an effective and more fulfilling way to see areas like downtown Scottsdale and Tempe. These two companies repair and sell bicycles as well as rent a range of bikes for out-of-towners who need the ride:

Arizona Outback Adventures
16447 N. 91st St., Scottsdale
(480) 945-2881, (866) 455-1601
www.aoa-adventures.com/bikes
Arizona Outback Adventures has been leading hiking and biking tours since 1990. Tours vary depending on what you want to see and how long you can go. The more independent-minded can rent a bike and strike out on their own. There is a wide variety of cruisers and mountain bikes ranging from $50 to $95 per day and $170 to more than $300 per week. All rentals include the free use of a helmet.

Tempe Bicycle
405 W. University Dr., Tempe
(480) 446-3033
www.tempebicycle.com
Tempe Bicycle is located just a bit off Mill Avenue in downtown Tempe. The shop rents bikes from $45 to $60 a day. Weekly rates are more than $100. Other Tempe locations are at 715 S. Rural Rd. (480-966-6896) and 922 E. Apache Blvd. (480-361-5260).

Hiking & Biking

A number of Valley cities have bike paths along urban streets, but also along the canals that run through the Valley. These canal paths are shared by bicyclists, hikers, joggers, and horseback riders, but they generally offer a tranquil route through the Valley. Be sure to take adequate water along with you for your trip, even if you're in the city. Check with your local municipality's parks or recreation department for maps or trail information.

GRAND CANAL

The Grand Canal travels across the Valley from where it emerges from an underground aqueduct southwest of the intersection of Washington Street and Mill Avenue in Tempe. The canal path heads northwestward into Phoenix, north of Indian School Road and past the Phoenix Indian Medical Center before it heads almost due west between Phoenix Central High School and Brophy College Preparatory School and then curves southwest. South of Indian School Road and I-17, the canal begins to travel west. It travels to the northwest a little north of 56th Avenue and Osborn Road. It travels into Glendale at 75th Avenue and Camelback Road, continuing northwest to Bethany Home Road and 83rd Avenue, where it heads due west to about 107th Avenue and ends.

✳HIEROGLYPHIC TRAIL
Superstition Mountains
South Kings Ranch Road, Gold Canyon,
about 10 miles east of Apache Junction
If you're looking for a memorable hike that's not to steep and not too boring, this is the one. The round-trip hike is about 2.5 miles. The elevation change is about 200 feet difference over some varying sand and rock, so it's manageable and quite scenic with the mighty Superstition range as the backdrop. At the top you can explore some truly bizarre rock formations marked with ancient Native American petroglyphs. The Superstitions are known as a fantastic day trip, and the spot puts you about 12 miles south of the Goldfield Ghost Town attractions for another place to explore with family.

MORMON & NATIONAL TRAILS
South Mountain Park
10919 S. Central Ave., Phoenix
(602) 495-0222
These are fun trails for mountain biking, although they're shared by hikers, so be careful and courteous. From the mountain-bike point of view, Mormon Trail is a technical singletrack. The trail climbs to a mountain ridge, follows it, and then hooks up to the National Trail. At this point you can choose to return to the trailhead by turning left down the National Trail. By turning right you continue upward on the National Trail. At "the waterfall" riders are forced to carry their bikes up a short distance, and then it's 3 to 4 miles back to the parking lot. The bike ride down is very bumpy.

i Our list of Valley hiking and mountain biking trails is just a starting point. There are dozens and dozens of trails across the Valley. A great source for insider info is Cosmic Ray's *Hiking Phoenix: Favorite Day Hikes* and *Fat Tire Tales and Trails,* which are respected by hardcore locals yet introductory enough for visitors.

✳SUMMIT TRAIL
Echo Canyon Recreation Area
East McDonald Drive at Tatum
Boulevard, Phoenix
(602) 256-3220

At 2,700 feet Camelback Mountain happens to be the tallest in Phoenix, so its Summit Trail takes hikers to the top of the Valley. However, you don't get the reward of a magnificent view without work. This is a popular place among overachievers, and the park rangers rate it a strenuous hike. The mile-long path is a vertical ascent with slippery patches of gravel, but it's well worth the effort.

Hockey Organizations

Desert Youth Hockey Association
1520 McClintock Dr., Tempe
(480) 941-0944
www.dyha.org
This association organizes youth hockey leagues and tournaments and coordinates participation in national tournaments.

Valley of the Sun Hockey Association
(602) 957-9966
www.vosha.com
In addition to youth ice hockey leagues and tournaments, its tiered system of teams gives kids of all skill levels a chance to compete. Its home rink is Arcadia Ice, 3853 E. Thomas Rd. in Phoenix.

SUMMIT TRAIL AT PIESTEWA PEAK
Phoenix Mountains Park and
Recreation Area
2701 E. Squaw Peak Ln., Phoenix
(602) 262-7901
We hesitate to mention the Summit Trail at Piestewa Peak because it's already so popular and crowded. This 1.2-mile trail doesn't go as high as Camelback's Summit Trail (it's only 2,600 feet), and it isn't as difficult. The trail has several places to stop and rest, and you don't have to climb very high to get a nice view.

Horseback Riding

Phoenix is not far removed from the Wild West, so you can bet that horseback riding is a passion for many residents who cling to their equestrian heritage. People who own horse properties out on the fringes of the Valley get on their horses and ride out into the rural area or wilderness nearby, which is not advisable for people who don't know the area. It's easy to get lost. If you ride from the stables listed below, you will have a trail guide regardless of your experience with horses. Remember to take plenty of water; you're sitting in the sun, even on horseback. Parents can also read about kid rides at MacDonald's Ranch in Scottsdale in the Kidstuff chapter.

ARIZONA HORSE LOVERS PARK
19224 N. Tatum Blvd., Phoenix
(602) 534-4657
www.phoenix.gov/PARKS/phxequct.html
This park has 4 equestrian arenas open to local horse owners Wed to Sun. Trails in the surrounding Reach 11 Recreation Area are open sunrise till sunset.

DONNELLY'S D-SPUR RANCH & RIDING STABLES
15189 E. Peralta Rd., Gold Canyon
(602) 810-7029
www.dondonnelly.com
For a unique way to tour the lovely Superstition Mountains, saddle up and take an hour-long trail ride through washes and cactus and desert terrain. Or, for more adventure, try a guided 2-hour Tenderfoot Ride, a half-day Wrangler Ride, or a full-day Top Hand

Tour that takes you to Weaver's Needle and a host of other sights. Rides start at $32 and go up to $200 per person for the overnight ride, which includes a campfire steak dinner and breakfast in the Superstition wilderness.

MARICOPA COUNTY PARKS & RECREATION DEPARTMENT
234 N. Central Ave., Phoenix
(602) 506-2930
www.maricopa.gov/parks

The county Parks and Recreation Department can supply maps and information on the horseback trails at the network of regional parks (see Parks section earlier in this chapter for more on Estrella Mountain, McDowell Mountain, Spur Cross Ranch, and other regional parks with equestrian trails). Maps can be picked up at the parks' ranger stations and are also available online. The department is also the place to go for maps and information on the Sun Circle Trail, which travels through urban areas and wilderness alongside the Arizona Canal and other major canals in the Valley. The county parks and rec department has horseback-riding concessionaires on or adjacent to the Cave Creek Recreation Area (623-465-0431) and White Tank Mountain Regional Park (623-935-2505). These outfits have special-use permits that allow them to lead trips into the regional parks and recreational areas managed by Maricopa County.

PAPAGO RIDING STABLE
400 N. Scottsdale Rd., Tempe
(480) 966-9793

Papago Riding Stables will take you on trails through the red rocks of Papago Park. Trail rides are $30 per hour, per person. In summer the stables shut down at the hottest hours of the day and reopen in the late afternoon. It's best to call ahead for times. There are discounts for groups of 10 or more.

PONDEROSA STABLES
10215 S. Central Ave., Phoenix
(602) 268-1261
www.arizona-horses.com

Ponderosa Stables offers horseback riding in South Mountain Park. Trail rides are $33 per person, per hour. Ponderosa also gives riding lessons at $45 an hour per person. The lessons are usually one on one, but they are sometimes in small groups. Ponderosa's wranglers will take groups out on cookout rides, featuring steak and chicken or hamburgers and hot dogs. There's an eight-person minimum on cookouts, and reservations are needed.

Ice Skating

Ice hockey has been popular in the Valley forever—or at least dating from when the late, minor-league Phoenix Roadrunners came to town. Now, fans of the NHL's Phoenix Coyotes have suffered through a series of tumultuous seasons as the Canadian-born franchise considers leaving Glendale. For a desert metropolis, Phoenix has a few really excellent places to play. Check the Kidstuff section for details on two of the Valley's more popular spots for free-skating, Alltell Ice Den in Scottsdale and Oceanside Ice Arena in Tempe.

ARCADIA ICE
3853 E. Thomas Rd., Phoenix
(602) 957-9966
www.arcadiaice.com

Arcadia Ice is open for skating and lessons. Located inside the Desert Palms Power Center, it sometimes has public skating sessions during the day and evening, with skating

lessons on weekend afternoons. Skating sessions vary, so call ahead or check the website for times and rates. Pick-up hockey games run $15 per person and are open to all ages.

Off-Roading Tours

DESERT STORM HUMMER TOURS
15525 N. 83rd Way, Scottsdale
(480) 922-0020
www.dshummer.com
National Geographic Adventures dubs the Desert Storm Hummer tours "one of the top 100 adventures in America." In 1995 owner Jesse Wade pioneered the company after 20 years in the outfitter industry. Half-day tours leave twice a day year-round at 8 a.m. and 10 p.m. You'll be driven for 10 miles of off-roading through lush trails and incredible rock formations to see Sonoran Desert vegetation in the Goldfield Mountain area. Guides sometimes catch rattlesnakes, reptiles, and tarantulas to show off to visitors before releasing them back into the wild. Ten guests are allowed per Hummer. Rates change based on day tours or the equally popular night tours of the desert, but they are around $75 to $150 based on age and tour type. Note that the pick-up location is not at the address above. Call for pick-up location directions and specific rates.

Roller Skating

ROLLERO FAMILY ROLLER SKATING CENTER
7318 W. Indian School Rd., Phoenix
(623) 846-1510
www.rollero.com
Rollero has been in business for more than 45 years and maintains a family atmosphere. It's open on all major holidays, with open-skating sessions on most nights of the week.

Prices vary daily, ranging from $5 to $8 per person depending on the day and time. There is no charge for skate rental. The schedule changes depending on the season and to accommodate private parties (Rollero specializes in birthday parties), so it's best to call ahead. Rollero does not allow in-line or street skates.

UNITED SKATES OF AMERICA
10054 N. 43rd Ave., Glendale
(623) 842-1181
www.greatskateglendale.com
United Skates boasts the largest rink in Arizona, and it allows both in-line and roller derby-style skates. The skating schedule changes regularly, so call ahead for the current schedule. Prices vary considerably; ask about them in advance. Lessons are offered Saturday morning. The center specializes in birthday parties, and the rink is available for private parties. Be sure to check the website for coupons.

Soaring

ARIZONA SOARING
Estrella Sailport, Maricopa
(520) 568-2318
www.azsoaring.com
How about soaring silently through desert sky at about 4,000 feet? Although Estrella Sailport is well south of the Valley, you can see the Valley spreading northward from your perch. Weather and geography are kind to Estrella Sailport, offering conditions right for soaring almost every day of the year. Sailplanes are taken up and released at 3,500 feet and, by riding the air currents, generally reach an altitude of about 5,000 to 6,000 feet. The high-performance craft can soar to 10,000 feet on a good day. A nice, mellow 20-minute ride in a training glider costs

$105. Too tame? Try the Aerobatic Deluxe package for $210 for some loopty-loops. To get there, take I-10 east to exit 162 and head toward Maricopa. Follow the road for 15 miles and then turn west on AZ 238. You'll come upon Estrella Sailport 6.5 miles later.

Softball

Slow-pitch softball has been growing nationwide since the 1960s, when American men and women realized they could both share the field and drink beer simultaneously. If you have a softball team and you want to play more than an occasional pickup game, there are many different leagues and tournaments open. Company and industrial leagues, church leagues, and ethnic leagues are mostly closed to people outside those particular groups. City leagues are open to all participants, sometimes with a residency requirement or restriction (i.e., teams that have no residents from the specific city may be last in line to register). Call the parks and recreation department of your city for a schedule or visit the websites below.

- **Chandler,** (480) 782-2727, www.chandler az.gov
- **Fountain Hills,** (480) 816-5151, www.fh .az.gov/sports-programs.aspx
- **Gilbert,** (480) 503-6200, www.ci.gilbert .az.us/parks
- **Glendale,** (623) 930-2820, www.glendale az.com/ParksandRecreation
- **Mesa,** (480) 644-2352, www.mesaaz.gov/ parksrec
- **Peoria,** (623) 773-7137, www.peoriaaz .com
- **Phoenix,** (602) 262-6862, www.phoenix .gov/parks
- **Scottsdale,** (480) 312-7275, www.scotts daleaz.gov/Topics/Recreation

- **Tempe,** (480) 350-5200, www.tempe .gov/recreation

Swimming

So many people have pools in their backyards or at their condo complexes, but the municipal pool centers in the Valley are among the best in the West. Fees are typically only a couple of bucks, though they vary slightly per town. Hours also vary, but you'll be able to check for updated information through these links and phone numbers:

CHANDLER

Chandler has 6 municipal pools open from various dates in the spring and summer. Some are equipped with water slides, beach boats, and other toys for kids. The city runs an aquatics hotline at (480) 782-2749.

- **Arrowhead Pool,** 1475 W. Erie St., (480) 732-1064
- **Desert Oasis Aquatic Center,** 1400 W. Summit Place, (480) 732-1061, (480) 732-1062
- **Folley Pool,** 600 E. Fairview St., (480) 732-1063
- **Hamilton Aquatic Center,** 3838 S. Arizona Ave., (480) 782-2630, (480) 782-2631
- **Mesquite Groves Aquatic Center,** 5901 S. Hillcrest Dr., (480) 782-2635
- **West Chandler Aquatic Center,** 250 S. Kyrene Rd., (480) 783-8261, (480) 783-8262

GILBERT

Fast-growing Gilbert opened its Perry and Williams Field pools recently, adding them to the network open from mid-May through mid-August. Swim passes are available through Gilbert Parks and Recreation, (480) 503-6200. Lessons are available. Call

for hours or visit www.gilbertaz.gov/parks/aquatics.cfm.

- **Greenfield Pool,** 35 Greenfield Rd., (480) 892-2414
- **Mesquite Aquatic Center,** 100 W. Mesquite St., (480) 503-6292
- **Perry Pool,** 1775 E. Queen Creek, (480) 503-6227
- **Williams Field Pool,** 1900 S. Higley Rd., (480) 503-6226

GLENDALE

Glendale operates its city pools from June through August. Schedules vary for each pool. Cactus Pool (at Cactus High School) and Ironwood Pool (at Ironwood High) are for lessons only. For the full range of aquatic activities, it's best to call (623) 930-2041 or visit www.glendaleaz.com/parksandrecreation.

- **Aquatic Playground/Splash Pad,** 83rd Avenue and Berridge Lane
- **Cactus Pool,** 15500 N. 63rd Ave.
- **Foothills Recreation & Aquatic Center,** 5600 W. Union Hills Dr.
- **Ironwood Pool,** 12603 W. 61st Ave.
- **Rose Lane Aquatics Center,** 5003 W. Marlette Ave.

MESA

Pool hours vary at different times of the summer, so check updated schedules by calling Mesa Parks and Recreation, (480) 644-2351, or visit www.mesa.gov/parksrec/aquatics. Rhodes Aquatic Complex features the Flow Rider wave pool. Others offer space for group parties. Swim passes and lessons are available. The city also runs discounts on family season passes if you buy them early in the season.

- **Brimhall Aquatic Complex,** 4949 E. Southern Ave., (480) 644-5087
- **Carson/Westwood Aquatic Complex,** 525 N. Westwood St., (480) 644-2550
- **Fremont Aquatic Complex,** 1001 N. Power Rd., (480) 644-2369
- **Kino Aquatic Center,** 848 N. Horne St., (480) 644-2376
- **Rhodes Aquatic Complex,** 1860 S. Longmore Rd., (480) 644-2550
- **Shepherd Aquatic Complex,** 1407 N. Alta Mesa Dr., (480) 644-3037
- **Skyline Aquatic Center,** 845 S. Crismon Rd., (480) 644-6040
- **Stapley Aquatic Complex,** 3250 E. Hermosa Vista Dr., (480) 644-4977
- **Taylor Pool,** 705 S. 32nd St., (480) 644-3036

PEORIA

Peoria has 3 pools open from Memorial Day weekend through early August daily and on weekends through Labor Day weekend. The city features the "Dive in Movie" event, which allows swimmers and their kids to cool off to a family-oriented flick in the evening. Call the parks department at (623) 773-7137 for more details.

- **Centennial Pool,** 14388 N. 79th Ave.
- **Peoria High School Pool,** 11200 N. 83rd Ave.
- **Sunrise Pool,** 21321 N. 86th Dr.

PHOENIX

Pools are open for Memorial Day weekend and reopen the first week of June for the long, hot summer. Learn-to-swim programs, water-safety and specialty classes, and recreational team programs are offered throughout the summer months. Most city pools have separate wading pools for very young children. Paradise Valley pool has a large mushroom in its wading area, which provides a cool shower of water for the children.

Telephone Pioneer is equipped with lifts, dry- and wet-access ramps, and a separate therapy pool for swimmers with disabilities. Lessons are available. For more information on the city's aquatic programs, call the city's Swim Line at (602) 534-7946. As of 2011, some pools were under construction or limited to shorter hours due to budget cuts, so check with the city for updates as to which pool is closest to you.

- **Alkire Pool,** 1617 W. Papago St., (602) 261-8787
- **Cielito Pool,** 4551 N. 35th Ave., (602) 262-4752
- **Coronado Pool,** 1717 N. 12th St., (602) 262-6709
- **Deer Valley Pool,** 19400 N. 19th Ave., (602) 534-1842
- **Eastlake Pool,** 1549 E. Jefferson St., (602) 261-8729
- **Encanto Pool,** 2125 N. 15th Ave., (602) 261-8732
- **Falcon Pool,** 3420 W. Roosevelt St., (602) 262-6229
- **Grant Pool,** 714 S. 2nd Ave., (602) 261-8728
- **Hermoso Pool,** 5749 S. 20th St., (602) 261-8731
- **Holiday Pool,** 4530 N. 67th Ave., (602) 261-8031
- **Maryvale Pool,** 4444 N. 51st Ave., (602) 262-6685
- **Mountain View Pool,** 1104 E. Grovers Ave., (602) 534-1347
- **Paradise Valley Pool,** 17648 N. 40th St., (602) 534-5161
- **Pecos Pool,** 17010 S. 48th St., (602) 534-9255
- **Perry Pool,** 3131 E. Windsor Ave., (602) 262-7367
- **Roadrunner Pool,** 3502 E. Cactus Rd., (602) 262-6789

- **Roosevelt Pool,** 6246 S. 7th St., (602) 262-6832
- **Starlight Pool,** 7810 W. Osborn Rd., (602) 495-2412
- **Sunnyslope Pool,** 301 W. Dunlap Rd., (602) 262-7165
- **Telephone Pioneer Pool,** 1946 W. Morningside Dr., (602) 495-2404

i For an excellent list of pool amenities and equipment, visit www .phoenix.gov/SPORTS/aquamap.html and click on the map. You can also find a schedule of swim classes on the website.

SCOTTSDALE

Scottsdale has 4 municipal pools; the Cactus and Eldorado pools are open year-round and heated in the fall and winter. Lessons are available. Call for hours.

- **Cactus Aquatic & Fitness Center,** 7202 E. Cactus Rd., (480) 312-7665
- **Chaparral Aquatic Center,** 5401 N. Hayden Rd., (480) 312-2484
- **Eldorado Aquatic & Fitness Center,** 2301 N. Miller Rd., (480) 312-2484
- **McDowell Mountain Ranch Park & Aquatic Center,** 15525 N. Thompson Peak Pkwy., (480) 312-6677

TEMPE

One of the city's coolest features is the Kiwanis Park Wave Pool inside the Kiwanis Park Recreation Center, 6111 S. All America Way (480-350-5201). The pool season runs from the last week of May through mid-August. Fees and hours are available at www.tempe.gov/pools. The city also has a number of kiddie splash pads at other city parks.

Tennis

Racquet sports have always been trendy here, though hardly as popular as golf. Most of the parks and recreation departments offer tennis courts—many lighted after dark—that are available in local parks on a first-come, first-served, no-charge basis. Call the respective city parks department for a complete list of courts. The following are some of the public, pay facilities in the Valley.

GENE AUTRY TENNIS CENTER
4125 E. McKellips Rd., Mesa
(480) 654-3787
www.mesatennis.com
This complex features 16 lighted tennis courts, a practice wall, showers, and a small pro shop. The facility is open Mon to Thurs. It's closed Friday and only open in the morning on the weekends. A court costs $4.50 in the daytime and $5.50 in the evening for 90 minutes of play. You can rent a ball machine for an hour for $10.

KIWANIS PARK RECREATION CENTER
6111 S. All America Way, Tempe
(480) 350-5201
www.tempe.gov/Tennis/
The Kiwanis Park Recreation Center has 15 lighted hard courts. It has been recognized by the US Tennis Association as one of the outstanding public tennis facilities in the country. Fees are $4.50 per court for 90 minutes before 7 p.m. and $6 per court after 7 p.m. The center also offers lessons and tennis leagues.

MOUNTAIN VIEW COMMUNITY CENTER
1104 E. Grovers Ave., Phoenix
(602) 534-2500
This center has 24 lighted tennis courts. Use of the courts costs $1.50 for 90 minutes during the day, plus $2.20 light fee for the same period at night.

PASEO RACQUET CENTER
6268 W. Thunderbird Rd., Glendale
(623) 979-1234
The Paseo Racquet Center features 19 hard courts, all lighted. Fees are $2.50 per person for 90 minutes. At night add on a $4 light fee per court. Reservations are taken 24 hours in advance and are recommended. The facility has a pro shop, lockers, and showers. Group and private lessons are available. The center also hosts about 20 tournaments per year.

PHOENIX TENNIS CENTER
6330 N. 21st Ave., Phoenix
(602) 249-3712
www.phoenix.gov/sports/tennis.html
The Phoenix Tennis Center features 22 lighted, hard-surface tennis courts. It's best to call the day before you want to play to make reservations. The facilities include lockers and showers, a stocked tennis shop, a ball machine court, backboards, and vending machines.

Tubing

✳SALT RIVER TUBING & RECREATION
1320 N. Bush Hwy., Mesa
(480) 984-3350
www.saltrivertubing.com
The lazy river ride provided by the folks at Salt River Tubing is an Arizona tradition. Visitors rent tubes as part of "Arizona's floating picnic," which takes them from the Salt River in Mesa for anywhere from 2 to 5 hours downstream from some gorgeous launch spots in Tonto National Forest back toward the main office off Usery Pass Road in Mesa. Friends tie their tubes together, pop a cooler filled with beer in the middle, and gently roll

down the scenic Rio Salado. It's around $15 for a tube rental and shuttle ride. The river rolls along pretty nicely, so there are only a few playful light whitewater splash-splash moments to worry about. The rest is pure relaxation.

i Yoga is huge in the Phoenix area, since so many wellness-conscious people prefer to work out indoors when it's hot. At One Yoga has locations in Phoenix and Scottsdale. The sites offer couples workshops and meditation programs. Information: www.atone yoga.com.

YMCA

YMCA VALLEY OF THE SUN
350 N. 1st Ave., Phoenix
(602) 404-9622
www.valleyymca.org
The YMCA offers a wide variety of athletics, fitness, and sporting activities, from basketball leagues and in-line hockey to swimming pools and aerobics. Locations, including the immaculately clean Scottsdale facility on Shea Boulevard, are listed on the website.

GOLF

When it comes to the links, Phoenix is home to everything from its namesake professional golf tournament to some of the top municipal courses in the US. It's difficult to find a dirty or chopped-up course. Even the cheap executive links are in great shape.

Golf is hardly a retiree's sport in Arizona. Young kids play. Teens compete in major tournaments. Executives play hooky to hit their country clubs. Average Joes play regularly with buddies and a cooler filled with adult beverages. Pros like Arizona State University alum Phil Mickelson and Tom Lehman, among others, live in Phoenix and Scottsdale.

Dubbed the "Golf Capital of the World" by the National Golf Foundation, Phoenix is considered one of the world's top golf destinations. A few mind-boggling statistics: A report by the Golf Industry Association of Arizona states that golf has an economic impact of $3.4 billion every year. The industry employs nearly 20,000 Arizonans.

The Valley's courses are known as some of the most exclusive and expensive in the US. Flawlessly designed desert courses at the Tournament Players Club of Scottsdale (home of the PGA's Waste Management Phoenix Open), Troon North, the Phoenician, and other major resorts run pretty high greens fees in the pleasant cooler months. Fees at these top courses, and most courses, drop in the summer if you can stand the heat.

In 2005 the city of Phoenix first offered its Phoenix Golf Card, which gives players the ability to book tee times up to 9 days in advance. To take advantage, visit www.phoenix.gov/recreation/rec/facilities/golf or phone the call center at (866) 865-GOLF. You can also register in person at any Phoenix course pro golf shop. The card costs $100 per year and has a slew of added benefits, such as discounted rates and advance notice of specials, but it cannot be used at Papago Golf Course. A Premium Phoenix Card, which costs $50, is available to residents of Maricopa County only and may be used at all golf courses, including Papago.

For information on the Phoenix Open, see the Spectator Sports chapter. What follows is a list of some of the semiprivate and public courses in the area. Of course there are many exclusive private and members-only courses in town, but these are not open for public play. Keep in mind that greens fees change by the season, so you'll want to contact individual pro shops for accurate quotes.

i Scottsdale is home to Hot Stix, the masters of custom clubs. After a consultation and a swing analysis, they'll provide clubs exactly suited to your style. A team of golf scientists (who knew?) stands at the ready to shave strokes off your game. Information: www.hotstixgolf.com or (877) 513-1333.

PHOENIX

ARIZONA BILTMORE GOLF CLUB
2400 E. Missouri St.
(602) 955-9656
www.azbiltmoregc.com

The Arizona Biltmore has represented the upper crust of Valley accommodations for decades, and the Biltmore's Adobe course has been part of the amenities since 1932. The Links course, equally top-notch, offers a modern alternative to the Adobe. These are semiprivate courses, with resort guests having priority on tee times.

As you might suspect from its age, the Adobe is a traditional 18-hole course. The par-72, 6,455-yard course features landscaping that's an extension of the hotel grounds' lush greenery. The signature hole is the third, a 423-yard par 4 that features water before the hole, a bunker to the right, and a pine tree to the left.

The par-71, 6,300-yard Links course wraps around the outer edge of the Biltmore grounds and offers good views of Camelback Mountain and downtown Phoenix in the distance. Seven lakes add challenges to your game.

Amenities include a clubhouse, pro shop, driving range, the resort hotel's restaurant and swimming pool, and mango-scented towels in the summer. Greens fees, cart included, are $185 in high season, $79 in the shoulder season, and $49 in summer. There's also an 18-hole putting course, which is free to guests.

CAVE CREEK GOLF COURSE
15202 N. 19th Ave.
(602) 866-8076
www.phoenix.gov/SPORTS/cavecree
.html

Averaging about 100,000 rounds a year, Cave Creek Golf Course surpassed Papago Park as the most popular Phoenix municipal golf course in recent years. Like the other Phoenix courses, this is a traditional 18-hole course. Unlike the other courses, this land was once a landfill reclamation project. Cave Creek runs through the middle of the course, and nearby hills and mountains add color. The 6,290-yard, par-72 course is difficult, with the toughest being the 450-yard, par-4 eighth hole.

Greens fees for the public are $43 to walk and $55 to ride. With a Phoenix Golf Card, expect to pay a morning rate of $29 to walk and $40 to ride. Seniors with a Phoenix Golf Card pay $22 all day if they walk or $33 to ride. After 2 p.m. the fees drop. Amenities at Cave Creek include a clubhouse, pro shop, driving range, putting and chipping greens, and snack bar.

i Goodyear's Estrella Mountain Ranch Golf Club now sports the latest in high-tech golf gear. It's called the K-Vest. You strap on equipment with special sensors and watch your swing on a computer screen. The bad news? It stings when your posture is out of whack. But hey, it's worth it to lower your handicap. For lessons, visit 11800 S. Golf Club Dr. or call (623) 386-2600.

ENCANTO GOLF COURSE
2755 N. 15th Ave.
(602) 253-3963
www.phoenix.gov/SPORTS/encant18
.html

Encanto Park is a green central Phoenix respite known for its giant trees and wide-open spaces, so it's only natural that its golf course, enhanced by mature palm and salt cedar trees, is known for the same. The par-70, 6,386-yard municipal course was designed by William P. Bell and is a favorite among local golfers. Completed in 1935, Encanto is billed as the third-oldest golf course in Arizona. Encanto has level, wide fairways and a limited number of hazards. The ambience is relaxed and amiable, a perfect place for the average golfer to just enjoy being out there knocking the ball around. The course features several par 4s that are more than 377 yards.

Greens fees for the public are $43 to walk and $55 to ride. With a Phoenix Golf Card, expect to pay a morning rate to walk of $29. In addition to its clubhouse, golf shop, driving range, practice area, and lessons, Encanto has a swimming pool and tennis court.

*PAPAGO GOLF COURSE
5595 E. Moreland St.
(602) 275-8428
www.papagogolfcourse.net

This 7,000-yard course undoubtedly is Phoenix's most attractive municipal golf course. Golfers play about 85,000 to 90,000 rounds a year at Papago. With the red rocks of the Papago Buttes dominating the views, golfers know full well they're in the desert Southwest even though they're walking through a traditional, tree-lined course. Designed by William F. Bell, the course features wide,

flowing fairways and large, rolling greens. It's playable but challenging for the average player, with demanding doglegs and interesting holes. For instance, the finishing hole, a par-4, 443-yarder, doglegs uphill to a wide green. Amenities include a clubhouse, pro shop, driving range, practice area, and lessons. Recent renovations gave Papago some extra tees and an upgraded practice facility.

Greens fees for the public are $43 to walk and $55 to ride. With a Phoenix Golf Card, expect to pay a morning rate of $29 to walk and $40 to ride. Seniors with a Phoenix Golf Card pay $22 all day to walk or $33 to ride. After 2 p.m. the fees drop.

> **i** In 2008 *Golf World* selected the Wildfire Golf Shop at JW Marriott Desert Ridge Resort as one of the top 100 golf shops in America. The JW Marriott is at 5350 E. Marriott Dr., Phoenix (480-293-5000). Information: www.wildfiregolf.com.

THE RAVEN GOLF CLUB AT SOUTH MOUNTAIN
3636 E. Baseline Rd.
(602) 243-3636
www.theravensouthmountain.com

The Raven, designed by David Graham and Gary Panks, opened in November 1995 on what used to be farmland at the base of South Mountain. It has quickly earned a favorable reputation for its enjoyable course layout and top-of-the-line service that rivals members-only clubs. A 6,264-yard, par-72 course, The Raven offers well-manicured, wall-to-wall grass in the Midwestern traditional golf style. Thousands of pine trees line the wide, undulating fairways, giving the golfer a sense of solitude. The Raven is very playable, with challenging holes. The par-3

seventh hole is very intimidating. It has water and sand all the way down the left-hand side of the fairway. The 18th hole, a par 4, is one of the best finishing holes around. A lake sits in front of the green, and to the right is a 3-tiered waterfall. South Mountain rises in the background.

The Raven has played host to the Southwest section of the PGA Championship, the LPGA Mitsubishi Invitational, and the Arizona Golf Association's State Stroke Play Championship.

Greens fees in high season run from $99 to $125, depending on time of play. Rates include use of the practice area and a golf cart. Amenities include a golf shop, locker facility, Raven Grill with an outdoor pavilion and banquet facilities, and a highly regarded practice facility with a golf academy, putting green, and chipping area.

SOUTHEAST VALLEY

ASU KARSTEN GOLF COURSE
1125 E. Rio Salado Pkwy., Tempe
(480) 921-8070
www.asukarsten.com

Karsten, opened in 1989, was designed by Pete Dye to accommodate players of all skill levels. Dye molded land near the Salt River into a stunning Scottish-style links course, with rolling hills, plenty of bunkers, and water. The 6,200-yard, par-72 course is adjacent to Tempe's Town Lake, a project that reclaimed part of the river bottom for use as an urban lake. Views of the man-made lake add beauty to the surroundings, which already provide a great view of ASU's Sun Devil Stadium leaning against "A" Mountain. With water lining the left-hand side, bunkers on the right-hand side, and water on the approach, the 18th hole has a lot of character.

Karsten serves as the practice facility for ASU's men's and women's golf teams and hosts NCAA and other regional championships. The amenities include a learning center, clubhouse and golf shop, driving range and practice area, private dining room, lessons, and the Trophy Room restaurant. In addition, the staff stresses service, treating players well in the fashion of the best resort courses. The PING Learning Center offers private, technologically advanced instruction, club fittings, and other coaching.

Greens fees on a weekend in high season, golf cart included, are about $110 for non-residents. Residents can expect to pay about $15 less. In the summer, that rate drops to about $40. Students and faculty are eligible for discounts.

i The PGA Tour Superstore holds 60,000 square feet of golf and tennis gear. It sells clubs and balls, but also includes golf bays, an indoor tennis court, and more. You'll find it at 2031 N. Arizona Ave., Chandler (480-214-4370). There's another location at 8740 E. Shea Blvd., Scottsdale (480-214-4350).

DOBSON RANCH GOLF COURSE
2155 S. Dobson Rd., Mesa
(480) 644-2291
www.dobsonranchgolfcourse.com

Dobson Ranch, sequestered in a suburban Mesa neighborhood, rivals Phoenix's Cave Creek and Papago Park courses as one of the busiest municipal courses in the state. Built in 1972, this 6,593-yard, par-72 course is a traditional, playable, and forgiving course. Dobson Ranch is well groomed with fast, often undulating greens. The layout is open, but the course features many trees to make

it more scenic. It's also an easy course to walk. The eighth hole, sitting next to a creek that runs down the whole right side of the course, is the signature hole. The sloped green of this par-4 hole sits among bunkers on three sides.

The course features a golf shop, clubhouse, lessons, putting greens, chipping area, lighted driving range, and sports grill. Greens fees in high season are $31 walking or $43 with a cart. After 10 a.m. you pay less. Juniors under age 17 must walk, and that fee is $8.

KEN MCDONALD GOLF COURSE
800 E. Divot Dr., Tempe
(480) 350-5250
www.playkenmcdonaldgolf.com
The traditional municipal course sees quite a bit of use and hosts nearly 100,000 rounds a year. The 6,743-yard, par-72 course is like a little park tucked away in a suburban development. The flat layout is easy to walk among the tree-lined fairways. Playing here is not overly demanding, either. The landing areas off the tees are relatively generous. One of the more interesting holes is the 17th, a par 3. There is water to the right and bunkers to both left and right, and the green undulates.

Tempe residents have preference in reserving tee times. Greens fees are $30 to walk and $42 to ride in high season. Juniors and seniors are eligible for a small discount. The amenities include a pro shop, clubhouse, lessons, club repair, practice areas, 2 putting greens, chipping green, and a full-service restaurant and bar.

OCOTILLO GOLF RESORT
3751 S. Clubhouse Dr., Chandler
(480) 917-6660
www.ocotillogolf.com

A basic description of Ocotillo Golf Club would mention water, houses, and grass. Ocotillo's 27 holes—3 separate nines called Blue, White, and Gold—feature 27 miles of shoreline. The nines are built on a traditional design, with 23 of the 27 holes involving water and houses surrounding the perimeter. Designed by Ted Robinson, Ocotillo opened in 1986 as something of a break from the beat-you-up target courses. The fairways are wide, though the water threatens. The Blue course is shortest but has the most water, while the Gold has the least, making for the safest and easiest passage. The White has the toughest hole in No. 9. The Blue-Gold combination is perhaps the most difficult rotation.

The signature fourth hole on the White course is a par 4 with water down the left side and water on the approach to the green. It's very pretty but not too forgiving. With a waterfall to the left of the green and the clubhouse behind the green to the right, this is the prettiest hole on the course.

Greens fees are $175, cart included, in the high season, $115 in the shoulder season, $65 May 22 through October 1, $125 October 2 through December 31, and $125 in January.

Ocotillo has a 28,000-square-foot clubhouse facility that includes a restaurant, outdoor dining area, and special-events pavilion. The amenities also include a golf shop, lessons, putting green, and a full driving range.

SAN MARCOS GOLF RESORT
1 San Marcos Place, Chandler
(480) 963-3358
www.sanmarcosresort.com
The San Marcos has a claim to being the oldest golf course in Arizona because its

original nine, which is now where the Chandler Public Library sits, was built back in 1912 by Harry Collis and Will Robinson. The San Marcos was a ritzy getaway when such celebrities as Fred Astaire, Bing Crosby, Errol Flynn, Clark Gable, and Jimmy Stewart played here in their heyday. Even Al Capone played here.

The 6,500-yard, par-72 course is a traditional, Midwestern style, built long before current water restrictions began to limit the amount of turf. Because of its age, it has a mature ambience and plenty of grass and trees, such as salt cedar, eucalyptus, willow, and palm, which offer shade from the desert sun.

Greens fees on weekends in high season, cart included, are $89. Arizona residents pay $55. Call or go online to check rates for other times of the year. The amenities include a clubhouse, pro shop, driving range, putting and chipping greens, and a restaurant.

TOKA STICKS GOLF CLUB
6910 E. Williams Field Rd., Mesa
(480) 988-9405
www.tokasticksgolf.com
Toka Sticks began as an Air Force golf course as part of Williams Air Force Base. The Gila River Indian Community bought the course in 1996 and renamed it for a traditional field-hockey game played by the women of the Pima tribe. The Pimas upgraded the course to the tune of $2 million, adding new cart paths and bunkers and sprucing up the greens. The 6,680-yard, par-72 traditional course was built in two phases. The Air Force built the first nine holes in the early 1950s, and the second nine, designed by civil engineers, were added in the early 1980s. The course is lined with trees such as eucalyptus and salt cedar. The toughest hole on the course—a par 5 of 541 yards—is saved for last. Amenities include a clubhouse, pro shop, driving range, putting and chipping greens, and a snack bar.

The morning greens fees, including cart, in high season are $45, 7 days a week, but afternoon tee times drop the rates quite a bit. In May the fees drop by $10; they drop again in August.

NORTHEAST VALLEY

✳THE GOLF CLUB AT EAGLE MOUNTAIN
14915 E. Eagle Mountain Pkwy., Fountain Hills
(480) 816-1234
www.eaglemtn.com
Eagle Mountain lets you look down on the East Valley as you golf. Perched as it is in the foothills of the McDowell Mountains, many prominent peaks add to the course's picturesque quality. Eagle Mountain has grass from tee to green, though its landscaping is nontraditional and it's not a true target course. When you're off the fairways and greens, you're in the desert, where saguaros and desert scrub dot the surroundings. The 6,755-yard, par-71 course, designed by Scott Miller and opened in January 1996, takes advantage of desert ravines to make the course, which wraps around Eagle Mountain, seem set apart rather than an expected part of the Eagle Mountain master-planned community. One of the best examples of the course's scenic charms is the closing hole, one of the most beautiful in the Valley and a demanding par 5. The tees are at the highest point on the golf course, with the green at the bottom of a slope. A lake and bunkers sit to the right, and the hole is framed by a dramatic view of Red Mountain.

Greens fees, including cart, range from $195 in high season to $65 from June to mid-September. Twilight rates are available.

The service and ambience of Eagle Mountain are comparable to those of a private country club. The amenities include a clubhouse, full practice facility, golf shop, lessons, locker rooms, and showers.

✳GRAYHAWK GOLF CLUB
8620 E. Thompson Peak Pkwy., Scottsdale
(480) 502-1800
www.grayhawkgolf.com
Grayhawk features 2 desert-style courses—Talon and Raptor. Set in the foothills in north Scottsdale, it offers views of the McDowell Mountains, Pinnacle Peak, and the Valley. Talon, designed by David Graham and Gary Panks, is a 6,391-yard, par-72 course. Despite its wide landing areas, Talon features 14 fewer grassy acres than Raptor and plays more like a target course. Take, for example, the stunningly beautiful 17th hole, a par 3 with an island green. Raptor, a 6,620-yard, par-72 course designed by Tom Fazio, features its own challenges, such as the 16th hole. A lake and a creek run alongside this par 3 that plays anywhere from 185 yards to 200 yards. It's definitely challenging. Greens fees, including cart, range from $225 in the high season to $75 in the summer months. There are discounts for weekdays during the warmer months, as well as for twilight golfing.

Grayhawk features a 42,000-square-foot clubhouse, 2 dining areas, a golf shop, lessons, the Kostis-McCord Learning Center, and Phil's Grill. Phil Mickelson is the PGA tour representative at Grayhawk.

i A number of courses offer price breaks for twilight rounds. Golfers leave work early, grab their clubs, and play until sunset. Some courses offer special rates in the morning, others in the late afternoon. The mornings are cooler, even cold in the winter. In summer the late afternoon is very hot, but doable if you're a well-hydrated fanatic.

KIERLAND GOLF CLUB
15636 N. Clubgate Dr., Scottsdale
(480) 922-9283
www.kierlandgolf.com
Kierland, which opened in 1996, features three 9-hole layouts—Ironwood, Acacia, and Mesquite—that golfers can combine for a 27-hole, par-72 round. Scott Miller designed a lush parkland with undulating greens for all three nines. Each layout, named for the predominant trees in its landscape, has its own identity. A wide-open topography allows for views of Pinnacle Peak, Camelback Mountain, and the McDowell Mountains. In fact, the beginning holes are oriented to each of these landmarks. Interestingly, Miller's design takes advantage of golden-colored native grasses—instead of rocks and cactus—to give strong definition to the fairways. So it looks like a target course, though it is less forgiving. With lakes at all three finishing holes and dry washes throughout the course, Kierland offers playability and drama.

In 2003 the club saw some big changes as the Westin Kierland Resort & Spa was opened, offering the usual amenities for those tired out from long hours on the greens. The course added a new 19,000-square-foot clubhouse, as well as enhanced bunkers and TifEagle greens.

Amenities include a clubhouse, pro shop, food and beverage service, practice facility, and the *Golf Digest* Golf School under the direction of pros Mike and Sandy LaBauve.

Morning greens fees, including cart, range from $210 in the high season to $85 during shoulder seasons. Twilight tee times give nice discounts.

THE PHOENICIAN GOLF RESORT
6000 E. Camelback Rd., Scottsdale
(480) 423-2450
www.thephoenician.com/golf

Since luxury is the calling card of the Phoenician resort, no one should be surprised that its semiprivate resort-golf experience is equally luxurious, featuring impeccably manicured grass and gorgeous landscaping. The Phoenician has 27 holes in three distinct nines. These wrap around the resort so that they can be played in three 18-hole patterns. Before the Phoenician opened in 1988, a public course sat on this site, but it was completely redone for the resort. The Phoenician's facility opened with 18 holes designed by Homer Flint. Ted Robinson Sr. designed the other nine holes, which opened in 1996.

The Oasis Course lives up to its name with plenty of water features that please the eye but trouble golfers; the Desert Course is a challenging target course that skirts the base of Camelback Mountain; and the Canyon Course is lushly landscaped and undulates across the southern slope of Camelback. The three 18-hole combinations are each a par 70. The par-3 eighth hole on the Desert Course is an especially gorgeous hole.

The clubhouse and golf shop are as well appointed as the resort's hotel. The package is completed by a driving range, club rentals, and lessons augmented with the Swing Solution video-analysis system, which offers a complex analysis of a player's swing.

Winter is the high season, though there's no set date when the winter rates begin, because overseeding with winter grass plays havoc with the schedule. High-season rates go into effect sometime around October. Rates are the same for guests and nonguests and range from $200 in high season to $60 in summer. Twilight tee times give nice discounts.

i The Arizona Golf Association keeps a tab on seasonal deals, getaway packages, and course maintenance updates, and even gives golfers access to blogs and RSS feeds of just about everything links-related in the state. Its searchable golf course database is a helpful tool. Now only if our sand wedges could work as efficiently. Information: www.azgolf.org.

TOURNAMENT PLAYERS CLUB OF SCOTTSDALE
17020 N. Hayden Rd., Scottsdale
(480) 585-4334, (888) 400-4001
www.tpc.com/tpc-scottsdale

As the home of the Waste Management Phoenix Open, the Tournament Players Club of Scottsdale can be thought of as the premier professional challenge in the Valley. There are 2 courses at TPC—Stadium and the Champions Course (formerly Desert Course). The team of Tom Weiskopf and Jay Morrish designed the courses to take advantage of the desert setting and excellent views of the McDowell Mountains. Both courses feature lush fairways surrounded by desert landscaping and punctuated by lakes and bunkers. The 7,089-yard, par-71 Stadium course is aptly named, using mounds and

terracing to provide a stadium-like area for spectators to watch PGA Tour events such as the annual Open that happens every winter around the Super Bowl (see the Spectator Sports section for more). The brand-new par-71 Champions Course, designed by Randy Heckenkemper, blends in with the Sonoran Desert and offers tough, rugged play. Get set for a dramatic finish. Starting at the 15th hole, the course brings challenge after challenge. The major renovation features a new clubhouse as well.

Morning greens fees range from $260 in peak season, down to $72 in the summer. The club has several shoulder seasons and twilight rates, so call for information. Maricopa County residents get a discount, as do juniors, seniors, and those who walk rather than ride a cart.

*TROON NORTH GOLF CLUB
10320 E. Dynamite Blvd., Scottsdale
(480) 585-5300
www.troonnorthgolf.com
Troon North offers 2 courses—Monument and Pinnacle. Monument, the older of the courses, was designed by Tom Weiskopf and Jay Morrish before they went their separate ways. Weiskopf designed the Pinnacle course. Both of these courses are tough for the average player and are routinely ranked among the best in the US.

Monument's flow through its 6,636 yards is smooth, yet the par-72 course is a desert target style—very tough. Every hole presents a challenge. The third hole is the Monument hole, a par 5 with a 25-foot-tall boulder in the middle of the fairway. The views of the McDowell Mountains, Pinnacle Peak, and the Valley provide a sense of solitude, heightening the singular experience of golf. Pinnacle's front nine are the most

scenic holes at Troon North. For example, the 6th hole of this 7,044-yard, par-72 course runs up the side of a hill where Pinnacle Peak dominates the background.

Troon North is a semiprivate facility, and members have preference for booking tee times. Greens fees, including cart, vary immensely depending on the season and how far in advance tee times are booked. Weekend peak fees come in at a high of $345; low season fees are down around $90.

The amenities include a clubhouse, pro shop, driving range for players with tee times, practice area, lessons, dining facilities, conference rooms, and The Dynamite Grill.

NORTHWEST VALLEY

THE LEGEND AT ARROWHEAD
21027 N. 67th Ave., Glendale
(623) 561-1902
www.legendatarrowhead.com
Arnold Palmer and Ed Seay designed this traditional, grass-from-tee-to-green course as the centerpiece of the master-planned Arrowhead Ranch community in Glendale. This area is booming because its gray-black hills and generous lots keep suburbia looking like the desert. Although the Legend is a traditional course featuring six lakes, it is built on those dark hills and can't be mistaken for a Midwestern-style course. This 6,969-yard, par-72 course becomes much more difficult when played from the championship tees, but if you choose your tee boxes well, it can be very enjoyable. In fact, golf doesn't get any better than the fifth hole. It's a 426-yard, par 4 that's played from elevated tees to an hourglass-shaped green with water on the right.

Greens fees, cart included, vary seasonally, with a high of $85 between December

and mid-April. Call or check online for low-season fees. Amenities include a clubhouse, restaurant, pro shop, lessons, driving range, practice area, and an all-grass chipping and putting green.

SOUTHWEST VALLEY

THE WIGWAM RESORT
300 Wigwam Blvd., Litchfield Park
(800) 909-4224
www.wigwamresort.com/arizona-golf-resorts.php

The Wigwam Resort is another bastion of the old high life of Arizona resorts. Originally built as the private domain of Goodyear executives, the Wigwam is open to those who can pay the price for these elegantly rustic surroundings. And the same goes for its 3 golf courses. The Wigwam has earned *Golf Magazine*'s Silver Medal Resort honors and *Links Magazine*'s Best of Golf Award. In addition, the Gold course was ranked as the top resort course on *Golf Digest*'s list of Arizona's Best Courses. In 2005 a $5 million renovation restored both the Gold and Blue courses to their original grandeur.

The Gold course features a traditional layout designed by Robert Trent Jones Sr. A 7,430-yard, par-72 course, the Gold is a tough one to play with elevated greens, narrow landing areas, bunkers, and water. At 6,085 yards, the par-70 Blue course is the shortest layout at the Wigwam, but that doesn't make it the easiest. It's a fairly unforgiving links-style course. The 6,865-yard, par-72 Red course was designed by Arizona's Robert "Red" Lawrence and V. O. "Red" Allen, and features lakes, creeks, and huge greens. It's a traditional layout that is something like comfort food compared with the others, although it still presents a challenge.

Greens fees for the Gold course are $129 in high season. The Red and Blue courses charge $109 in high season. All fees decrease after 10 a.m., and all fees include carts. Amenities include a clubhouse, pro shop, driving range, and practice area, as well as tennis courts, spa, dining facilities, and lessons. The Wigwam includes a staff of fully certified instructors, video bays, target greens, and putting greens.

SPECTATOR SPORTS

The Valley has a deep sports tradition that covers four major pro sports teams, two PAC-10 conference universities, and one of the most successful women's pro basketball franchises in history.

The Arizona Diamondbacks and WNBA's Phoenix Mercury are the sole champions in the mix. The D-Backs shocked the New York Yankees in the 2001 World Series on a chip-shot, walk-off base hit by local hero Luis Gonzalez. The Mercury, led by superstar Diana Taurasi, has won two titles. Both teams generate their share of excitement in downtown Phoenix at Chase Field and US Airways Arena, which is also home to the Phoenix Suns and Arizona Rattlers.

In 2006 the Arizona Cardinals moved to their new home, University of Phoenix Stadium in Glendale, and went to their first Super Bowl 2 years later. The stadium has all the latest high-tech gear, from air-conditioning throughout the entire building to a retractable roof and field. Glendale and the Valley played host to the 2008 Super Bowl and will surely earn the right to host another.

Each March brings the four greatest words in the English language for any true baseball fan: "Pitchers and Catchers Report." That means the Cactus League season is underway, as teams like the Oakland Athletics, Los Angeles Dodgers, and Chicago Cubs make their way to their spring training facilities to prepare for the season. See the Close-up on the Cactus League in this chapter for a glimpse at a few of the Cactus League's newest stadiums. For baseball purists there's nothing quite like it, except for the sister Grapefruit League in Florida. You're able to watch games for $10, sitting on a beach towel on a sunny outfield lawn. The players are approachable, and the smaller stadiums allow you to reconnect with your team.

In addition to the professional sports, Arizona State University and the University of Arizona have a heated rivalry that extends across every sport. The annual Territorial Cup football game is one of the best matchups of the PAC-10 season. The Valley is also home to such annual events as the Waste Management Phoenix Open, one of the best-attended pro golf tournaments on the PGA Tour, and the Fiesta Bowl, which hosted the first unified national college championship game in 1999. The Fiesta Bowl is played in Glendale's University of Phoenix Stadium. The Valley loves NASCAR, and the races at Phoenix International Raceway draw some of the largest crowds on the circuit.

ARENA FOOTBALL

ARIZONA RATTLERS
US Airways Center
201 E. Jefferson St., Phoenix
(485) 985-3292
www.azrattlers.com

In many ways, the Rattlers are more popular in Arizona than the long-suffering Cardinals. Arena ball is fast and explosive, so it attracts footballs fans with a shorter attention span than Xs- and Os-loving NFL fans. Everyone in Arena League plays offense and defense with the exception of the kicker, quarterback, offensive specialist, kick returner, and 2 defensive specialists. The high-scoring games help football-starved fans get through the spring. The off-field atmosphere is raucous, with lots of flashing lights, ear-splitting music, and sound effects. There are plenty of giveaways. Halftime and pregame festivities feature the team mascot, Fang, a fierce-looking biker who rides into the arena on a huge Harley to rev up the crowd (and his motorcycle).

The Rattlers played under coach Danny White, the former Dallas Cowboys and Arizona State University quarterback, until 2006, when they burned through a couple of coaches. In 2003 wide receiver Randy Gatewood was named the league's Ironman of the Year, and the Rattlers became the first team in AFL history to score 80-plus points in consecutive games. The team sports a sharp rattlesnake logo, easily recognizable in the Valley. Rattlers' gear is available at the Team Shop in the arena. The team is involved in many community events and sponsors a flag-football tournament.

The Rattlers' 16-game season begins in February and ends in June. Single-game tickets range from $10 in a single upper end zone to $110.

AUTO RACING

FIREBIRD INTERNATIONAL RACEWAY
20000 Maricopa Rd., Chandler
(602) 268-0200
www.firebirdraceway.com

Drag racing rules at Firebird. Funny cars and jet dragsters roar around 1 of 3 tracks, so the events are noisy and festive. The east track is 1.25 miles long and features 10 turns. The west track is 1.2 miles long with 11 turns. The Firebird Course is 1.6 miles with 14 turns. Drag racing is held most Friday nights throughout the year. Major annual events at Firebird include the NHRA Arizona Nationals in October and the NAPA Auto Parts Monster Truck Nationals in April. Adjacent Firebird Lake also is the site of drag-boat racing. Admission varies with events. Firebird Raceway is easily accessible from I-10, just west of the Wild Horse Pass Boulevard exit.

PHOENIX INTERNATIONAL RACEWAY
7602 S. 115th Ave., Tolleson
(623) 463-5400
(888) 408-7223 (box office)
www.phoenixintlraceway.com

Situated in view of the ruggedly gorgeous Estrella Mountains, Phoenix International Raceway serves as a setting for many TV commercials that highlight cars moving against a pristine desert backdrop. The track is in use 300 or more days a year for auto testing, driving schools, commercials, and especially racing events. Using private money, PIR track officials have spent more than $50 million on capital improvements within the past few years. In 2011 the track received its first full repaving of the course since 1990. The surface was removed and replaced with a new surface that encourages more-competitive NASCAR races. The track now has 26 new suites and an extra

14,000 seats for the huge fan base. Bars like the Speed Cantina give fans a place to party if the massive sea of trucks and trailers that form in the parking areas for NASCAR events doesn't provide enough entertainment.

The raceway, described as the fastest 1-mile oval in the world, opened in 1964 in an unincorporated part of Maricopa County about 30 miles west of downtown Phoenix. Back then its location was way, way out in the Valley, and even now, with tendrils of development creeping out that way, it remains an isolated desert experience. The NASCAR Subway Fresh Fit 500, held in November, draws about 100,000 people to the D-shaped track. Smaller 100- and 200-lap events are also held in the spring and fall.

To reach the track from Phoenix, go west on I-10 to 115th Avenue. Head south on 115th about 4 miles until 115th Avenue takes a turn to the west into Baseline Road.

BASEBALL

ARIZONA DIAMONDBACKS
Chase Field
401 E. Jefferson St., Phoenix
(602) 462-6500
http://arizona.diamondbacks.MLB.com

The Diamondbacks game 7 walk-off victory over the New York Yankees in the 2001 World Series is burned into the memory of every Arizona baseball fan. The expansion franchise toppled the mighty Yanks just weeks after the terrorist attacks of September 11 in New York, making for a memorable and patriotic championship. The twin-tower aces of co-MVPs Randy Johnson and Curt Schilling brought then-owner Jerry Colangelo and the state of Arizona its first and only World Series title.

The Diamondbacks' story began with the Phoenix Suns basketball team. Suns former owner Jerry Colangelo announced in 1993, the year his basketball team went to the NBA Finals, he was putting together an ownership group to try to purchase a Major League Baseball franchise for Phoenix. In 1995 Colangelo received the franchise, which would start play in 1998.

Almost immediately, work began on Bank One Ballpark (now renamed Chase Field), a retractable-roof stadium with a natural-grass playing surface. It was built in the current MLB fashion to offer the old-time, single-use baseball stadium feel. At the same time, it is air-conditioned to make a capacity crowd of 49,033 comfortable. Chase Field even boasts a swimming pool for patrons who want to stay wet during a game or dive in after a home run. The opening of the roof even has its own dramatic theme music.

When former New York Yankees coach Buck Showalter signed on in 1995, 18 months before the Diamondbacks would play their first game, the tone was set for good, fundamental baseball. Alas, it was still an expansion team despite having a team of talented veterans, including gold glover Matt Williams at third base. The Diamondbacks stuck to the bottom of the National League West in 1998. The next year, the D-Backs, with the help of "The Big Unit" Johnson, took the National League's Western Division Championship. Since 2001 the D-Backs have appeared in one National League Championship Series. It's been mostly rebuilding since then, though new manager and World Series hero Kirk Gibson is expected to promote a new aggressive style of play for young studs like Justin Upton and Chris Young.

Full-season tickets range from $415 for the uppermost level to $3,000-plus for the

Club Box level. Single-game tickets range from around $10 to $220.

There are approximately 33,600 parking spaces available within a 15-minute walk of Chase Field. Garages like the one on Monroe Street near Heritage Square will validate if you have a beer after the game at a bar like Rose and Crown. Cheap parking is available in lots south of the stadium and further east on Jefferson Street. The Diamondbacks' home schedule overlaps with home games of the Phoenix Suns, Phoenix Mercury, and Arizona Rattlers on many nights, which means an additional 10,000 to 19,000 people downtown on some game nights. You should allow extra time to park if you want to arrive in time for the national anthem.

The light rail line drops off along Jefferson Street on the north side of the stadium for even easier access. The trains after the game get a little packed, but it's nothing compared to what you have to deal with on public transportation in Chicago or Boston.

> **i** Phoenix Suns games are usually sold out, but fairly often you can buy a ticket from a season ticket holder who is unable to attend a certain game. Go to www.nba.com/suns and look for "Ticket exchange."

CACTUS LEAGUE
www.cactusleague.com

The Cactus League includes 15 Major League Baseball teams that play in March across 10 cozy Valley stadiums that provide fans a much more intimate look at the game. The spring training venues give fans the chance to see their teams preparing for the season ahead, which means a close look at high-priced free agent acquisitions and rookie phenoms in their new uniforms. This is the place where Barry Bonds hit tape-measure home runs through his BALCO steroids scandal. It's where Rickey Henderson teaches the next generation of Oakland A's players how to steal bases. It's where legends like Fergie Jenkins, Rollie Fingers, and George Brett routinely pose for photos with fans. The late Bob Feller and Ron Santo were also fixtures in the crowd at Indians and Cubs games.

The league has humble roots, as only eight teams played in the Valley and Tucson in the 1980s. Its popularity as a spring destination spot exploded in the 1990s and around the turn of the century as new stadiums like Scottsdale Stadium (1992, San Francisco Giants) and Surprise Stadium (2002, Texas Rangers and Kansas City Royals) sprang up to give fans more options. Since 2009 six teams have moved into 3 new parks that combine luxury and old-school baseball amenities. Today you can spend a long weekend traveling between different Valley communities to get a taste of the old and new. Tailgate with bratwurst-grilling Brewers fans at the no-frills Maryvale Stadium in west Phoenix on Saturday before driving on Sunday to the Salt River Fields in Scottsdale for a luxury-like experience at the new home of the Diamondbacks and Rockies.

The Cactus League is an economic force for Arizona. Sales generate around $200 million annually as fans travel to the Valley from Chicago, the Bay Area, and Colorado to see their teams in action. Locals also watch several games each March, if not more. The parks are the place to be to enjoy the 80-degree weather and teasingly phone friends or family back East.

• **Arizona Diamondbacks/Colorado Rockies,** Salt River Fields at Talking Stick, 7555 N. Pima Rd., Scottsdale, www.saltriverfields.com

⊙ Close-up

Cactus League

Cactus League baseball means sunshine and cheap tickets. Yeah, you can walk right in for $12 or sit on the outfield lawn for less in some parks. But for baseball fans, it's the springtime window to rub shoulders with players, to examine fights for roster spots, to scout the top rookies, and see the latest free agent signings in their new uniforms.

This is baseball at its most pure. And unlike the Grapefruit League in Florida, all the stadiums are so close together, it's easy to see three or four games in a long weekend without driving across the state. Most teams allow fans to watch their practices either at the stadiums or at their neighboring training complexes. For autograph hunters it's paradise. For young fans getting an up-close glimpse of their heroes, it's a memory that will last long into adulthood.

The Chicago Cubs and San Francisco Giants tend to draw the biggest crowds. But the Cactus League's three stadiums will also prove to be a more difficult ticket to get than the low-key older stadiums in Phoenix, Tempe, and Peoria.

- **Chicago Cubs,** Hohokam Stadium, 1235 N. Center St., Mesa, www.hohokam stadium.com
- **Chicago White Sox/Los Angeles Dodgers,** Camelback Ranch, 10710 W. Camelback Rd., Glendale, www.camel backranchbaseball.com
- **Cincinnati Reds/Cleveland Indians,** Goodyear Ballpark, 1933 S. Ballpark Way, Goodyear, www.goodyearaz.gov/ballpark
- **Kansas City Royals/Texas Rangers,** Surprise Stadium, 15754 N. Bullard Ave., Surprise, www.surpriseaz.gov/files/springtraining
- **Los Angeles Angels of Anaheim,** Tempe Diablo Stadium, 2200 W. Alameda Dr., Tempe, www.tempe.gov/diablo
- **Milwaukee Brewers,** Maryvale Baseball Park, 3600 N. 51st Ave., Phoenix, www.phoenix.gov/sports/marystad.html
- **Oakland Athletics,** Phoenix Municipal Stadium, 5999 E. Van Buren St., Phoenix, www.phoenix.gov/sports/phxmuni.html

- **San Diego Padres/Seattle Mariners,** Peoria Sports Complex, 16101 N. 83rd Ave., Peoria, www.peoriasportscomplex .com
- **San Francisco Giants,** Scottsdale Stadium, 7408 E. Osborn Rd., Scottsdale, www.scottsdaleaz.gov/stadium

ARIZONA FALL LEAGUE
Valley-wide stadiums
www.mlb.com/mlb/events/
winterleagues
Compared with spring training and the Diamondbacks, MLB's Fall League is a well-kept secret with a total attendance of about 50,000 people at 138 games. You can pretty much sit wherever you want and get a close glimpse of the next Bryce Harper or Albert Pujols. That's right. Both played in Arizona in the heavily scouted league. So did Mike Piazza, Jason Giambi, Nomar Garciaparra, Todd Helton, and many others.

The Fall League, which began in 1992, is essentially an all-star league of AA and AAA players on the cusp of being everyday big leaguers. Each MLB team sends several prospects to the league, and they are assigned to one of the league's six teams. In 1994 the league drew its biggest crowds ever because of Michael Jordan, who had already made his name on the basketball court before trying to catch on in the White Sox's minor league system.

The schedule is set by about the middle of June, and the games are played from the beginning of October through November. Game times are 1:05 and 7:05 p.m. Plenty of walk-up tickets ($6 for adults, $5 for seniors and children) are available on game days at the individual stadiums.

The teams use the same stadiums that serve as Cactus League spring training headquarters for their parent clubs:

- **Grand Canyon Rafters,** Surrise Stadium, 15754 N. Bullard Ave., Surprise
- **Mesa Solar Sox,** Hohokam Stadium, 1235 N. Center St., Mesa
- **Peoria Javelinas,** Peoria Sports Complex, 16101 N. 83rd Ave., Peoria
- **Peoria Saguaros,** Peoria Sports Complex, 16101 N. 83rd Ave., Peoria
- **Phoenix Desert Dogs,** Phoenix Municipal Stadium, 5999 E. Van Buren St., Phoenix
- **Scottsdale Scorpions,** Scottsdale Stadium, 7408 E. Osborn Rd., Scottsdale

CAMELBACK RANCH
Chicago White Sox and Los Angeles Dodgers
10710 W. Camelback Rd., Glendale
www.camelbackranchbaseball.com
After more than 60 years in Vero Beach, Fla., the Dodgers opened a new 140-acre spring training home in the Cactus League. The White Sox abandoned Tucson to join their American League roommate to open the 2009 season. The ballpark west of the Loop 101 in Glendale gives fans a third option with the stadiums in Peoria (Mariners and Padres) and Surprise (Rangers and Royals) in the Northwest Valley.

GOODYEAR BALLPARK
Cincinnati Reds and Cleveland Indians
1933 S. Ballpark Way, Goodyear
www.goodyearaz.gov/ballpark
The slightly sunken diamond ballpark offers a unique game day experience for fans who want to make the trek to Goodyear. In 2011 attendance was down, though Ohio sports fans still consider the new park a little slice of heaven against the backdrop of the Estrella Mountains. The outlying location and lower attendance make it a great place to buy a cheap ticket and slide down into better seats.

SALT RIVER FIELDS AT TALKING STICK
Arizona Diamondbacks and Colorado Rockies
7555 N. Pima Rd., Scottsdale
www.saltriverfields.com
The fully loaded stadium was the talk of baseball during its inaugural 2011 season as fans took note of the high-definition scoreboard, perfectly manicured lawns, and upscale vendors that top the typical ballpark frank. It's located on the Salt River Pima-Maricopa Indian Community, but only a short drive from central Scottsdale. Parking is a nightmare, so park for free at Scottsdale Pavilions shopping center and avoid the Loop 101 around game time.

BASKETBALL

PHOENIX MERCURY

US Airways Center
201 E. Jefferson St., Phoenix
(602) 379-7900
(602) 252-9622 (box office)
www.phoenixmercury.com

In 1997 the WNBA's inaugural year, the Phoenix Mercury professional women's basketball team won the Western Conference title. The team drew an average attendance of 13,703, tops in the eight-team league. Team owner Jerry Colangelo, confident there was an untapped market in women's basketball, hired Cheryl Miller to be head coach and general manager of the Mercury. Miller was known for building winning records as a coach at USC from 1993 to 1995.

Since then the WNBA has seen more expansion with new teams and a 33-game regular-season schedule. After Colangelo left, the team was taken over by Robert Sarver, who also owns the Phoenix Suns. Former UConn standout and No. 1 overall draft pick Diana Taurasi is the most popular player in the team's history. The Mercury won the WNBA title in 2007 with Taurasi as its young leader and repeated in 2009.

Ticket prices range from $11 to $65 per game, while season tickets range from $189 to $2,295 on the floor. Season tickets include a preseason game and first dibs on postseason tickets.

PHOENIX SUNS

US Airways Center
201 E. Jefferson St., Phoenix
(602) 379-7900
(602) 379-7867 (box office)
www.nba.com/suns

The Phoenix Suns opened up shop in 1968 as an NBA expansion franchise, the first pro club in Phoenix. To this day, they are the most widely beloved of the Valley's four major pro sports teams, though they have never won a title. Befitting an expansion franchise, their first few seasons were terrible. Their bad luck didn't end with a 16–66 mark in their first season. Thanks to the last-place finish, the Suns had the opportunity to flip a coin with expansion mates the Milwaukee Bucks to decide who would get the No. 1 pick in the 1969 draft. The Bucks won the toss and got Lew Alcindor (soon to be much better known as Kareem Abdul-Jabbar). In 1971 he led the Bucks to the NBA Championship. The Suns are still waiting for their turn.

The team made a run to the finals in the 1975–76 season, parlaying a 42–40 season record. When they met the Boston Celtics in the finals, the series was tied after four games. The Suns took game 5 to triple overtime at the Boston Garden before losing to the Celtics. They lost the series in the next game. The NBA finals didn't see another triple overtime game for 17 years, until (guess who?) the Phoenix Suns met the Chicago Bulls in 1993. Although the Suns, led by the irrepressible Charles Barkley, won the triple overtime this time, the Bulls still prevailed in six games thanks to Michael Jordan. The list of impressive Suns players goes on to include Shaquille O'Neal, Amare Stoudemire, and Steve Nash, the 2004–05 and 2005–06 NBA Most Valuable Player.

The Suns have sold out US Airways Center's 19,023 basketball seats ever since the arena opened in the fall of 1992. Tickets range from $10 in the uppermost seats to $1,550 on the floor. Season tickets are sold on a per-game basis. In a 44-game season, season tickets range from $10 to $1,000 per game per ticket, but there is a long waiting list.

COLLEGE SPORTS

ARIZONA STATE UNIVERSITY SUN DEVILS

Sun Devil Stadium (and other venues in Tempe)
500 E. Veterans Way, Tempe
(480) 965-2381
www.thesundevils.cstv.com

When the Sun Devils football team made its 1996 run to the Rose Bowl, it captivated the Valley, often outdrawing the NFL's Cardinals in the same stadium each fall weekend. Average home-game attendance was 63,884 that year.

The university's athletics programs have been an important part of Valley sports since their inception. As is the case with most sports programs, the men's teams—football, basketball, and baseball—have the highest profile. However, there is a strong following for the women's basketball and softball teams.

ASU has competed in the Pacific 10 Conference in 20 varsity sports and has won 129 national championships, including 11 in women's golf and 5 in baseball. Former Sun Devils include "Mr. October" Reggie Jackson, infamous home run king Barry Bonds, former Dallas Cowboys quarterback Danny White, and golfer Phil Mickelson. But perhaps the most adored of all Sun Devils is Pat Tillman, the local boy who fought his way through the NCAA and later the NFL with his hometown Cardinals before quitting football to join the Army. He was killed in a firefight in 2004 in Afghanistan while serving in the elite Army Rangers.

Football far and away is the dominant sport in terms of fan support and can fill many of Sun Devil Stadium's 73,379 seats. The team has seen some high rankings in recent years, though the product on the field hasn't met expectations. The annual game with archrival University of Arizona, known as the Territorial Cup, is one of the most spirited and competitive events in college football.

Men's and women's basketball teams play at Wells Fargo Arena, a 14,198-seat facility that was built in 1974 at a cost of $8 million. Baseball players try to knock it out of the park at Packard Stadium, a 7,875-capacity ballpark built in 1974. A left-handed hitter can slug a home run beyond the right field wall into oncoming traffic on Rural Road. Softball pitchers do their windmill windup at Farrington Stadium, a 1,500-seat field. Track and field events take place at the Sun Angel Stadium/Joe Selleh Track, which has a 5,000-seat grandstand and movable bleachers that can accommodate another 4,000 for big events such as the annual Sun Angel Track Classic. There's an aquatic center for the swimming teams, and ASU Karsten Golf Course gives the golf teams dedicated space for practice. The Sun Devil Ticket Office has information on all sports tickets at ASU. Each of the venues is located within walking distance of Sun Devil Stadium.

i Professional players are fond of eating at Don & Charlie's, a steakhouse at 7501 E. Camelback Rd. in Scottsdale (480-990-0900). You'll find an impressive collection of sports memorabilia on the walls, from autographed jerseys to signed baseballs and bats. MLB Commissioner Bud Selig has a steak named after him there, so you'll know where to go with your complaints about the designated hitter or extended playoffs.

TOSTITOS FIESTA BOWL
University of Phoenix Stadium
1 Cardinals Dr., Glendale
(480) 350-0911
www.fiestabowl.org

The Fiesta Bowl is part of the College Football Bowl Alliance, formed in 1997 to create a system to guarantee a true national championship game each year. The championship game rotates among the four members of the alliance, which also include the Sugar, Orange, and Rose bowls.

The idea that the Valley should have a football bowl game was first floated in a speech by ASU president B. Homer Durham at an athletic awards banquet in 1968. Boosters seized on the idea and formed a group called the Arizona Sports Foundation. They prepared a pitch emphasizing that the Rose Bowl was the only bowl game being played outside the South, that Arizona's climate would be a natural ally in the game's success, and that a number of worthy Western Athletic Conference teams had been overlooked by the existing bowls. They also framed it as a charity event that would aid the fight against drug abuse. They made the pitch to the NCAA in 1970 and were turned down. The next year, though, the NCAA gave its approval. Since then the Fiesta Bowl has seen its share of controversy, most recently with key members of the nonprofit organization placed under investigation for glad-handing with lobbyists and politicians.

The first Fiesta Bowl was played December 27, 1971, with ASU beating Florida State before a crowd of 51,098. Over the years the Fiesta Bowl spawned dozens of auxiliary events, including the Fiesta Bowl Parade, 4 tennis events, a 3-on-3 basketball tournament, and a gigantic New Year's block party in downtown Tempe. In 2006 the Fiesta Bowl moved across the Valley to Glendale's new University of Phoenix Stadium. Its more notable games include the 43-42 overtime victory by Boise State over Oklahoma in 2007, which is widely considered one of the wildest games in NCAA postseason history.

FOOTBALL

ARIZONA CARDINALS
University of Phoenix Stadium
1 Cardinals Dr., Glendale
(602) 379-0102
www.azcardinals.com

The short course in Arizona Cardinals history goes like this: 1899, Morgan Athletic Club (Chicago); 1900, Racine (Chicago) Normals; 1901–1921, Racine (Chicago) Cardinals; 1922–1959, Chicago Cardinals; 1960–1987, St. Louis Cardinals; 1988–1993, Phoenix Cardinals; 1994–present, Arizona Cardinals. The oldest continuously operating professional sports franchise (dating from 1898) represented the NFL's youngest team in 2001.

Since then the team has been bad enough to earn top-5 draft picks and good enough to make the Super Bowl. The Cardinals lost their first-ever in February 2009 to the Pittsburgh Steelers on a last-minute drive that sucked the wind out of long-suffering Arizona football fans. That team, led by quarterback Kurt Warner and standout wide receiver Larry Fitzgerald, proved the Cardinals could dominate the weaker NFC West conference. But it didn't stick. Since then the team faded from the playoff picture as head coach Ken Whisenhunt struggled to find a long-term replacement for Warner.

After 18 years in Arizona, the Cardinals have a home of their own. In 2006 the Cardinals bid farewell to the sweltering heat of Sun Devil Stadium in Tempe and

Close-up

Best Seats in the House: Valley Sports Bars

We understand if you can't miss a game. True fans refuse to. So if you can't find the game on TV, or it's sold out at the stadium, or you're just looking to get out of your house for a cold beer with buddies, here are the best options in the Valley:

AHWATUKEE

CK's Tavern and Grill
4142 E. Chandler Blvd.
(480) 706-5564
www.ckgrill.com

CAVE CREEK

Harold's Cave Creek Corral
6895 E. Cave Creek Rd.
(480) 488-1906
www.haroldscorral.com

CHANDLER

Dark Horse Sports Bar & Grill
4929 W. Ray Rd.
(480) 753-4772
www.darkhorsesportsbar.com

Regal Beagle
6045 W. Chandler Blvd.
(480) 961-4488

Stadium Club
940 N. Alma School Rd.
(480) 963-3866
www.stadiumclubchandler.com

GLENDALE

Padre Murphy's
4338 W. Bell Rd.
(602) 547-940
www.padremurphy.com

MESA

Brick's Family Sports Grill
2235 S. Power Rd.
(480) 218-0404

R.T. O'Sullivan's
1010 W. Southern Ave.
(480) 844-1290
www.rtosullivans.com

PHOENIX

Half Moon Sports Grill
288 E. Greenway Pkwy.
(602) 993-6600
www.halfmoonsportsgrill.com

Hazelwood's First Place
3626 E. Indian School Rd.
(602) 957-2462
www.hazelwoodsfirstplace.com

inaugurated University of Phoenix Stadium in Glendale. The stadium, with its retractable roof and playing field, received rave reviews from a huge 2008 Super Bowl audience. At long last, the Cardinals will have home-field advantage, and fans hope that will spark the team to victory.

Tickets have been so popular that management had to cancel mini-season packages like the popular 4-pack. Instead, season tickets can be purchased for as little as $25 per seat, per game, up to Club-level goal-line seats, which sell for $325 per seat, per game. Or you can buy bulk premium seats in The Loft, with preferred parking, a private entrance, and access to cutting-edge technology. These are available for 5-, 7-, and 10-year leases. Prices range from $85,000 for

Santisi Brothers
2710 W. Bell Rd.
(602) 789-7979
www.santisibrothers.com

Zipps Sports Grill
3647 E. Indian School Rd. (and 7 other locations)
(602) 957-2112
www.zipps-sportscafe.com

SCOTTSDALE

Brennan's Sports Bar
13610 N. Scottsdale Rd.
(480) 951-8837

Goldie's Neighborhood Sports Cafe
10135 E. Via Linda
(480) 451-6269
www.goldiessportscafe.net

Prankster's Too
7919 E. Thomas Rd.
(480) 990-1114
www.prankstersgarandbrill.com

Sugar Shack Sports Grill
6830 E. 5th St.
(480) 533-7833
www.sugarshackaz.com

Upper Deck Sports Grill
4224 N. Craftsman Ct.
(480) 941-9333
www.upperdecksportsgrill.com

TEMPE

Devil's Advocate Bar & Grill
955 E. University Dr.
(480) 921-2585
www.devilstempe.com

Doc & Eddy's
909 E. Minton Dr.
(480) 831-0635
www.docandeddystempe.com

Monkey Pants Bar & Grill
3223 S. Mill Ave.
(480) 377-8100
www.monkeypantsbar.com

Philly's Sports Bar and Grill
1826 N. Scottsdale Rd.
(480) 946-6666

18 seats up to $125,000, but you'll have to join the long waiting list. Single-ticket prices change each season, so call (602) 379-0102 for more information.

Parking at the new stadium is plentiful, and the design team made sure to add plenty of trees for shade, so tailgating is excellent.

GOLF TOURNAMENTS

WASTE MANAGEMENT PHOENIX OPEN
Tournament Players Club of Scottsdale
17020 N. Hayden Rd., Scottsdale
www.wastemanagementphoenixopen.com

The Phoenix Open is the one of the top-drawing sporting events in Arizona, usually attracting 500,000 spectators for the

weeklong event, held in late January or early February. Sure, you can't bring cell phones onto the course and golf is a quiet game where you're not supposed to make too much noise, but this event is one of the most exciting experiences in sport, let alone golf. The culture, party scene, and entertainment surrounding the tournament are part of the attraction, which caters to the average Joe as much as the career-long golfer.

The par-3 16th hole seems more like a frat party than a golf tournament. Fans chant and holler at golfers before and after their vertical approach to the green, which is enclosed by the canyon-like walls of surrounding bleachers that pack thousands inside. Like other key holes around the event, the 16th is a place to drink (heavily) and eat (much less). It's one of the rowdiest holes in golf. If you want to hear birds chirping as one of your favorite golfers strikes a crisp 7-iron into the breeze, you'll want to set up on a fairway far away.

The tournament wasn't always so popular. Only about 600 people were in the gallery to see Ralph Guldahl finish 5 strokes better than John Perelli to win the tournament in 1932. The tournament was abandoned during the depths of the Depression but was revived by the special events committee of the Phoenix Chamber of Commerce in 1939. The committee was expanded to become the Thunderbirds, a service group that has been putting on the Phoenix Open ever since. The Thunderbirds put on the Thunderbird Collegiate Invitational and the Thunderbird Junior and Senior Golf Classics each summer.

The Thunderbirds have donated an astonishing $53 million to hundreds of local charities over the years. Each year the Thunderbirds contribute to needy children and families and help improve the quality of life for all Arizonans. The Phoenix Open PGA event includes such pretournament activities as a junior golf clinic, 4 Pro-Am events, a pro-celebrity shootout, and a long-drive contest. Prices are $25 for general admission each day. Children 17 and younger get in free with an adult.

i During the Phoenix Open, the fully enclosed 16th hole is known as the "Loudest Hole in Golf." The 165-yard par 3 rarely sees a hole in one, though the crowd erupts when it does, like the 2011 shot by underdog Jarrod Lyle.

HOCKEY

PHOENIX COYOTES
Jobing.com Arena
9400 W. Maryland Ave., Glendale
(623) 772-3200
www.phoenixcoyotes.com

The Coyotes were formed in 1996 when the Winnipeg Jets left Canada for the desert. Arizona sports fans were thrilled when hockey legend Wayne Gretzky—the NHL's all-time greatest player—joined developer Steve Ellman in the purchase of the team. When the new ownership team took over the hockey club in February 2001, Gretzky assumed the role of managing partner and wasted no time making changes to the Valley's ice-hockey team. "The Great One" also coached for a spell, despite never playing for the Coyotes.

With so many Midwesterners in the Valley, the Coyotes have a loyal following. The team rallied to consecutive playoff appearances in 2010 and 2011—helping fans briefly forget about the team's financial

challenges—only to lose in both seasons to the mighty Detroit Red Wings. The Coyotes filed for bankruptcy in 2009, which led to a series of high-profile squabbles with the NHL and the City of Glendale. By 2011 the NHL took ownership of the 'Yotes as the city negotiated with the league and potential buyers to keep the team in the West Valley. So the future of NHL hockey in Arizona was very much up in the air at press time. Rumors flied like errant slap-shots about the team's possible return to a Canadian city or even Las Vegas or Europe.

Single-game tickets sell for $15 to $25; season-ticket prices start at $396, which includes all 41 regular-season games, 3 pre-season contests, and first dibs on playoff tickets for the "White Out." Local media advertise special offers on single tickets from time to time that sometimes include a drink and a hot dog.

HORSE RACING

TURF PARADISE
1501 W. Bell Rd., Phoenix
(602) 942-1101
www.turfparadise.com

Want to bet the ponies? Turf Paradise features live thoroughbred racing and betting on simulcast races from late September to early May. Although the main attraction is horse racing, the track's floral gardens, olive grove, 3 lakes, orchid trees, palm trees, and waterfall let the track live up to its name. The exotic avian wildlife includes swans, flamingos, and herons. The tranquil setting contrasts with the high adrenaline in the grandstand.

Walter Cluer announced he would build a horse track on the 1,400-acre site back in 1954, when the spot was many miles from Phoenix. Now, although encircled by growth, it maintains its desert oasis atmosphere.

The raceway features book-style betting carrels and a trackside, resort-style swimming pool, in addition to 2 restaurants (the elegant Turf Club and the casual Clubhouse). There are also 2 rooms for banquets and the top-level Director's Suite. All provide good views of the racing action. Admission is $2 for the grandstand and an additional $2 for the clubhouse levels.

DAY TRIPS

You're in the desert, so it's all about cactus and triple-digit temperatures, right? Not quite. Arizona is such a massive state and covers such a wide variety of landscape that there's quite a bit of pine-studded high country to explore up north. Between Flagstaff, Sedona, and Tucson to the south, there's a range of hiking and outdoors events in other communities if you want to get out of the Valley.

The Grand Canyon is a 4-hour drive from Phoenix, and based on how much time you have, it is certainly worth the trek. But you really don't have to drive that far north. Locals like to get out of the heat in the summer and drive to Prescott, Payson, and Pine for a breather. It's about 10 degrees cooler in the summer, which makes a huge difference in August or September. It also snows heavily in the winter in Flagstaff. Major holiday weekends like Labor Day and Memorial Day tend to clog I-17 between Phoenix and Flagstaff. The college town about an hour and half north of the Valley is home to some outstanding mountain hiking and other outdoor adventures. Places like Lowell Observatory, Humphrey's Peak, and the downtown shopping district make for a great jaunt out of Phoenix.

Sedona, known for its breathtaking red rock buttes and energy vortexes, is just over an hour's drive north of the Valley. It's far more touristy than Flagstaff, but still worth your time if you've never been. The hiking and sightseeing are sensational. It's unlike anywhere else in Arizona, with the color of the rocks and the otherworldly buzz of certain spots shrouded in juniper and prickly-pear. Plus, it's an artists' haven, with everything from traditional oil paintings to far-out New Age stuff on sale in dozens of shops.

Tucson is less than 2 hours to the south. It's also a draw for its museums, hiking, and college-town vibe in its central core. The city's history museums, Sonoran Desert Museum, Biosphere, and Titan Missile Museum are major draws.

UP I-17

Arcosanti

Visitors may know about our famous architect, Frank Lloyd Wright, but few know about his student, Paolo Soleri, known for his experimental city that is the antithesis of Phoenix's urban sprawl. Arcosanti, about 50 miles north of Phoenix, is east of I-17 at the Cordes Junction exit. This prototype city is compact and is meant to leave little impact on the surrounding landscape—a refinement of Italian hill villages, where people live in clustered housing while the fields where they work stretch out for miles around.

The cement structures, although cast in futuristic geometric shapes, look rustic, at least in part because they're unfinished—something like a ghost town from tomorrow. Privately funded—with most of the legwork being done by students and volunteers—Arcosanti may never be completely finished. The environmentally sensitive philosophy behind the project has made it attractive to ecological idealists and artisans, and fascinates anyone interested in ways to solve the problems of diminishing energy resources and a dwindling supply of open land. Soleri has been internationally recognized for his innovative designs.

Some of the funding for the project comes from the sale of distinctive Soleri-designed wind bells, which are sold in the gift shop. More on the Cosanti foundry in Paradise Valley is listed in the Attractions chapter. Guided tours of Arcosanti take about an hour, but you can walk around the grounds, visit the cafe and bakery, and even stay overnight if you wish. For details call (928) 632-7135 or visit www.arcosanti.org.

Flagstaff

Flagstaff—140 miles north of Phoenix on I-17—makes an easy day trip from the Valley, but be aware that the two cities are practically polar opposites when it comes to weather. While you may be enjoying a round of golf in February in the Valley, the 58,000 residents of Flagstaff are likely to be hunkered down in their homes, staying warm by the fire. While Phoenix is one of the warmest cities in the nation, Flagstaff is one of the nation's snowiest cities, with 99 inches a year. Not surprisingly, the annual snowfall bodes well for Flagstaff's ski area, the Arizona Snowbowl, nestled in the San Francisco Peaks.

Come summer, Flagstaff is bustling with Valley residents escaping the blistering heat for the pines, the peaks, and temperatures that usually top out in the low 80s. Many Phoenix residents have summer cabins in the Flagstaff area. The highway to the north continually dips and rises as the Sonoran hills become more mountainous and the landscape of saguaro and cholla turns green with cottonwoods and other trees. After a drop down into the Verde Valley, you climb up into the thick forests of pine that form the gateway into Flagstaff, elevation 7,000 feet. The city's backdrop is the San Francisco Peaks, where you will find 12,643-foot Mount Humphreys, the highest point in Arizona.

In the mid-1990s Flagstaff completed extensive downtown renovations, which spruced up the city considerably. We recommend a day in Flagstaff if you enjoy browsing arts-and-crafts stores and soaking up the historic ambience of this major east-to-west railroad stop. Northern Arizona University is also interesting to see, as is the Museum of Northern Arizona. You will want to combine Flagstaff with two or three other sights in

the northern and central parts of the state. See this section for descriptions of Sedona, Jerome, Montezuma Castle National Monument, and Tonto Natural Bridge State Park, which are all within about a 90-minute driving radius of Flagstaff. We've put Flagstaff, or "Flag" as many call it, in the day trips section, but it really is worth staying for a night or two. Use it as a base for seeing the Grand Canyon and the numerous archaeological sites in the area. (For further information on these destinations, check out the *Insiders' Guide to Grand Canyon and Northern Arizona.)*

Here's the lowdown on a few of Flagstaff's major attractions, places to stay, and restaurants:

The Arizona Snowbowl's ski season usually runs from December to mid-April. There are more than 30 trails and 4 chairlifts. In summer those chairlifts turn into the Scenic Skyride, lifting you to an elevation of 11,500 feet. The Snowbowl is 14 miles north of Flagstaff on US 180. For information call (928) 779-1951 or visit www.arizonasnowbowl.com. For the Snow Report call (928) 779-4577.

About a mile from downtown is Lowell Observatory, where Pluto was discovered in 1930. Lowell has a visitor center, hands-on exhibits, tours, lectures, and sky shows. It is at 1400 W. Mars Hill Rd. (928-774-2096; www.lowell.edu). The Museum of Northern Arizona, 3101 N. Fort Valley Rd. (928-774-5211; www.musnaz.org), is a good place to learn about the anthropology, biology, and geology of the Colorado Plateau region. Also, there is often an exhibit focusing on Native American arts and crafts. The museum's short nature trail with its cliff overlooks is worth walking. Fairly close to Flagstaff are two interesting natural attractions: Sunset Crater Volcano National Monument, an extinct volcano surrounded by a surreal landscape of cooled lava flows; and Walnut Canyon National Monument, with a paved nature trail leading to Sinagua cliff dwellings built into steep canyon walls. Sunset Crater is 15 miles north of Flagstaff on US 89 (928-526-1157; www.nps.gov/sucr). Walnut Canyon is 7 miles east of Flagstaff on I-40 (928-526-3367; www.nps.gov/waca).

Lodging is plentiful in Flagstaff because of its ski industry and its reputation as an Arizona summer getaway. The city is also convenient for those traveling cross-country on I-40. Reservations are essential in the height of summer. Radisson Woodlands Hotel, 1175 W. Route 66 (928-773-8888), is one of the fancier spots in the city. If you want to be more in the center of things, the historic Weatherford Hotel, at 23 N. Leroux St., has been a favorite for more than a century. There are two bars—a relaxing one upstairs that has a great view of the town and mountains and a loud one downstairs that features live music. The rooms are somewhat basic, and noise filters up from the carousing downstairs, but the convenience and great atmosphere outweigh any disadvantages. The hotel can be reached at (928) 779-1919 or www.weatherfordhotel.com.

A great bed-and-breakfast is the Aspen Inn Bed and Breakfast, which is inside a home built in 1912. The inn has 3 large bedrooms with king-size beds and private baths, and a smaller room with a queen-size bed. It is located at 218 N. Elden St. (888-999-4110; www.flagstaffbedandbreakfast.com). The Hotel Monte Vista, 100 N. San Francisco St., is located close to the Weatherford. It's a similar local historic spot, though a bit grittier (and more fun, in some ways) than its stately neighbor. The rooms date to 1926, and the bar and cafe in the lower levels are

enough to keep visitors from straying too far into the cold. Information: (928) 779-6971 or www.hotelmontevista.com.

Campgrounds include the KOA Campground at 5803 N. US 89 (928-526-9926; www.koa.com/campgrounds/flagstaff) and the Fort Tuthill Coconino County Park Campground off I-17 just south of Flagstaff (928-774-3464).

Flagstaff's dining choices have become more sophisticated over the years. A menu of American cuisine can be found at Josephine's Modern American Bistro, 503 N. Humphreys St. (928-779-3400; www.josephinesrestaurant.com). For American and continental food, try Buster's Restaurant & Bar, 1800 S. Milton Rd. (928-774-5155; www.busters-restaurant.com), which has been known as one of the best bar-restaurants in Flag since it opened in 1983. For Italian food try Pasto Restaurant at 19 E. Aspen Ave. (928-779-1937; www.pastorestaurant.com). Racha Thai serves great Thai dishes at $6 to $10 per entree. It's located at 104 N. San Francisco St. (928-774-3003). The place for a greasy spoon breakfast before your hike into the woods is the Downtown Diner, 7 E. Aspen Ave. (928-774-3492; www.downtowndinerflagstaff.com). As a college town, Flagstaff attracts coffeehouse intellectuals, artists, and outdoors enthusiasts. Their hangouts include Macy's, 14 S. Beaver St. (928-774-2243; www.macyscoffee.net), which serves great vegetarian dishes, coffees, and pastries, and Beaver Street Brewery, 11 S. Beaver St. (928-779-0079; www.beaverstreetbrewery.com).

One of Flagstaff's major annual events is Winterfest in February. Highlights include sled-dog races, sleigh and snowmobile rides, snow sculpture contests, concerts, art shows, winter stargazing, and various winter sports. Every New Year's Eve is also a party in Flag.

The city drops a giant electric pinecone from the top of the Hotel Weatherford for the crowds to cheer. During the summer you'll find various art and music programs like A Celebration of Native American Art held at Northern Arizona University (928-774-5213; www.musnaz.org).

For more information contact the Flagstaff Convention and Visitors Bureau at 323 W. Aspen Ave. (928-779-7611; www.flagstaffarizona.org) or the Flagstaff Visitor Center, 1 E. Route 66 (800-842-7293).

i On the Hualapai Reservation, which is about 250 miles northwest of Phoenix, crews have assembled an amazing glass-bottomed skywalk. The brave can wander out 70 feet over the Grand Canyon and look straight down. The cost is about $75. Information: www.grandcanyonskywalk.com.

Grand Canyon

If you haven't seen it, prepare to be awestruck. Some people spend weeks hiking through Grand Canyon. For others it's an inspirational day trip to peer over the rim into the abyss of the ages. There's something indefinably limitless about the canyon.

If you only have the time to do the canyon as a day trip, do it, but pace yourself. The South Rim is a 4-hour drive from Phoenix, and half the trip is on interstates. To get there take I-17 north for about 2.5 hours to Flagstaff, then get on US 180 heading north for about another 2 hours. It's about 220 miles from Phoenix. Private vehicles pay $25 to enter Grand Canyon National Park. Many of the park's scenic overlooks are accessible by car, but because of the large number of visitors at the park, some are closed parts of the year and you should be prepared to

catch a shuttle bus to the rim. The East Rim Drive (AZ 64) is open year-round and follows the canyon rim for 26 miles east of Grand Canyon Village to Desert View, the park's east entrance. The West Rim Drive is closed to private automobiles from mid-March through mid-October, during which time the park runs a free shuttle bus. When the road is open, you can follow the rim for 8 miles from Grand Canyon Village west to Hermits Rest.

Backcountry hiking through the 1.2-million-acre Grand Canyon National Park requires a permit. The cost is $5 per person, per day, plus the $10 permit fee. Write to: Backcountry Information Center, Grand Canyon National Park, PO Box 129, Grand Canyon, AZ 86023, or call (928) 638-7875. Please note that the phone is answered only between 10 a.m. and 5 p.m. Be sure to apply for any permits well in advance.

North Rim

Since the North Rim is quite a way from Phoenix and is better reached from Colorado or Utah, we'll give only a quick overview and then focus on the South Rim. To reach the North Rim from Phoenix, take I-17 north to Flagstaff, then take I-40 east to US 89 north. This is a mostly two-lane road of more than 100 miles through some rather desolate stretches of the Navajo and Hopi Reservations. But you're not done yet—at Bitter Springs, take US 89A west, cross the Colorado River at Navajo Bridge, and continue on to Jacob Lake. Head south on AZ 67 through beautiful pine forests to the North Rim entrance. This is an all-day drive, but you will be rewarded with a more peaceful Grand Canyon experience. Park Service cabins are available for overnight lodging. For details call Grand Canyon National Park at (928) 638-7888 or visit www.thecanyon.com or

www.nps.gov/grca. Since the North Rim is a couple of thousand feet higher than the South Rim, many Park Service facilities there are open only from mid-March through late October.

i The Arizona Office of Tourism puts out several helpful visitor packets of interest to anyone touring the state. You can visit the visitor center at 1111 W. Washington St. in Phoenix. Information: (866) 275-5816 or www.arizonaguide.com.

South Rim

The trails to the Colorado River below are more winding than a coiled snake; they are steep, rocky, and dusty—and rather dangerous in spots. We don't recommend a hike to the bottom if you're doing the canyon as a day trip. But you can set out on the popular Bright Angel Trail for a spell just to see what it's like. Be sure to wear your best sneakers with treads or, better yet, hiking boots. Also, pack water and sunscreen. There is no water along the trail, and you will need it no matter what time of year it is. Hiking is advised only when it is not snowing or raining at the canyon. In fact, spring and fall are excellent times to see the South Rim because the crowds lessen a bit (actually, it's gotten to the point where there is no downtime for tourism here) and because the walking is easier in balmier weather. Summer temperatures at the canyon are about 80 degrees on the rim and about 100 degrees at Phantom Ranch along the Colorado River. However far you take the trail, remember that the hike back up will take almost twice as long as the hike down. If you don't feel like hiking, you can arrange to descend the canyon on your ass (by mule, that is).

Don't feel bad if you decide to skip the hiking. The scenic drives give excellent views, and there are several observation points where you can get out of the car to meditate on the views. To best capture the definition and depth of the red rocks, gray cliffs, and tree-studded mesas, try taking pictures at sunrise or sunset.

If you want to learn more about the park or simply catch a shuttle bus, visit the Canyon View Information Plaza. Here visitors catch their first glimpse of the canyon in relative serenity away from the noise of traffic. You also get an overview of the park's recreational options, including information on shuttle buses, biking, hiking, and ranger-guided activities.

You'll need to do more research about the Grand Canyon if you plan an extended stay here. Here are a few other things to think about as you plan your trip:

If you take the Bright Angel or South Kaibab Trail all the way down, you might consider arranging for overnight lodging at Phantom Ranch, which has bunkhouses, cabins, and a few other simple amenities to revive you after the hike. But reservations are a must; in fact, you should make them a year in advance. Call (888) 297-2757. Rafting trips through the canyon are equally, if not more, difficult to secure.

During the canyon's busiest times, it's likely that portions of the scenic drive along the rim will be closed to private automobiles and you will be asked to take one of the free shuttle buses operated by the Park Service. It's part of an effort to reduce pollution and parking problems at this tourist haven, which receives more than 5 million visitors a year from all over the world. Eventually the Park Service hopes to bring visitors in by light-rail mass transit from Tusayan, 7 miles south of the South Rim.

Have you considered taking a train to the Grand Canyon? From a depot in Williams, west of Flagstaff, you can catch the scenic Grand Canyon Railway to the South Rim. For information call (800) 843-8724 or go to www.thetrain.com.

Still other ways to see the canyon include small airplane and helicopter flights; mule rides; motor-coach tours; mountain biking; and guided walks with a park ranger.

At Grand Canyon Village you have a choice of 6 different lodges, including the rustic Bright Angel Lodge, Thunderbird Lodge, Maswick Lodge, Yavapai Lodge, the Kachina Lodge, and the historic El Tovar. Prices range from $76 to $256 per night, with many options in between. The El Tovar, dating from 1905, recently underwent $1 million in renovations. Once visited by the likes of former President Theodore Roosevelt and Western writer Zane Grey, many of the rooms offer wonderful views. The hotel decor resembles an elegant hunting lodge with massive wood-beam ceilings, fireplaces, and chandeliers. All reservations are made by calling (303) 29-PARKS or visiting www.grandcanyonlodges.com. You can also call (888) 297-2757. The hotel and lodges have various high-end restaurants, steakhouses, cocktail lounges, coffee shops, and cafeterias. You can also find several reasonably priced restaurants and motels in Tusayan. Campers should call the Grand Canyon National Park Campgrounds at (800) 365-2267 for reservations.

See the Grand Canyon on a 7-story IMAX screen at the Grand Canyon National Geographic Theater in Tusayan, 7 miles south of the South Rim. A film gives a history of the 277-mile-long canyon, including the story of Major John Wesley Powell and his trip down the Colorado River in 1869. For information

call (928) 638-2468 or go to www.explorethe canyon.com.

For a trip planner and other information, write to Grand Canyon National Park at PO Box 129, Grand Canyon, AZ 86023; or call (928) 638-7888 and visit www.thecanyon .com or www.nps.gov/grca.

i If you're traveling with four-legged companions, don't leave them in the car while you get out and explore in the daytime. Temperatures inside a car climb quickly and will overpower a small creature in just a few minutes. Remember your water and a water dish for your pet.

Jerome

Located 130 miles north of Phoenix in the central Arizona hills, Jerome has evolved from a mile-high ghost town into an eclectic artist community. Browse art galleries, sip latte at an outdoor cafe, and admire the buildings that survived Jerome's long-gone heyday as a copper mining town. To get there from Phoenix, head north on I-17, then take AZ 260 west until you hit US 89A, which passes through the small towns of Cottonwood and Clarkdale. You practically have to climb into Jerome, which is set on the side of Cleopatra Hill, overlooking the Verde Valley. The short, steep, and winding drive is only mildly unnerving.

Miners struck it rich in Jerome in the mid-1800s. The population boomed in the 1920s to about 15,000, but that didn't last. Today Jerome's population totals about 300 residents.

Don't expect a ghost town in the sense that it's devoid of people. Actually, they come in droves, especially on weekends with good weather. Jerome is a popular day

trip for Phoenix residents. Word has gotten out—don't be surprised to see license plates from all over the country. Motorcyclists also love the drive into town and the no-frills attitude once they arrive.

Wander around the historic buildings, or what's left of them. A "traveling jail" still stands, even though a dynamite explosion in the 1920s moved it 200 feet from its original foundation. The mansion of mining king "Rawhide Jimmy" Douglas has been turned into Jerome State Historic Park. Old photographs and exhibits of the region's copper mining days can be seen at the Jerome Historical Society Mine Museum, Main Street and Jerome Avenue (928-634-5477). The Gold King Mine Museum, Perkinsville Road (928-634-0053), is considered the top attraction in town by many regulars. It has a replica of a mine shaft. Several of Jerome's historic homes open each May for the town's annual home tour. Call the Jerome Chamber of Commerce for more information about the tour or any other aspect of the town. The chamber, at 50 N. Main Street, can be reached at (928) 634-2900. The historical society lists useful information about the town at www.jeromehistoricalsociety.org.

You might want to combine a trip to Jerome with a look at Tuzigoot National Monument near Clarkdale, where you'll see the ruins of a 100-room pueblo inhabited by the Sinagua from the 12th to 15th centuries. For information call (928) 634-5564. Clarkdale is the departure point for the Verde Canyon Railroad, which affords a scenic 40-mile round-trip through cottonwood groves and desert mesas. For more information contact the Cottonwood/Verde Valley Chamber of Commerce at 1010 S. Main St., Cottonwood (928-634-7593; www .visitcottonwoodaz.org). You can also call

the railroad directly at (800) 582-7245 or visit www.verdecanyonrr.com.

ℹ️ **Dead Horse Ranch, located about 90 miles north of Phoenix in Cottonwood, is known as one of the top birding spots in Arizona. You'll see lots of domestic songbirds and neotropical migrants. Information: (928) 639-0312 or www.pr.state.az.us/Parks/DEHO. Additional info is available through the Verde Valley Birding and Nature Festival at www.birdyverde.org.**

Both Jerome and the Cottonwood area have plenty of lodgings, many in historic buildings. Choices include the Jerome Mile High Inn, 309 N. Main St. (928-634-5094; www.innatjerome.com); the Ghost City Inn, 541 N. Main St. (888-634-4678; www.ghost cityinn.com); and the Surgeon's House, 100 Hill St. (928-639-1452, 800-639-1452; www .surgeonshouse.com), a bed-and-breakfast converted from the home of a mining-company surgeon. All of these inns are several decades old but have been carefully restored.

Prescott

Arizona's first capital, Prescott (pronounced *press-KIT*) sprang up amid the nation's largest contiguous forest of ponderosa pines back in 1863, shortly after gold was discovered in the nearby hills. Today Prescott is the county seat of Yavapai County (named for a local Native American tribe) and an easy 2-hour trip from Phoenix. Take I-17 north to the Cordes Junction exit and head west on AZ 69 until the junction with AZ 89, where a quick jog south puts you in the heart of the city.

AZ 69 winds through pretty, mountainous country on the way to Prescott. Most of the highway has been widened to four lanes in recent years to accommodate local residential traffic and the increasing number of visitors from the Valley. You'll pass the tall smokestack of a long-abandoned smelter in the one-time mining town of Mayer.

Just before the turn onto AZ 89, you traverse the Yavapai Reservation, where casino gambling adds another attraction for visitors.

A more challenging "back way" from the West Valley offers a scenic ride through the ponderosas of Prescott National Forest. From Phoenix take Grand Avenue northwest to Wickenburg. In Wickenburg US 60 splits off to the west. From that point continue northwest for about 7 miles and take the turnoff for AZ 89 and the town of Congress. From Congress AZ 89 climbs northeast up steep Yarnell Hill. The view back toward Wickenburg becomes a bird's-eye view panorama, and the scenery near Yarnell Hill quickly becomes mountainous evergreen forest. AZ 89 brings you into Prescott on Montezuma Street, which is better known as Whiskey Row.

If you choose to take this route for a day trip, it's advisable to take it one way, either into or out of Prescott, and to use the I-17 route for the other portion of the trip. The back way adds an hour or more, mostly because you're heading farther west and then cutting back to Prescott. Mountain switchbacks tend to slow the progress of even the most intrepid driver.

Young professionals are likely to motor up to Prescott on the weekend to soak up the local nightlife around Whiskey Row (so named because it is where all the town's saloons and brothels used to be), stay the night, and then head back down to the Valley. Prescott also offers plenty of attractions for families.

The city boasts 525 buildings listed on the National Register of Historic Places—a pleasant contrast to the Valley's penchant for tearing down any building that's been up for a while.

Courthouse Plaza—bounded by Gurley Street on the north, Montezuma Street on the west, Goodwin Street on the south, and Cortez Street on the east—is the heart of Prescott. Tree-shaded and cool (Prescott averages about 20 degrees cooler than Phoenix), the plaza invites visitors to dawdle while checking out the courthouse, which dates from Prescott's stint as the territorial capital.

Prescott's pace feels slower than the Valley's. The restored brick buildings that house the restaurants, antiques stores, saloons, and other businesses around the plaza are authentic reminders of Arizona's Wild West days. Shopping for antiques certainly fits the setting.

To get a full appreciation of Prescott's past, visit the Sharlot Hall Museum, 2 blocks west of the plaza at 415 W. Gurley St. (928-445-3122; www.sharlot.org). Sharlot Hall came to the territory at age 12 in 1882. Her fascination with Arizona, its history, and its artifacts led her to become the official territorial historian in 1909. The museum she opened in 1928 encompasses the original Governor's Mansion, a log home built in 1864, two 1870s vintage homes, and utilitarian buildings such as a blacksmith's shop and a schoolhouse, among others. The Sharlot Hall Building, opened in 1934, is itself old enough to be considered historic in this neck of the woods. It houses the museum's exhibits on Prescott and Native American history. The museum also is host to major annual events such as the Folk Arts Fair during the first weekend of June

and the Indian Arts Market in July. Admission is $5.

Another Prescott museum, The Smoki Museum at 147 N. Arizona St. (928-445-1230; www.smokimuseum.org), displays artifacts from many Native American tribes, including clothing, ornaments, and ceremonial paraphernalia from the Sioux, Apache, and Woodland tribes. Many items in the collection were donated by Arizona son Barry Goldwater, who was a member of the Smoki People.

Of the many annual events in Prescott, the Frontier Days/World's Oldest Rodeo celebration around the Fourth of July is the city's biggest draw. Prescott also plays host to an Intertribal Powwow in June, and the Yavapai County Fair in September.

Prescott's setting at the edge of a mountain-studded plain makes it a natural spot for hiking, fishing, boating, and other activities that take in the scenery. Off Thumb Butte Road west of downtown, Thumb Butte—which resembles a giant thumb—offers a picnic area and hiking trails. North of town, on AZ 89, the Granite Dells, giant slabs of yellowish-brown granite, rise on both sides of the highway. Sparse vegetation clings to the sides of these smooth, rounded rock towers, which will take much longer to wear away than the soil that once covered them.

As you might expect, the nearby Prescott National Forest is well worth a visit for hiking and camping. Maps and information are available at the Prescott National Forest main office, 344 S. Cortez St. (928-443-8000).

If you want to spend the night in Prescott, the Hassayampa Inn at 122 E. Gurley St. (928-778-9434, 800-322-1927; www.hassayampainn.com) is one of Prescott's many historic buildings and offers accommodations in the $135-a-night range. The

Hotel St. Michael, 205 W. Gurley St. (928-776-1999, 800-678-3757; www.stmichaelhotel .com), offers accommodations from $69 and up. The supposedly haunted hotel sits next to a Whiskey Row cowboy bar.

If you want to grab a bite while you're in Prescott, forget all the national fast-food chains and check out Kendall's Famous Burgers and Ice Cream, 113 S. Cortez St. (928-778-3658). The burgers are big and tasty. For Southwestern-style prime rib, go to Murphy's at 201 N. Cortez St. (928-445-4044). Murphy's offers its own microbrews and private-label wine. To dine elegantly, the Peacock Room at the Hassayampa Inn, 122 E. Gurley St. (928-778-9434), is the place for continental cuisine.

These are just a few of the accom-modations, activities, and points of interest in Prescott. For more information contact the Prescott Chamber Tourism Information Center, 117 W. Goodwin St. (928-445-2000, 800-266-7534; www.prescott.org).

Sedona

The artists' community of Sedona, named for one of the town's original settlers, Sedona Schnebly, nestles among towering red rocks that form one of the most beauti-ful spots in Arizona. The rock formations are imbued with deep hues from iron oxides; their names—Cathedral Rock, Bell Rock, and the Cockscomb Spires—are inspired by their strange, windblown shapes. A top tourist attraction, Sedona nevertheless offers plenty of natural places to sequester oneself from the photo-clicking throngs of out-of-towners. Some locals and many visitors believe that the area's natural elec-tromagnetic fields—dubbed "vortexes"—have rejuvenating properties. Decide for yourself by making the fairly easy 2-hour

drive to Sedona from Phoenix. Follow I-17 north to AZ 179, then turn west toward Sedona.

You'll find plenty to do walking through town, especially if you like arts and crafts. Possessing much the same ambience as the Scottsdale art scene, but with more of a crowd, Sedona's galleries showcase top-notch paintings and sculptures in a variety of media, from Native American arts and crafts to modern studio art glass. The Worm at the Factory Outlet Mall (928-282-3471; www .sedonaworm.com), on the corner of AZ 179 and Jack's Canyon Road, has a large selection of books, maps, and music.

Sedona has more than 3 dozen galleries, which congregate not only along the main road, US 89A, but also at Tlaquepaque Arts and Crafts Village at 336 AZ 179, (928-282-4838; www.tlaq.com), a re-creation of an old Mexican village graced with all manner of galleries. Tlaquepaque is located on your left just off AZ 179 on your way into town. Another must-see is the Sedona Arts Center, at US 89A and Art Barn Road (928-282-3809; www.sedonaartscenter.com), in the center of town, which has changing exhibits by regional artists.

Sedona's weather is usually pleasant much of the year, but be warned that it does snow there in the winter, and summer temperatures can go as high as 100 degrees Fahrenheit. Because of the nice weather, out-door festivals are popular. Some of the town's biggest annual events involve the perform-ing arts: the Sedona International Film Festi-val in late February (www.sedonafilmfestival .com), the Sedona Bluegrass Festival in May, and Sedona Jazz on the Rocks in October (www.sedonajazz.com). In December folks come from all around Arizona to see Sedona Red Rock Christmas Fantasy, where more

than 1 million lights illuminate several acres at Los Abrigados Resort.

If you feel spiritually uplifted after your visit, it's probably because of the vortexes that draw New Agers from around the country. There are said to be about a dozen such vortexes, including those at Cathedral Rock and Bell Rock. Nonbelievers can still enjoy earthly delights such as massages and spas offered by Sedona's New Age stores and traditional resorts. There are plenty of places to have your aura or palm read, or to channel past-life spirits.

If the city shops make you feel fenced in, there are better things to do out of town. Stop by the Sedona Heritage Museum at 735 Jordan Rd., Sedona Historical Park (928-282-7038; www.sedonamuseum.org), for a peek at Sedona's past, including its location as a site for old western movies. Hiking along Oak Creek Canyon is remarkable with the high canyon walls of varying colors of rock rising above the oak tree-lined stream. A great place to enter is the West Fork Trail (928-527-3600), which is on the north of Slide Rock State Park (928-282-3034) on 89A in Oak Creek Canyon.

Northern Light Balloon Expeditions runs hot-air flights above Sedona (928-282-2274; www.northernlightballoon.com). The red rock area is also prime territory for 4-wheeling, horseback riding, and mountain biking. Several companies in town offer excursions, but the oldest one is Pink Jeep Tours (800-873-3662; www.pinkjeeptours.com). The Pink Jeep office is at 204 N. US 89A. If you drive a high-clearance vehicle, try Schnebly Hill Road, which connects Sedona with I-17 and Flagstaff and offers great views of the red rocks and Verde Valley. In the opposite direction, after heading west on US 89A, take FR 152 north toward Devil's Bridge.

The 400-foot climb up, partly on a naturally occurring red rock staircase, leads to a giant red rock arch with spectacular views of the surrounding mountains.

For many people Sedona feels so much like home (there's something very familiar about it), they are tempted to stay overnight. This is difficult during peak seasons because the town and nearby villages get so packed with vacationers. But there are some excellent lodgings. Known for a long time to Phoenix residents wishing to splurge on a romantic creek-side getaway is L'Auberge de Sedona, a re-creation of a French country inn at 301 L'Auberge Ln. (928-282-1661; www.lauberge.com). We also recommend Junipine Resort on US 89A (928-282-3375; www.junipine.com); Los Abrigados Resort, 160 Portal Ln. (928-282-1777); and Poco Diablo Resort, 1752 AZ 179 (928-282-7333; www.pocodiablo.com).

There are several nice bed-and-breakfasts, some along Oak Creek Canyon north of town. Look into the Lodge at Sedona, 125 Kallof Place (928-204-1942; www.lodgeatsedona.com); the Territorial House, 65 Piki Drive (800-801-2737; www.territorialhouse.com); Canyon Villa Bed & Breakfast Inn, 40 Canyon Circle Dr. (928-284-1226; www.canyonvilla.com); or the Inn on Oak Creek, 556 AZ 179 (800-499-7896; www.innonoakcreek.com). The budget-conscious traveler might consider the Kings Ransom Inn, 725 AZ 179 (928-282-3132; www.kingsransominn.com); or the Sedona Super 8 Motel, 2545 US 89A (928-282-1533; www.sedonasuper8.com). The Manzanita Campground in Oak Creek Canyon is small but scenic. It has about 18 sites for non-RV campers. There are no hookups, but you will find tables, grills, toilets, and drinking water. Reservations can be made at (877) 444-6777.

There are also several Forest Service campgrounds along Oak Creek, north of Sedona. Pine Flat Campground has 58 unreserved camping spots on two sites and can also be reached at (877) 444-6777.

Sedona has more than 60 restaurants covering the spectrum from fast food to Mexican to gourmet. We recommend the Heartline Cafe, 1600 W. US 89A (928-282-0785; www.heartlinecafe.com), arguably the best in town with its continental cuisine. Rene at Tlaquepaque is another upscale option located in the Tlaquepaque shopping area. The tile work at the door is warm and welcoming. The restaurant is open for lunch and dinner. Call (928) 282-9225 for reservations, or visit www.rene-sedona.com.

The Sedona Chamber of Commerce at 332 Forest Rd, can be reached at (928) 282-7722, (800) 288-7336, and www.sedona chamber.com.

i Sedona is home to one of the top 10 most beautiful swimming holes, according to Time magazine. It's at Slide Rock State Park, 6 miles north of Sedona in Oak Creek Canyon. You can picnic and hike before cooling off in the creek. Information: (928) 282-3034.

UP THE BEELINE HIGHWAY (AZ 87)

Payson

Located approximately 95 miles away from downtown Phoenix, Payson is the closest summer getaway for people in the East Valley. From downtown you get on the Red Mountain Freeway (AZ 202 east) to its junction with AZ 87. It's a simple buzz north up the Beeline Highway, through the

Salt River Pima-Maricopa and Fort McDowell Yavapai reservations, through the Mazatzal (pronounced, *ma-tah-zall*) Mountains, and into the cool pine forests of Payson.

At an elevation of 5,000 feet, the temperature in Payson is typically 20 degrees lower than in the Valley. The Payson area also enjoys about 21 inches of rain a year, about three times the Valley's annual rainfall. Payson sits in the Tonto Basin, about 20 miles south of the Mogollon Rim, the steep lip of a 7,000-foot plateau that stretches eastward to New Mexico. The Rim separates Arizona's northern plateau area from the state's central and southern regions. The huge rock wall stands like a shorter Grand Canyon wall. The Rim dominates the landscape; hence the Payson area is also known as Rim Country.

Founded in 1882 as a mining settlement, Payson has gone through phases as a ranching and lumber town. Today tourism and retirement industries dominate the local economy. You'll find 15 antiques shops in the area, 9 motels, a number of bed-and-breakfasts, and cabin facilities, plus several RV parks and campgrounds.

Payson bills itself as the Festival Capital of Arizona, and the annual events in Payson include the World's Oldest Continuous Rodeo in August. There are a number of other festivals as well, including the Arizona State Old Time Fiddlers' Contest in September.

Set in the middle of the Tonto National Forest, Payson is a place to enjoy outdoor activities year-round. It's a place to view spring wildflowers, to stay relatively cool in summer, to view colorful foliage in the fall, and to do cross-country skiing in winter. The area's mountains, lakes, and streams lure anglers, bird-watchers, boaters, campers,

hikers, horseback riders, hunters, swimmers, and water-skiers.

Western novelist Zane Grey fell in love with the Rim Country and set many of his cowboy novels in this region. He built a hunting lodge near Payson in 1920, writing there often. For many years after his death in 1939, the cabin was preserved as a historic site featuring exhibits on the novelist and the Wild West. Unfortunately, it was one of 61 homes that burned down in a forest fire in 1990, the effects of which still can be seen outside Payson, where the forest is slowly growing back. The Zane Grey cabin site is now owned by a private developer and no longer open to the public, but you can find plenty of Zane Grey history in Payson proper.

The Rim Country Museum, 700 Green Valley Pkwy. (928-474-3483, www.rimcountry museums.com), has rebuilt the Zane Grey cabin on its grounds in Payson to complement its exhibits on the author. The museum resides in the original Tonto National Forest Ranger Station, built in 1907. While you're out that way, you may want to tour the Tonto Creek Fish Hatchery (928-478-4200). It's a 17-mile drive from Payson to the turnoff to the hatchery on AZ 260. The road is marked with a sign, and you'll turn north on FR 289. The hatchery has been stocking Rim Country creeks and lakes with trout for 50 years. You can tour the facility free of charge 7:30 a.m. to 3:30 p.m. daily, excluding holidays. Stop by the visitor center, where you'll learn more about the whole process.

Down the same road as the hatchery is the Tonto Creek campground. The campground's upper section features 9 sites, while the lower has 17. You're in the forest out here—nestled amid ponderosas, junipers, and oaks. Tonto Creek flows nearby, and it's stocked with rainbow trout. This is a rustic site with no toilets or electricity. It's open April 1 to October 30. Information: (928) 474-7900.

Payson is just 10 miles south of Tonto Natural Bridge State Park, on AZ 87 (928-476-4202). The natural rock formation that gives the park its name is the largest travertine bridge in the world. The bridge is 400 feet wide and 180 feet high and crosses a 150-foot-wide canyon. In fact, it is so big that when you arrive at the old lodge and park your car, you have no idea you are actually on the bridge. Viewpoints are easily accessible, but most exciting is a steep climb down a trail at the side of the canyon wall, which will lead you under the bridge. The site was discovered by prospector David Gowan in 1877 during a skirmish with Apaches. Admission is $5 per adult. Hours vary, so call ahead.

On the way to Tonto Natural Bridge, you may want to check out the Shoofly Indian Ruin. It's just north of Payson, 1 mile off AZ 87 on Houston Mesa Road. The only remains of this ancient settlement are primitive rock pit houses, abandoned by their residents about AD 1250. No one knows why they left or where they went.

About 19 miles north of Payson on AZ 87 is the town of Strawberry, home of the oldest schoolhouse in Arizona. Turn left at Strawberry Lodge in the center of town and about 1.5 miles later you'll find the log schoolhouse, built in 1884. The last classes were held there in 1916.

Strawberry is just below the Mogollon Rim. You can climb AZ 87 another 10 miles to the top of the Rim. Watch for the signs to FR 300, which turns off to the east. This gravel road, maintained only in summer and passable by passenger car, offers spectacular lookouts from the edge of the Rim as well as picnic areas and campgrounds. It also

🔍 Close-up

Tonto Natural Bridge

If you're a little tired of hiking around cacti and cholla, drive about an hour north of the city to Tonto Natural Bridge State Park near Payson. The site features the largest natural travertine bridge in the world.

The park is a pleasant experience for the entire family. There are grassy picnic areas at the main area, an old lodge with a gift shop, and trails that are tolerable for anyone. From the base of the bridge, you can look up at the 183-foot-high bridge into the sun and feel the cool waterfall trickling over the entrance to the 400-foot-tunnel.

The hike through the bridge gets a little hairy. The rocks are slippery from the runoff and the creek that winds through the area. The rocks are uneven in parts and a bit difficult to negotiate, but the Pine Creek Trail hike from the tunnel up through the creek is worth the effort. You get a sense of the lush valley located between Payson and Pine.

There are usually a couple of park rangers down in the tunnel to share facts about the geological features of the park. They'll warn you about rattlesnakes if you're taking the Pine Creek Trail, since the chilly rocks along the water lead up to the warm, dry rocks that snakes like to hide under. Tonto Natural Bridge is also an outstanding place to spot javelina wallowing in the shallow water. The viewing areas are a great place to catch a glimpse.

The park is closed Tuesday and Wednesday. Information: Tonto Natural Bridge State Park, west of AZ 87 about 6 miles north of Payson; 928- 476-4206 or www.pr .state.az.us/parks/TONA.

affords access to a number of lakes that are great for fishing. If you follow the road for its entire 45-mile length, you'll end up on AZ 260, approximately 30 miles east of Payson.

Anglers can pick up information on good fishing locations in Rim Country lakes and streams (as well as other information on Payson-area attractions and activities) by visiting the Rim Country Regional Chamber of Commerce at the corner of AZ 87 and Main Street (928-474-4515; www.rim countrychamber.com). The chamber also has information about lodgings in the area; there are lots of nice cabins to rent if you have a bigger group willing to spend a bit more.

For hikers, a number of trails wander through the area. A popular choice is the Highline National Recreational Trail, which travels for 51 miles beneath the Mogollon Rim. Some trails branch off from the Highline up to the Rim itself. From the Pine Trailhead, 15 miles north of Payson off AZ 87, the Highline heads toward the 260 Trailhead, 27 miles east of Payson off AZ 260. For more details on trails in the Tonto National Forest, pick up trail guides available at the USDA Forest Service Ranger's District Office at 1009 E. AZ 260 in Payson (928-474-7900). The office also has information on nearby Forest Service campgrounds.

Saguaro Lake

Boating, jet-skiing, fishing, picnicking, and camping can be enjoyed at a number of different lakes, though Saguaro Lake is a favorite for Valley residents who welcome the hour-and-a-half drive to ensure a bit more seclusion from crowds. From Scottsdale take Shea Boulevard east to Fountain Hills, then catch AZ 87 going north. About 10 miles past Fort McDowell Casino, you will see the signs directing you to Saguaro Lake. You can also get to AZ 87 (the Beeline Highway) from Mesa, where Country Club Drive turns into the Beeline as it heads north.

Saguaro Lake is part of a chain of four lakes formed by Salt River dams built in Tonto National Forest over several decades of the 20th century. The most famous of these is Roosevelt Dam. Completed in 1911, it is the world's largest masonry dam, constructed entirely of quarry stone. The dams provide the Valley of the Sun with hydroelectric power, irrigation, and flood control. Roosevelt Lake is the easternmost of the four lakes, and the chain moves to the west with Apache and Canyon Lakes, then Saguaro—the second-smallest at 1,200 acres.

Anglers catch bass and trout in Saguaro. Jet-Skiers and boaters ply the elongated stretches of the lake throughout the summer. If you want something a little tamer, consider a 1.5-hour paddleboat cruise on the Desert Belle. It allows you to see much of the lake's 22-mile shoreline, and the captain provides occasional commentary to enhance your visit. You have your choice of sitting in an open or covered area. The weather will be a bit cooler than in the Valley, and you'll get a breeze off the lake, so dress appropriately. The scenery is an intriguing juxtaposition of rocky desert outcroppings against blue water. You will pass dozens of rock formations, narrow canyons, and caves as well as cliffs streaked with black varnish where waterfalls once cascaded. Flora includes many varieties of cacti, desert trees, and, in the spring, a good smattering of desert wildflowers. Wildlife sightings are part of the fun. It's not unusual to see coyotes, javelinas, rabbits, squirrels, mule deer, and bighorn sheep. Birds are quite abundant, and if you're lucky you'll see turkey vultures, hawks, owls, blue herons, and even bald eagles. From Oct through Jan, the Desert Belle leaves the dock as early as 12:30 p.m. though departure times and availability vary based on the season. Sunset summer cruises are also popular. The cost is $20 for adults and $10 for children. For more information on the Desert Belle, call (480) 984-2425 or visit www.desertbelle.com.

Information on other amenities at Saguaro Lake is also available from the Tonto National Forest Service by calling (602) 225-5200. Those with boats and personal watercraft should be considerate of water-skiers and kayakers. For boat storage contact the marina at (480) 986-5546 or www.saguaro lakemarina.com); for service and rentals call (480) 986-0969. Boating maps are available at the Mesa District Ranger Station, 5140 E. Ingram St., Mesa (480-610-3300), and at the Tonto National Forest Office, 2324 E. McDowell Rd., Phoenix (602-225-5200). The entry fee is $6 per day, per vehicle, with $4 extra charged for watercraft.

Canyon Lake also offers cruises, in this case aboard the Dolly Steamboat, a 100-foot replica of an old double-decker riverboat. You have to take a different route to reach Canyon Lake, which lies 16 miles north of Apache Junction off AZ 88, also called the Apache Trail. Cruise times vary by season, but generally the 90-minute Nature Cruise,

which costs $20 plus tax, departs at noon and 2 p.m. daily. The Twilight Astronomy Dinner Cruise varies depending on the season and costs $60. Call ahead for the latest prices, schedules, and reservations at (480) 827-9144 or visit www.dollysteamboat.com.

DOWN I-10

Tucson

For a look at Arizona's second-largest city, you need only drive about 2 hours southeast of Phoenix on I-10. The distance is 115 miles, and Arizonans joke that it is the most boring drive in the state. Luckily, the 75-mph speed limit helps you breeze past the desert scrub toward the more interesting sight of Tucson's Santa Catalina Mountains. One stop to consider along the way, though, is Picacho Peak, near Eloy, site of Arizona's only Civil War battle. It is commemorated with a monument and a flagpole.

Like Phoenix, Tucson is a highly livable desert metropolis seeing tremendous growth. It has beautiful residential developments and a respectable cultural scene. Plus, it's in a lovely setting surrounded by five mountain ranges, including the blue-tinged Santa Catalinas. The fact that it's a university town, with University of Arizona, also makes it more of a draw for young professionals.

Metropolitan Tucson encompasses about 1 million people in an area of 500 square miles. Its residents by and large love their "Old Pueblo," preferring it to Phoenix, which they see as being way too urbanized and sprawling. You'll often hear residents of the two cities banter over which place is better.

Tucson does seem to have a slight advantage concerning weather. It boasts 350 days of sunshine a year, compared with Phoenix's 300 days. Also, those familiar with both cities say the summer daytime heat is somewhat less oppressive, and the nights are crisper in Tucson, although 105 degrees Fahrenheit in June is not uncommon. Tucson is 1,000 feet higher than Phoenix, which partially explains the weather difference. Winters feel a bit more like winter thanks to the sight of snowcaps on the surrounding mountains. As expected, for at least 6 months of the year, Tucson's weather is ideal for Arizona.

i **Visitors to Tucson's Arizona-Sonora Desert Museum can observe daily animal demonstrations, including with birds of prey, as well as bird walk tours. The show times change, so call first; (520) 883-2702 or www .desertmuseum.org.**

Tucson makes an effortless day trip from Phoenix, but its scenery, major attractions, and resorts make it a fine vacation destination in and of itself. What follows are several suggestions on making the most of your excursion. For further details, see *Insiders' Guide to Tucson*.

The Arizona-Sonora Desert Museum alone is worth the trip. It's located about 10 miles west of Tucson at 2021 N. Kinney Rd. It offers a terrific look at the plant and animal life of the Sonoran Desert, with more than 300 animal species and 1,300 kinds of plants in a natural landscape. One exhibit features nocturnal desert dwellers such as kit foxes and tarantulas. An underwater viewing area lets you see beavers, river otters, and desert fishes. There are also a hummingbird aviary and a prairie dog colony. A walk-through cave leads you to an exhibit of gems and minerals from this region. All around are

blooming desert gardens and displays of cacti. Admission is $14.50 for adults, September to May; $12 June to August; children get discounts. Information: (520) 883-2702 or www.desertmuseum.org.

The mission at San Xavier del Bac is easy to reach from I-19. Heading south about 10 miles from Tucson, look for the San Xavier Road exit. The gleaming white towers and domes of the mission are unmistakable. Against a clear blue sky, this mission—dating from 1783—is a one-of-a-kind image, so be sure to bring your camera. The interior architecture is wonderful as well, thanks to many years of meticulous restoration work. Called the "Sistine Chapel of North America," the mission features artwork on practically every square inch and in practically every nook and cranny. This includes paintings, frescoes, and statues. Arizonans know the mission as the "White Dove of the Desert." As you wander around, learn about the Jesuit missionary and explorer Father Eusebio Francisco Kino and other men of the cloth who served here. Located on the Tohono O'odham Reservation, the mission is one of the last Spanish churches still serving its Native American parishioners. No admission is charged, though donations are welcome. Masses are held each morning and four times on Sunday. For more information call (520) 294-2624 or visit www.sanxavier mission.org.

If you're exploring Tucson by car, don't miss a drive through Saguaro National Park, where you will find the largest concentration of saguaro cacti in the state—in the world, for that matter, since saguaros grow only in the Sonoran Desert. For Saguaro Park West, the western district, or the area surrounding the Tucson Mountains, exit at Ina Road from I-10 and drive west, following the signs. For

Saguaro Park East, the eastern district, or the area surrounding the Rincon Mountains, continue on I-10 until you reach southern Tucson, then take Houghton Road north and follow the signs for about 8 miles. Information: (520) 733-5100 or (520) 733-5153.

For a taste of the Old West, one of the best bets in Arizona is Old Tucson Studios, originally built as a set for the movie *Arizona* in 1939. It has since been used as the backdrop for more than 200 movies, TV shows, commercials, and documentaries. Old Tucson is tourist friendly, with lots of staged gunfights, stunt shows, trail rides, costumed characters, tours of movie sites, films, old-fashioned shops, stagecoach rides, cowboy-style dinners, and saloons. It's 12 miles west of Tucson, next to Saguaro National Park's western entrance. The address is 201 S. Kinney Rd. Admission is $17 for adults, $11 for children ages 4 to 11, and free for children younger than 4. Information: (520) 883-0100 or www.oldtucson.com.

Another Tucson-area attraction worth visiting is the Pima Air & Space Museum, 6000 E. Valencia Rd. (520-574-0462; www .pimaair.org). It has more than 250 civilian and military airplanes on display. Admission is $15.50 for adults. Children are $9 and seniors $12.75.

The University of Arizona also makes an interesting stop. Highlights of the campus include the planetarium and observatory at the Flandrau Science Center (520-621-4515), the Ansel Adams collection at the Center for Creative Photography (520-621-7968; www .creativephotography.org), and the exhibits on Native American cultures at the Arizona State Museum (520-621-6302; www.state museum.arizona.edu).

If you don't mind going a little farther afield, the Biosphere 2 Center in Oracle is

an unusual sight. About 30 miles north of Tucson on AZ 77, Columbia University's Biosphere 2 is the new incarnation of the original Biosphere, which you may remember as the place where several scientists lived under a roof of glass and steel in a small version of Earth and its various climates. The scientists no longer live there; it is now a research center with daily tours and plenty of interesting exhibits, including global warming and rain forest plant life. Admission is $20 for adults, $13 for ages 6 to 12; kids under 6 free. For more information call (520) 838-6200 or visit www.b2science.org.

Tombstone, with its famed OK Corral, is about 70 miles southeast of Tucson. The Birdcage Theater Museum and mock gunfights give visitors a sense of what it was like in the era of Doc Holliday and Wyatt Earp. Information: www.tombstone.org.

Tucson is known as the "Astronomy Capital of the World," thanks in large part to clear desert night skies and to Kitt Peak National Observatory, 950 N. Cherry Ave., which houses the largest collection of telescopes anywhere, including the largest solar telescope. You can reach it about 50 miles southwest of Tucson via a steep and winding mountain road. The visitor center at the observatory offers guided tours. Inquire about evening stargazing programs. For information call (520) 318-8000 or visit www .noao.edu/kpno. The Titan Missile Museum, about 30 miles south of Tucson, features a tour of the underground silo housing the world's only Titan II ICBM. The phone number is (520) 625-7736.

Hiking enthusiasts can head up to Sabino Canyon in north Tucson. From I-10, exit east on Grant Road, then turn left at the Tanque Verde Road turnoff. Tanque Verde leads to Sabino Canyon Road and the visitor center. Sabino Canyon Tours helps with your trip in and can direct you to some of the area's most gorgeous spots. Information: (520) 749-2861 or www.sabinocanyon.com.

i Arizona highways have a high glare factor. Bring or buy a pair of sunglasses for the road. And remember to wear sunscreen even in the car during summer.

Should you decide to stay at a hotel overnight in Tucson, consider: Windmill Inn at St. Philips Plaza, 4250 N. Campbell Ave. (800-547-4747); or Hilton Tucson East, 7600 E. Broadway Rd. (520-721-5600), with 233 rooms in an atrium-style upscale hotel. Tucson also has several nice bed-and-breakfasts, including Adobe Rose Inn, near the university in the historic Sam Hughes neighborhood, at 940 N. Olsen Ave. (800-328-4122; www.aroseinn.com), and the El Presidio Inn, 297 N. Main Ave. (520-623-6151).

First-class resorts help feed Tucson's economy. Those with a national reputation include the Arizona Inn, a restored hotel dating from 1930. It is at 2200 E. Elm St. (520-325-1541; www.arizonainn.com). Spa enthusiasts can't go wrong with Canyon Ranch and its full slate of fitness activities, nutrition counseling, beauty treatments, and gourmet meals. It's tucked away at 8600 E. Rockcliff Rd. (520-749-9000, 800-742-9000; www.canyonranch.com). Golf resorts, all brimming with amenities, include: Loews Ventana Canyon Resort, 7000 N. Resort Dr. (520-299-2020, 800-234-5117; www.loews hotels.com/en/Ventana-Canyon-Resort); and Westin La Paloma, 3800 E. Sunrise Dr. (520-742-6000, 800-937-8461; www

.westinlapalomaresort.com). Expect rooms at these resorts to go for at least $400 a night double occupancy in high season.

If you're looking for Mexican or Southwestern food, Tucson is better than Phoenix in a lot of ways. A classic, can't-miss pick is El Charro Mexican Cafe, the oldest family-operated Mexican restaurant in the US, at 311 N. Court Ave. (520-622-1922; www.elcharrocafe .com). Another is the well-reviewed Cafe Poca Cosa, 110 E. Pennington St. (520-622-6400; www.cafepocacosatucson.com).

Contact the Metropolitan Tucson Convention & Visitors Bureau, 110 S. Church Ave., at (800) 638-8350 or www.visittucson.org.

Appendix

LIVING HERE

In this section we feature specific information for residents or those planning to relocate here. Topics include real estate, education, health care, and much more.

RELOCATION

More than 90,000 residents moved to Arizona from other states in 2007, but those numbers dwindled in the following years due to the national economic crisis. Arizona was known as one of the fastest-developing states. Things have slowed down substantially, but there is plenty of positive possibility going forward. Original forecasts showed the population doubling over the next quarter-century, but by 2010 the rate of population growth was around 1 percent, or about 2.5 percent less than the booming years of 2004–2005, according to US Census data.

Still, the Valley remains a draw for businesses, families, and young people. High-tech companies continue to expand to Phoenix. Since the housing bubble burst, the Valley has seen an uptick in the rental market. Schools like Arizona State University and University of Phoenix remain a driving force in higher education and job-development. In spite of the economic slowdown, Phoenix remains a destination spot for people seeking to expand their career or improve their family's way of life.

In this chapter we introduce you to some of the Valley's well-known neighborhoods and to some of the area's established real estate agents who can help you find the perfect home. The Valley is known for its retirement communities, and we have listed those in greater detail in the Retirement chapter. For information on Valley school districts, see the Education & Child Care chapter.

LIBRARIES

All Maricopa County residents are eligible for a free Phoenix public library card with proof of ID. To get one, stop by any Phoenix Public Library branch, or register online and then go to any branch to pick up your card. A list of locations is available at www.phoenixpublic library.org.

HEALTH CARE

Home to several top hospitals, including the world-renowned Phoenix Children's Hospital and the Mayo Clinic in Scottsdale, the metro area is a hub for medical professionals and innovators. The Health Care chapter provides an exhaustive and detailed list of all the major hospitals and medical services in the greater Phoenix area. For additional information or an overview, you can also contact:

**ARIZONA DEPARTMENT OF HEALTH
  SERVICES**
(602) 542-1025
www.azdhs.gov

ARIZONA MEDICAL ASSOCIATION
(602) 246-8901
www.azmedassn.org

ARIZONA MEDICAL BOARD
(480) 551-2700
www.azmd.gov

i If you're looking for comprehensive information on relocating to the Phoenix area, check out the *Phoenix Relocation Guide*. It provides vital statistics, detailed housing information, and listings of relocation professionals. Order the book online (for $10 shipping) and get free information at www.reloguide.net.

MOTOR VEHICLE INFORMATION

If your car is already titled or registered in another state, you must get an Arizona title, registration, and license plate when you become an Arizona resident. If you work in Arizona, remain in the state for 7 months or longer during any calendar year, or put children in school without paying nonresident tuition rates, you are considered a resident.

VEHICLE REGISTRATION
Arizona Department of Transportation
Motor Vehicle Division
(602) 255-0072
www.azdot.gov/mvd

Emissions

For the metro Phoenix area, your vehicle must first be emissions-tested if it is a model year 2001 or older, including diesels. For more information contact the Department of Transportation at (877) 692-9227, or check the Arizona Department of Environmental Quality's website at www.azdeq.gov.

Driver's License

If you have a valid license from another state, you have to present it and one other form of ID to get an Arizona license. A vision test is required, but not a written test. For motor vehicle department locations, call the Arizona Department of Transportation at (602) 255-0072. The website www.azdot.gov/mvd has a list of locations.

RELOCATION SERVICES

ARIZONA RELOCATION ALLIANCE
www.azrelocationalliance.com
(602) 912-1535
The organization was formed in 2001 to facilitate professional networking and relocation to the Valley and Arizona. The nonprofit group brings together a list of member relocation experts who can help newcomers get their foot in the door with corporations, real estate groups, and other business ventures.

RETIREMENT

A leader in the development of "active-adult" communities, the Valley of the Sun affords lots of choices for retirees of all types. Looking for an active retirement? You'll find year-round golf, tennis, swimming, and lots of senior-friendly activities to choose from. Check out the Retirement chapter for details and listings of retirement services and communities. A terrific central resource is the Area Agency on Aging, (602) 264-2255; www.aaaphx.org.

CHAMBERS OF COMMERCE

These are great resources for local information, and many provide free relocation packages. Here are some of the larger chambers of commerce in the Valley:

CAREFREE/CAVE CREEK
(480) 488-3381
www.carefree-cavecreek.com

CHANDLER
(480) 963-4571
www.chandlerchamber.com

GLENDALE
(623) 937-4754
www.glendaleazchamber.org

GREATER PHOENIX
(602) 495-2195
www.phoenixchamber.com

MESA
(480) 969-1307
www.mesachamber.org

SCOTTSDALE AREA
(480) 355-2700
www.scottsdalechamber.com

SOUTHWEST VALLEY
(623) 932-2260
www.southwestvalleychamber.org

NEIGHBORHOODS

Most Valley housing is relatively new. So are most neighborhoods. Those that people can pick out by name usually have some history to them. In Phoenix neighborhoods such as Encanto, Arcadia, Maryvale, Paradise Valley, and Sunnyslope are among the best known.

To the rest of the Valley, a neighborhood usually means the name of a development. In Scottsdale master-planned communities like Scottsdale Ranch and Grayhawk prevail rather than traditional boroughs. With so many new developments popping up, any listing would quickly become a litany of names and features without any context. It's much more useful to think of the Valley outside Phoenix

in geographic terms. North and South Scottsdale are distinct from one another; so are North and South Tempe and East and West Mesa. The neighborhoods and developments within each geographic area are very similar.

With very few exceptions, the great truth about development is the farther you get from the Valley's core, the houses being built are bigger and the landscaping is more desert-like.

The oldest Valley neighborhoods were built to help the residents forget they were in the desert. Greenery abounds thanks to lawn irrigation. In these neighborhoods lawns were often sunk an inch or two below the surrounding sidewalks and bounded by grass-covered mounds. The lawns are flooded at night so that they look a bit like rice paddies. They stay green.

As time went on, the Valley became more water-conscious. The neighborhoods built in the 1950s through the 1970s saw a mixture of green lawns and desert landscaping, with grass lawns still tending to outnumber the desert landscapes. By and large, these neighborhoods are full of ranch-style houses built without basements on concrete pads. Because the elements (except for the sun) were relatively kind to autos, many homes built in that era featured carports rather than garages. Most of these homes were built in cozy proximity for young, blue-collar, and lower-middle-class families.

The developments built in the past 15 to 20 years tend to have a more spacious feeling. Two-story houses have become more common. Garages are the norm. The developments themselves have sunken greenbelts for flood protection, which opens up the landscape of a neighborhood. The greenbelts become places to jog, walk the dog, or ride your bike. Many newer

developments are built around artificial lakes or golf courses to add a touch of cool, green relief to the surroundings. On the higher end of the price scale, most communities are gated and have their own security.

Homeowner associations have become more common, both in older neighborhoods and in new developments. In new developments especially, they act as a form of low-level government, enforcing various restrictions in the property deeds in an effort to keep property values up for all association members. Enforcement is usually through fines, after the homeowner has been given some warnings. The associations use their dues to keep up common areas, such as greenbelts and roadside landscaping. Restrictions can be as loose as making sure that all the houses are painted in a similar palette of colors or as tight as not allowing outdoor speakers in a patio area. Outdoor remodeling and building additions often have to be reviewed by the associations to ensure they comply with the deed restrictions. This review is in addition to any review procedure that a city might have.

The associations evolved because of the vast differences in neighborhood upkeep, especially in Phoenix proper. You can drive down one half mile of a street in a development and find nothing but immaculately kept homes and landscapes, and then proceed the next half mile through blocks of badly kept rentals. The associations help keep this patchwork from developing any further.

Phoenix

Sprawling for more than 400 square miles, the city of Phoenix encompasses many neighborhoods. The following are some of the more identifiable.

Arcadia

Arcadia is one of the more mature neighborhoods. Sitting beside Camelback Mountain and stretching to Scottsdale, this neighborhood developed mostly in the postwar era. Within its confines a mix of wood-frame, brick, and painted cinder-block homes can be found. The landscaping is mature, and the streets are lined with trees, making it an attractive area for middle-class families and young urban professionals. The houses have more character than many of the homes built in later years, although some of the older ranch-style homes are being torn down and replaced with large, Tuscan- and Southwestern-style residences. In 2004 voters approved a $217-million bond to modernize Arcadia high schools. Work is still in progress.

Downtown Phoenix

Downtown Phoenix, considered the area from McDowell Road south to the Southern Pacific railroad tracks and 7th Street west to 7th Avenue, is undergoing a revitalization spearheaded by the location of two major venues in the area: US Airways Center and Chase Field. The new CityScape development, Dodge Theater, and First Friday art community are other main attractions. This growth has brought an explosion of interest in opening businesses—particularly restaurants, coffeehouses, and nightclubs— that take advantage of the sudden influx of nighttime foot traffic in the area.

What little housing there was in the area before downtown's resurgence was older and housed mostly lower-income people. This housing—generally small, single-story houses with mature, water-intensive grass-and-tree landscaping—is being torn down to make way for upscale condominium and

townhomes. However, it is an area where concerns about crime and personal safety are legitimate. It's now referred to as Copper Square, and the Downtown Phoenix Partnership is working with residential developers, the business community, civic leaders, and current residents to attract housing here that fits the urban character of downtown, including lofts, upscale apartments, and housing priced to meet many budgets. The partnership has greatly increased the number of services available in the downtown area. There are security guides, streetscape improvements, parking and traffic assistance, the DASH (a free downtown area shuttle), and downtown information directories. Downtown residents also have access to the new light rail system, making the 20-minute commute unnecessary. If you work downtown, living close by might be a better option than living in the 'burbs.

Encanto

The neighborhood around the 222-acre Encanto Park, called Encanto Village, forms a good portion of the square mile defined by 7th Avenue, Thomas Road, 19th Avenue, and McDowell Road. It is very good-looking and home to most of Phoenix's historic district. The homes are older, dating from as far back as the 1920s, and feature mature landscaping. There's a sense of being in an oasis that has a bit of a Midwestern look. Unlike developments built after water restrictions came in, this is a neighborhood that relies on grass for landscaping rather than desert styles. Being in a relatively flat area of central Phoenix that is only a few miles from the Salt River, the neighborhood's trees and grass insulate and isolate the area. You don't notice the surrounding mountains so much here, just the neighborhood. As a desirable little

enclave close to downtown Phoenix, Encanto's housing is relatively expensive, filling the neighborhood with professionals and their families. In fact, it's been dubbed the "Bel-Air of Phoenix." The Encanto neighborhood is of a similar character to a number of neighborhoods within 5 miles of downtown Phoenix, including the Willo, Coronado, and Phoenix Country Club neighborhoods.

Christown

By and large, the homes in the area around Christown are affordable and close to the amenities of downtown and the state fairgrounds. The neighborhood streets, developed from the 1950s through the 1970s, are wider than those in older neighborhoods such as Encanto, so it doesn't seem so isolated from the desert.

The postwar housing reflects a suburban imperative. Single-story structures, either of wood-frame or painted cinderblock construction, dominate, with mature landscaping and grass-blanketed yards. If not for the palm trees and desert mountains visible in the distance, this would be a suburban area that fits comfortably in any part of the country.

In many ways the Christown area is mirrored east of Central Avenue by similar unnamed neighborhoods (or neighborhoods whose names are obscure) and west of I-17 by the vast Maryvale neighborhood. They present a line of demarcation between the old Phoenix of the 1950s, with its working-class ambience, and the outlying upper-middle-class areas (often defined by desert landscaping) farther out from the city's core.

Maryvale

Maryvale has become almost synonymous with the west side of Phoenix. In actuality

Maryvale was a 1950s development by builder John F. Long. (He named it for his wife, Mary.) The units were affordable for young families, looking something like desert versions of the house in the *Dick Van Dyke Show*. The streets were broader than the old cozy developments like Encanto, but the general suburban desert feeling was the same. Occasionally, you see some desert landscaping, but most reminders of the desert are the occasional cactus or saguaro that's part of a conventional grass lawn. Maryvale still attracts working-class and lower-middle-class folks.

Many builders followed Long's lead in subsequent decades, and the effect is a similar style of single-story tract housing for many miles around. The only difference is that with newer developments, desert landscaping began to catch up with and rival the predominance of grass lawns.

Some areas of Maryvale have deteriorated and face high crime, although westside business has been growing since the completion of I-10. The housing, which depended on lower-cost materials for its affordability, goes south very quickly when not maintained properly. That desert sun is murder on asphalt shingles and sprayed-paint exteriors.

Metrocenter

The area around Metrocenter mall, which runs alongside I-17 from the Arizona Canal to Peoria Avenue, is newer than Christown. Looked at as a geological exercise, this neighborhood reflects the next strata in the Valley's growth. The developments around the mall are more likely to feel like suburban enclaves than those in Christown. The Metrocenter neighborhood's streets feature more twists and turns that keep nonresidents

from cutting through, a legitimate concern in light of the mall's heavy traffic. Here some desert landscaping starts to creep in among the suburban lawnscape. The landscaping is mature, and houses may be just a tad farther apart. Again, single-story structures dominate, and there is less of the painted cinderblock and more of the wood-frame type of house. By and large, this area is a bedroom community for middle-class families or professionals who work downtown or in nearby office-industrial parks.

North Central

From the 1920s on, an address along the northern parts of Central Avenue meant the occupants were wealthy. Keep in mind that northern is a relative term. The city has expanded far to the north of Northern Avenue, which once was the northern boundary of the city. This well-heeled section of Central Avenue begins at Camelback Road on the south and extends to just north of Northern Avenue. Houses here were built over a long period. Some reflect an older, statelier style, while others are upscale suburban ranch houses. The streets are narrow and cozy. You'll find a tree-shaded walking path on both sides of Central Avenue, the remains of an old riding trail for horses. The landscaping is mostly a lush green. The neighborhood is upscale and filled with professionals.

Sunnyslope

Sunnyslope began as a place where indigent people came to seek cures for lung ailments. The Valley's dry climate made it the perfect place for such cures, but cure seekers were banned from pitching tents in Phoenix proper. So they went north to around Dunlap and Central Avenues to the foothills, where they would sit on the "sunny slopes"

and recover their health. Eventually a sanatorium was built there, and a small, thriving lower-middle-class community arose.

The beauty of Sunnyslope is that the neighborhood feels cozy. It's a strange perception because the houses aren't really any closer together than elsewhere. Perhaps the maturity of the landscaping and the way the community nestles at the foot of the North Mountain Preserve make it feel more enclosed than some other areas. Homes in the area are mainly ranch style, and the character of the neighborhood is generally middle class to lower middle class.

Paradise Valley

The Paradise Valley neighborhood of Phoenix borders the town of Paradise Valley, but don't confuse the two. The Paradise Valley neighborhood is a visually busy area that creeps up to the north end of North Mountain. It also rises toward the foothills to the north. Houses here appeal to blue- and white-collar types. The construction is generally single-story tract homes, with many taking advantage of desert landscaping, which tends to become more of the norm in the areas immediately around Phoenix's mountains.

South Phoenix

Technically, South Phoenix would include Ahwatukee and an extremely wide variety of houses and neighborhoods. Farms, ranches, nurseries, orchards, and industrial parks, as well as the luxurious area around the Pointe South Mountain Resort—all are part of South Phoenix.

Unfortunately, in popular parlance, South Phoenix is the wrong side of the tracks—actually, the wrong side of the Salt River. Some (and we stress the word *some*) sections of South Phoenix come as close as you'll find to an urban war zone in the Valley. But over the years, there's been a strong effort among community members to fight blight and crime.

South Phoenix, like many other Valley areas, is an area of suburban tract homes, many of them built in the past 20 to 30 years. Many developers are rediscovering the area and building pockets of upscale homes near the base of South Mountain. These developments offer great values on mountain-view housing. Even when you exclude the more luxurious areas of South Phoenix, the income levels vary widely, from middle class to poor.

Ahwatukee

Sitting south of South Mountain, Ahwatukee began growing in the 1980s and 1990s and is still growing today. Terracotta roofs and stucco predominate, and the neighborhood is generally walled off from the main streets, with a few entry points. This is a neighborhood full of young urban professionals, a mix of families, and a small pocket of retirees. Be warned that commuter traffic during rush hour can be slow. The housing, generally single-story or 2-story homes and a wide variety of upscale apartments and townhomes, ranges from the moderately priced to the expensive.

Southeast Valley

Chandler

Chandler has a small downtown core with some housing that dates from the city's founding. Chandler didn't see an immediate postwar growth boom and thus remained a largely agricultural community until residential developments began sprouting at a rapid clip in the late 1970s and early 1980s.

In recent years Chandler has continued to grow at a fast pace, with residential subdivisions taking the place of farms and ranches. Again, the newer developments are predominantly of the tile-roof and stucco style, but there are also wood-frame neighborhoods and neighborhoods akin to Maryvale in the older sections. Chandler is attractive to young families and middle-class professionals, particularly since Intel became a major employer here. Its retail sectors are also a main attraction, with the refurbishment of the downtown business district and the addition of Chandler Fashion Center mall. Early in 2006 Chandler deployed citywide Wi-Fi Internet service, joining Tempe and Gilbert in forming the largest contiguous network in the US.

Gilbert

Like Chandler, Gilbert had been an agricultural community for most of its existence. Then in the 1980s residential development started to boom. In recent years the city has exploded with new residential and retail developments. The vast majority of housing in Gilbert is relatively new, which means tile roofs and stucco. The older places in town—those that are still left—are a mixture of horse properties and small ranches. The city of Gilbert attracts young families and middle-class professionals.

i The journalists at The Arizona Republic designed a list of resources at www.azcentral.com/real estate/relocation to help Valley newcomers. The site lists information on jobs, schools, neighborhoods, and city services. It's considered one of the best one-stop shops for Phoenix rookies.

Mesa

At 122 square miles, Mesa is not as vast as Phoenix. Still, the east-west drive across Mesa is long and makes the city seem to stretch on forever. Most of the city's growth in the past two to three decades has been in housing developments that spread eastward from the more mature area surrounding downtown.

Downtown Mesa—The center of downtown spreads out from the intersection of Center and Main Streets. It is at this intersection that Mesa's beautiful new arts center stands in all its grandeur. The streets are wide and lined with trees. There's plenty of space for parking, and a number of the streets are wide enough so that you can park diagonally head on to the curb. Many of the streets have substantial grassy medians. Much of the housing is from before World War II. Exteriors of red brick, painted brick, and painted cinder block and stucco are the norm here. The area ranges from middle class to blue-collar.

East Mesa—The eastern portion of Mesa is a progression of new housing developments. The farther east you travel, the stucco and tile-roof style that predominates in the Valley's new developments is just as predominant here. However, you're also more likely to see wood-frame housing reminiscent of the East or Midwest here than you are in other new areas. These new suburban developments are encroaching upon older areas that contain horse properties and little clusters of old trailer parks and rentals.

The spaces between the old development clusters and the new are still fairly wide open as you near Apache Junction and the Superstition Mountains; however, this land is also slowly being gobbled up by development. These older areas grew up around

the old alignment of US 60, which followed Main Street and the Apache Trail to points east. (Main Street becomes Apache Trail as it heads east of Power Road.) The alignment of US 60 along the Superstition Highway and the completion of the highway through Mesa make it an easy hour's drive to downtown Phoenix, fueling the building boom.

With the addition of Phoenix-Mesa Gateway Airport, the growth of east Mesa has also expanded southward, again with new developments of tile-roof and stucco housing. The area features a mixture of young families and middle-class professionals.

West Mesa—Much of this area was developed from the 1960s through the 1970s and features suburban housing tracts that are similar to the Maryvale, Christown, and Metrocenter areas of Phoenix. You'll find a mix of lawns and desert landscaping here and more shingle roofs than tile. The vast majority of homes are single story. The developments are very similar in character to those in neighboring areas of Tempe. The area's residents include young families, blue-collar workers, and middle-class professionals.

Tempe

Although there are many smaller neighborhoods in Tempe, the city breaks down into essentially three areas—north of the Salt River, the Arizona State University area, and south Tempe.

The area north of the Salt River resembles and is adjacent to south Scottsdale. A quick rise from the river toward the Papago Buttes gives the well-kept, single-story tract housing an attractive background. The neighborhoods up here are pretty well settled with mature landscaping, usually grass and palm trees.

Redevelopment and the addition of Tempe's Town Lake have changed the face of downtown Tempe, which is adjacent to the ASU campus south of the Salt River. The neighborhoods surrounding downtown and ASU are mostly older areas, with mature trees and grass landscaping. The wood-frame and brick houses are small but have individual character. These are pleasant and shady neighborhoods of old-time flavor, almost a stereotype of the college town. The area attracts mostly students and faculty. However, some new high-end loft homes have recently gone up and are attracting urban professionals to downtown.

South of Southern Avenue, Tempe essentially becomes the land of red tile roofs and stucco. Housing here tends to start from the mid-$200,000s, and in some enclaves goes well beyond that. As you move south, the lots grow larger with a few horse properties and even pricier homes. So the area attracts middle-class, upper-middle-class, and, depending on the development, a few wealthy folk.

Northeast Valley

Carefree

Carefree was founded in the 1950s and is one of the earliest planned communities in Arizona. Famous for its giant sundial (the largest in the Western Hemisphere) and unique rock outcroppings, Carefree is 36 miles from downtown Phoenix and encompasses about 8.8 square miles. With a population of around 4,000, this upscale community has a reputation for a laid-back lifestyle; city streets are named Ho and Hum Roads and Easy Street. This is an area of affluence that retains somewhat of a bohemian, artist vibe in part of the community. However, many of the homes are gorgeous and

on par with the larger properties found in north Scottsdale.

Cave Creek

Cave Creek was settled in the 1870s by miners and ranchers but did not become incorporated as a municipality until 1986. Just northwest of Scottsdale, it's only 36 miles from downtown Phoenix and has a population of about 4,000. People are attracted to Cave Creek's Old West feel and cozy atmosphere. There's a sizable artist community in Cave Creek, and while some live in pretty humble abodes up in the hills, others live in upscale manors with huge pool patios and 3-car garages.

i Professionals might want to contact the Arizona Internet Professionals Association at www.azipa.org. It's a cross-functional group for people working in the fields of business, art, finance, law, education, technology, and others. What they have in common is Internet-related work. It's a good way to connect when you arrive.

Fountain Hills

Isolated from the rest of the Valley by the ridge of the McDowell Mountains, Fountain Hills revels in its small-town atmosphere. Residents swear by the friendliness of neighbors. A planned "bedroom" community, Fountain Hills set its sights on retirees when it opened in 1970. The area had previously been a cattle ranch. The houses were intended to be small to fit the needs of the retired couple. Life would center on the golf course that wends its way through town along Saguaro Boulevard and on Fountain Park, where the world's tallest fountain can send a jet of water up to 560 feet into the air. The town's master developer, MCO Properties Inc., says the market changed and demanded larger houses. Most of what's available in Fountain Hills is of the stucco and tile-roof variety, but there's more variation within that style than you'll see in many recent developments. Fountain Hills is attractive to older families, professionals, and retirees.

Paradise Valley

Now, if you really want to go upscale, check out the town of Paradise Valley, which is adjacent to (but not to be confused with) the Paradise Valley neighborhood of Phoenix. Surrounded by Phoenix and Scottsdale, this community boasts a vast array of well-to-do celebrities and highly successful businesspeople. With the reddish-brown rock of Camelback and Mummy Mountains dominating the hilly landscape, this is a place where desert landscaping abounds. Exclusively zoned for single-family residents, many of the houses are done in variations of Southwestern or Tuscan home architecture, giving them a cool quality in the bright heat of the sun. People with money are buying up perfectly good older homes, tearing them down, and building mansions on the expensive earth. The spaces between houses are vast and peppered with desert plants.

Scottsdale

Scottsdale essentially is two cities—north and south. The southern portion of the city is the area developed from the 1950s through the 1970s as a result of booming employment in aerospace and other industries. Palm trees dot the landscape and let the sun shine through. The housing, mostly single-family tract homes, is affordable and has been, for the most part, well maintained. It's an area that attracts faculty and students

from nearby ASU as well as middle-class families.

As you move northward, toward Shea Boulevard and beyond, the housing values rise from the mid-$400,000 range up to the millions. New developments of the red-tile roof and stucco variety seem to be going up constantly, eating up more of the pristine desert that two decades ago wasn't even part of the city. Some communities offer Tuscan-style architecture. These are all upscale developments—some of them feature artificial lakes, while others depend on golf courses— all basking in the splendor of the nearby mountains. You can't forget you're in the desert up here, even though most of the subdivisions have plenty of trees and greenery.

Northwest Valley

Glendale

Glendale has three faces. The part of Glendale that bounds the north-central section of Phoenix is much like that part of Phoenix in character. As you go north from the Glendale line at Camelback Road and 43rd Avenue, the developments get newer. The southern end is much like the Christown neighborhood of Phoenix, giving way to developments more like those around Metrocenter. The southern end has more young families. In the northern end more established professionals predominate.

Downtown Glendale has been through quite a face-lift in recent years. It has a charming, small-town quality that belies the city's status as the third largest in the Valley. This is where you'll find the city's oldest prewar houses (some of them pre-World War I), a number of which are being reclaimed by professionals who like their charm. As with most housing from the

Valley's early days, red brick and white stucco are the norm.

Then, there's the rest of Glendale, which has boomed and expanded over the past two to three decades to the southwest and to the north. The growth has been in areas that once were covered with farm fields and orchards. True to the character of most suburban development in the area, there is much tile-roof and stucco. Given that Glendale once had a reputation as a blue-collar town—old industrial parks dot Glendale's south end—the new development is surprising: It's not only middle class, but also upper middle class in character. Arrowhead Ranch in northwestern Glendale typifies this up-and-coming face of the city. The 4,000-acre development features artificial lakes with 14 miles of shoreline and 2 championship golf courses.

The biggest thing to hit Glendale in recent years is the Westgate City Center, a complex that includes the 17,000-seat Jobing.com Arena—home to Arizona Coyotes hockey, along with other sporting events, shows, and concerts—and the new University of Phoenix Stadium, which opened in August 2006. Glendale hosted the Super Bowl in 2008 at the new stadium.

Peoria

Peoria was founded in 1886 as a small farming community. The housing developments that have exploded across Peoria in the past few decades are mostly of the tile-roof and stucco variety with desert landscaping, although you'll also find some wood-frame styles mixed in. The city is attractive to both younger and older families and also to a number of retirees residing in Westbrook Village, which is just east of Sun City. Shopping and entertainment at the malls around

Arrowhead Towne Center are enough to satisfy Peoria families.

Sun City

Sun City is a well-planned retirement community that offers every amenity to its residents. Life here revolves around the golf courses and recreation centers, where senior citizens defy old stereotypes with an active lifestyle. The 1,200 acres of golf links create belts of green relief among houses that were built from 1960 through 1980. Sun City is an unincorporated area of Maricopa County. (See the Retirement chapter for more about Sun City.)

Sun City Grand

Like its sister communities, Sun City Grand, located in Surprise, is a growing retirement community for active adults. The 4,000-acre community has about 10,000 homes. Sun City Grand, now owned by Pulte Homes, offers a full complement of recreational facilities, including 4 golf courses, a fitness center, the Cimarron Day Spa, and a lifelong learning center affiliated with Arizona State University.

Sun City West

Separated from Sun City by the usually dry Agua Fria River, the Sun City West retirement community opened when Sun City was just about built out in 1980. Sun City West is a bit grander in scale than Sun City. The houses are bigger and essentially for more well-to-do seniors. Sun City West also reflects a general housing trend in the Valley toward bigger, less-crowded development. However, in its basics, Sun City West is much like Sun City, revolving around golf courses and recreation centers. Sun City West is an unincorporated area of Maricopa County. (See the Retirement chapter.)

Surprise

Surprise officials have a new plan in place that calls for 9 new urban villages, so the old town is quickly disappearing. Surprise has attracted new development as young families look farther from the Valley's core to find lower-cost property. Surprise also includes 2 large retirement communities: Arizona Traditions and Sun City Grand.

Southwest Valley

With the advent of Loops 101 and 303 on the west side of Phoenix, the Southwest Valley has absolutely exploded with growth, both residential and commercial. As this part of the Valley becomes more accessible, and more affordable than the east side, people from all over are flocking here, where mostly master-planned communities are being built.

Avondale

Avondale was founded during World War II to provide housing for workers from the tire and rubber factory in nearby Goodyear. Homes in the older section retain their small-town feel, and this downtown neighborhood reflects Avondale's history as an agricultural community. Three rivers traverse the city—the Gila, Salt, and Agua Fria—and their banks serve as recreation areas. However, with all the new development occurring in Avondale, the town is certainly changing. The new communities, aimed at young families and professionals, are heading in the tile-roof and stucco direction. Years ago the city annexed the area around Phoenix International Raceway, and although this neighborhood used to be surrounded by an area of large, relatively isolated homes, you can now find new subdivisions and strip malls here, too.

Buckeye

Buckeye was once a small farming community, with most of its housing contained in a small town center. Not anymore. With the construction of master-planned communities like the 8,800-acre Verrado, with 14,000 homes and its own city hall, this once-sleepy little town was booming before the economy slowed down. Much of the planned development has been halted. The tile-roof and stucco neighborhoods now under construction in Buckeye offer a plethora of amenities—such as lakes, golf courses, and hiking trails—and are luring single professionals, families, and even retirees. Plans are under way for as many as 240,000 homes around the White Tank Mountains, and Del Webb opened Sun City Festival in 2006, which sports 7,000 homes. Buckeye's proximity to Phoenix, about 30 to 45 minutes via I-10, makes it desirable to anyone who wants to get away from the hustle and bustle of Phoenix and get more house for their money.

Goodyear

In 1917 the Goodyear Tire and Rubber Company purchased 16,000 acres in Arizona to grow cotton to be used in making rubber tires. The town of Goodyear grew up around these fields, and in the 1940s, when the cotton market declined after the war, the company opened an airplane plant in town. For years Goodyear had a company-town feel to it, since its single-family homes were initially built for plant workers. Over the years, however, Goodyear's cotton fields gave way to other crops, and this land has now been used for residential development. The planned communities moving into Goodyear offer everything from affordable starter homes to a variety of upscale residences, including casitas and mountainside or equestrian estates. Currently, the largest development in Goodyear is the 20,000-acre community of Estrella Mountain Ranch, which is nestled at the base of the Estrella Mountains and offers single-family and custom home sites, along with 2 lakes, a yacht club, a golf course, and a 40-acre park. Goodyear is attractive to both young families and professionals, many of whom commute to Phoenix.

Litchfield Park

Litchfield Park was also founded by the Goodyear Tire and Rubber Company, and as Valley sizes go, it is a small town both in area and population. In the older part of town, the streets are shady and the homes are situated on large lots. No walls separate Litchfield Park from the rest of the Valley, but it nonetheless feels like an enclave. The town has developed over the past three and a half decades in the shadow of the Wigwam Resort, which remains the town's top employer. However, even though Litchfield Park has little room for growth in area, a few new tile-roof and stucco housing developments have sprung up in recent years. Litchfield Park has, in a sense, merged with the town of Goodyear, since Litchfield Park is so small and Goodyear is expanding so greatly. Litchfield Park is also just 3 miles from Luke Air Force Base, and many of its residents are retired military personnel.

Tolleson

Tolleson is a largely Hispanic town with a farming-community past. Like other Southwest Valley cities, it, too, is evolving. In recent years new tile-roof and stucco subdivisions have been built next to the town's older single-family homes, and its proximity to I-10

has made it attractive for both residential and commercial growth. The town is home to a variety of manufacturing and distribution companies.

APARTMENT LIVING & OTHER RENTALS

Extensive growth in the Valley has put upward pressure on the rents charged by apartment complexes. Still, the Valley remains a very affordable place for renters. Broadly speaking, good one-bedroom units with a minimum 6-month lease range from the low $650s per month in Phoenix to $840-plus monthly in north Scottsdale. In Tempe the average runs about $725 per month. Expect to pay about $625 in Glendale. These are all ballpark figures.

APARTMENT FINDERS
Offices Valleywide
(602) 957-7000
www.aptfind.com
In business since 1981, Apartment Finders has a computer network that offers current information on more than 300,000 units in the Valley of the Sun. The information available includes floor plans, amenities, school information, and other details. The company's licensed agents can help find long-term and short-term leases for winter visitors and corporate relocators. They even escort apartment seekers to the properties and are experts in handling challenging rental issues such as income and credit problems or finding properties that allow large dogs. The company is paid by the property owners, so its services to renters are free. It has 5 offices (three in Phoenix, one each in Tempe and Mesa) serving the entire Valley. Information: (602) 957-7000.

REAL ESTATE AGENCIES

ARIZONA ASSOCIATION OF REALTORS
255 E. Osborn Rd., Phoenix
(602) 248-7787
www.aaronline.com

CENTURY 21 A.M. REALTY
1730 E. Warner Rd., Tempe
(480) 831-1114
www.century21.com
Century 21 A.M. Realty opened its doors in 1980 and is the oldest Century 21 franchise in Maricopa County. The agency focuses on the East Valley, although it can find and sell homes across the Valley. Through Century 21 and the VIP Referral System, the agency can accept and refer relocation clients worldwide. Century 21 has dozens of independently owned and operated affiliates in the Valley that offer similar services.

i Tech Oasis, an alliance of industry and government founded in 1999, sponsors monthly get-togethers for tech workers at various locations in Phoenix, Scottsdale, and Tempe. It's an opportunity to meet and network with other techies. Visit www.techoasis.com to learn where and when the next meeting will be held.

COLDWELL BANKER RESIDENTIAL BROKERAGE
8525 E. Pinnacle Peak Rd., Scottsdale
(480) 585-0809
www.cbscottsdale.com
Coldwell Banker has more than 25 sales offices serving every portion of the Valley of the Sun. The company has a full-fledged relocation division. Coldwell Banker is a full-service real estate company and also offers

relocation services, a developers' marketing service, and concierge services.

ERA ENCORE REALTY
678 E. Thunderbird Rd., Phoenix
(602) 938-2000
www.era.com

Encore Realty is one of the top 50 offices in sales in ERA's international franchise network. Based in Phoenix, Encore handles sales in all areas of the Valley with more than 50 agents. Encore is a member of the National Military Broker Network and specializes in meeting the needs of service members from Luke Air Force Base.

JOHN HALL & ASSOCIATES
11211 N. Tatum Blvd., Phoenix
(602) 953-4000
www.johnhall.com

John Hall and Associates, in business in Arizona since 1974, has four offices and more than 800 real estate professionals covering the Valley. It is a full-service agency that offers complete relocation services for individuals, brokerages, and corporations.

KELLER WILLIAMS REALTY
11010 N. Tatum Blvd., Ste. 101, Phoenix
(602) 787-2000
www.kw.com

Keller Williams Realty maintains 13 sales offices in the Valley of the Sun. This is the north Phoenix location. The firm provides local sales and relocation services as part of the Keller Williams network.

MCO REALTY INC.
9617 N. Saguaro Blvd., Fountain Hills
(480) 837-2500
www.mcorealty.com

You can't miss MCO Realty, because its 2-story headquarters stands prominently at the busy intersection of Saguaro and Shea boulevards. Another Fountain Hills office can be found at the Plaza Fountainside, next to Fountain Park. A wholly owned subsidiary of MCO Custom Properties, the master developer of Fountain Hills, MCO Realty focuses on selling both new and resale homes as well as custom home sites in Fountain Hills.

RUSS LYON REALTY
7135 E. Camelback Rd., Scottsdale
(480) 991-2929
www.russlyon.com

Russ Lyon Realty, a Valley firm that opened for business in 1947, has more than 575 sales associates in 7 Valley sales offices. This is their corporate and relocation office. Russ Lyon is an affiliate of RELO, a nationwide relocation service, and is also an affiliate of Sotheby's International Realty, specializing in luxury properties.

i Okay, seriously, the best way to learn about a new area is to listen to the people who live there, right? And that's exactly what we suggest. We went looking for some interesting Phoenix blogs relating to real estate. Of course, the bloggers have a lot to say about other local topics, too. Settle back and click to find out what these local bloggers really think: www.phoenixrealestateguy.com, www.christophschweiger.com, http://phoenixrealtors.featuredblog.com, and www.arizonarealestatenotebook.com.

REALTY EXECUTIVES
4427 N. 36th St., Phoenix
(602) 957-0444
www.realtyexecutives.com

This is the central Phoenix office of the Realty Executives franchise operation, which was born in the city in 1965. Today there are more than 1,000 Realty Executives franchises worldwide. Reflecting its hometown roots, Realty Executives Phoenix has scads of offices in the Valley of the Sun, as well as its corporate headquarters.

RE/MAX ALL STARS
8079 N. 85th Way, Scottsdale
(480) 998-6000
www.movetoarizona.com

RE/MAX All Stars is one of many RE/MAX offices across the Valley of the Sun. It offers full-service real estate sales and relocation services through RE/MAX's international network.

WEST USA REALTY
7047 E. Greenway Pkwy., Phoenix
(480) 948-5554
www.westusa.com

West USA Realty is a Phoenix firm that opened its doors in April 1986 and has since grown to six branch offices and 7 franchise offices, with a network of more than 1,400 real estate professionals in the Valley. The Kierland office serves the metro Phoenix area. West USA's other offices are scattered Valleywide.

RETIREMENT

In Phoenix you can talk to retirees who have traveled the world for leisure, business, or military service—people who know they have a wealth of choices for a retirement nest—and they'll tell you why they chose this city above everywhere else: climate, of course. Tired of shoveling snow and skidding on ice, many retirees opt for the Valley of the Sun. They also like the fact that Phoenix is so welcoming to seniors. The cost of living is relatively low, the people are friendly, there's plenty to do, and the active retirement communities here have gained international fame.

Many part-time winter residents, who are usually at least 50 years old, are known as snowbirds. These folks flock to a variety of Valley roosts—apartments and condos with short leases, relatives' homes, their own part-time homes, and, most notably, mobile homes and RV parks. In many cases they find enclaves of like-minded seniors, easing their way into feeling at home in the big city.

Seniors tend to congregate on the fringes of the metropolitan area. In Apache Junction, in the far Southeast Valley, for instance, there are literally dozens of mobile home and RV parks that attract the older set, those here either year-round or part of the year. Diagonally across the Valley, in the far northwest, is the world-famous, first-of-its-kind Sun City, along with similar age-restricted communities marketed as havens for seniors.

There is plenty to choose from in the Valley, both permanent and temporary. For seniors, it's an ideal place to enjoy the twilight years with families and friends.

ACTIVE-ADULT COMMUNITIES

Ever wonder how "active adult" became the catchphrase for seniors-only communities? The concept of vibrant retiree neighborhoods—where grannies biding their time on rockers are far from the norm—got its start in the Valley of the Sun. In 1960 pioneer builder Del Webb completed Sun City, a tidy community of homes northwest of Phoenix. Sun City homes were built on circular streets, with major roads bisecting those streets and leading the way to clusters of activity—shops, banks, and recreation centers as well as acres and acres of golf courses. Now, the community is so self-contained that many residents prefer to get around in golf carts instead of cars. Cultural life flourishes thanks to the 7,000-seat Maricopa County Events Center, a well-tended art museum, and various musical, dance, and theatrical groups. Over the years the place has filled to the brim with social groups catering to a wealth of interests. The requirement for buying into this paradise: At least one member of the family has to be 55 or older, and no one younger than 18 is allowed, except for visits.

i Phoenix offers a service called Reserve-A-Ride, which picks up those who are certified as disabled or over 60 and delivers them anywhere within an 8-mile radius. All vans are wheelchair accessible. The service is free, but donations are accepted. You must first register at (602) 262-4400. Information: www.phoenix.gov/PUB TRANS/reserve.html.

The concept has taken off like Tiger Woods with a 9-iron. Developers' billboards all over the Valley display the happy faces of couples that look just barely older than 55—playing golf, swimming, and reveling in a lifestyle that, supposedly, is "like being on vacation every day!"

Sun City remains the largest retirement community in the country, and it set the standard for other active-adult communities from Florida to California.

After Sun City, Del Webb Corp. followed up with two other communities in the Northwest Valley, opening Sun City West in the late 1970s and launching Sun City Grand in 1996. While these original communities are all sold out and available for resale only, Del Webb continues to build new ones, including Fireside at Norterra in Phoenix, Solera at Johnson Ranch in Queen Creek, and Sun City Festival in Buckeye. In the Southeast Valley, Robson Communities got on the bandwagon with Sun Lakes in the 1970s. More than a dozen other active-retirement communities—designed by different developers but offering similar amenities—dot the Valley, mainly in the suburbs. Here's a quick rundown of those by Robson and Del Webb, the two leaders in the concept, followed by the names of Valley developers whose projects include age-55-and-older communities.

CORTE BELLA
22135 N. Mission Dr. Sun City West
(623) 328-5068
www.cortebella.net

Corte Bella is Del Webb's first active-adult country club and the first club of its kind in the Phoenix area. With only 1,650 homes, it is considered small and intimate compared to most communities. Like all Del Webb operations, the amenities are top-notch. The golf club's par-72, 18-hole championship course by designer Greg Nash offers 4 sets of tees, from 5,145 yards to 7,000 yards, with an expansive putting green, short-game practice area, and generous driving range with target greens. There are separate men's and women's locker rooms and a fully equipped pro shop as well. A 7,500-square-foot social club is a great spot for casual dining at the cafe, with large patios overlooking the golf course. The fitness club and spa at Corte Bella offer more than 10,000 square feet of basic cardio- and weight-training areas and an aerobics studio. Services include spa treatment rooms, separate men's and women's lounges and locker rooms, indoor whirlpool and steam rooms, and private sun patios. Additional services such as massages and facials can be arranged by request. The minimum age for this Del Webb community is 55. *Arizona Business* magazine frequently selects Corte Bella as the best active adult community in the area.

i For information on active-adult communities in the Valley, visit www.retirearizonastyle.com. The site breaks down short sales and foreclosure listings, in addition to the top senior communities in the area.

SUN CITY
16824 N. 99th Ave., Sun City
(623) 977-5000
www.suncityaz.org

In this first active-adult community built by Del Webb, the prices range from $93,000 to $185,000. Although sold out, resale homes are available through real estate brokers and directly from owners, and there may be additional homes in the future. There are about 40,000 residents and 27,000 homes, with a median age of 75 in this amazing miniature city. You can visit anytime; make your first stop the visitor center.

The Sun City Visitor Center, 16824 N. 99th Ave., located in the Bell Recreation Center (623-876-3040; www.sunaz.com/centers/bell), is chock-full of pamphlets, maps, fliers, and magazines describing the dozens of recreational opportunities, housing options, social clubs, and more for would-be residents. It's also the place to arrange for a guided tour.

Sun City's 7 recreation centers are conveniently dispersed around town. A look around will tell you in an instant that residents in these parts don't like sitting still. The centers encompass 7 swimming pools (6 outdoor and 1 indoor); 2 libraries; a variety of classes in crafts, hobbies, and fine arts; square dancing and ballroom dancing; fitness rooms; and bowling alleys. Add to that therapy pools, lawn bowling, tennis courts, miniature golf, and shuffleboard; 8 golf courses belong to the recreation centers and 3 country clubs. Check with the visitor center for specifics on the community's amenities.

The motto "Keeping Sun City Beautiful" rings true thanks to the Sun City residents who volunteer for the Sun City Prides. They spend untold hours picking up litter, raking the landscaped medians, trimming bushes, painting the trunks of the community's 1,800 orange trees, caring for the automatic watering systems, and reporting needed street repairs. County government officials once estimated the Prides' services to be worth more than $500,000 a year. The Sun City Sheriff's Posse, volunteers coordinated by the Maricopa County Sheriff's Office, helps Sun City maintain one of the lowest crime rates for a US city of its size. Posse members help with neighborhood watches, search and rescue, and home-security surveys.

SUN CITY GRAND
19753 N. Remington Dr., Surprise
(623) 546-7444
www.grandinfo.com

Sun City Grand opened October 1, 1996, in Surprise, just west of Sun City. The 400-acre community has 9,800 homes and around 26,000 residents. The community was the first in the Del Webb family to target the newly retiring baby boomer and has been the best-selling master-planned community in Arizona since its opening and is one of the top-selling active-adult communities in the country. Although Sun City Grand is completely sold out, it is still possible to buy in through real estate brokers or individual homeowners. Recently, the age limit was lowered to 45. Since floor plans vary widely, it's best to ask a Realtor for pricing information. Expect homes to start a bit higher than $200,000.

Designed to reflect a Southwestern desert resort with all the related resort amenities, Sun City Grand features state-of-the-art recreational facilities, championship golf courses, and Del Webb's trademark amenities. The Village Center is located at the community's hub. With its inviting, pleasant courtyard design, cascading water features,

and lush landscaping, the Village Center provides an ideal environment for socializing and meeting neighbors. The centerpiece for that mingling is the Sonoran Plaza, a beautiful 21,000-square-foot structure that offers a 9,100-square-foot ballroom, a performing-arts stage, several smaller meeting rooms, a reading room/lounge, an outdoor patio area with fireplace, and the offices of the Community Association Management. It also provides the setting for the Adobe Spa and Fitness Center, a sophisticated facility with the latest exercise and weight training equipment, indoor and outdoor pools, an indoor walking track, and aerobics classrooms.

The center also includes bocce and tennis courts, lawn-bowling greens, and a fishing pier, as well as an outdoor amphitheater for festivals and special events and activity rooms for interests ranging from billiards to computers. The 4 golf courses include Desert Springs Golf Course, a public course designed by Billy Casper and Greg Nash, featuring playability for players of all levels, 17 lakes, and panoramic views. Granite Falls South, a second course designed by Casper and Nash, opened in December 1997. Designed more like Midwestern courses with rolling fairways and large greens, Granite Falls South offers a picturesque 18th hole that features 2 lakes linked by a cascading waterfall and a fountain as a backdrop. Granite Falls North, the third Casper- and Nash-designed 18-hole golf course, features more than 20,000 native shrubs and trees, including burrage, brittlebush, mesquites, palo verdes, and a variety of cacti. A fourth full-facility course, Cimarron, was designed by the Casper and Nash team and has a slope of 123 to 117, depending on the tee. The course is considered excellent.

SUN CITY WEST
13823 Camino del Sol, Sun City West
(623) 214-8629
www.suncitywest.org

Buoyed by the success of Sun City, Del Webb Corp. moved 2 miles west in 1978 to begin building a second active-adult community. The first homes were completed in 1978, and the final home was delivered in 1998, for a total of 17,000 homes and 31,000 residents. Like its neighbor, Sun City West, now owned by Pulte Homes, is self-contained, with dozens of shops, banks, restaurants, several golf courses, 4 recreation centers, and a hospital. In the same vein, it mandates that at least one member of a household be age 55 or older.

Sun City West also has a Sheriff's Posse to keep crime down and a Prides volunteer organization to keep neighborhoods tidy. It calls itself "Flag City U.S.A." owing to the hundreds of American flags lining the major thoroughfare, R.H. Johnson Boulevard, under the guidance of the local American Legion post.

The residents' get-up-and-go attitude is reflected in the diversity of clubs and social groups at their disposal. A club list from the visitor center, for instance, lists over 100 organizations, from the Agriculture Club to the Yoga Club. Folks regularly get together for jazz dancing, water therapy, bicycling, and other sports.

And don't forget the golfing. Sun City West has 10 golf courses, 7 of which are owned by the residents. All are private. The community also has 4 recreation centers. Call the visitor center at (623) 214-8629 for hours and fees. Amenities include an Olympic-size swimming pool at each of the centers as well as tennis, bowling, billiards, racquetball, miniature golf, fitness rooms, slow-pitch softball,

and horseshoes. Social halls host various kinds of dancing, bingo, and other weekly activities. Arts and crafts rooms let rec center members try their hands at ceramics, stained glass, painting, woodworking, and many other endeavors.

ℹ️ **White Tank Mountain Regional Park offers summer evening walks geared toward children and seniors. It's a chance for the older folks to pass along their knowledge. Information: (623) 935-2505.**

SUN LAKES RESORT COMMUNITY
9666 E. Riggs Rd., Sun Lakes
(480) 895-9600
www.sunlakesofarizona.com
On the opposite end of the Valley from the Sun Cities lies the community of Sun Lakes, which has grown to more than 35,000 people. It's about 20 miles from downtown Phoenix, but is still considered part of the Valley because of its proximity to I-10. As you're heading southeast to Tucson, Sun Lakes springs out of agricultural fields like an oasis of towering trees and ample golf courses. Here, too, active adults find plenty of ways to have fun and stay busy with social clubs, recreation opportunities, places of worship, and performing arts.

You'll find travel groups, social groups, 81 holes of golf, aerobics, dancing, card groups, and computer clubs—to name just a few of the hundreds of activities listed at clubhouses and in community newspapers. Every major holiday brings some kind of get-together at the luxurious clubhouses.

Sun Lakes was conceived about 30 years ago when developer Ed Robson envisioned an active-adult community with a "youthful spirit." The community was built in three phases, beginning in 1972, and is currently sold out.

Its 3,500 acres are organized around the 5 country clubs, called Sun Lakes, Cottonwood, Palo Verde, Ironwood, and Oakwood. Many of the streets are circular, with the golf courses and lakes as the focal points. The homes range in price from $150,000 to $500,000 and range in size from 1,444 to 3,497 square feet. Sun Lakes also offers luxury 1- and 2-bedroom retirement apartments for independent senior living.

Although the growing city of Chandler and regional shopping malls are fairly close to home, Sun Lakes residents can get much of their shopping done within the community. Supermarkets, banks, professional offices, a health center, and specialty shops are at the major intersections.

OTHER COMMUNITIES

LEISURE WORLD
908 S. Power Rd., Mesa
(480) 832-7451
www.leisureworldarizona.com
One of the more established active-adult communities, Leisure World, located 30 miles from metropolitan Phoenix, consists of 2,664 homes and over 4,000 residents. It has 2 large recreation centers, two 18-hole golf courses, security gates, a 24-hour mobile patrol, and minibuses that shuttle to nearby shopping centers. Resale homes are 1-, 2-, or 3-bedroom. You can also choose from 1-, 2-, or 3-bedroom condominiums, garden homes, and duplexes, with prices starting around $170,000.

PEBBLECREEK RESORT COMMUNITY
3003 N. 164th Ave., Goodyear
(800) 795-4663
www.robson.com

Voted one of the best master-planned communities in the country by *Where to Retire* magazine, PebbleCreek is located in Goodyear, 17 miles west of downtown Phoenix. With 6,500 units, this community is for age 40-plus. Priced from the $150,000s to $800,000s, the homes range in size from 1,532 to 3,421 square feet and feature 20 floor plans in 3 home series. The country club amenities include 2 clubhouses, on-site restaurants and lounges, 2 golf courses, a swimming pool, and a lap pool; a new sports club opened in 2007. A variety of arts and crafts classes are offered.

RIO VERDE
18934 Avenida Del Ray, Rio Verde
(480) 471-1962, (800) 233-7103
www.theverdes.com

An adult golf community (age 55-plus) in the Northeast Valley (Scottsdale area), Rio Verde began development in 1973 and today is close to completion. There are approximately 1,080 residential home sites (single family and townhomes) priced from around $300,000 to $2 million, 6 commercial buildings, 3 recreation buildings, and a church. Rio Verde's population is over 1,800. The country club offers 2 private 18-hole championship golf courses, a driving range, and several putting and chipping greens interspersed within the community. A 26,000-square-foot clubhouse contains 2 dining rooms. Amenities include 6 lighted tennis courts, a large swimming pool with four 75-foot lap lanes, Jacuzzi, fitness center, and hiking trails. The community center also has a library, arts-and-crafts room, pool table, table tennis, multipurpose room, and 2 large card rooms. Ice-cream socials, theater events, potluck dinners, Western dance classes, art classes,

and other special-interest group activities are all available to residents.

SUNLAND SPRINGS VILLAGE
2233 S. Springwood Blvd., Mesa
(480) 984-4999, (800) 777-7358
www.sunlandsprings.com

Located in Mesa, close to the Superstition Mountains, the slightly more affordable active-adult community (age 55-plus) of Sunland Springs Village offers 3,000 units of 2- to 3-bedroom homes and condominiums with prices ranging from around $190,000s to the $350,000s. You'll find pools, tennis, shuffleboard, and an 18-hole golf course with driving range and chipping and putting greens.

Frequently Called Numbers

The Phoenix area has an ever-growing number of community services that, if not directly related to seniors, can still be of help. Here are the telephone numbers for some important resources:

AARP—(866) 389-5649

Alzheimer's Association Helpline—(602) 528-0550

Area Agency on Aging Help Line—(888) 264-2258

Catholic Social Services Phoenix Area—(602) 997-6105

Community Information & Referral—(602) 263-8856

Foundation for Senior Living—(602) 285-1800

TONTO VERDE

18934 Avenida Del Ray, Rio Verde
(480) 471-1962, (800) 233-7103
www.theverdes.com

Deep in the valley between the McDowell and Mazatzal Mountains, Tonto Verde is an upscale adult community with 750 elegant homes. One member of the household must be at least 55 to buy in. All the new homes have been sold; however, it is possible to buy from a real estate agent or directly from a homeowner. Homes start in the 2,000-square-foot range and go up to 5,500 square feet. Prices begin in the $300,000 range and work up to over a million dollars. Amenities include a 26,000-square-foot clubhouse, two 18-hole championship golf courses, a swimming pool with lap lanes, an exercise facility, 6 lighted tennis courts, a beauty salon, and a dentist office. The community sponsors monthly hikes, a fly-fishing club, and numerous other clubs and events.

WESTBROOK VILLAGE

19281 N. Westbrook Pkwy., Peoria
(623) 561-0099
www.westbrookvillage.org

Westbrook Village includes about 4,000 single-family homes. It's an active-adult community open to those age 40 and older. No children are allowed as permanent residents. Amenities include 2 championship golf courses, a golf club, 2 recreation centers with swimming pools, tennis courts, and a fine-arts-class center.

MOBILE-HOME COMMUNITIES

With its alluring climate and long-standing reputation as a haven for seniors, the Valley of the Sun has developed a variety of lifestyle options for those ready to settle into retirement. Age-restricted (55-plus) mobile-home communities are an option to consider. Like the Sun Cities and Sun Lakes, many of these parks are happy to assist you in your pursuit of an active retirement full of recreation and socializing. If quiet and solitude are more to your liking, they can accommodate that, too. Plus, mobile-home parks are usually the more economical route.

Mobile-home parks in the Valley number literally in the hundreds and can accommodate as few as two dozen homes or as many as 600. An alternative term for mobile homes is manufactured homes, referring to the large, prefabricated homes trucked into a community from a factory. Once a site is chosen, the homes pretty much stay put for decades until they're replaced by newer models.

Manufactured homes are a growing trend in the US housing market. The Valley of the Sun is keeping up with the trend, judging from the number of manufactured-home communities developing on its fringes. Their architectural amenities rival those of custom homes, yet manufactured homes can save buyers 25 to 50 percent per square foot. At Crescent Run in Mesa, there are seven styles of model homes available; they range in size from 970 to 1,706 square feet.

Mobile and manufactured homes are the favorite roosts of snowbirds. Each mobile-home community varies in its ratio of permanent residents (those who brave the summer) to winter residents, who tend to stay from 3 to 8 months each year and either leave their homes vacant during the summer or rent them out.

Following are several of the larger age-55-plus mobile- and manufactured-home parks scattered around the Valley. Being larger, they are more likely to offer their

residents a potpourri of leisure activities and social groups. Amenities typically include heated pools, billiards, shuffleboard, tennis courts, card groups, bingo games, holiday-themed parties, and small golf courses.

Phoenix

FRIENDLY VILLAGE OF ORANGEWOOD
2650 W. Union Hills Dr.
(623) 869-7498

This gated community likes the fact that it has 75 percent permanent residents—a fairly high number among mobile-home communities. In addition to planned activities, residents enjoy the village's 5-hole golf course, pool, hot tub, shuffleboard, and other recreational opportunities.

PARADISE PEAK WEST
3901 E. Pinnacle Peak Rd.
(480) 515-2043

Boasting a view of the McDowell Mountains, this community has 415 spaces for manufactured homes. It's known for its 9-hole golf course.

Southeast Valley

CRESCENT RUN
8500 E. Southern Ave., Mesa
(480) 373-8500
www.hometownamerica.com/
CrescentRun

An 11,000-square-foot recreation center is the centerpiece of this community of 300 manufactured homes with over 330 lots available. It's also a gated community, with amenities that run the gamut from pools, putting green, and tennis to craft rooms, exercise classes, and a library. On the grounds is an 8-acre park with a natural grass amphitheater.

i Every February in Buckeye, the best seniors in the country "cowboy up" and put on a rodeo, complete with bull riding, roping, steer wrestling, and other events. Check the newspaper for location and time.

HACIENDA DE VALENCIA
201 S. Greenfield Rd., Mesa
(480) 832-6081
www.mhchomes.com

The Hacienda has room for 365 mobile homes. Amenities include 2 pools, a hot tub, a horseshoe pit, a gazebo area for barbecues, a social hall, a card room, a billiards room, an exercise room, and community center.

LA CASA BLANCA
2208 W. Baseline Rd., Apache Junction
(480) 983-1344

This gated, 198-space community has pools and other recreation amenities and hosts hiking and golfing trips, potlucks, and lectures. About 70 percent of the residents call it home all year. A sister community, Desert Harbor, is nearby, with 207 spaces.

LAS PALMAS
215 N. Power Rd., Mesa
(480) 396-2172
www.laspalmasmesa.com

Las Palmas is huge—539 spaces to be exact. Recreation facilities include swimming and therapy pools, with a continuous roster of planned activities within the community. There's also tennis, shuffleboard, bocce, horseshoes, hiking trails, and a large clubhouse with meeting and game rooms.

PALMAS DEL SOL COUNTRY CLUB

6209 E. McKellips Rd., Mesa
(480) 641-3385
www.palmasdelsolmesa.com
There are courts aplenty here, along with pools, hot tubs, and shuffleboard. The manufactured-home sites number 467.

Northeast Valley

ROADRUNNER LAKE RESORT

1149 N. 92nd St., Scottsdale
(480) 945-0787
www.roadrunnerlakeresort.com
This 627-space community promotes resort living with a miniature-golf course, a pool, 2 heated spas, a computer room, and shuffleboard, as well as many activities in its large clubhouse.

SHADOW MOUNTAIN VILLAGE

8780 E. McKellips Rd., Scottsdale
(480) 947-8393
Conveniently located near the new Pima and Red Mountain Freeways, this 55-plus community has 586 spaces and a number of recreation amenities, including a tennis court, a horseshoe pit, shuffleboard, pools, exercise equipment, and billiards, all located in and around 2 clubhouses and a dance hall. Planned activities include holiday parties, pancake breakfasts, and dances.

Northwest Valley

BLUE SKY MOBILE HOME ESTATES

4800 W. Ocotillo Rd., Glendale
(623) 939-5425
Blue Sky, a 55-plus community, has only 160 spaces but plenty of amenities—a clubhouse, pool, hot tub, exercise room, billiards area, and library. Add to that lots of Bunco and bingo games, potlucks, and breakfasts.

GRAND MISSOURI MOBILE HOME PARK

4400 W. Missouri Ave., Glendale
(623) 937-7721
www.grandmissouri.com
Retirees 55-plus with an interest in ceramics will find company here in the various classes offered. Planned activities include bingo games and potlucks; exercise options include swimming and therapy pools, tennis, shuffleboard, and aerobics. The park has 303 spaces.

PALM SHADOWS MOBILE HOME PARK

7300 N. 51st Ave., Glendale
(623) 934-1308
Bingo every night? You'll find it here, along with horseshoes, shuffleboard, billiards, pools, and spas. Palm Shadows also has an auditorium. A mix of winter and permanent residents occupy the 294 spaces.

INFORMATION & ASSISTANCE FOR SENIORS

Valleywide

AMERICAN ASSOCIATION OF RETIRED PERSONS

201 E. Washington St., Phoenix
(866) 389-5649
www.aarp.org/states/az
AARP is a nonprofit, nonpartisan service organization for people age 50 and older. By design and mission AARP helps members achieve goals of independence, dignity, and purpose. There are several active AARP chapters in the Valley. The number above is for the statewide office, which can put you in touch with local groups.

AREA AGENCY ON AGING
1366 E. Thomas Rd., Phoenix
(602) 264-2255
www.aaaphx.org

The Area Agency on Aging's Region One office serves the elderly and disabled adults in all of Maricopa County. It administers contracts with various services and agencies for benefits assistance, transportation, counseling, home repair, assisting the homebound, recreation, socialization, and respite services. It also runs specialized programs, for instance, dealing with elder abuse prevention or assisting someone in making the transition from hospital to home.

DUET PARTNERS IN HEALTH & AGING
555 W. Glendale Ave., Phoenix
(602) 274-5022
www.duetaz.org

Formerly known as the Beatitudes, this organization lends a hand in a variety of ways, including a parish nursing/ministry network, a library with books and videos related to aging, caregiver support groups, a volunteer base that makes home visits and phone calls to seniors living on their own, and an interfaith volunteer network that runs errands and does small home repairs for those in need.

FOUNDATION FOR SENIOR LIVING
1201 E. Thomas Rd., Phoenix
(602) 285-1800
www.foundationforseniorliving.com

The foundation's aim is to protect seniors as well as adults with disabilities from institutional placement that may be both costly and inappropriate. Its many flexible, individualized personal care programs are the means to do that, through counseling, adult day care, home health care, low-cost remodeling, apartments and supervised private homes geared to their needs, and senior centers. They have a wide offering of programs, including home care, adult day health service referrals, and housing information. Your best bet is to call these friendly people.

MEALS ON WHEELS
Residents who are unable to prepare their own meals are eligible for this service. Hot and cold meals are prepared and then delivered by volunteer drivers for a nominal fee.

AHWATUKEE
(602) 264-HELP

SCOTTSDALE
(480) 312-2375

SUN CITY
(623) 974-9430

SUN HEALTH
13180 N. 103rd Dr., Sun City
(623) 876-5350
www.sunhealth.org

Many of the health care services in the Sun Cities come under the aegis of Sun Health, including Boswell Memorial Hospital in Sun City and Del E. Webb Memorial Hospital in Sun City West. Sun Health also runs a physician referral service, a community education program, and hospice and home health care services.

HEALTH CARE

Phoenix and the Valley of the Sun are home to a number of nationally prominent health-care facilities, such as Barrow Neurological Institute, the Arizona Heart Institute, and the Mayo Clinic. This reflects a forward-looking attitude toward health-care innovations that the Valley has maintained since the earliest days of Maricopa Medical Center, the oldest health-care institution in the Valley, which was established in 1883.

Today all of the hospitals feature state-of-the-art equipment and the latest ideas in patient care—such as single rooms where mothers can go through labor, delivery, and recovery in relative comfort, instead of being wheeled around from the labor area to the delivery room and then to the recovery room.

Most of them also offer preventive medicine, either in the form of classes or wellness programs. In this chapter we give you a selection of Valley hospitals with some details that are valuable if you're visiting or if you've just moved here.

HOSPITALS

Phoenix

ARIZONA HEART HOSPITAL
1930 E. Thomas Rd.
(602) 532-1000
www.azhearthospital.com
The 59-bed Arizona Heart Hospital, dedicated to the diagnosis and treatment of heart disease, opened in early 1998 and has received international recognition for its work. It has close ties to the Arizona Heart Institute (see next listing). The facility was built to function as an advanced coronary-care unit and has a staff of more than 300 physicians, including the world's leading cardiologists and cardiovascular surgeons. The hospital has 4 operating rooms; 4 cardiac catheterization and electrophysiology suites; 59 private inpatient rooms, including 14 cardiac intensive-care rooms; a special peripheral vascular suite, and a 24-hour emergency center. It also encompasses the Wound Healing and Hyperbaric Oxygen Center, which treats nonhealing wounds such as diabetic ulcers, and a congestive heart failure clinic, which offers individualized intensive programs to congestive heart failure patients.

i Phoenix Children's Hospital dispenses a van to various Valley locations to provide free health care to homeless kids. The van is called Crews'n Healthmobile, and it's outfitted with high-tech gear and a team of doctors and nurses. To get a list of places the van visits, go to www.phoenixchildrens.com or call (602) 546-1000.

ARIZONA HEART INSTITUTE
2632 N. 20th St.
(602) 266-2200
www.azheart.com

The nation's first freestanding outpatient clinic devoted to cardiovascular diseases was founded in 1971. Affiliated with the Arizona Heart Hospital, where the institute's patients are referred if necessary, its multi-specialty outpatient facility is dedicated to the prevention, detection, and treatment of cardiovascular, pulmonary, and neurological disorders. The Heart Institute has an open-door policy and offers same-day service for testing and exams. It specializes in advanced nonsurgical interventional therapies that replace traditional scalpel-and-suture treatment for heart and blood vessel disease and is currently conducting research on myoblastic and gene-cell therapies.

The Arizona Heart Institute keeps relatively standard business hours Monday to Friday. Treatments offered include advanced alternatives to surgery, angioplasty, cardiac rehabilitation, general medical care, cardiovascular and thoracic surgery, pulmonology, checkups, and preventive medicine. The institute's Vein Clinic provides treatment for varicose veins, with most procedures taking place in the doctor's office.

BANNER ESTRELLA MEDICAL CENTER
9201 W. Thomas Rd.
(623) 327-4000
www.bannerhealth.com
Banner Estrella Medical Center opened in 2005 with a 50-acre campus that includes a 172-bed hospital, a surgery center, and a medical office building. It serves the rapidly growing West Valley communities of Avondale, Glendale, Goodyear, Litchfield Park, Peoria, and Tolleson. The hospital was designed with an eye toward the future and incorporates the latest in health-care technology and health-care delivery processes. The hospital prides itself on being paperless

and very high-tech. In fact, it's been chosen by *Newsweek* magazine as one of the top 10 most innovative hospitals. Services include inpatient and outpatient surgery, cancer care, cardiac services, ambulatory care, emergency services, and a comprehensive women and infants services center. An electronic physician information system eliminates handwritten flip-charts to reduce or eliminate medical errors. In 2008 the new hospital expanded baby facilities to include a nursery and more labor rooms to accommodate the mini baby boom. The expansion added 36 beds, bringing the total count to 208. Banner Estrella was designed with soothing colors and comfortable furnishings, and all the hospital's rooms are private and look like bedrooms. The hospital also offers room-service meals to all patients and their families.

i A list of top Phoenix doctors can be found at www.phoenixmag .com/top-docs.

BANNER GOOD SAMARITAN MEDICAL CENTER
1111 E. McDowell Rd.
(602) 239-2000
www.bannerhealth.com
Banner Good Samaritan began its days as a tuberculosis sanitarium, the Deaconess Hospital and Home, which was founded by a Methodist group in 1911. In 1928 it was renamed Good Samaritan Hospital and began to offer a wider range of services to the local community. Today Banner Good Samaritan Medical Center is run by Banner Health and is one of the largest hospitals in Arizona, with 673 licensed beds. Banner Good Samaritan has 2,000 physicians representing 54 specialties. It features 16 inpatient

operating suites and 8 outpatient operating suites. The hospital leads the state in heart procedures and is a prominent research center for Alzheimer's and spinal-cord injuries. The hospital specializes in heart and cancer care and is a leader in kidney and liver transplants, high-risk obstetrics, and multiple births. It also offers general maternity services, a sleep-disorders program, a Level I trauma center, rehabilitation, and outpatient services. The institute's Vein Center provides treatment for varicose veins, mostly in the doctor's office.

The hospital has 92 beds dedicated to intensive-care and intermediate-care services. Banner Good Samaritan's emergency room trauma center treats patients from around the Southwest and Mexico. The hospital has the state's first positron emission tomography (PET) scanner, which is used to monitor the chemical activity of living cells within tissue. Oncology services include a bone-marrow transplantation program run in conjunction with the City of Hope National Medical Center in Los Angeles. The campus also houses the 60-bed Banner Good Samaritan Rehabilitation Institute, one of the top rehab centers in the state, and Banner Good Samaritan Behavioral Health Center, which offers both inpatient and outpatient mental health services. Banner Poison Control Center is also on campus. Its phone number is (800) 222-1222. The hospital has attained Magnet status, one of only two in the Valley.

BARROW NEUROLOGICAL INSTITUTE
St. Joseph's Hospital and Medical Center
350 W. Thomas Rd.
(602) 406-6281
www.thebarrow.com
Barrow Neurological Institute opened at St. Joseph's Hospital in 1962 as advances in brain surgery and neurology made such a center feasible. It is recognized as a leader in neurological innovations. The institute treats aneurysms, vascular tumors, malformations, occlusions, ischemia, epilepsy, chronic pain, and trauma. Barrow is one of the largest neuroscience centers in the Southwest, with 8 dedicated surgical suites, a postanesthesia care area, 24 intensive-care beds, 15 intermediate-care beds, 24 acute-care beds, a 38-bed neurorehabilitation inpatient unit, a stroke unit, a spine unit, an epilepsy monitoring unit, a subacute rehabilitation unit, and outpatient neurology specialty clinics. A pediatric neurosurgery section helps children with complex conditions such as spina bifida, cerebral palsy, craniofacial abnormalities, brain tumors, and head injuries. The institute is part of a Level I trauma center for brain and spinal cord injury victims in central Arizona. It is also a teaching hospital and a research facility. Treatments pioneered at Barrow are now being used around the world.

CARL T. HAYDEN VETERANS AFFAIRS MEDICAL CENTER
650 E. Indian School Rd.
(602) 277-5551
www.phoenix.med.va.gov
In 1947 Senator Carl T. Hayden was approached by a group of Maricopa County residents who believed that Phoenix needed a hospital to serve veterans recently returned from World War II. A land deal was arranged with the Phoenix Indian School for a 27-acre parcel on the northwestern corner of 7th Street and Indian School Road. Approximately 290,000 veterans live in Maricopa County, and the facility serves about 60,000 of them annually through its programs. The hospital has 192 medical and

surgical beds, 104 nursing-home beds, and 48 mental-health beds. It is also a teaching and research hospital. Its services include an emergency life-support unit, services for homeless veterans, a substance-abuse disorders program, and a post-traumatic stress disorder program.

General medical and surgical services are offered, as are mental health and behavioral science services, physical medicine, rehabilitation, and neurology. In addition, the hospital has its own pharmacy and complete laboratory services and a 60,000-square-foot ambulatory-care center.

HACIENDA DE LOS ANGELES
1402 E. South Mountain Ave.
(602) 243-4231
www.haciendainc.org
Hacienda de Los Angeles is a long-term residential care and hospital-to-home transition center serving infants, children, and young adults. It was founded in 1967 by Eileen Butler, who shared her mobile home on South Mountain to care for these patients. In 1970 a group of supporters called the Madrinas secured funding for a proper facility, and in 1976 Hacienda de Los Angeles moved to its current location. The hospital serves patients who have genetic disorders or have suffered from birth trauma, physical abuse, or accidents such as near-drowning and car accidents. The hospital-to-home transition program is meant to speed recovery and the patient's return home. A respite-care program provides short-term care (including medical services and recreation) to allow the families of the patients to take a respite from caregiving. The long-term care program is a home away from home for chronically ill patients. Services include medical and therapeutic care, on-campus and public-school

education, social and recreational activities, respiratory therapy, and physical, occupational, and speech therapy.

Emily Center

If you have a sick child, you might want to check out the Emily Center, a pediatric health library at Phoenix Children's Hospital. Founded in 1990 by the family of Emily Anderson—who lost her life to leukemia at age 7—the Emily Center is the most comprehensive pediatric health library in the Southwest. It is free, open to the general public, and provides accurate and up-to-date information on children's health and diseases. A large collection of resources in Spanish is available. The center is located on the main corridor of the Phoenix Children's Hospital at 1919 E. Thomas Rd. Hours vary, so call ahead. Information: www.phxchildrens.com/health-information/the-emily-center or (602) 546-1400.

JOHN C. LINCOLN HOSPITAL–DEER VALLEY
19829 N. 27th Ave.
(623) 879-6100
www.jcl.com/deervalley
The Deer Valley location of John C. Lincoln Hospital began its days as Phoenix General Hospital, and for most of its existence it has been known as Phoenix General Hospital and Medical Center. It was purchased by John C. Lincoln Health Network in 1997. The hospital's 174-bed facility, with all-private rooms, offers inpatient and outpatient

medical and surgical care. The hospital also offers a 24-hour, 35-bed emergency department with a Level II trauma center, an intensive-care unit, cardiac care, and diagnostic imaging, among other services. Its pediatric center, called Mendy's Place, is the only pediatric emergency room in the North Valley. The Deer Valley hospital is known for its excellence in treating emergency heart conditions, pediatric health care, and other conditions.

JOHN C. LINCOLN HOSPITAL–NORTH MOUNTAIN
250 E. Dunlap Ave.
(602) 943-2381
www.jcl.com/northmountain

John C. Lincoln Hospital has its roots in the Desert Mission Sanitarium, which was opened by the Presbyterian Church in then-remote Sunnyslope to serve poor people who were ailing from tuberculosis. It grew through the years and became John C. Lincoln Hospital. This facility was the first in the Valley to earn the coveted Magnet status, which places the hospital in the top 3 percent of the nation's hospitals for nursing care. Today it's a 266-bed facility that provides 24-hour Level I trauma and emergency services, intensive-care and cardio intensive-care units, inpatient and outpatient surgery, an orthopedic unit, a breast care center, a sleep disorders center, diagnostic imaging, oncology services, and outpatient rehabilitation services. Part of its legacy as a onetime tuberculosis sanitarium is the respiratory wellness and pulmonary rehabilitation programs, which combine exercise and education to make daily life easier for people with chronic conditions such as emphysema. The birthing center at the hospital was designed by women. It features private rooms with whirlpool tubs and a quiet, calming atmosphere.

LOS NIÑOS HOSPITAL
1402 S. Mountain Ave.
(602) 243-4231
www.haciendahealthcare.org/careproviders/losninos

This 15-bed facility opened in 1994 and is the acute-care facility for Hacienda de Los Angeles. The children's hospital offers medical care for children suffering from a variety of ailments. It specializes in acute care for infants, children, and teens, including medical monitoring, urgent care, and transitional care. The hospital also offers physical, occupational, and speech therapy and training to prepare family members and others for patients' post-hospital care. Los Niños Hospital allows 24-hour visitation by parents and encourages them to spend the night. The hospital is locally owned and features a cheerful, homelike setting.

MARICOPA INTEGRATED HEALTH SYSTEM
2601 E. Roosevelt St.
(602) 344-5011
www.mihs.org

Maricopa Integrated Health System was honored in 1999 as one of the best hospitals in the country by *US News & World Report*. The original Maricopa County Hospital was built at 7th Avenue and Roosevelt Street in 1883 to handle smallpox victims. The site was very close to downtown Phoenix even then, so the county was pressured to move the contagious patients farther out. The county bought a site at 35th Avenue and Durango Street in 1885, where the hospital was built. By the early 1960s the Valley had outgrown its existing hospitals, and a

$10.8 million bond issue was approved to fund a new 425-bed county hospital. Site selection dragged into the late 1960s, when a document was uncovered showing the county owned a site at Roosevelt and 24th Streets. The new hospital opened in 1971. The Arizona Burn Center was established at Maricopa County Hospital in 1965 and is the state's only regional burn center. Maricopa Medical Center was the first Arizona hospital to establish a Level I trauma unit to handle all types of life-threatening injuries and emergencies.

The 449-bed hospital also features one of the few emergency centers in Phoenix dedicated to the special needs of children, a pediatric intensive-care unit, a neonatal intensive-care unit, 3 adult intensive-care units, and a family birthing center, among other services. Maricopa Medical Center (MMC) is part of the Maricopa Integrated Health systems, a network that includes not only the MMC but also 13 family-health centers throughout the Valley, a behavioral-health care center in Mesa, and 3 health plans. Maricopa Medical Center is a teaching hospital affiliated with the University of Arizona College of Medicine, Arizona State University, and the Mayo Graduate School of Medicine.

MAYO CLINIC HOSPITAL
5777 E. Mayo Blvd.
(480) 515-6296
www.mayoclinic.org/mchospital-sct
The Mayo Clinic Hospital opened in 1998 and about 10 years later received approval to expand by about 2 million square feet to about 8 million square feet total. Mayo is the first hospital planned, designed, and built by the Mayo Clinic. A 205-bed facility, its focus is to provide inpatient care to support the 65

medical and surgical specialties practiced at the Mayo Clinic Scottsdale. The hospital has 244 licensed beds and 18 operating rooms. It also has a Level II emergency department and a full-service clinical laboratory, urgent-care services, an intensive-care unit, a bone-marrow transplant facility, and a sleep studies lab for the diagnosis and treatment of sleep disorders. The hospital also offers a liver, kidney, and pancreas transplant program, with success rates higher than the national average. The recent expansion plans slated a new building for specialized cancer treatment, such as proton-beam therapy.

PARADISE VALLEY HOSPITAL
3929 E. Bell Rd.
(602) 923-5000
www.paradisevalleyhospital.com
As the Northeast Valley grew in the early 1980s, the need for a hospital became apparent. This 130-bed facility was built in 1983 to serve an area within a 10-mile radius of 40th Street and Bell Road. Today Paradise Valley Hospital is owned by Vanguard Health Systems and is run by their Abrazo Health Care, with a staff of 700 physicians. The hospital has 8 surgical suites available for outpatient procedures and general surgeries. The diagnostic imaging department features an open-scan MRI unit. Paradise Valley Hospital also has a Women's Center that provides women's health-care services and includes a labor and delivery center. In addition to recovery units for orthopedic, oncology, and pediatric patients, the hospital also has a 14-bed intensive-care and coronary-care unit and a 28-bed ER with cardiac monitors. The hospital offers outpatient surgery, rehabilitation services, spinal treatment, and hyperbaric wound treatment. Since 2006 it has undergone nearly about

$50 in renovations, including updates to its emergency room and diagnostic imaging area. All rooms are now private, so no more roommates here.

ℹ️ **The Banner Poison Control Center can be reached 24/7 at (800) 222-1222.**

PHOENIX BAPTIST HOSPITAL
2000 W. Bethany Home Rd.
(602) 249-0212
www.baptisthealth.com

Phoenix Baptist Hospital began as a small children's hospital in 1963. As the Valley grew, the hospital expanded its focus to all-purpose care for patients of all ages. Since 2000 Phoenix Baptist has been owned by Vanguard Health Systems and is part of their Abrazo Healthy Care network of hospitals. Phoenix Baptist is a 219-bed facility that offers general medical and surgical services, an emergency room, an intensive-care and coronary-care unit, oncology services, a cardiology center, the Center for Arthritis and Joint Replacement, a mammography center, maternity services with labor-delivery-recovery-postpartum suites, and a perinatal department that can handle premature infants. Phoenix Baptist also houses a 6-bed hospice unit and provides home health care. In 2005 PBH opened the Sunnyslope Prenatal Care Clinic to provide care at significantly discounted cost. Later expansions have included a state-of-the-art emergency room with shorter waiting times and 27 private rooms with flat-screen TVs.

PHOENIX CHILDREN'S HOSPITAL
1919 E. Thomas Rd.
(602) 546-1000
www.phoenixchildrens.com

The concept of a children's hospital had languished for about a decade when, in 1978, the Maricopa County Pediatric Society began considering ways to make the concept a reality. In 1980 a group of community leaders joined the pediatric doctors to form the nonprofit Phoenix Children's Hospital Inc. The founders decided that Phoenix Children's Hospital would best accomplish its mission in conjunction with an existing hospital, and hospitals throughout the Valley were invited to submit proposals. A blue-ribbon committee accepted a proposal from Good Samaritan Regional Medical Center (now called Banner Good Samaritan Medical Center). Phoenix Children's Hospital opened in 1983 in space leased from Good Samaritan. There were no construction or equipment costs incurred. Instead, Good Samaritan transferred its pediatric services and beds to Phoenix Children's Hospital through the lease arrangement.

Recently the hospital outgrew its facility at Banner Good Samaritan, and in 2002 Phoenix Children's Hospital moved into its current 20-acre campus, at which a $538 million state-of-the-art hospital was completed in 2011. The hospital is the largest freestanding children's hospital in the US and the only licensed pediatric hospital in Arizona. It also runs 3 outpatient specialty care centers, in Glendale, Mesa, and Scottsdale. The hospital has expanded to more than 600 beds, playrooms, schoolrooms, and family sleep areas in patient rooms and throughout the hospital. Services include pediatric critical care; the state's only 24-hour, 7-day-a-week pediatric emergency department; neonatal intensive care; a blood and marrow transplant unit; a kids' kidney center; a children's cancer center; a cystic fibrosis center; a neurosciences center for neurology and neurosurgery; a

children's heart center; a hemophilia center; and endocrinology, gastroenterology, pulmonology, and rehabilitation services.

PHOENIX INDIAN MEDICAL CENTER
United States Department of Health and Human Services
4212 N. 16th St.
(602) 263-1200
www.ihs.gov

The Phoenix Indian Medical Center started its days as a tuberculosis sanitarium for Native American children. The sanitarium opened in 1909 on land owned by the Phoenix Indian School, and it was administered by the school until 1931. After a few years as an independent facility, the sanitarium administration changed its mission, deciding to serve adults as well as children, and Phoenix Indian Hospital was born. Today it serves the medical needs of six Native American communities under the aegis of the Phoenix Area Indian Health Services. The hospital has 127 acute-care beds and a complete array of health services, including an HIV center. Because diabetes is a serious health issue for tribal members, the National Institutes of Health maintains a National Institute of Diabetes, Digestive, and Kidney Diseases at the hospital. The hospital's Auxiliary Association provides scholarships for Native American students who are pursuing education in the health field. The auxiliary also purchases equipment for various departments and donates time and money to hospital-sponsored community events.

ST. JOSEPH'S HOSPITAL & MEDICAL CENTER
350 W. Thomas Rd.
(602) 406-3000
www.stjosephs-phx.org

The Sisters of Mercy came to Phoenix in 1892 to teach. When they got here, they were moved by the suffering of tuberculosis victims. By 1895 the sisters had raised enough money to rent a 6-room cottage at 4th and Polk streets, where the original St. Joseph's Sanitarium was established. A year later the sisters were forced to find larger quarters and changed the name to St. Joseph's Hospital. As the city grew, so did the hospital. The sisters opened a school of nursing in 1910. They moved the hospital to its current location in 1953, and it continued to grow, adding a kidney dialysis unit in 1956, the Barrow Neurological Institute in 1962 (see listing), a coronary-care unit in 1965, a neonatal intensive-care unit in 1967, a respiratory intensive-care unit in 1968, and pediatric intensive-care unit in 1972. The hospital also changed its name to add the words "medical center" to reflect its expanded role. On his trip to Phoenix in 1987, Pope John Paul II visited the hospital.

The Sisters of Mercy continue to guide the institution in partnership with secular hospital professionals. Its services include more than 500 patient beds, a Level I trauma center, general surgery, hyberbaric medicine, the Heart & Lung Institute, a research enterprise with numerous clinical trials, maternity services, the Muhammad Ali Parkinson's Research Center, outpatient surgery, an adult-day hospital, an audiology center, behavioral and developmental pediatrics, a blood bank, a cardiac catheterization lab, cardiac rehabilitation, a child-abuse assessment center, dialysis, general medical education, and much more. The hospital has a neuro-rehabilitation center for brain and spinal cord injuries, and also a new lung transplant program.

ST. LUKE'S MEDICAL CENTER
1800 E. Van Buren St.
(602) 251-8100
www.stlukesmedcenter.com

St. Luke's Medical Center opened in 1907 as the St. Luke's Home serving tuberculosis patients. Tuberculosis was pretty well under control in 1947, when St. Luke's expanded its mission. As St. Luke's Hospital, the facility specialized in respiratory and cardiovascular diseases as well as general medicine and surgery. Today St. Luke's Medical Center is a 235-bed facility that provides services and programs in cardiology, pulmonology, orthopedics, general medicine and surgery, neuroscience, emergency medicine, gastroenterology, oncology, and ophthalmology. Facilities include the Charles A. Barrow Heart Lung Center, an inpatient Physical Rehabilitation Center, and the Bridges Center for Surgical Weight Management, which opened in 1996 and is the oldest center of its kind in the Valley. The hospital also offers robotic surgery for heart, prostate, and other ailments, and a wound care center that treats nonhealing wounds such as diabetic ulcers. A $6 million expansion of the Emergency Department nearly doubled the capacity to 27 treatment rooms.

Southeast Valley

BANNER BAYWOOD HEART HOSPITAL
6750 E. Baywood Ave., Mesa
(480) 854-5000
www.bannerhealth.com

Banner Baywood Heart Hospital is the second-largest freestanding heart hospital in the United States. After completing a $13.2 million expansion, the hospital is now a 111-bed facility. The hospital offers a wide variety of cardiac services, including advanced capabilities in cardiac catheterization, electrophysiology, noninvasive cardiology, heart surgery, and vascular care. The facility has 4 operating room suites and 5 cardiac catheterization labs.

BANNER BAYWOOD MEDICAL CENTER
6644 E. Baywood Ave., Mesa
(480) 321-2000
www.bannerhealth.com

Banner Baywood Medical Center, formerly known as Valley Lutheran Hospital and now owned by Banner Health Systems, opened in 1984 with 120 beds. It has grown into a 365-bed, full-service hospital providing general surgery and medical care, critical care, and maternity care. The hospital opened its $35 million expanded emergency department in 2009. It also has a women's health center, a joint-replacement program, and an outpatient services center. In 2006 the hospital underwent a $90-million expansion project that added a 7-story tower that holds 123 beds, of which 26 are in the intensive-care unit. Lots of high-tech gear was also installed, as was an additional parking lot.

BANNER DESERT MEDICAL CENTER
1400 S. Dobson Rd., Mesa
(480) 412-3000
www.bannerhealth.com

Banner Desert Medical Center, formerly known as Desert Samaritan Hospital, opened in 1973, but its roots go back to 1921 when Genevieve LeSueur donated her 2-story, 12-room house to become Mesa Southside District Hospital. As Mesa grew, so did the hospital. By 1958 it had moved to Main Street and Country Club Drive and expanded to become a complete hospital facility with operating rooms, a recovery room, and an emergency room. In 1968 Southside merged with Good Samaritan Hospital (now known

as Banner Good Samaritan Medical Center), and Samaritan Health Service was born. The corporation built Desert Samaritan to replace Southside Hospital, and in 2003 the hospital was purchased by Banner Health Systems and renamed Banner Desert Medical Center. Banner Desert primarily serves Mesa, Tempe, Chandler, Gilbert, and Apache Junction. A full-service community hospital, Banner Desert has 611 licensed beds, including private rooms with patios. It features a Level II emergency room with 53 beds. Banner Desert also provides 26 private labor-delivery-recovery rooms. Banner Desert Children's Center is a Level III neonatal intensive-care unit and also offers pediatric intensive-care facilities. Thousands of inpatient and outpatient surgeries are performed each year at Desert Banner, including more than 500 open-heart surgeries. The hospital also has a radiation oncology department, 88 critical-care and intermediate-care beds, a 32-bed orthopedic and neurology unit, and a sleep disorders center. Banner Desert also offers various therapy programs, such as aquatic therapy, community health education classes, and an orthopedic and sports-rehabilitation program.

BANNER GATEWAY MEDICAL CENTER
1900 N. Higley Rd., Gilbert
(480) 543-2000
www.bannerhealth.com
Opened in 2007, Banner Gateway represents an investment of $190 million into Valley health. The 60-acre center features 176 beds, in all-private rooms, 8 operating suites, and a 37-bed emergency department. The focus of the newest Banner facility will be on obstetrics, pediatrics, emergency services, and general surgery. Eventually the facility will be upgraded to hold 500 beds. The

center is built with a canyon theme that blends the outdoors with the indoors in a relaxing atmosphere. This is a high-tech kind of place, with room service, access to the Internet, a quiet environment, and state-of-the-art recordkeeping.

CHANDLER REGIONAL HOSPITAL
475 S. Dobson Rd., Chandler
(480) 728-3000
www.chandlerregional.org
A citizens group established Maricopa County Hospital District No. 1 in 1961 and, through it, built Chandler Regional Hospital. The 209-bed facility provides all-private rooms. Its major services include an emergency center featuring Level II trauma care, an intensive-care unit, inpatient and outpatient surgery, physical rehabilitation services, a pediatrics unit, and cardiopulmonary services. The Family Birth Center offers full-service care and features labor-delivery-recovery suites. In addition, the East Valley Regional Cancer Center, which offers comprehensive oncology services, is on the campus. The Wound Healing and Hyperbaric Oxygen Center is the only center of its type in Arizona to win international accreditation. Recent construction expanded the emergency surgery center and diagnostic imaging services and added a heart vascular center, which offers a full range of cardiovascular services.

MERCY GILBERT MEDICAL CENTER
3555 S. Val Vista Dr., Gilbert
(480) 728-8000
www.mercygilbert.org
Opened in 2006, the Mercy Gilbert Medical Center pays tribute to the Sisters of Mercy, the sponsoring congregation. It's a full-service, acute-care institution that opened with 92 beds. Expansion efforts added a new

tower in 2007, and plans for further expansion are underway. The hospital has a 33-bay emergency room, a perioperative team for health care before and after surgery, a family birth center, and a center specializing in cardiology, neurology, and pulmonary issues.

MOUNTAIN VIEW MEDICAL CENTER
1301 S. Crismon Rd., Mesa
(480) 358-6100
www.mvmedicalcenter.com
Mountain View Medical Center, built in 2007, houses 178 beds in all-private rooms. It's one of the perks of living in a brand-new developing area. The hospital also has room service and valet parking. The facility offers emergency services, surgical services, wound management, child-care services, senior programs, and diagnostic imaging. More than 300 physicians serve on the staff.

TEMPE ST. LUKE'S HOSPITAL
1500 S. Mill Ave., Tempe
(480) 784-5500
www.tempestlukeshospital.com
Tempe St. Luke's Hospital opened in 1944 as a small, 10-bed community hospital in the home of Dr. Ernest Pohle. It remains the only acute-care hospital in Tempe. A 103-bed facility, Tempe St. Luke's has an emergency room, general surgery, a radiology lab, a sleep disorders center, a wound care center, and outpatient surgery. Also on the hospital campus is a 63,000-square-foot medical office complex housing more than 50 specialized medical practices.

Northeast Valley

MAYO CLINIC SCOTTSDALE
13400 E. Shea Blvd., Scottsdale
(480) 301-8000
www.mayoclinic.org/scottsdale

Mayo Clinic Scottsdale opened in 1987 and, owing to the Mayo Clinic reputation, it serves a varied clientele. More than 280 physicians are available to patients at the Mayo Clinic Scottsdale. It is also part of an integrated, multicampus system that includes the 205-bed Mayo Clinic Hospital, located in northeast Phoenix, several primary care centers throughout the Valley, and the Mayo Center for Women's Health. It is a multispecialty outpatient clinic with more than 240 exam rooms, an outpatient surgery center, a full-service laboratory, a pharmacy, a patient-education library, and an endoscopy suite. The Mayo Clinic's Samuel C. Johnson Medical Research Building is a basic science research lab and is currently conducting research in such areas as molecular genetics and cellular and molecular biology. Clinical research trials give patients access to the latest medical treatments. It is also a teaching institution. More than 65 medical and surgical specialties are practiced at the clinic, which includes an NCI-designated comprehensive cancer center, organ transplantation, a breast clinic, a gastrointestinal endoscopy program, a sleep disorders center, and state-of-the-art radiation oncology treatment. The Mayo Clinic Scottsdale also offers a patient-education library and a 188-seat auditorium for patient- and physician-education programs. Also on the clinic's campus is Courtyard by Marriott, a 124-room hotel that is available for overnight stays for patients and their families.

SCOTTSDALE HEALTHCARE OSBORN
7400 E. Osborn Rd., Scottsdale
(480) 882-4000
www.shc.org
City Hospital of Scottsdale was founded in 1962 as a 120-bed facility. As the Northeast

Valley grew, so did the hospital and its mission. For most of its existence, it has been known as Scottsdale Memorial Hospital, but in 1998 changed its name to Scottsdale Healthcare Osborn. It is a 285-bed, full-service hospital, known for its cardiovascular medicine, obstetrics, orthopedics, and oncology services. Its emergency department is a Level I trauma center that serves the East Valley and much of south-central Arizona. The hospital also provides an urgent-care center; outpatient surgery and recovery care; inpatient and outpatient facilities for physical, occupational, and speech therapy; a cardiac center; 15 operating suites, including 2 specifically equipped for open-heart surgery; a critical-care unit; a freestanding birth center with 12 couplet care rooms and 9 labor and delivery rooms; and a Level II nursery. The hospital also houses hyperbaric oxygen treatment, a total joint center, a sleep disorder center, weight loss surgery, a diabetes center, and primary care through the Family Practice Center.

SCOTTSDALE HEALTHCARE SHEA
9003 E. Shea Blvd., Scottsdale
(480) 323-3000
www.shc.org
Scottsdale Healthcare Shea, consistently ranked among top hospitals in the nation, is a 400-bed hospital that features almost all-private rooms and is known for its cardiology, oncology, and women's and children's services. The hospital's Kenneth M. Piper Outpatient Surgery Center offers surgical specialties, such as reconstructive, orthopedic, urology, and gynecology, and houses the Scottsdale Healthcare Reproductive Medicine program. The Piper Center contains 8 operating rooms and a 9-room overnight-services pavilion to serve patients requiring

postsurgery observation, pain control, or IV therapy. The hospital also has an emergency room; cardiology services that include open-heart surgery, cardiac catheterization, and inpatient and outpatient cardiac rehabilitation facilities; an intensive-care unit; medical and surgical services; obstetric services; a bone-marrow transplant unit; a 24-bed oncology unit; a sleep disorders center; and an epilepsy monitoring center. Also available through the hospital are pediatric services; outpatient physical, occupational and speech therapy; laboratory services; and lithotripsy, a special treatment for kidney stones.

On campus is the Virginia G. Piper Cancer Center, an outpatient center that provides a myriad of programs and services including hematology, bone marrow transplants, a genetic risk program, occupational therapy, diet and nutrition advice, and a team of medical oncologists. There is also a boutique featuring makeup and prosthetics. The center is affiliated with the Arizona Cancer Center of Tucson and participates in various clinical trials and special research programs.

Northwest Valley

ARROWHEAD COMMUNITY HOSPITAL
18701 N. 67th Ave., Glendale
(623) 561-1000
www.arrowheadhospital.com
This 220-bed facility has served the Northwest Valley since 1988. The hospital offers state-of-the-art equipment and technology. Services available include angioplasty, a cancer resource center, cardiac catherizaton lab, cardiac rehab, a Level II obstetrics unit, oncology and mammography services, labor and delivery suites, orthopedic and outpatient surgery, and a variety of wellness programs such as exercise classes and a diabetic education course through the Wellness

Connection, just north of the main hospital building at 6670 W. Sack Dr. An expansion doubled the size of the ICU, which now has 18 beds, and added 3 operating rooms, for a total of 10. The ER now has 30 beds.

BANNER DEL E. WEBB MEDICAL CENTER
14502 W. Meeker Blvd., Sun City West
(623) 214-4000
www.bannerhealth.com
The 297-bed Del E. Webb hospital, built in 1988, serves the communities of the Northwest Valley. Focused on medicine for adults, the hospital offers an emergency center, general medical and surgical services, a cardiac catheterization laboratory, outpatient surgery and services, rehabilitation services, medical-psychiatric services, mobile MRI and lithotripsy services, and extended-care facilities. It is a leading center for hip and knee replacement, as well as other follow-up rehabilitation programs. It is the site for the Sun Health Pain Management Center and the Sun Health Center for Adult Behavioral Health, the Valley's only nursing home unit . for med-psych care. The hospital is particularly noted for its diagnosis and treatment of strokes. The Louisa Kellam Center for Women's Health offers extensive services for women, including obstetrics and gynecology. A new tower with an ER opened in 2009 as part of a major expansion.

BANNER THUNDERBIRD MEDICAL CENTER
5555 W. Thunderbird Rd., Glendale
(602) 865-5555
www.bannerhealth.com
Northwest Hospital—Glendale's first hospital—opened in 1960. In 1983, when it had outgrown its original site, the hospital moved to its current location and was renamed Thunderbird Samaritan Medical Center. Today the hospital is called Banner Thunderbird Medical Center and is owned by Banner Health Systems. It has undergone a lot of major expansion in the past several years, capped by $290 million that added a 16-bed pediatric unit and heart and vascular center, among other updates. The hospital has 397 licensed beds, plus 62 licensed behavioral-health and rehabilitation beds, and primarily serves residents of the Northwest Valley. Its emergency department features 45 fully equipped treatment rooms. The hospital also offers a complete range of gynecological and obstetrical services, including a labor, delivery, and recovery unit, and a nursery that provides expert care for premature infants. The hospital has 12 operating rooms, including several suites for open-heart surgery. Banner Thunderbird offers general surgery, orthopedics, pediatrics, pulmonary care, a critical-care and intensive-care unit, an oncology and urology unit, occupational therapy and rehabilitation services, cardiac care, and renal care. A sleep-disorders program, an outpatient center, and a hospice program are also available. In addition, Banner Thunderbird Behavioral Health offers psychiatric, behavioral-health, and substance-abuse treatment for adults and adolescents on an inpatient basis. The recent overhaul added a 7-story, 200-bed tower and expanded emergency services.

SUN HEALTH BOSWELL MEMORIAL HOSPITAL
10401 Thunderbird Blvd., Sun City
(623) 977-7211
www.bannerhealth.com
When Boswell Memorial Hospital was built in 1970, Sun City was a long way from

Glendale, Peoria, and the mainstream of the Valley. Reflecting the nature of the retirement community, Boswell focused on adult care and medicine. As the Northwest Valley has grown, Boswell has maintained that focus. This recently expanded 422-bed community hospital provides inpatient and outpatient medical and surgical services as well as a skilled-nursing facility. Boswell offers an emergency center, an outpatient center, a cancer program, cardiovascular surgery, an intensive-care unit, and extended-care and rehabilitation services. The Heart Center in the hospital includes catheterization labs and office space on-site for cardiologists and surgeons.

Southwest Valley

CANCER TREATMENT CENTERS OF AMERICA AT WESTERN REGIONAL MEDICAL CENTER
14200 W. Fillmore St., Goodyear
(800) 931-9299
www.cancercenter.com/western-hospital
.cfm
The fourth cancer center of its kind opened in 2008 in Goodyear. The site provides integrated cancer care to oncology patients. Like other Cancer Treatment Centers hospitals, the Southwest Valley site provides advanced diagnostic and therapeutic resources. The 213,000-square-foot facility has 37 outpatient suites, an infusion center, 14 private inpatient rooms, and an intensive-care unit. The facility and organization take pride in blending conventional treatments with other medicine and therapy to restore cancer patients to long-term health.

WEST VALLEY HOSPITAL
13677 W. McDowell Rd., Goodyear
(623) 882-1500
www.wvhospital.com
West Valley Hospital opened in 2003 and is part of the Vanguard Health Systems/Abrazo Health Care network. A recent expansion brought the total bed count up to 131, and further expansions are in the works. The hospital added a cardiac rehabilitation center and expanded the ICU to 20 beds. It provides general medical care to Phoenix's West Valley communities and also offers obstetrics services, a cardiovascular operating room, a 19-bed emergency room, and radiology services. In 2008 it added a Level II nursery.

EDUCATION & CHILD CARE

There's much to praise about higher education in the Phoenix area: the ever-improving Arizona State University, one of the largest community college systems in the nation, and private schools whose fame reaches beyond Arizona's borders. In comparison, though, the Valley's public school system is not as dynamic as it could or should be for such a large metropolitan area. Those who rank livable cities say Phoenix's public school system is part of the reason the city doesn't make it to the top echelon. The question is why we don't perform better. Some have suggested that heavier reliance on high-performing charter schools and private schools might ease that burden. For now, Arizona sits at an educational crossroad as legislators search for a promising path.

If you talk with Phoenix area residents with young children, you'll find that many of them shop for school districts as much as they do for real estate when they are ready to move into new homes. (Home buyers should consult the Relocation chapter.)

In this chapter we start our list of educational facilities with public and private universities, including Arizona State University, which for many years was considered a distant afterthought to the University of Arizona in Tucson as far as overall education. Some would argue that the two schools are now about equal.

Education opportunities also trickle down to the youngest of Arizonans. The Valley of the Sun has a number of outstanding preschool programs, including ones endorsed by the National Association for the Education of Young Children, Montessori programs, and parent-cooperative programs. See the Child Care section of this chapter for important phone numbers, as well as information on finding babysitters, nannies, and child care centers.

EDUCATION

Arizona State University

From a humble teachers' college more than a century ago, Arizona State University has grown to a multipurpose institution of around 64,000 students on 4 campuses, including the new downtown Phoenix campus, which opened in 2006. It has undergone several name changes over the decades. It started out as Tempe Normal School in the 1890s, later became Arizona State Teachers College, then Arizona State College, and finally Arizona State University in 1958. The university is one of the top 5 largest universities in the nation. ASU is very much a part of the Valley community based on its contributions to education, research, business, and the arts. The campuses are a source of pride for local residents, because ASU has been able to continually ascend in the ratings of universities nationwide. In addition,

ASU continues to improve in reputation as a research university. For instance, it has been highly involved in the Mars Pathfinder project and the fields of bioengineering and biomedicine.

In athletics ASU is known for having an excellent overall program, one that has risen to the national rankings in several of its more than 22 varsity programs. The football team went to the Rose Bowl in 1987 and 1997. In the 2004–05 season, the baseball, women's golf, and cross-country squads posted top 10 finishes. The teams' mascot, Sparky, is the maroon-and-gold Sun Devil, an impish-looking devil complete with pitchfork. Top-notch athletic amenities include Sun Devil Stadium, the Karsten golf course, and the Plummer Aquatic Center. The softball team won the 2011 NCAA Women's College World Series.

ASU has more than 400 student organizations, including those that have religious or ethnic affiliations and certain political or environmental interests. The ASU library system boasts 3.2 million volumes, making it the 37th-largest research library in the US and Canada, according to the Association of Research Libraries. Hayden Library on the main campus houses the Arizona Collection and research sites in Chicano and Native American studies. A 2-level underground addition to Hayden opened in 1989. Also on campus are the Noble Science & Engineering Library, housing a vast map collection and data on US patents, and law, music, and video research libraries.

ASU's newspaper, the State Press, is published Monday to Friday. A literary magazine called *Hayden's Ferry Review* comes out twice a year and highlights local and national writers and artists. It is considered one of the best literary magazines in the country. The

Arizona Board of Regents is the governing board for the state's public university system, which also includes the University of Arizona in Tucson and Northern Arizona University in Flagstaff.

ASU MAIN CAMPUS
University Drive and Mill Avenue, Tempe
(480) 965-9011
www.asu.edu

Counts seem to vary based on how you judge enrollment, but around 58,000 students take a variety of classes at ASU's Tempe campus. The 700-acre campus takes up several city blocks in downtown Tempe, and it regulates the pulse of the city. When the students leave for the summer, the usually bustling Mill Avenue falls quiet. There's little open space and landscaping between campus buildings and Tempe businesses, so there's an overall feeling that this is an urban, commuter campus. On the other hand, the interior of the campus has several malls—wide, tree-lined pedestrian walkways—that give the feeling of seclusion and seriousness associated with institutions of higher learning. Plus, there are 16 residence halls and ASU-run apartment complexes, proving that the campus is a good mix of commuters and those who hang out close to campus.

The school's top programs include the W.P. Carey School of Business, which has various MBA programs for full-time and part-time students. The Graduate College, Sandra Day O'Connor College of Law, Ira A. Fulton Schools of Engineering, and other programs are located at the Main Campus.

Architecture buffs should have a look at Grady Gammage Memorial Auditorium on Mill Avenue, a grandly executed circular building with lighted ramps leading out from it. It was the last public building

designed by Frank Lloyd Wright. Nearby you will see the round and tiered Music Building and the futuristic Nelson Fine Arts Center.

ASU Main students pursue a choice of 87 undergraduate degrees, 95 master's degrees, 48 doctoral or terminal degree programs, and 1 law degree program. The colleges ASU is best known for are in liberal arts and sciences, engineering, fine arts, architecture and environmental design, business, nursing, and education. The huge Computing Commons is near the center of campus.

ASU DOWNTOWN PHOENIX
411 N. Central Ave., Phoenix
(602) 496-1000
www.campus.asu.edu/downtown
ASU used to be all about Tempe. The satellite campuses were an afterthought. Now the downtown campus is a destination for undergraduates who want to live in the urban core of the city. By 2010 more than 13,000 students attended classes downtown. ASU opened the new state-of-the-art building for the Walter Cronkite School of Journalism and Mass Communication in 2008, adding it to the growing campus that also includes undergraduate exploratory programs at University College, the College of Nursing and Health Innovation, and the Phoenix Urban Research Laboratory. The new ASU campus is centered in the heart of Copper Square and is a full-service arm of the main campus. Student services include computer labs, the massive Taylor Place dorms, a bookstore, library facilities, recreational facilities, and the Mercado area at 502 E. Monroe Ave.

ASU EAST
7001 E. Williams Field Rd., Mesa
(480) 727-3278
www.east.asu.edu

ASU's easternmost campus is the home campus for ASU's College of Technology and Applied Sciences, the Morrison School of Agribusiness and Resource Management, and East College, serving about 6,000 students.

ASU WEST
4701 W. Thunderbird Rd., Phoenix
(602) 543-5500
www.west.asu.edu
Established in 1984 to serve the West Valley, ASU West continues to grow, serving more than 6,500 students. Undergraduate and graduate-level courses lead to 41 degree programs, plus professional certificates offered through the Colleges of Arts & Sciences, Education, and Human Services as well as the School of Management and Division of Collaborative Programs.

Other Universities

GRAND CANYON UNIVERSITY
3300 W. Camelback Rd., Phoenix
(602) 639-7500, (877) 860-3951
www.gcu.edu
Arizona's premier private Christian university was founded in 1949. GCU is regionally accredited and emphasizes individual attention for both traditional undergraduate students and the working professional in 6 colleges: the Ken Blanchard College of Business, the College of Education, the College of Nursing, the College of Arts and Sciences, the College of Fine Arts and Production, and the College of Doctoral Studies. GCU offers traditional campus-based programs, as well as online bachelor's, master's, and doctoral degree programs. The University's curriculum fuses academic and clinical rigor with Christian values to prepare its students to be skilled, caring professionals. More than

42,000 students are enrolled on campus and online. The GCU Antelopes compete in a wide selection of intercollegiate sports.

i The Arizona State Braille and Talking Book Library at 1030 N. 32nd St. in Phoenix provides scads of material to the visually challenged. Information: (602) 255-5578 or www .lib.az.us/braille.

UNIVERSITY OF PHOENIX
www.phoenix.edu
The Arizona-based University of Phoenix is the nation's largest accredited for-profit university. University of Phoenix classes are offered at more than 200 campuses and learning centers across the US, Puerto Rico, Mexico, Canada, and around the world via the Internet and currently enroll more than 470,000 students. The faculty roster is 32,000 strong. The University of Phoenix bills itself as the nation's leading university for working adults, with degree programs in areas such as business, information systems, counseling, nursing, and education. An important note, though: The university accepts only gainfully employed students age 21 and older. A recent study indicated that nearly half of all higher-education students are in this age group. Flexible scheduling of classes allows working professionals to earn degrees or certifications without interrupting their careers. This means weekend and evening classes, usually lasting for compressed amounts of time compared with similar classes at traditional universities.

CHANDLER LEARNING CENTER
3075 W. Ray Rd., Chandler
(480) 557-2802

MESA LEARNING CENTER
1620 S. Stapley Dr., Mesa
(480) 557-2000

NORTHWEST LEARNING CENTER
2550 W. Union Hills Dr., Phoenix
(602) 557-2762

PHOENIX HOHOKAM CAMPUS
4635 E. Elwood St., Phoenix
(602) 557-2000

WEST VALLEY LEARNING CENTER
9520 W. Palm Ln., Phoenix
(480) 557-2000

Community Colleges

MARICOPA COMMUNITY COLLEGES
District Office
2411 W. 14th St., Tempe
(480) 731-8000
www.maricopa.edu
Ten colleges, 2 skill centers, and several satellite campuses in Maricopa County are organized into the Maricopa Community College District, which is the largest provider of postsecondary education in Arizona and one of the largest in the country. The district formed in 1962 with a single college and has since grown to serve more than 400,000 students annually in credit and noncredit programs. Students have their choice of professional, occupational, special interest, and continuing education programs. In other words, you can study just about anything somewhere within the Maricopa Community College system. Many students attending Arizona State University have taken prerequisites in the liberal arts and other subjects at a community college, either before starting at ASU or while at ASU. Dramatic growth, innovative partnerships, and outstanding faculty and staff

have created a community college district known for contemporary programming, technological advances, and an imaginative environment for learning. Maricopa Community Colleges and Northern Arizona University penned an agreement allowing NAU to develop a physical presence on every Maricopa Community College campus. The Maricopa Community Colleges offer almost 10,000 credit courses and about 1,000 occupational programs as well as 7 degrees, including Associate in Arts (AA), Associate in Science (AS), Associate in Applied Science (AAS), Associate in Business (ABus), Associate in Transfer Partnership (ATP), Associate in Elementary Education (AEE), and Associate in General Studies (AGS).

The colleges serve many diverse communities, with students ranging from teenagers to 90-year-olds. Currently about 40 percent of all adults residing in Maricopa County have received educational services at one of the Maricopa Community Colleges. More than half of all Arizona State University baccalaureate degree recipients transfer credits from the Maricopa Community Colleges, and articulation agreements exist with numerous public and private colleges and universities in Arizona and nationally.

Campuses, for the most part, have a few thousand students, but some are smaller. District growth has enabled campuses to build not only classroom buildings, but also such things as fitness centers, child care centers, and computer labs.

Flexible scheduling and evening classes help accommodate working adults. Rio Salado Community College is known as the college without walls, because most of the classes take place at various satellite learning centers. Some of its campuses also offer distance learning via the Internet. These programs help make the community college experience accessible to everyone.

The community colleges pride themselves on being able to serve every corner of the Valley. For addresses and phone numbers, call the district's 24-hour hotline at (480) 731-8333.

Important Phone Numbers

Here are several addresses and phone numbers you might find helpful as you research the education scene in the Valley.

Arizona Department of Education
1535 W. Jefferson St., Phoenix
(602) 542-5393
www.ade.state.az.us

Arizona Association of Parents & Teachers/PTA
2721 N. 7th Ave., Phoenix
(602) 279-1811
www.azpta.org

Arizona Private School Association
7776 S. Pointe Pkwy. West, Ste. 110, Phoenix
(602) 254-5199
www.arizonapsa.org

Arizona State Board for Charter Schools
1700 W. Washington St., Ste. 164, Phoenix
(602) 364-3080
www.asbcs.az.gov

Maricopa County Education Service Agency
4041 N. Central Ave., Ste. 1100, Phoenix
(602) 506-3753
www.maricopa.gov/schools

Other Higher Education Institutions

EAST VALLEY INSTITUTE OF TECHNOLOGY (EVIT)
1601 W. Main St., Mesa
(480) 461-4000
www.evit.com

EVIT is a regional, technological public school district, open to students in 10th through 12th grades in the East Valley. It's free for students, although adults out of high school pay a small tuition. Financial assistance is available. The school prepares students for immediate employment in health occupations, commercial art, computer programming, electronics, welding, construction, culinary arts, and other areas of business and industry. Students typically spend half the school day at their regular school and the other half at EVIT.

SCOTTSDALE CULINARY INSTITUTE
8100 E. Camelback Rd., Scottsdale
(480) 990-3773, (888) 356-6666
www.chefs.edu/scottsdale

With its many resorts, hotels, and fine restaurants, the Valley is a natural location for training chefs. The institute, in operation since 1986, offers an Associate of Occupational Studies degree in Le Cordon Bleu Culinary Arts, a 15-month program, and the Le Cordon Bleu Patisserie and Baking Certificate Program, which lasts 9 months. The school also offers certificates in Le Cordon Bleu Hospitality and Restaurant Management and Le Cordon Bleu Culinary Management. All programs provide intensive, hands-on learning, and the school's graduates have gone on to great jobs, locally and elsewhere, as sous chefs, pastry chefs, and banquet managers. The Institute's L'Ecole Restaurant, which boasts a four-star rating on Yelp, is a classroom, laboratory, and public restaurant.

The restaurant is open for lunch and dinner Tuesday to Friday. Call (480) 990-7639 for reservations. The institute has a second campus, Sky Bridge, in downtown Scottsdale, with additional classrooms, kitchens, and new student-run bistro-style cafes, L'Ecole and L'Academie Cafe, both of which are open for lunch and dinner Monday to Friday.

THUNDERBIRD SCHOOL OF GLOBAL MANAGEMENT
15249 N. 59th Ave., Glendale
(602) 978-7000
www.thunderbird.edu

This private graduate school enjoys a global reputation as one of the top schools of international business. It was established in 1946 on the principle that to do business on a global scale, one must be able to combine functional business skills—such as finance and marketing—with the ability to understand the culture, language, and business climate of one's customers and business associates. Thunderbird offers a three-part curriculum: the study of one or more languages, international studies, and international business. Students have their choice of studying Arabic, Chinese, French, German, Japanese, Portuguese, Russian, or Spanish. International students may opt for thorough training in English as a Second Language. Many international students are sent here by their home country's graduate schools or corporations for further polishing in international business. All students earn an MBA in international management, a master of science in global management, a master of arts in global affairs and management, master of global management dual degrees and post MBAs. Part-time and distance learning programs allow you to get an MBA in a specific area of focus. Thunderbird, with about 700

full-time students, bills itself as the oldest graduate management school in the world devoted exclusively to the education of college graduates for international careers. It also boasts a large multimedia library called the International Business Information Centre. The school says it has more than 40,000 alumni working in 140 countries, making for an impressive global network of contacts for graduates. About 5,000 students go through the school's non-degree executive programs annually, which offer short-term training, certification, and continuing education. Thunderbird students are required to study overseas as part of their education, traveling to countries that include Japan, France, Cuba, China, Brazil, and Mexico.

i Arizona now provides full-day classes for kindergartners. Parents still have the half-day option, but the all-day choice is proving popular. To learn more, call the Early Childhood Education Department at (602) 364-1530 or visit www.ade.az.gov/earlychildhood.

Valley School Districts

The Valley is a quilt of dozens of school districts serving more than a half million students. Some districts—especially in central Phoenix—have historically been at a disadvantage in regard to academic programs, staffing, facilities, and amenities. Districts in the suburbs centered in high-growth regions typically enjoy newer facilities and amenities, along with a variety of extra programs to expand students' knowledge. Home buyers tend to flock to these recently developed areas, which has led to difficulties in overcrowding when supply can't keep up with demand. The Arizona Legislature has

struggled to address this issue of inequality for years, not only in the Phoenix area but also around the state.

In 1997 Arizona schools began distributing the Stanford 9 Achievement test, which measured reading, math, and vocabulary, to select grades. Now students in public and charter schools must complete state assessments that include either the standards-based Arizona's Instrument to Measure Standards (AIMS) or the norm-referenced Stanford 10.

Arizona's open-enrollment law allows parents to send their child to a public school outside the designated home district, provided the school has room. Deadlines for open enrollment are usually early in the calendar year. Call the school district you are interested in for more information. State requirements for enrolling your children in public schools include birth certificates and immunization records. Some individual districts require a proof of residency. State law requires children to be 5 years old before September 1 or January 1 to start kindergarten.

PARADISE VALLEY UNIFIED SCHOOL DISTRICT
15002 N. 32nd St., Phoenix
(602) 449-2000
www.pvschools.net

This district—the state's seventh largest—encompasses all kinds of neighborhoods, from low-income housing to multimillion-dollar hillside homes. With some parts of the district experiencing high growth, most of the schools were built in the last 20 years. Organized in 1919, the district became a unified elementary and high school district in 1976 and currently boasts 31 elementary schools, 7 middle schools, and 5 high

schools. It also runs an alternative high school and middle school. There are more than 33,000 students.

PEORIA UNIFIED SCHOOL DISTRICT
6330 W. Thunderbird Rd., Glendale
(623) 486-6000
www.peoriaud.k12.az.us

As the Valley rapidly expanded, the Peoria Unified School District was nestled in the midst of two of the fastest-growing cities in the Phoenix metropolitan area—Glendale and Peoria. The school district grew to encompass nearly 150 square miles. The Peoria Unified School District now stretches south from Glendale Avenue all the way north to the Maricopa–Yavapai County borders. As Arizona's third-largest district in terms of enrollment, the Peoria Unified School District boasts 31 elementary schools, 7 high schools, and 1 alternative school, serving more than 36,000 students. Interestingly, 33 of the 38 schools have been built since 1972, indicating the area's rapid growth rate. Many of the original campuses have received improvements and renovations thanks to a voter-approved bond election in 1996.

PHOENIX UNION HIGH SCHOOL DISTRICT
4502 N. Central Ave., Phoenix
(602) 764-1100
www.phxhs.k12.az.us

Phoenix Union is one of the largest high school districts in the nation, serving more than 25,000 students. But what sets this district apart from other high school districts in the Valley is its 10 magnet programs and 1 magnet high school. The magnet concept is how the district complies with a federal court order to desegregate its schools.

Students often choose schools outside their neighborhoods because they're interested in a certain program at another school. Whatever their choice, they receive free transportation to that school. A magnet school, as described by the district, provides both specialized and advanced preparation to students with special needs or ambitions. In addition to specialized courses, the schools offer a full slate of basic curriculum, athletics, clubs, and student government. Here are a few examples of magnet programs: medical and health studies at Alhambra High School in west Phoenix; computer and marine/environmental studies at Carl Hayden High School in west Phoenix; an international baccalaureate program for college-bound students at North High School in central Phoenix; and performing/visual arts, aviation/aerospace, and law-related studies at South Mountain High School in south Phoenix. Camelback High School also launched a new program in 2010 called "GEARS" (Game and Web Design, Engineering, Architecture, Robotics, and Sustainability), which includes special classes for students interested in those subject areas. Central High School is now a Cambridge International Center, the first in Arizona.

Metro Tech High School, formerly a vocational-technical school, has now become a comprehensive 4-year high school and offers both regular academic classes and more than 25 career-vocational programs.

SCOTTSDALE UNIFIED SCHOOL DISTRICT
3811 N. 44th St., Phoenix
(480) 484-6100
www.susd.org

This district of about 26,000 students celebrated its centennial in 1996. It enjoys a

good reputation, although you may find newer schools in the growth areas of north Scottsdale are at an advantage in facilities and programs over older schools in south Scottsdale. The district incorporates Paradise Valley, most of Scottsdale, and portions of Tempe and east Phoenix. It has 16 elementary schools, 6 middle schools, 5 high schools, 3 K–8 schools, and one alternative school. One of the elementary schools is a "learning center," where the emphases are on hands-on learning, whole-language reading, and cross-grade classrooms in a multicultural environment. Another elementary school focuses on back-to-basics instruction.

Charter Schools

Arizona is a leader in the concept of charter schools—state-funded K–12 schools that market specialized programs and offer residents a choice outside of traditional public schools for free education.

Charter school statutes support flexibility and innovation in operations and structure, including governance, scheduling, curriculum, and instructional methodologies. Arizona's charter school laws are said to be among the most liberal in the nation.

Charter schools are owned and operated by private individuals or companies but funded by taxpayers. There are close to 450 charter schools in the state (at least half of them in Maricopa County), with enrollment of 93,000-plus students, and the number continues to rise.

In the past few years, many charter schools have sprung up in new buildings or have taken the place of existing schools. They are an eclectic bunch, and they receive state funding as long as they comply with established laws. Complex new regulations are hampering the establishment of charter schools. Since the end of 2005 charter schools have had to comply with about 100 regulations. As a result, some charter schools have decided to forgo public funding and go private.

Charter schools advertise various focuses; examples are science/technology, back-to-basics, workplace skills, Montessori, college preparatory, the arts, and integrated approaches. Most charter schools stick to either kindergarten through 8th grade enrollment or high school students. They are in a variety of neighborhoods. Some take hundreds of students, and others are as small as 50 students.

For a list of charter schools, call the Arizona Department of Education Charter School Info Line at (602) 542-5094 or visit www.ade.az.gov/charterschools/info.

i For a parent's guide to K–12 Valley schools, visit www.greatschools.net. This site lists top-rated area schools and allows parents to compare schools within Maricopa County.

Private & Parochial Schools

The Valley is home to several dozen private schools. In addition, there are Catholic, Protestant, Jewish, and Islamic schools. There's an enormous tuition range, with some of the parochial schools' fees starting at $1,000 to $3,000 for annual tuition; midrange private schools charge about $5,000 annually, and the more exclusive private schools ask for as much as $20,000 annually. Some schools test students prior to admitting them and require interviews. You'll also find that siblings of current students have the edge in admissions. Ask about financial assistance; some schools offer scholarships or can set up flexible payment plans.

i The Arizona Commission for Post-secondary Education publishes a directory of the state's private and public colleges and universities. The Arizona College and Career Guide costs $5 and may be obtained from the commission at 2020 N. Central Ave., Phoenix, or by calling (602) 258-2435. The directory is also available in the state's public libraries and online at www.azhighered.gov.

ALL SAINTS' EPISCOPAL DAY SCHOOL
6300 N. Central Ave., Phoenix
(602) 274-4866
www.allsaints.org

All Saints' philosophy is to identify academically talented youth and develop their abilities through a curriculum that balances academic excellence, physical education, and spiritual awareness. There are many enriching programs, such as computers and drama, as well as extracurricular activities, such as chorus, sports, and community service. The school opened in 1963 and now serves kindergartners through 8th-graders. The student–teacher ratio is 9-to-1.

BROPHY COLLEGE PREPARATORY
4701 N. Central Ave., Phoenix
(602) 264-5291
www.brophyprep.org

Brophy Prep sits on a 17-acre campus near Central Avenue and Camelback Road and encompasses a historically significant private chapel built when the school opened in 1928. The all-male Catholic Jesuit high school serves 9th- through 12th-grade students. The school's curriculum is college prep, and 99 percent of its graduates go on to 4-year colleges and universities. The ratio of students to teachers is 20-to-1.

PHOENIX COUNTRY DAY SCHOOL
3901 E. Stanford Dr., Paradise Valley
(602) 955-8200
www.pcds.org

This is a popular option for Northeast Valley parents who want the private-school experience. The school opened in 1961 and has expanded over the years to a sprawling 40-acre campus near Camelback Mountain. It's open to preschoolers through 12th graders. It dubs itself a student-centered school and has many electives and extracurricular activities. The student-teacher ratio is 9-to-1, and current enrollment is about 700.

RANCHO SOLANO PRIVATE SCHOOLS
5656 E. Greenway, Scottsdale
(602) 996-7002
www.ranchosolano.com

Founded in 1954, Rancho Solano has 5 campuses in the Valley. It's open to preschoolers through 8th graders, and adheres to the philosophy that basic skills and appropriate study habits—mixed in with lots of activities, a positive attitude, and fun—are necessary to accomplish optimum personal, educational, and career goals. Rancho Solano has a college-preparatory focus, with arts, athletics, and bilingual education as pluses. For grades K–8, the student-teacher ratio is 18-to-1, and for preschool students it's 15-to-1. In 2008 the school opened the Rancho Solano Upper School Program for high school students.

SCOTTSDALE CHRISTIAN ACADEMY
14400 N. Tatum Blvd., Phoenix
(602) 992-5100
www.scottsdalechristian.org

The Scottsdale Christian Academy, founded in 1968, boasts top-notch facilities on a sprawling campus in north Phoenix. Current

enrollment is approximately 900 students, preschool through high school. All students must sign a statement of faith in Christianity before admission. Older students receive a college-preparatory curriculum.

TESSERACT
4800 E. Doubletree Ranch Rd., Paradise Valley
(480) 991-1770
www.tesseractschool.org

The word *tesseract* comes from Madeleine L'Engle's book *A Wrinkle in Time* and refers to a fifth-dimensional learning experience. The school opened in Paradise Valley in 1988 and features an "inquiry-based way of learning" that emphasizes self-esteem and communication skills for preschoolers through 8th-graders. The school inaugurated a 9th-grade class in 2008 and plans to offer instruction for all high school grade levels in 2011. The student-teacher ratio is 8-to-1, and enrollment is about 350 students.

CHILD CARE

You are sure to find the type of child care you're looking for in an enterprising area like the Valley of the Sun. There are hundreds of options in day-care centers, in-home care, and preschools.

One of the best ways to start your search is by talking to your neighbors who have children. Usually you will want something close to home for a day-care center or preschool, and neighbors will be able to recommend nearby places. When seeking out child care, be sure to ask the provider about hours of operation, full-time versus part-time care, and cleanliness and safety standards. Look for a variety of toys and playground equipment and colorful surroundings. You'll

also want to investigate if it's a place where your child will have ample opportunities to learn, develop socially, and generally have fun. Find out if a preschool program tends to be open-ended and child-oriented or more academically oriented with a structured curriculum. The Valley has a number of parent-cooperative programs in which parents volunteer a few hours a week in the center. Many of these are affiliated with churches and temples.

To find a state-licensed day-care program, contact the following offices. For centers and family child-care homes serving more than five children, contact the Arizona Department of Health Services' Office of Childcare Licensing at (602) 364-2539 or www.azdhs.gov/als/childcare. For family child-care homes serving one to four children, contact the Arizona Department of Economic Security's Child Care Administration at (602) 542-4248 or www.azdes.gov/childcare. You can search the files of preschools and also complaints or violations listed against them. Remember, not all child-care facilities are required to have state licenses. You might also want to contact Arizona Child Care Resources and Referral, which runs a resource and referral service and other programs in support of child care for all income levels. Call (602) 244-2678 or visit www.arizonachildcare.org.

Montessori programs are well represented in the Phoenix area. The philosophy embraces learning activities that are related to real-life experiences and that are highly interactive and hands-on. The various schools cater to toddlers, preschoolers, and elementary school-age children. For more information on Montessori schools in the Valley, contact the Foundation for

Montessori Education, 9215 N. 14th St., Phoenix, at (602) 395-0292.

Among the child-care chains operating in the Valley are KinderCare Learning Centers, www.kindercare.com; Childtime Learning Centers, www.childtime.com; La Petite Academy, www.lapetite.com; and Tutor Time Child Care/Learning Centers, www.tutortime .com.

If you're looking for in-home care provided by a babysitter or nanny, try calling one of the Valley's nanny referral agencies. One longtime company is A Caring Nanny (480-946-3423; www.acaringnanny.com). Agencies will help you find a live-in nanny or someone who works in your home full-time or part-time. Typically the agencies have completed various background checks on potential babysitters before setting up interviews. If you're a visitor in town seeking babysitting services, your hotel or resort can put you in touch with a number of caregivers. One Valley company that specializes in serving the tourist market is Parent's Time Out (480-460-1200; www.ptofamily.com).

INDEX

INDEX

Scottsdale, 12, 267
Scottsdale Arabian Horse
   Show, 165
Scottsdale Artists'
   School, 182
Scottsdale Arts
   Festival, 167
Scottsdale Artwalk, 181
Scottsdale Center for the
   Performing Arts, 124
Scottsdale Christian
   Academy, 307
Scottsdale Civic Center
   Library, 159
Scottsdale Culinary
   Festival, 168
Scottsdale Culinary
   Institute, 303
Scottsdale Cultural
   Council, 182
Scottsdale Fashion
   Square, 136
Scottsdale Healthcare
   Osborn, 294
Scottsdale Healthcare
   Shea, 295
Scottsdale Kosher
   Market, 108
Scottsdale Municipal
   Airport, 33
Scottsdale Pavilions, 138
Scottsdale Seville, 138
Scottsdale Trolley, 26
Scottsdale Unified School
   District, 305
Scramble, 92
Seamus McCaffrey's, 93
Sedona, 247
Sedona Phoenix
   Shuttle, 33
Segal's, 108
Sens Asian Tapas & Sake
   Bar, 90
Shadow Mountain
   Village, 282

Shaker Room at Martini
   Ranch, The, 120
Shemer Art Center &
   Museum, 179
Sheraton Crescent
   Hotel, 51
Sheraton Phoenix
   Downtown, 51
Sheraton Wild Horse Pass
   Resort & Spa, 76
Shopping, 125
Shops at Gainey
   Village, 136
Shops at Town & Country,
   The, 128
Shuttles, 25
Siam Thai Cuisine, 112
Skydive Arizona, 202
Sleepy Dog Saloon &
   Brewery, 117
SMoCA Store, 139
Soaring, 209
Softball, 210
Southeast Valley, 9
South Mountain Park, 201
South Phoenix, 264
Southwest Shakespeare
   Company, 173
Southwest Valley, 18
Spanish Fly Mexican Beach
   Club, 120
Spectator Sports, 225
Sphinx Ranch Gourmet
   Market, 139
Sportsman's Fine Wines &
   Spirits, 130
SpringHill Suites, 62
Spur Cross Ranch
   Recreation Area, 197
Stadium Club, 234
State Park, 195
St. Francis, 89
Stinkweed's, 127
St. Joseph's Hospital &
   Medical Center, 291

St. Luke's Medical
   Center, 292
Stockyards, The, 99
Sugar Bowl, 139
Sugar Shack Sports
   Grill, 235
Summer Spectacular
   ArtWalk, 169
Summit Trail, 206
Summit Trail at Piestewa
   Peak, 207
Sun City, 17, 269, 276
Sun City Grand, 17,
   269, 276
Sun City West, 17, 269, 277
Sunflower RV Resort, 80
Sun Health Boswell
   Memorial Hospital, 296
Sun Lakes Resort
   Community, 278
Sunland Springs
   Village, 279
Sunnyslope, 263
SuperShuttle, 29
Superstition Farm, 162
Superstition Springs
   Center, 132, 157
Surface Streets, 23
Surprise, 18, 269
Sushi Eye, 100
Swimming, 210
Symphony Hall, 178

T
Taberna Mexicana, 110
Taliesin West, 13, 151
Talking Stick Resort, 70
Tammie Coe Cakes, 91
Taxis, 29
Taxis & Limousines, 34
T. Cook's, 93
Tempe, 10, 266
Tempe Beer Festival,
   The, 167
Tempe Bicycle, 205

Regional Travel at Its Best

INSIDERS' GUIDE®

The acclaimed travel series that has sold more than 2 million copies!

Discover: Your Travel Destination.
Your Home. Your Home-to-Be.

Albuquerque

Anchorage & Southcentral Alaska

Atlanta

Austin

Baltimore

Baton Rouge

Boulder & Rocky Mountain National Park

Branson & the Ozark Mountains

California's Wine Country

Cape Cod & the Islands

Charleston

Charlotte

Chicago

Cincinnati

Civil War Sites in the Eastern Theater

Civil War Sites in the South

Colorado's Mountains

Dallas & Fort Worth

Denver

El Paso

Florida Keys & Key West

Gettysburg

Glacier National Park

Great Smoky Mountains

Greater Fort Lauderdale

Greater Tampa Bay Area

Hampton Roads

Houston

Hudson River Valley

Indianapolis

Jacksonville

Kansas City

Long Island

Louisville

Madison

Maine Coast

Memphis

Myrtle Beach & the Grand Strand

Nashville

New Orleans

New York City

North Carolina's Mountains

North Carolina's Outer Banks

North Carolina's Piedmont Triad

Oklahoma City

Orange County, CA

Oregon Coast

Palm Beach County

Palm Springs

Philadelphia & Pennsylvania Dutch Country

Phoenix

Portland, Maine

Portland, Oregon

Raleigh, Durham & Chapel Hill

Richmond, VA

Reno and Lake Tahoe

St. Louis

San Antonio

Santa Fe

Savannah & Hilton Head

Seattle

Shreveport

South Dakota's Black Hills Badlands

Southwest Florida

Tucson

Tulsa

Twin Cities

Washington, D.C.

Williamsburg & Virginia's Historic Triangle

Yellowstone & Grand Teton

Yosemite

**To order call 800-243-0495
or visit www.Insiders.com**

Phoenix & Scottsdale